ERTÉ

ART DECO MASTER OF GRAPHIC ART & ILLUSTRATION

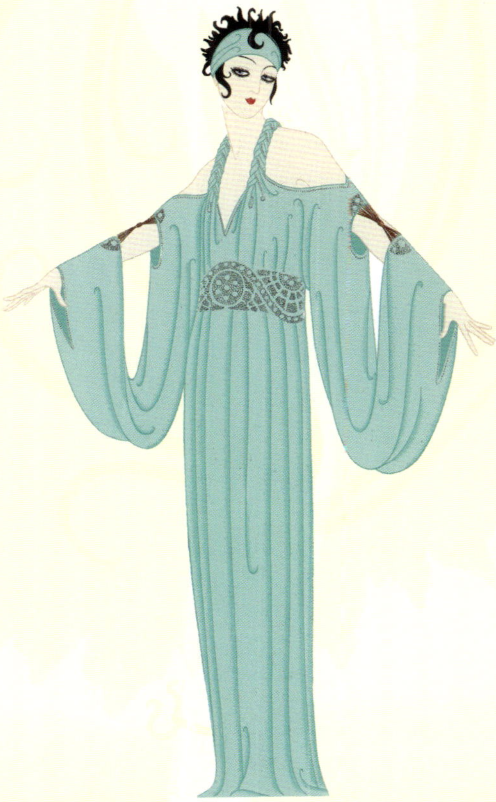

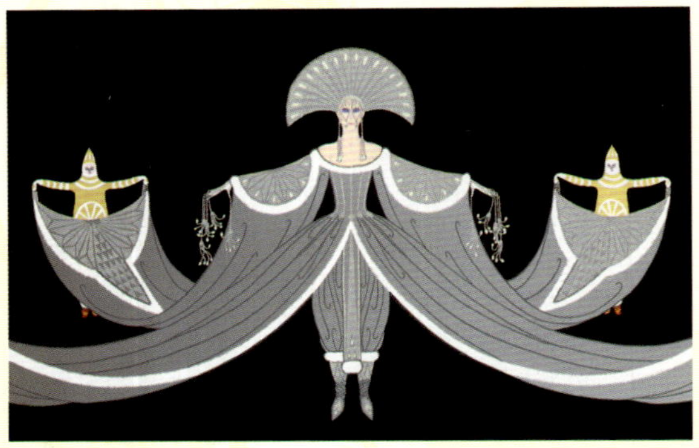

Publisher and Creative Director: Nick Wells
Project Editor: Catherine Taylor
Art Director: Mike Spender
Digital Manager: Chris Herbert

Special thanks to: Ray and Beverley Perman at Sevenarts, Anna Jim at Chalk & Vermillion and Mark Schachner at Ertémuseum.com – thank you for all your help and for putting up with all the to's and fro's! Thanks also to Matt Knight, Frances Bodiam, Vanessa Hinds, Laura Bulbeck and Eileen Cox.

Note to the reader: The magazine *Harper's Bazaar* was initially spelt '*Bazar*' until the extra 'a' was added in November 1929 but, for the sake of consistency in this book, unless it is used for the name of an illustration, it is always spelt the way it was to become known.

FLAME TREE PUBLISHING
6 Melbray Mews
Fulham, London SW6 3NS
United Kingdom

www.flametreepublishing.com

First published 2014

18 17
3 5 7 9 10 8 6 4

A CIP record for this book is available from the British Library upon request.

ISBN 978-1-78361-216-1

Printed in China

ERTÉ

ART DECO MASTER OF GRAPHIC ART & ILLUSTRATION

ROSALIND ORMISTON

FOREWORD BY RAY PERMAN

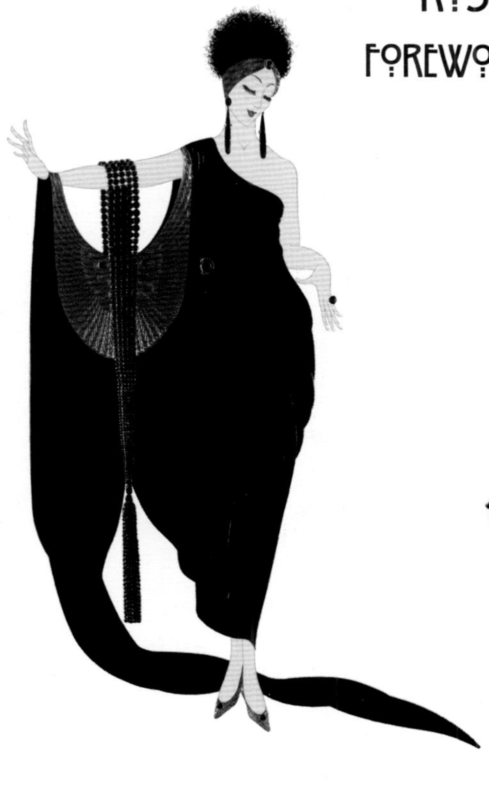

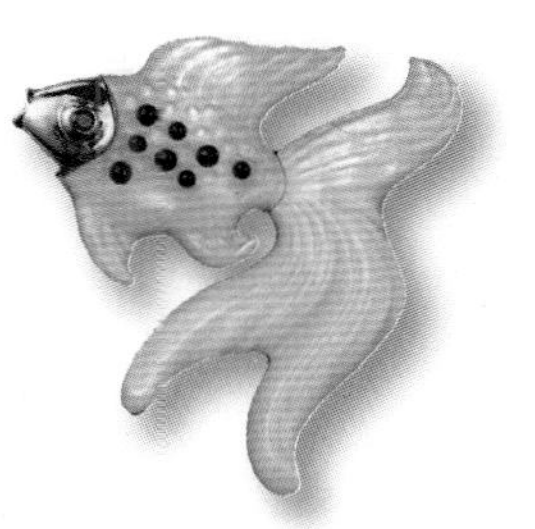

FLAME TREE
PUBLISHING

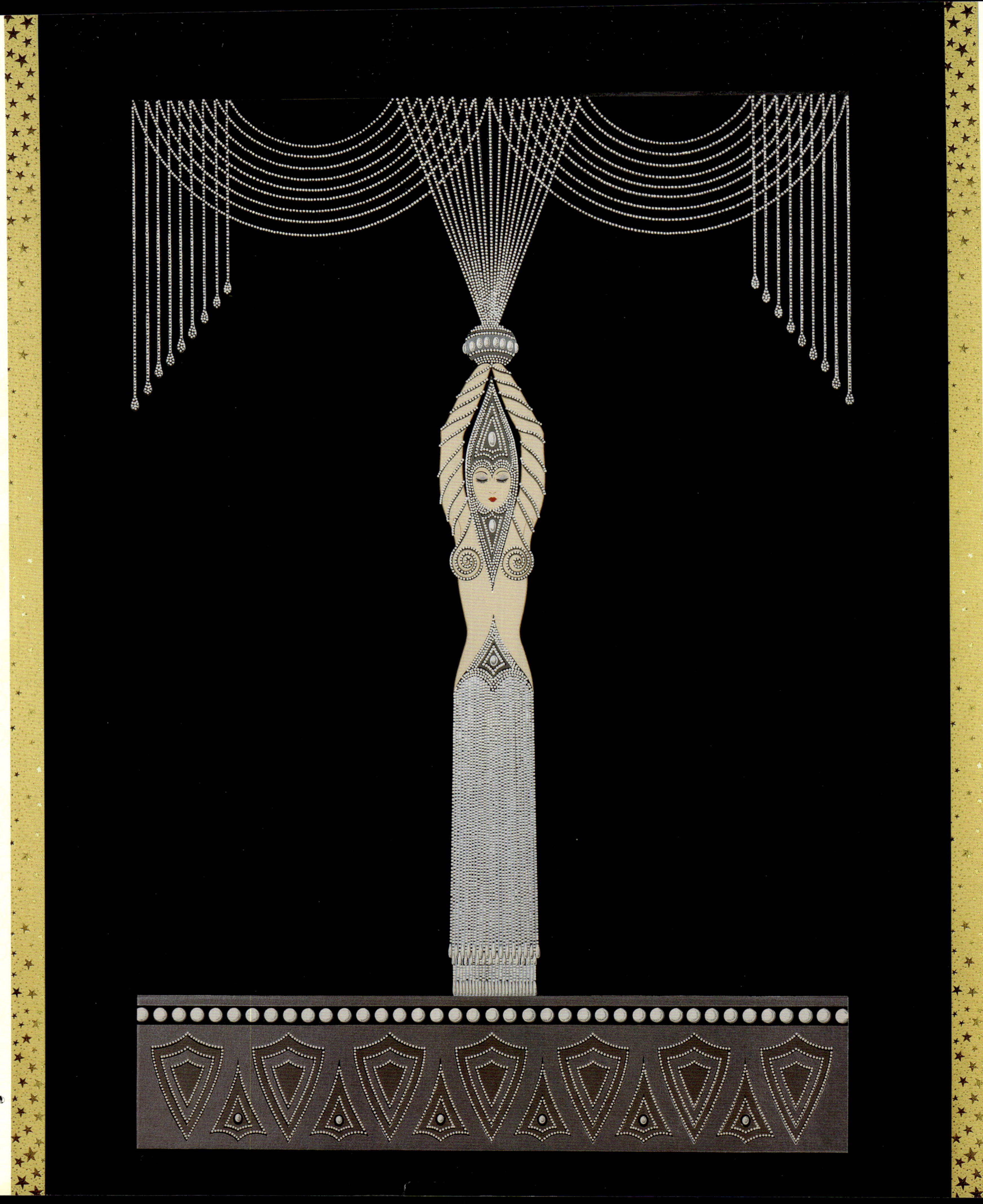

CONTENTS

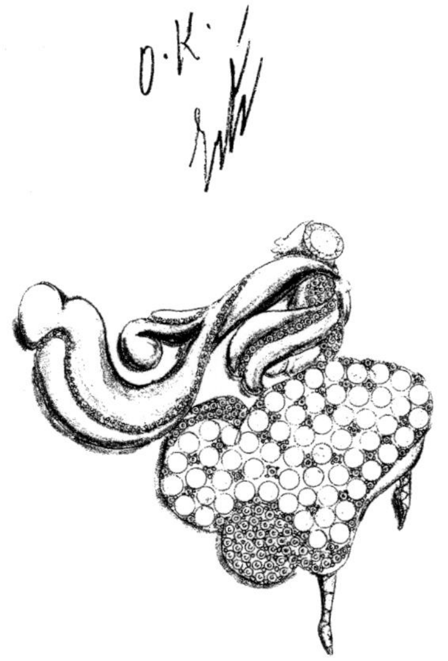

FOREWORD

ERTÉ – Prince of the Music Hall, Mirror of Fashion and Master of Art Deco – died on 21 April 1990. A pivotal figure in the history of design and illustration, a leading proponent of the Art Deco aesthetic who left us a legacy of work that continues to inspire and intrigue new and erstwhile collectors and fashion designers. As recently as December 2013, *Harper's Bazaar* produced a celebratory edition with an Erté cover of twenty years earlier: as fresh today as it was then and, inside, a mention that Gucci sent a phalanx of top models down its gleaming mirrored catwalk wearing dresses with patterns inspired by Erté.

I was first introduced to Erté – born Romain de Tirtoff but known as Erté from the age of twenty-one from the French pronunciation of his initials – when I joined the Grosvenor Gallery after a twenty-five-year tenure at Christie's. The gallery was owned by Eric and Salome Estorick, who had guided Erté in a new career from 1967 when they had sell-out shows of his work in London and New York and had been his exclusive agents since that time. The original intention was that I would be responsible for the sale of modern master works owned by the gallery whilst the Estoricks would focus solely on the Erté business – and a business it certainly was, with the exploitation of his designs for prints, sculpture, art objects, jewellery and much more. When it was suggested to Erté that this was a cottage industry he said, 'No, more of a mansion'. I was soon to take over the role of Salome, who had worked closely with the artist for two decades but now suffered ill health, which was to be the start of a great friendship and a new career for me.

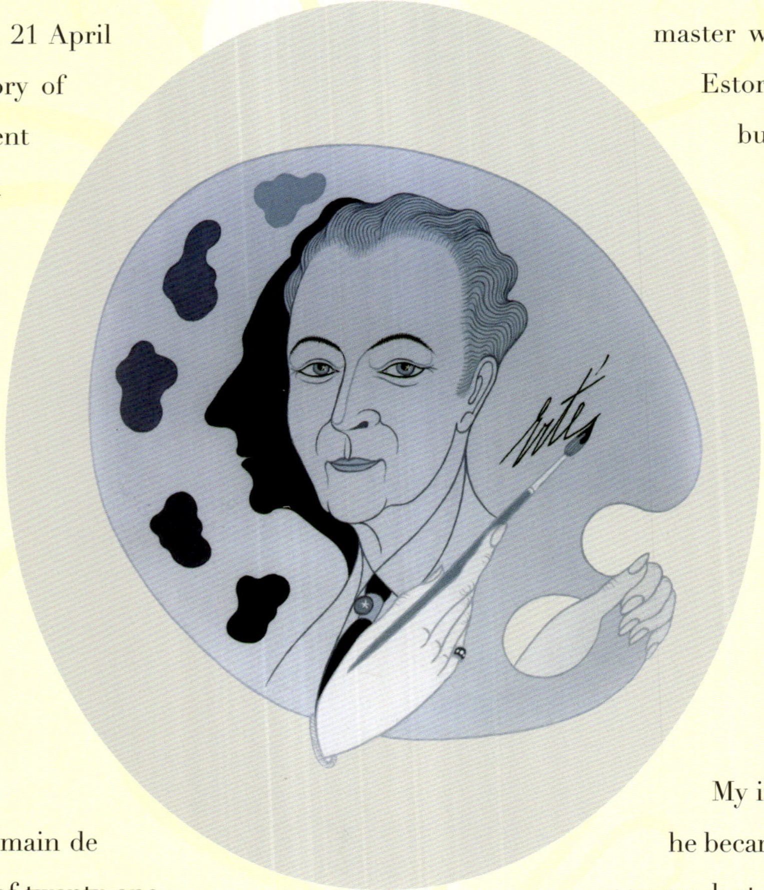

My initial role was to review with Romain, as he became to me, proofs of new prints, samples of new products and clays for sculpture. He endeavoured to create the elegant, extravagant and exotic without vulgarity. He was extremely demanding and we had extensive discussions on art works derived from his original designs which, far from being sketches or rough drawings, were precise and finely detailed due to the influence of Persian miniatures which had fascinated him as a boy. Fortunately, David and Leslee Rogath, who

(Page 1) **Pillow Swing** *(detail), 1985, embossed serigraph with foil stamping, 73 x 53.3 cm (28¾ x 21 in)*
(Page 2) **La Mer blanche**, *1986, serigraph with foil stamping, 55.9 x 78.7 cm (22 x 31 in)*

(Page 4) **Pearls and Diamonds**, *1986, embossed serigraph with foil stamping, 94.7 x 69.9 cm (37¼ x 27½ in)*
(Above) **Self-portrait**, *1969, pen, ink and gouache*

published the prints and later sculptures through their company, Chalk & Vermilion, were up to the challenge. Together they were able to develop new techniques in printing, and create new machines capable of foil stamping and embossing, resulting in art forms that have never been duplicated and possibly never will be.

I took my two young daughters, Alexandra and Charlotte, on a trip to Paris to meet Erté. He was enchanted by them and, after we had finished reviewing proofs of new print editions, he insisted we went shopping at Galeries Lafayette, where he bought each of them a dress and accessories to wear and arranged for us all to dine at Régine's, Ledoyen, off the Champs-Élysées. The restaurant had special memories as it was where he first met Nicolas, the love of his life. Acting now as agent, I accompanied Erté to numerous exhibitions of his work and celebrations of his birthday, as well as meetings with publishers and would-be licensees. For his ninety-fifth birthday, David and Leslee arranged a fabulous party at the Plaza Hotel, New York, where I shared a table with Erté and Andy Warhol, who collected Erté's work, as did Barbra Streisand, Elton John, Michael Caine and many others.

At the height of his fame, when he was represented in hundreds of galleries throughout America, had new fashion products being manufactured in Japan and was on the cusp of agreeing a perfume and cosmetics contract, he decided to take a holiday in Mauritius. I called to see if he had arrived safely and he said yes but felt unwell. He had contracted septicaemia and was in a coma by the time I reached him with a hospital plane and medical team. Fortunately, the neighbouring island of Réunion had dialysis equipment and were able to treat him. Once he was sufficiently recovered, I took him to the Hospital Cochin in Paris where he continued to improve. So much so that, during the next weeks, he insisted on working on what were to be the final limited editions of his prints. David Rogath made several visits with me to finalize the details of what Erté said would be the most extravagant and amongst the best to portray his designs.

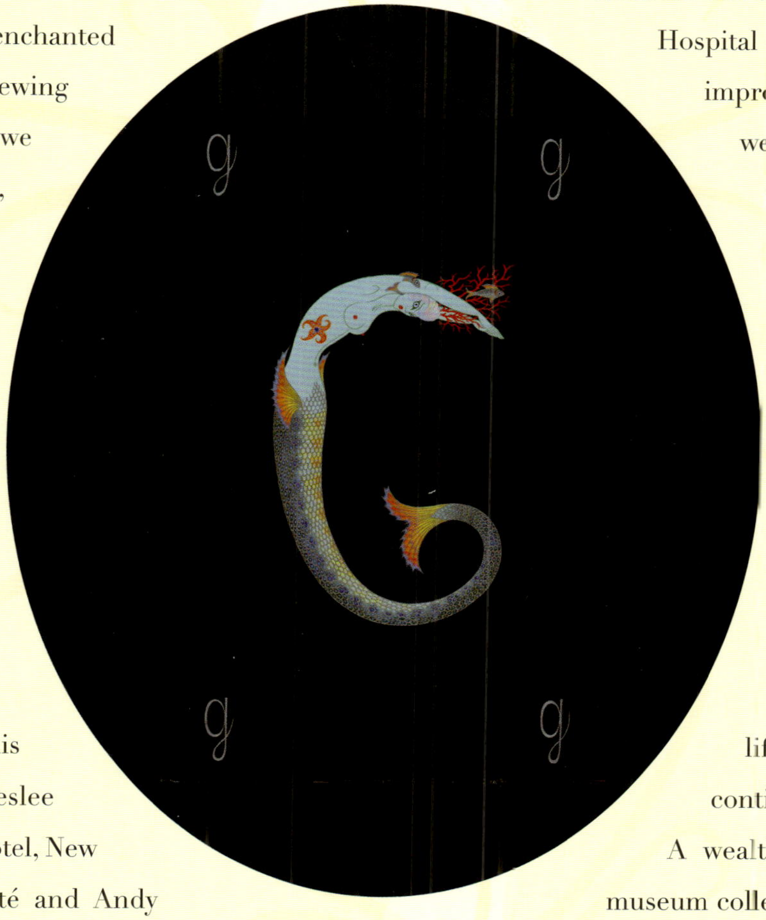

Sadly, Erté's recovery could not be sustained and he died after a short stay in the urological wing of the hospital prior to his intended homecoming. His life ended, but his creations live on and continue to influence the designers of today. A wealth of his original works are held in museum collections, by artists and collectors, as well as by the thousands of buyers of his limited editions, jewellery and art objects. This book contains just a small representation of his life's work of more than twenty thousand designs and a fashion career that spanned three quarters of a century.

Ray Perman, ***Friend, Associate and Executive Director, Sevenarts Ltd***

The Alphabet: 'G', *1979, lithograph/serigraph, 42 x 26.7 cm (15¾ x 10½ in)*

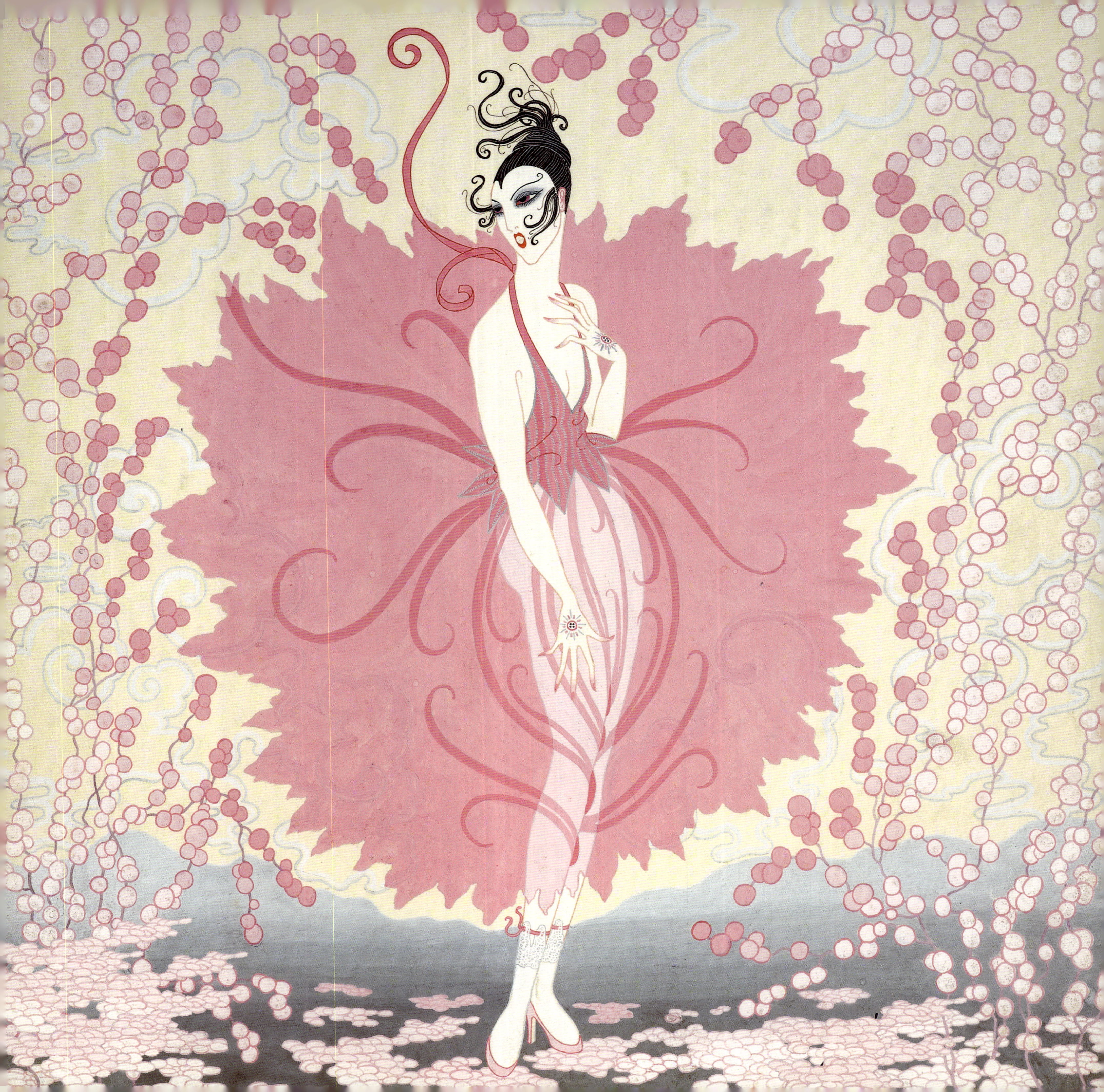

INSPIRATIONS

In 1975, at the age of 83, the acclaimed Russian-born designer Romain de Tirtoff (1892–1990), widely known as Erté, published his autobiography. He began *Erté: Things I Remember* with the story of his departure from St Petersburg, Russia in January 1912 at the age of 19. It was a momentous occasion for him. He was bound for Paris and what he hoped would be his future as an artist. At the station many members of his family had congregated to wish him well: his mother and father, his sister, his aunts and his cousins. From Erté's telling of the event, it is clear that he had the support of his close family, albeit not in the naval career they had originally planned for him. Who could have guessed that he would be later fêted worldwide as the 'Father of Art Deco'?

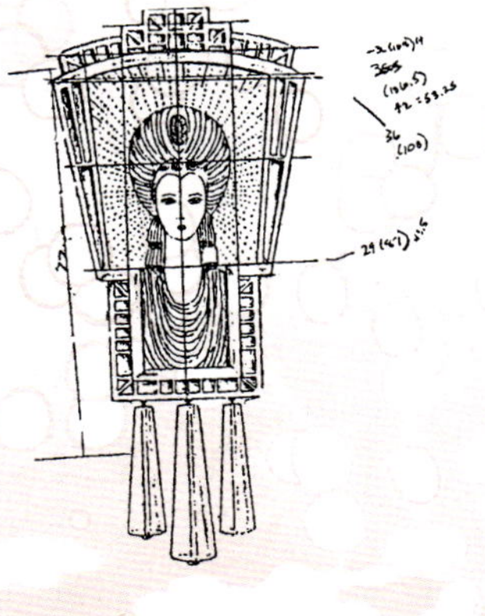

A MOMENTOUS BEGINNING

Erté is treasured as an icon of Art Deco design but much of his work was transitional, evoking *fin-de-siècle* Art Nouveau. Despite the fact that he said little influenced him other than medieval miniatures of India and Persia, one can see in his fashion illustrations, stage and film sets, and costumes, inspiration from many sources, such as European Orientalist art, Byzantine mosaics, Greek vases, Egyptian motifs and more. Moving to Europe would be the first key trigger of much of what was to influence his work.

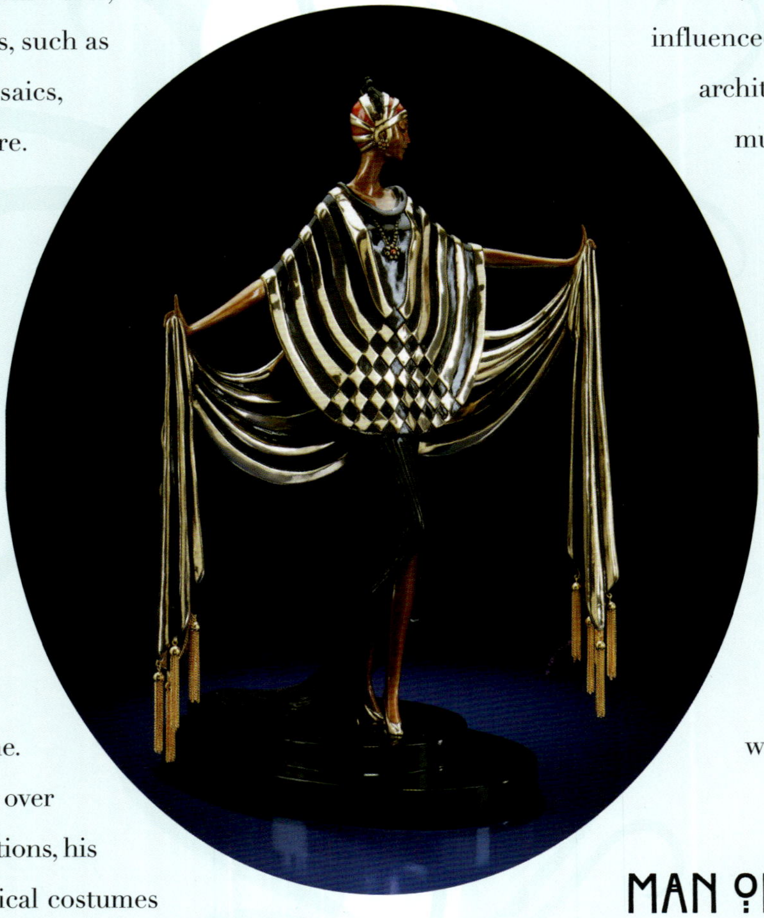

A LONG CAREER

'Erté', Romain de Tirtoff's professional title in use after 1912 when he moved to Paris, was created from the French and Russian phonetic sound 'Er-Tay' of the 'R' and 'T' in his name. Erté lived to be 97, with a career spanning over 75 years. What inspired his unique illustrations, his fashion and jewellery designs, his theatrical costumes and stage sets, and his bronze sculptures? Looking through Erté's vast catalogue of works, one can see the same intensity of detail in the early 'La Belladonne' costume in *Les Fleurs du Mal* in 1917 (*see* page 169), through to the much later *Dream Girl* sculpture of 1991, one of his last works (*see* page 74) – some works were released posthumously, but all were originated and supervised by Erté; he did not cast the bronzes himself. But where does one look for the essence of what inspired and influenced Erté? In his autobiographies (there were two: *Erté: Things I Remember, An Autobiography*, of 1975, and *Erté: My Life/My Art: An Autobiography*, of 1989) he stated that all his artistic ideas were his own, unique, without influence from other artists or designers. Yet studying his life and work, one can see that in his early years he was influenced by the avant-garde in art and fashion, architecture and decorative art, ballet and music in his home city of St Petersburg. His 1975 autobiography refers to it. He was immersed, too, in the city's rich cultural heritage. And in Paris from 1912, as part of the city's diverse wealth of artists, designers and architects, dancers and opera singers, he, amongst many others, brought a rich world of talent to the city. Erté, an aristocratic Russian émigré with perfect manners, who was fluent in English, Spanish, German and French, was at the centre of the very decorative arts.

MAN OF THE MOMENT

In 1913, from the moment he was employed in Paris by the French high society fashion designer Paul Poiret (1879–1944), Erté captured the mood of the city. His work picked up on dance crazes such as the tango and charleston, on masked balls and the mania for Russian ballet, particularly the avant-garde Ballets Russes,

(Previous page) **Pink Lady**, *1980, lithograph, 63.5 x 45.72 cm (25 x 18 in)*
(Above) **Opening Night** *sculpture, 1989, bronze, 51 x 36 x 30 cm (20 x 14 x 12 in).*

The Balcony, *1989, serigraph with foil stamping, 100 x 72 cm (391.4 x 28¼ in)*

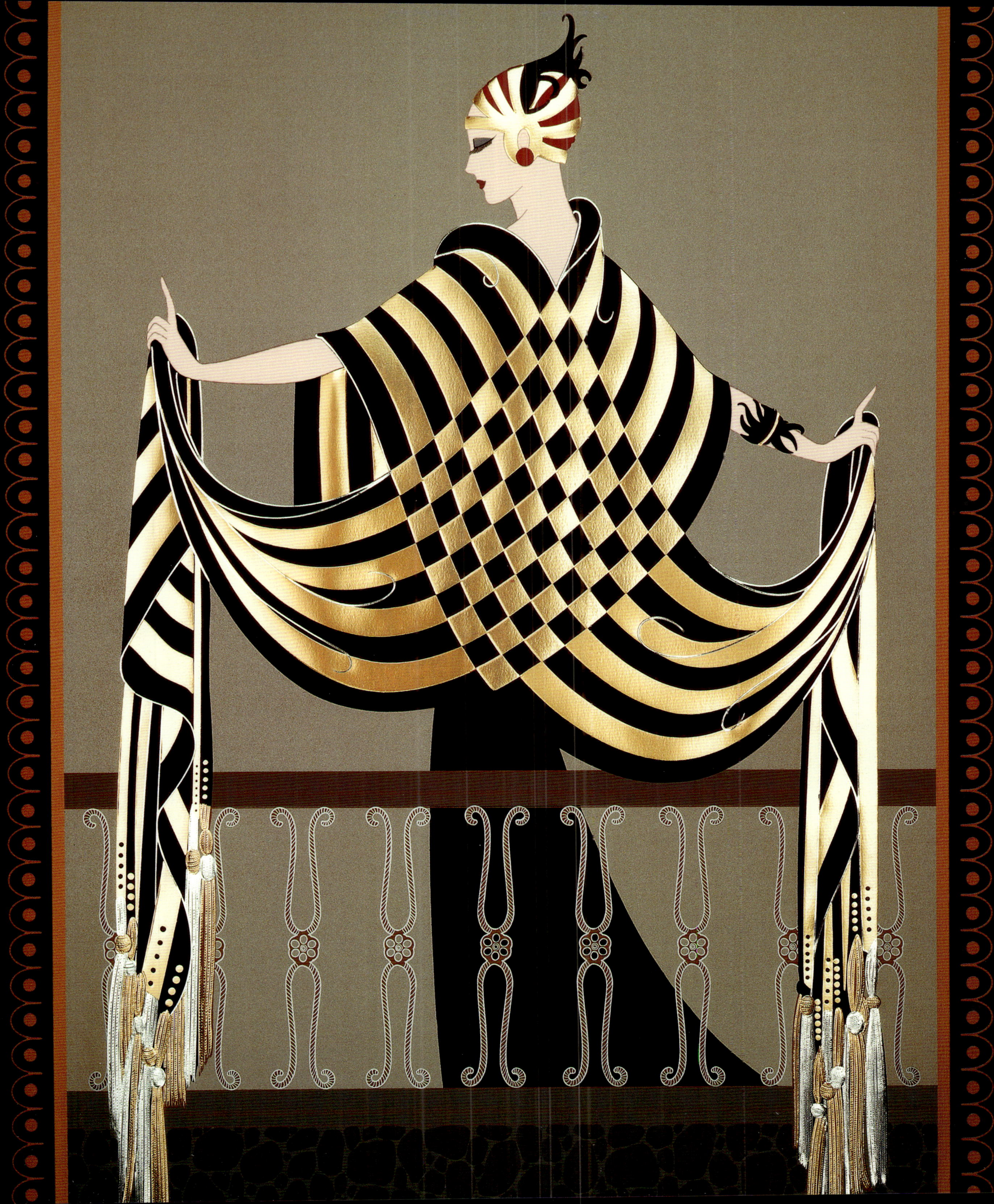

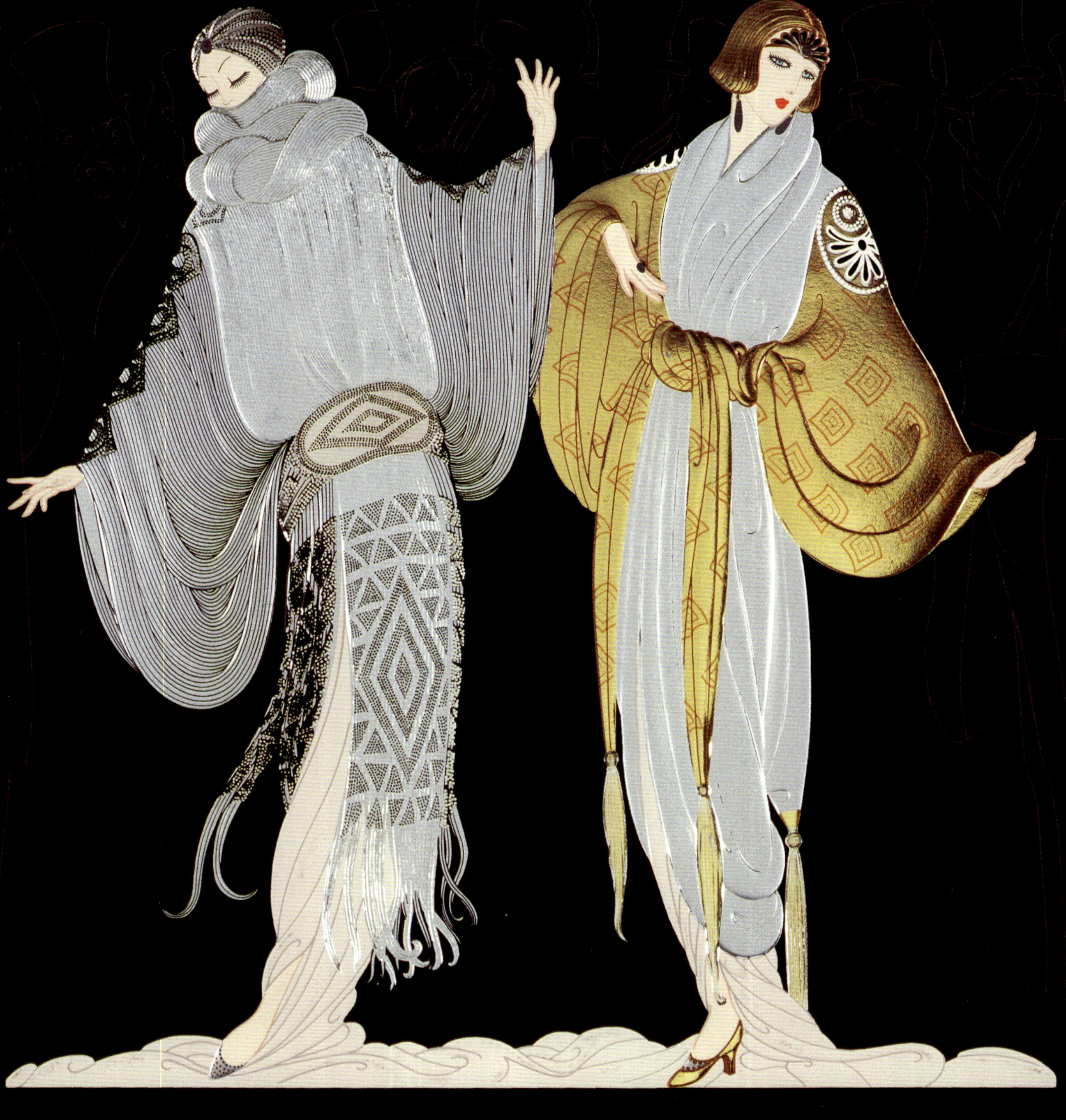

brought to Paris by Sergei Diaghilev (1872–1929). Through Erté one feels part of the excitement of pre-First World War Paris, and later in interwar years when he travelled to America and worked in Hollywood. With him we can 'listen in' to conversations with film mogul Cecil B. DeMille (1881–1959) and the American multi-millionaire publisher Randolph Hearst (1863–1951), or the successful impresario George White (1892–1968), the owner of 'Scandals' musical revues on Broadway. Erté's life takes us there in his autobiographies and through his remarkable design illustrations.

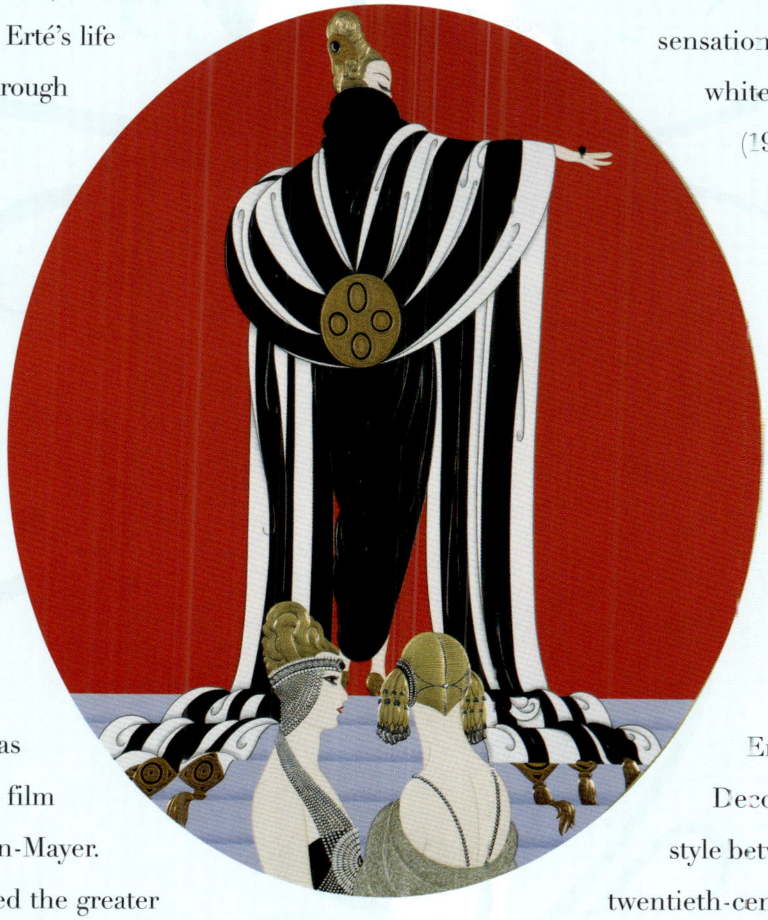

DEFINING ERTÉ'S STYLE

Does Art Deco define Erté's work? It is evident in some of his works, which confirms his view that he remained aware of fashionable movements and styles in art, decorative art, architecture and design, but it did not affect everything he created. When he embraced Art Deco the result was sensational, like the 'boudoir' set for the film *Paris* (1926), produced by Metro-Goldwyn-Mayer. His view was that Art Deco had influenced the greater part of the twentieth century, seeing it as 'an evolution from Art Nouveau in combination with the geometric forms of Cubism' (*Erté: Things I Remember*, 1975). There are, of course, many examples. One can see Art Deco in the androgynous kimono-style costume design *Michelle* (1925), remade as a limited edition serigraph *Michelle* in 1980 (*see* page 19), and his *Michelle* earrings of the 1980s, copied decades later from the original work. It is evident in the gouache *Geometric* of 1914, later echoed in his jewellery design of the same name from 1979. Erté could transfer the characteristics of Art Deco – the chevron or ziggurat, geometric lines, bold colours or chic black and white with metallic – to small items of jewellery. Or he could create a dramatic Art Deco effect on a large scale, like the sensational stage set design with its green and white geometric pattern for *Les Spectacles* (1928), for George White's 'Scandals' revue in New York. The Art Deco style transferred well to the bronze sculptures Erté created from earlier works, for example *Angel* (1985), based on the earlier *Angel Harpist* costume (1926, *see* pages 102–3).

FROM ART NOUVEAU TO ART DECO

Erté is often considered an artist of the Art Deco period but his art is of a transitional style between Art Nouveau and Art Deco. His late twentieth-century revival pieces created from the 1970s onwards were taken from figure illustrations he made in the 1920s and 30s, and embody the essence of Art Nouveau, a reminder of the passion amongst late nineteenth-/early twentieth-century aesthetes for Symbolist visual rhetoric, and the eroticism and 'other-world' of Orientalism. In many ways, Art Nouveau and Art Deco are defined by Erté's work. It informed

Opening Night, *1985, embossed serigraph with foil stamping, 64.3 x 75.6 cm (25½ x 29¾ in)*

Monaco, *1989, embossed serigraph with foil stamping, 99.1 x 80.3 cm (39 x 31½ in)*
The *Monaco* serigraph image was also created as a three-dimensional painted bronze sculpture, *Monaco* (1989). The image may have recalled personal memories for Erté, who lived in Monte Carlo, Monaco, from 1914 to 1922.

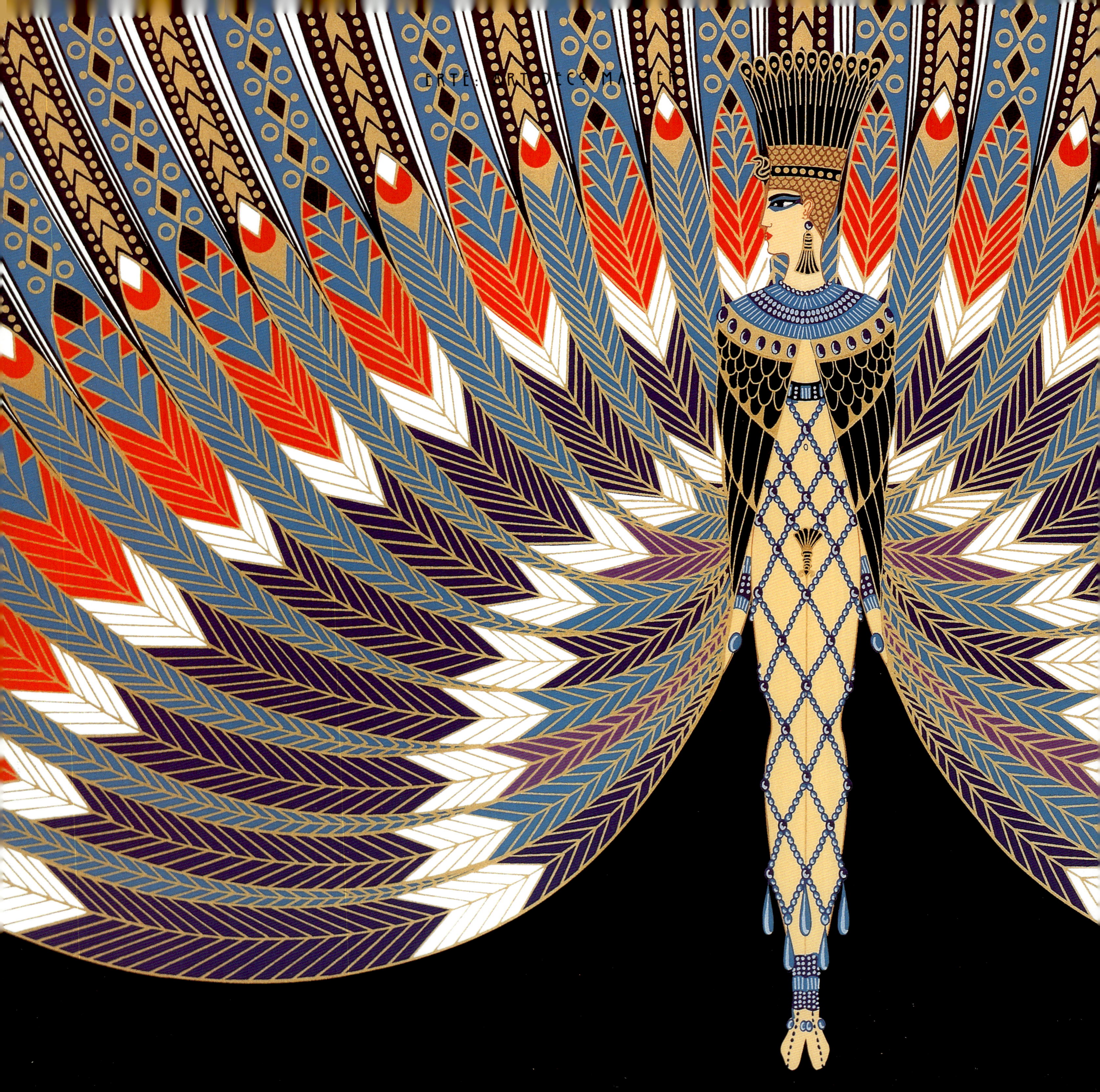

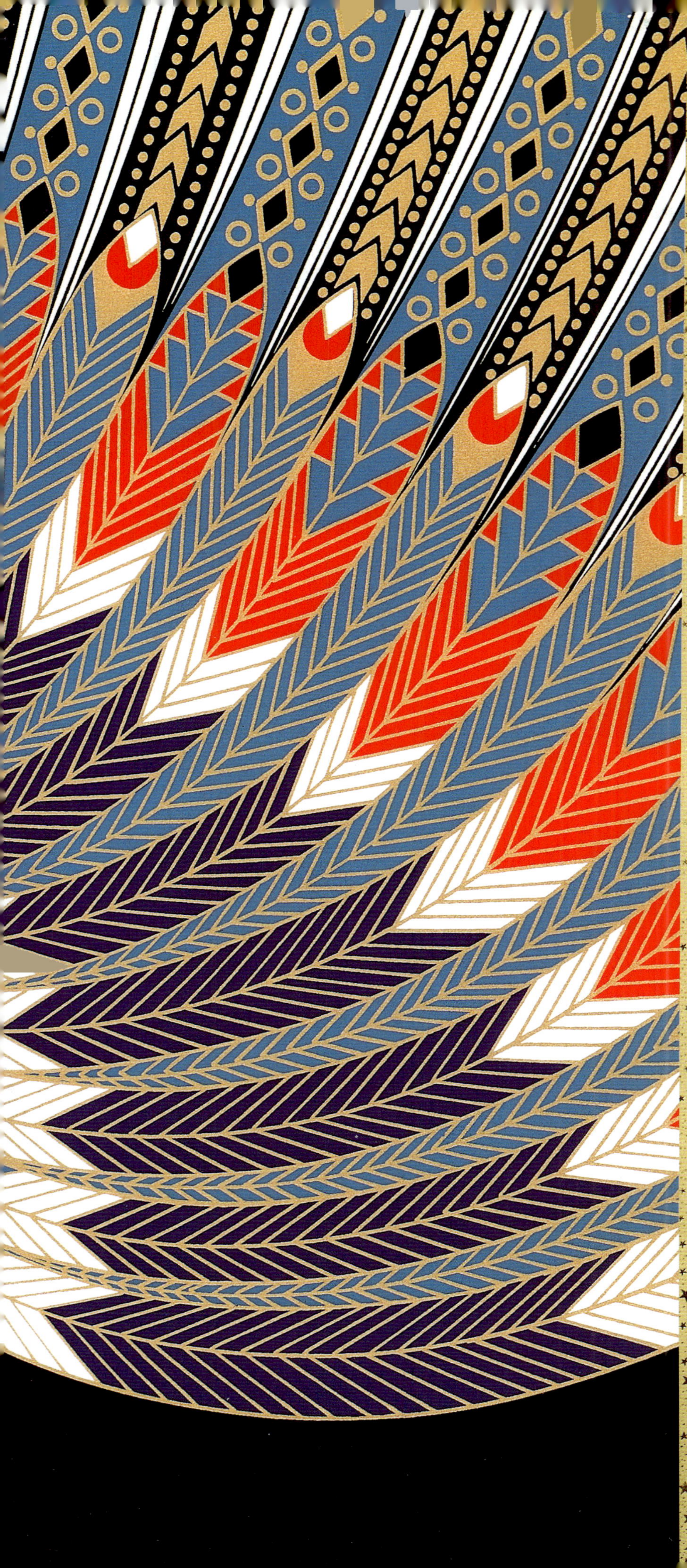

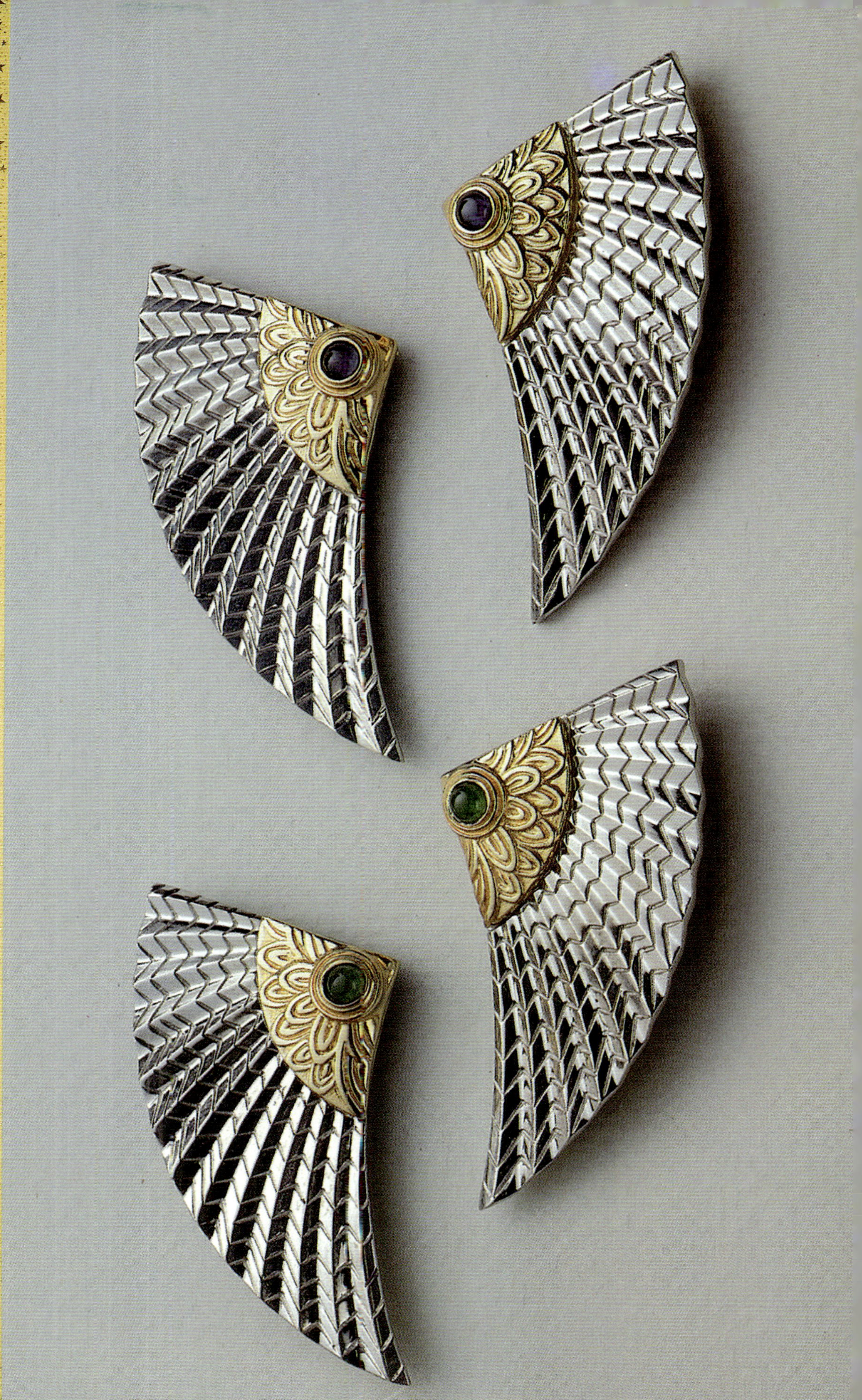

The Nile *earrings, 1979–90 – top: gold, silver, blue sapphires; bottom: gold, silver, emeralds.*

him as a fashion illustrator, a costume and set designer for theatre and films, a jewellery designer and a sculptor. What other influences surrounded him? From his privileged background he made many friends. His circle included the nobility and aristocracy, famous actors, actresses and models, film producers, directors and impresarios, editors, publishers, writers, gallery owners and art collectors. He inspired them, as they inspired him. His life was never dull. When he died, aged 97 in 1990, he was still enjoying a career peak.

A NAVAL FAMILY

To discover the inspirations that supported Erté's work, it is worth reading a little on his early years and the people, places and career opportunities that he embraced or rejected. He was born into a family of wealth and high status in Russian society and political life. His father Piotr Ivanovitch de Tirtoff (d. 1929), of Tartar origins, was an admiral of the Russian Imperial Fleet, following the family tradition of a naval career. When illness forced his father to stand down from the navy for two years, he became a member of the Tsar's cabinet. Piotr's brother was a chamberlain at the Imperial Court. In the history of Erté's ancestors – of which he was very proud and acknowledged in his autobiography *Erté: Things I Remember* (1975) – under the reign of Ivan III 'the Great' (1440–1505), Grand Prince of Moscow, all Tartar Khans (chiefs), with the exception of Erté's ancestor Khan Tirt, had surrendered Tartar Mongol rule to create a united Russia under the leadership of Ivan III. They were given princely titles. Erté's ancestor later surrendered his position during the reign of Ivan IV 'the Terrible' (1530–84), Grand Prince of Moscow, and Tsar of all Russias from 1547. Khan Tirt received a lesser title of 'hereditary nobleman', and was allowed to use the 'de' when abroad. The title ensured the place of the de Tirtoff family within Russian aristocracy.

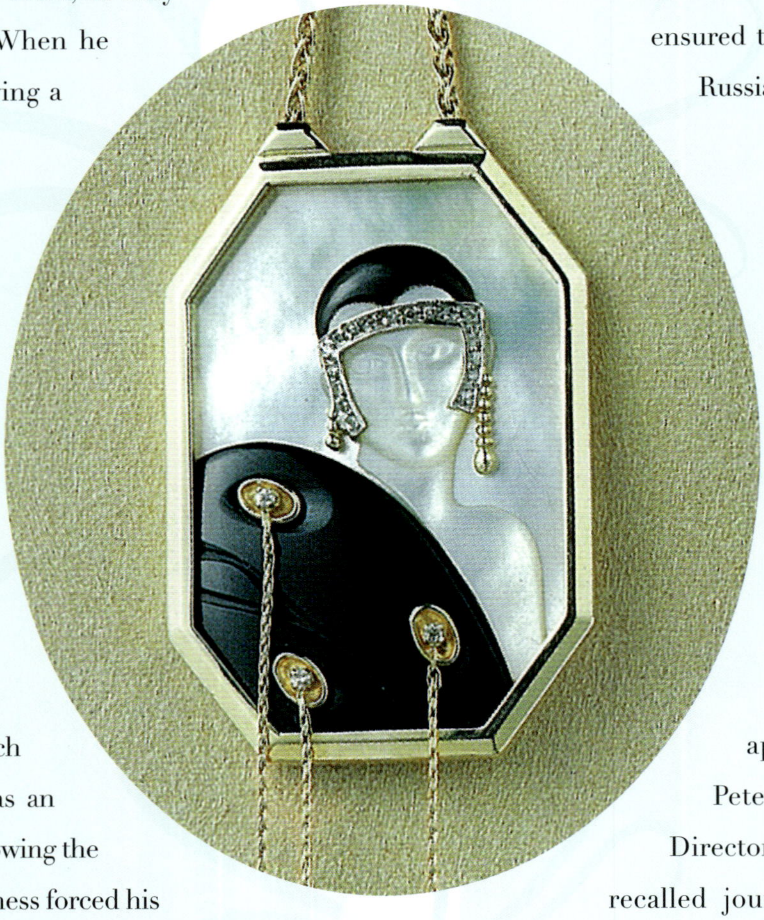

ROMAIN DE TIRTOFF

Erté, named Romain at birth, was born on 23 November (10 November in the Russian calendar) 1892 at the St Petersburg Naval School. He was the second child with an older sister. He spent part of his later childhood, from the age of 15, on Kronstadt, an island approximately 16 m (26 km) from St Petersburg, where his father served as Director of the Naval Engineering School. Erté recalled journeying in winter on a horse-drawn sleigh to cross the frozen waters of the bay to St Petersburg. In spite of his immersion into naval life, Erté knew from an early age that he did not want to pursue a military career. He relates a memory of throwing out of the window a box of wooden toy soldiers presented to him by an aunt. It was his own way of making his views felt, and he called it his 'peace

(Previous page) **The Nile**, *1982, serigraph, 57.4 x 70.1 cm (22½ x 27½ in)*
(Above) **Folies** *necklace, c.1979–90, gold, diamonds, mother-of-pearl, black onyx, gold chain.*

Loge de Théâtre, *1984, embossed serigraph with foil stamping, 83.8 x 68.6 cm (33 x 27 in)*
The final dress rehearsal night was the event high society dressed up for, to be seen and to be admired. This serigraph is based on one of Erté's covers for *Harper's Bazaar.*

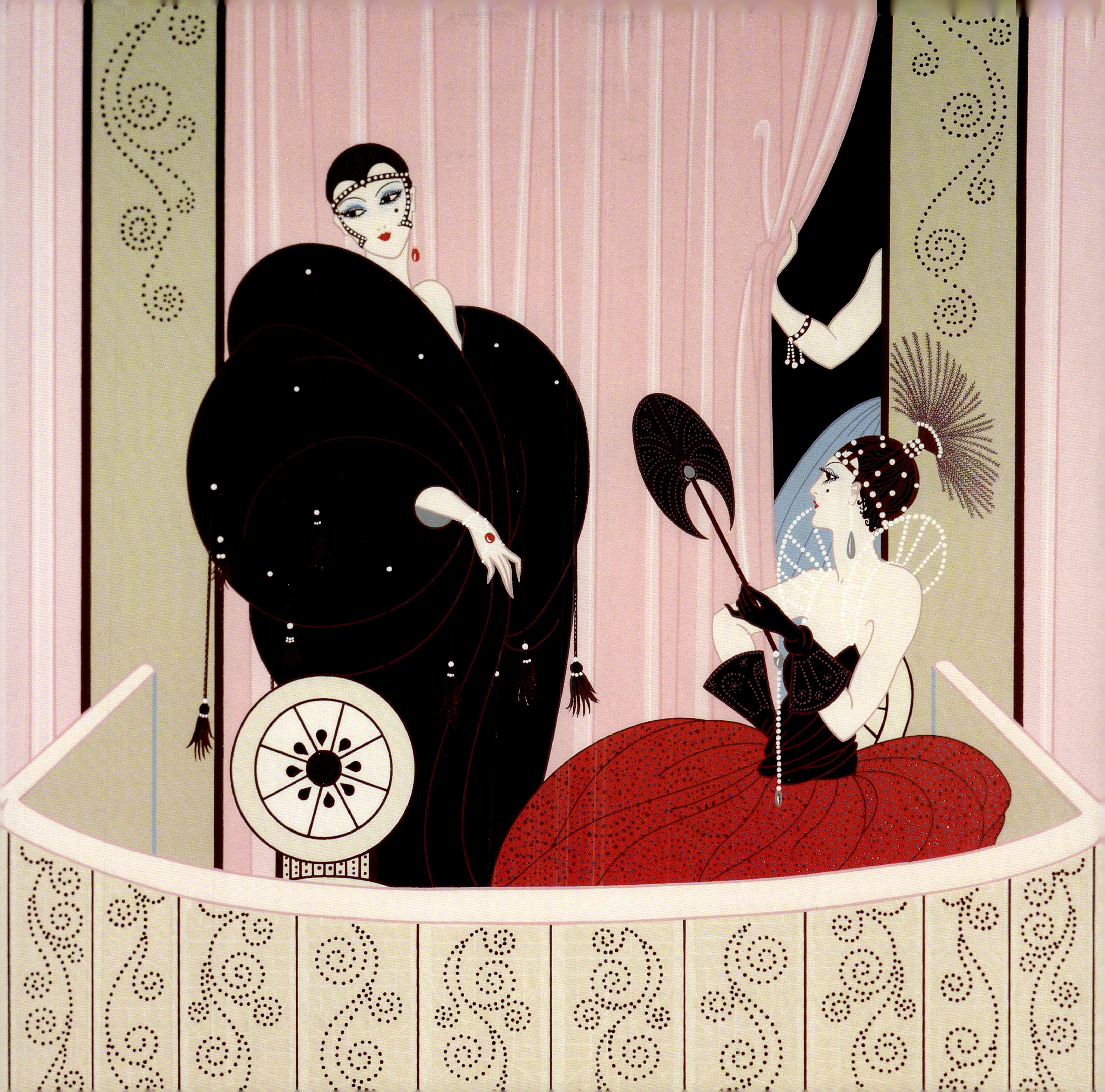

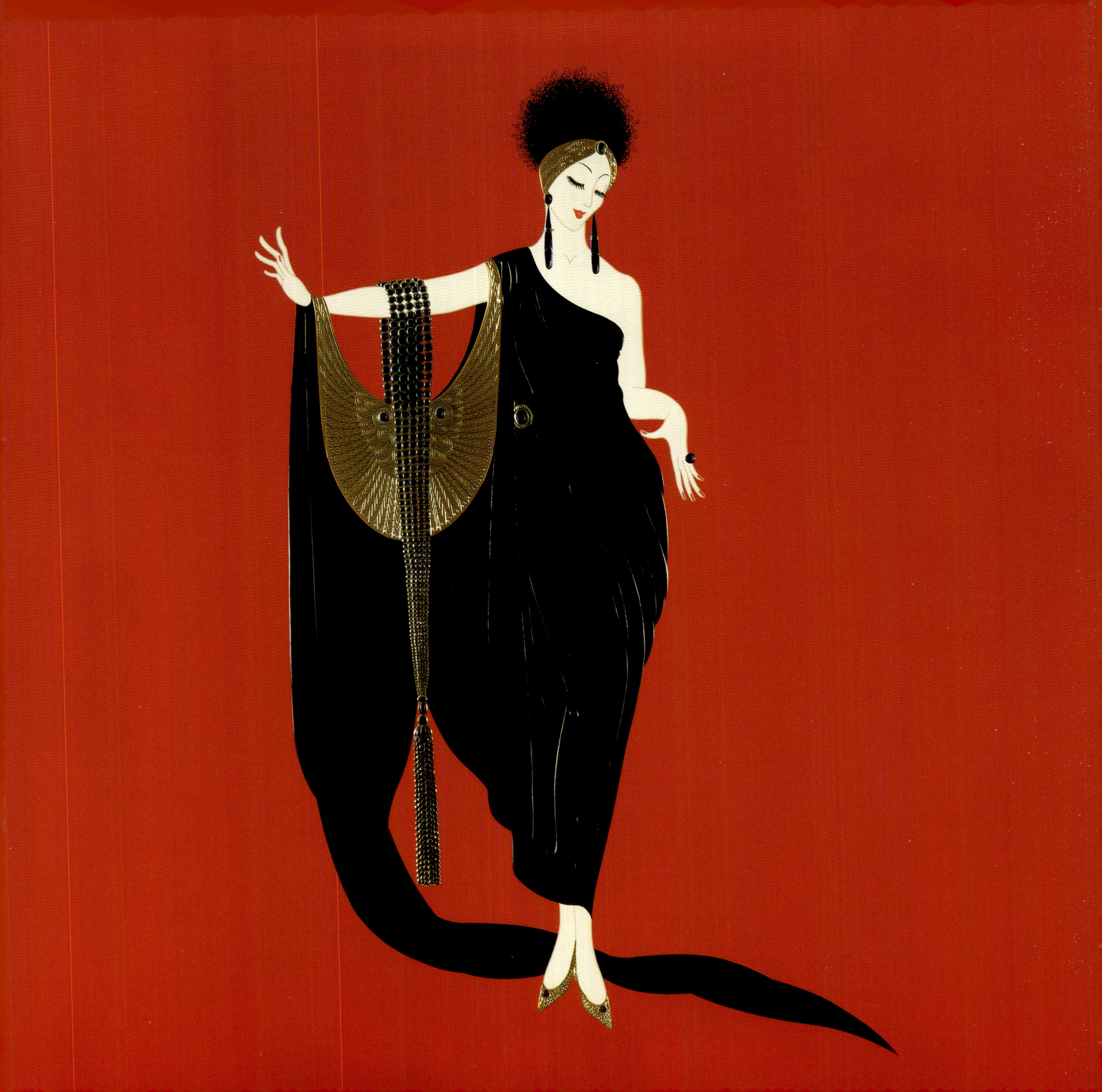

demonstration'. In his 1975 autobiography he stressed that he always hated war. He never served his country despite the fact that all his male relatives had served in a military or diplomatic capacity since the founding of the Imperial Navy by Peter the Great, including his maternal uncle and godfather, Nicolas, who became the youngest army general during the Russo-Japanese War (8 February 1904 – 5 September 1905). Erté described it as 'a struggle' not to conform, to choose a vastly different career than the one expected of him as the only son.

HOME LIFE

Erté was brought up surrounded by women. His mother, Natalia Mikhailovna Nikolenko – of Ukrainian heritage – supervized a large household of servants, which included her personal dressmaker Maria and a seamstress. He lived with his mother and his sister Natalia, nine years older than himself, and was looked after by a nursemaid Euphrosinia who had a daughter Aglaé. In addition, after his early years – until he attended school at the age of 12 – an English nanny was employed to teach him English, later followed by French and German governesses to teach him their mother-tongues. He spoke fondly of his grandmothers, particularly of summers spent at the house of his paternal grandmother, Eugenie, with her other grandchildren. Memories of his childhood included playing with her tame bear who loved the children.

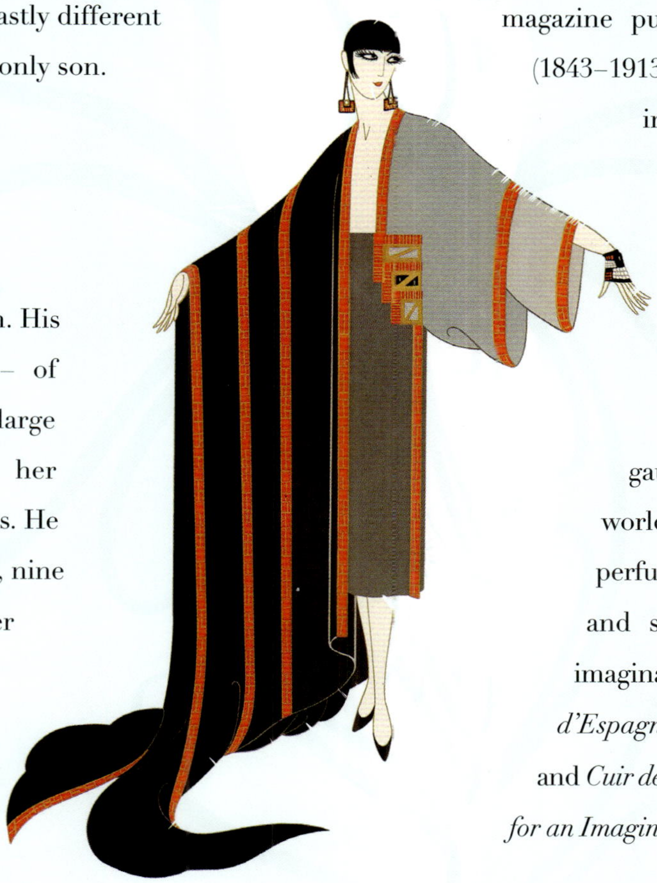

EARLY INSPIRATION

St Petersburg was a city with close links to France. The 1892 Franco-Russian Pact established cultural ties and a military bond. Natalia de Tirtoff and her daughter were enthusiastic followers of French and Viennese fashion. Natalia's dressmaker, Maria, made them costumes based on fashion designs copied from French magazine publications such as *Le Moniteur de la Mode* (1843–1913). The magazine's artist, Jules David (1808–92), initiated the idea to create 'conversation pieces', fashion plates showing women wearing the latest fashions in domestic settings and in daily activities outdoors, as well as at evening concerts and balls. While she was cutting out the material, Maria would give Erté tiny pieces of discarded lace, chiffon and gauze, and with them he created a theatre with a world of characters created from his mother's empty perfume bottles. Erté filled them with coloured water and stuck on the fabrics to create dancers for imaginary ballets. He recalled the perfume names: *Peau d'Espagne*, *Floramie*, *Orchidée*, *Trèfle Incarnat*, *Tuberues* and *Cuir de Russie*. One of his earliest extant works is *Design for an Imaginary Ballet* (1911).

FASHION INSPIRATIONS

Erté loved his mother's appearance, recalling her to be 'extremely beautiful' with rich black hair and pale skin. He enjoyed going on shopping trips with her to Morskaya Street in St Petersburg where,

Glamour, *1985, embossed serigraph with foil stamping, 69.3 x 52.7 cm (27¼ x 20¾ in)*

Michelle, *1980, serigraph, 63.5 x 45.72 cm (25 x 18 in)*

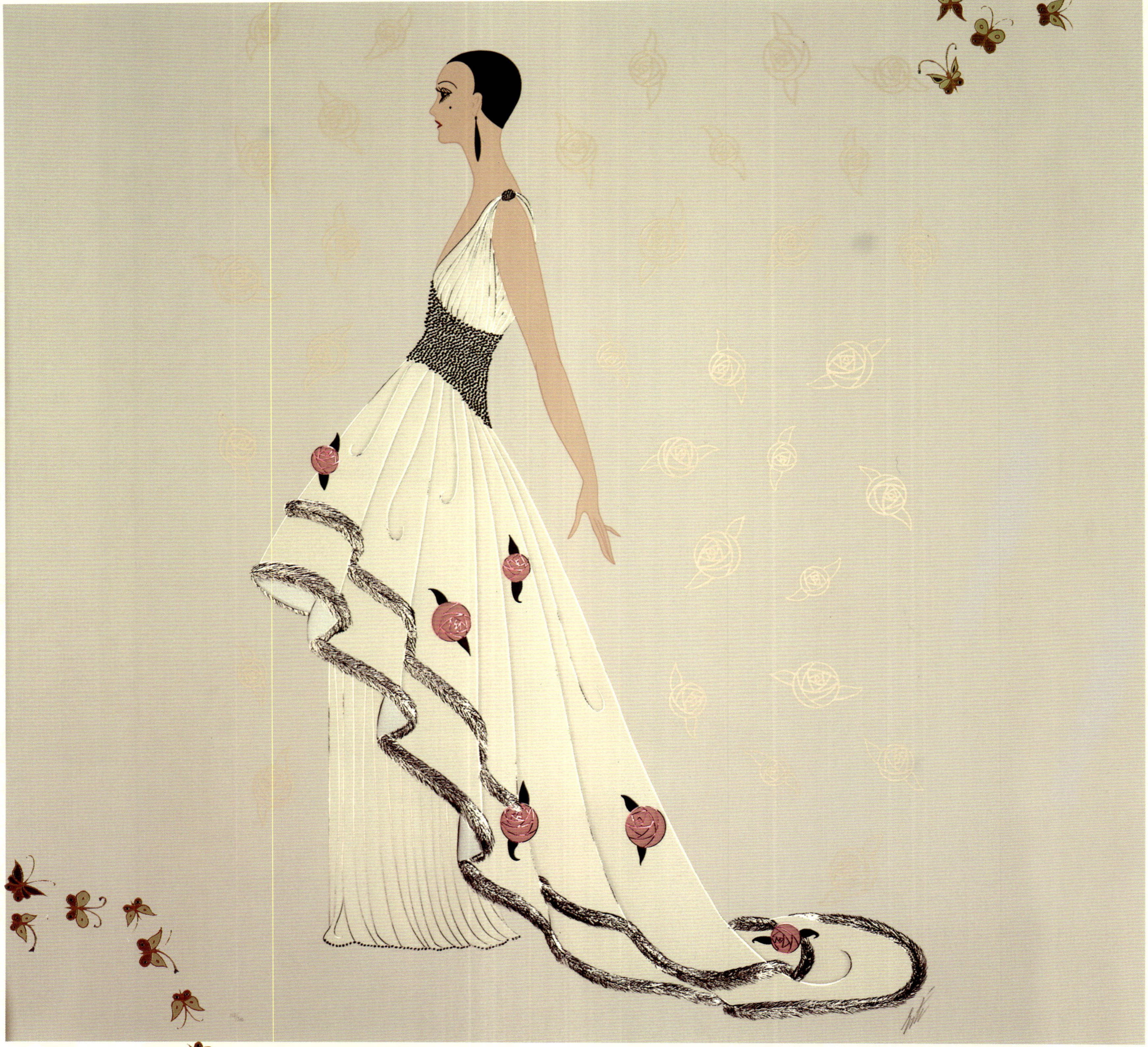

Rose Gown, *1989, embossed serigraph with foil stamping, 96.5 x 74.4 cm (38 x 29¼ in)*

Roses de Nuit, *1989, embossed serigraph with foil stamping, 96.5 x 74.4 cm (38 x 29¼ in)*

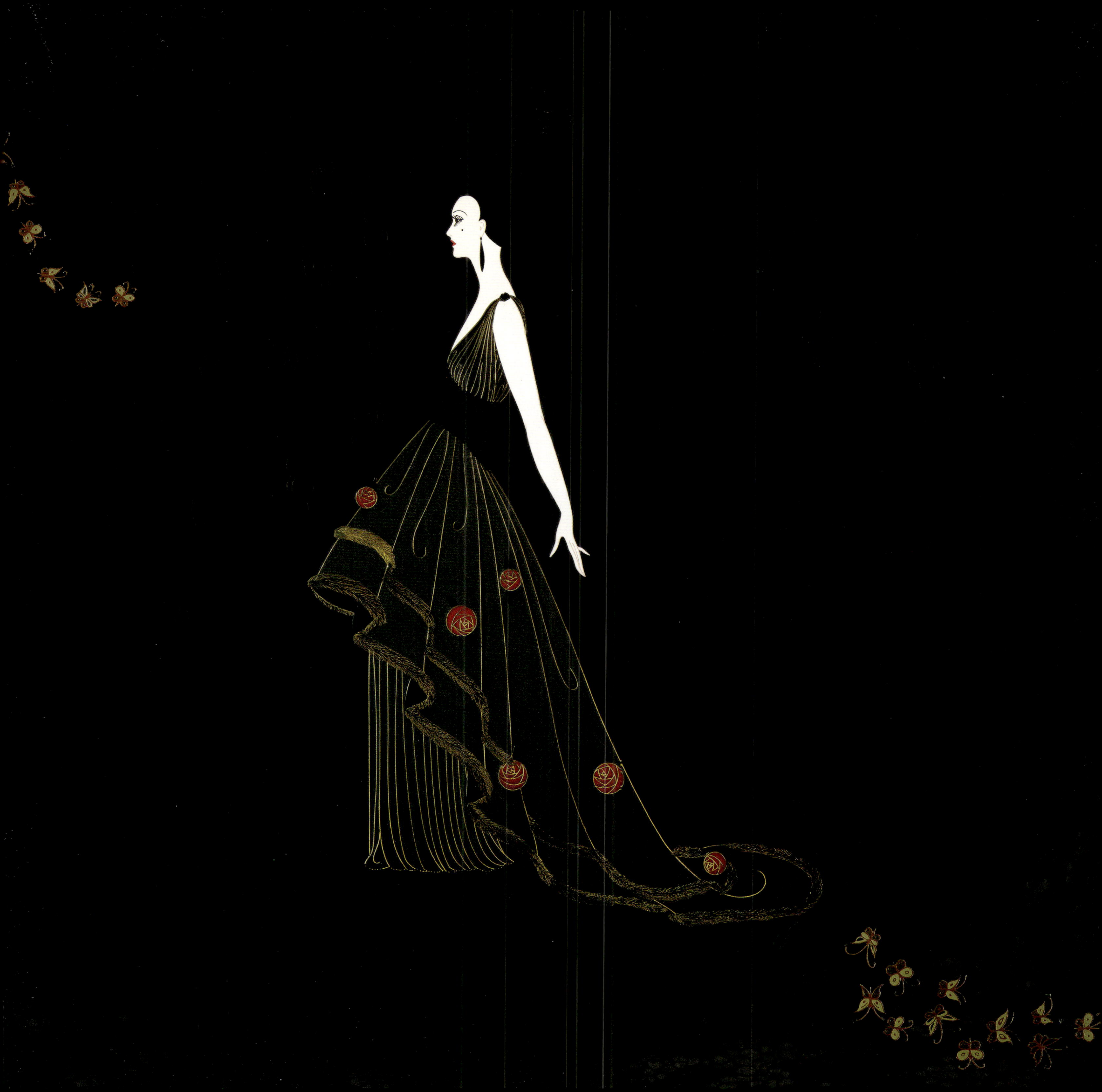

as he recalled, his mother's milliner had her shop, and to Nevsky Prospekt, the most well-known street in Russia, with its grand avenue of beautiful buildings. They would visit the Russian couturier Nadezhda Lamanova (1861–1941). The sign above her establishment proudly stated 'N. Lamanova, supplier to the Imperial Court'. In 1911, French fashion designer Paul Poiret – who would become Erté's employer in 1913 – on a European tour to exhibit his couture fashions, paid a visit to Lamanova, no doubt impressed by her aristocratic clientele. The regular visits Erté made with his mother to couture houses and retail establishments would have educated him about the world of fashion beyond St Petersburg. It was his first direct involvement with Paris haute couture. But he was not always taken with the high-fashion styles. In 1900 the fashion was for a hat to be perched on top of false hair to heighten the figure. His mother and sister's hats had elastic straps to stop them falling off. He remembered their hats rising up from their hair whenever there was a breeze, which made him laugh with its silliness. One can see from Erté's memories that fashion was his focus from a very early age.

ST PETERSBURG

St Petersburg was founded in 1703 by Peter the Great. The major buildings were built in the late Baroque or Neoclassical architectural style. The city's position on the Gulf of Finland, its waterways and beautiful buildings gave it the title 'Venice of the North'. Erté would have been familiar with the neoclassical architecture and interiors of St Petersburg's museums, galleries and palaces, as well as the Hermitage Museum which he visited regularly from the age of ten. He favoured the Egyptian, Assyrian, Classical Greek and Roman artefacts most of all. At this age he would have seen notable architecture emerging in the city, including the Church of Our Saviour on the Spilled Blood (from 1883, completed 1907), built on the spot where Tsar Alexander II was fatally wounded in an assassination attempt in 1881. The remarkable building design is informed by Russian church architecture of the sixteenth to seventeenth centuries. A prominent Art Nouveau building at Nevsky Prospekt no. 28, created as the Russian headquarters of the American Singer Sewing Machine Company, would also have been inspirational. It was designed by the Russian architect Pavel Suzor (1844–1919) and completed in 1904. In addition, the wealthy merchants, the Elisseeff Brothers, opened their flagship retail complex, the exotic 'Elisseeff Emporium', at the corner of Nevsky Prospekt and Malaya Sadovaya Ulitsa. The building was designed in the Art Nouveau style by the Ukrainian-born architect Gavriil Baranovsky (1860–1920), and completed in 1903. Both buildings eschewed the opulence, Orientalism and exoticism of the Art Nouveau style, and would have informed Erté's knowledge of decorative architecture and its accompanying interior design.

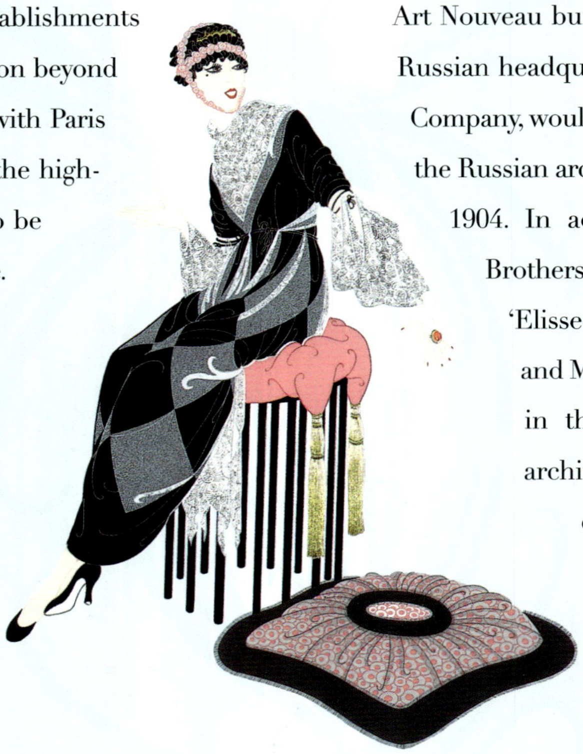

FIRST FASHION DESIGN

Erté's mother, Natalia, was a direct influence on his interest in women's style and dress design, and one of her dresses in particular remained long in his memory. It was made of black

Harmony, *1986, embossed serigraph with foil stamping, 83.8 x 70.5 cm (33 x 27¾ in)*

Fall, *1979, serigraph, 76.2 x 60.3 cm (30 x 23¾ in)*

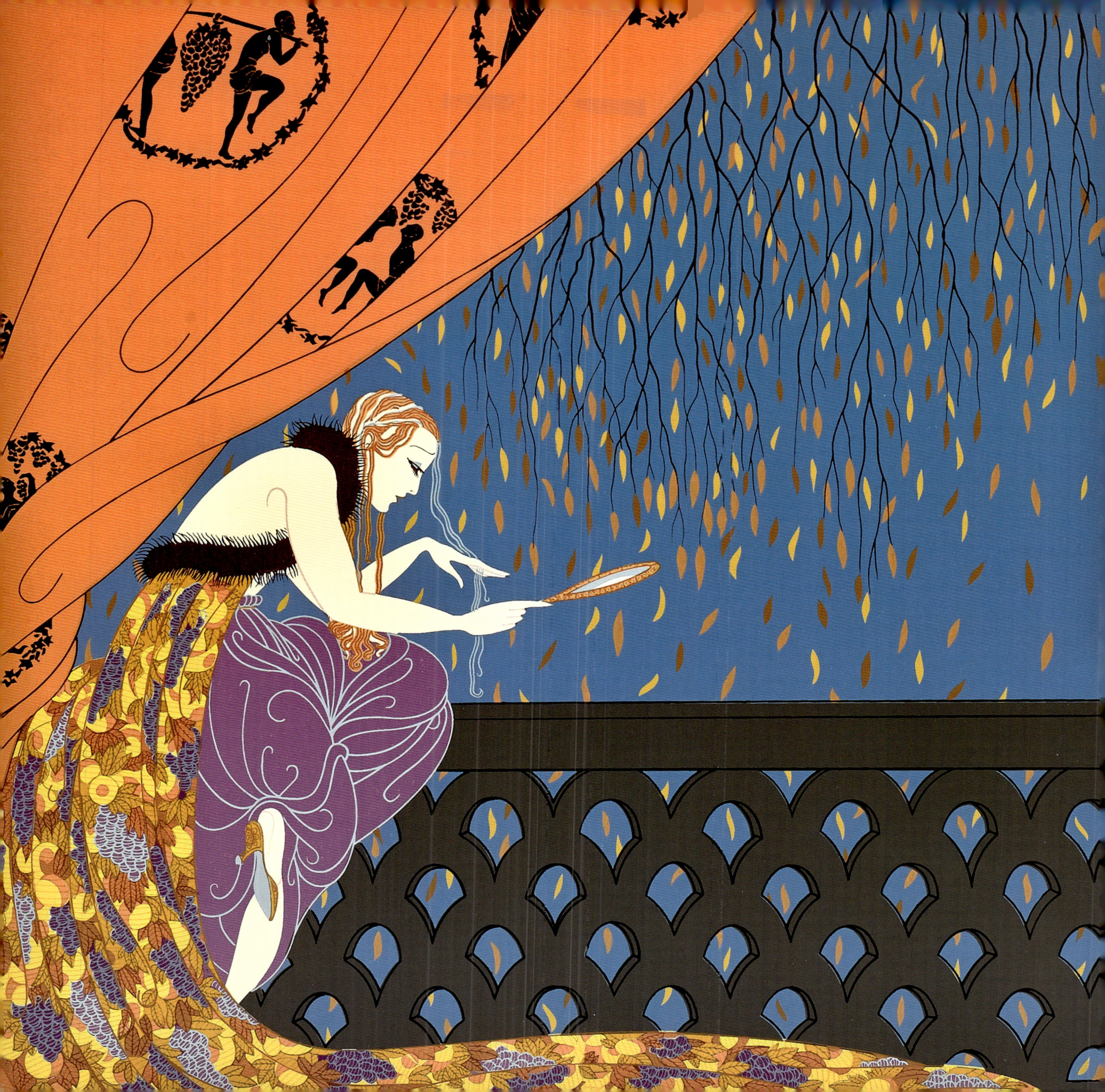

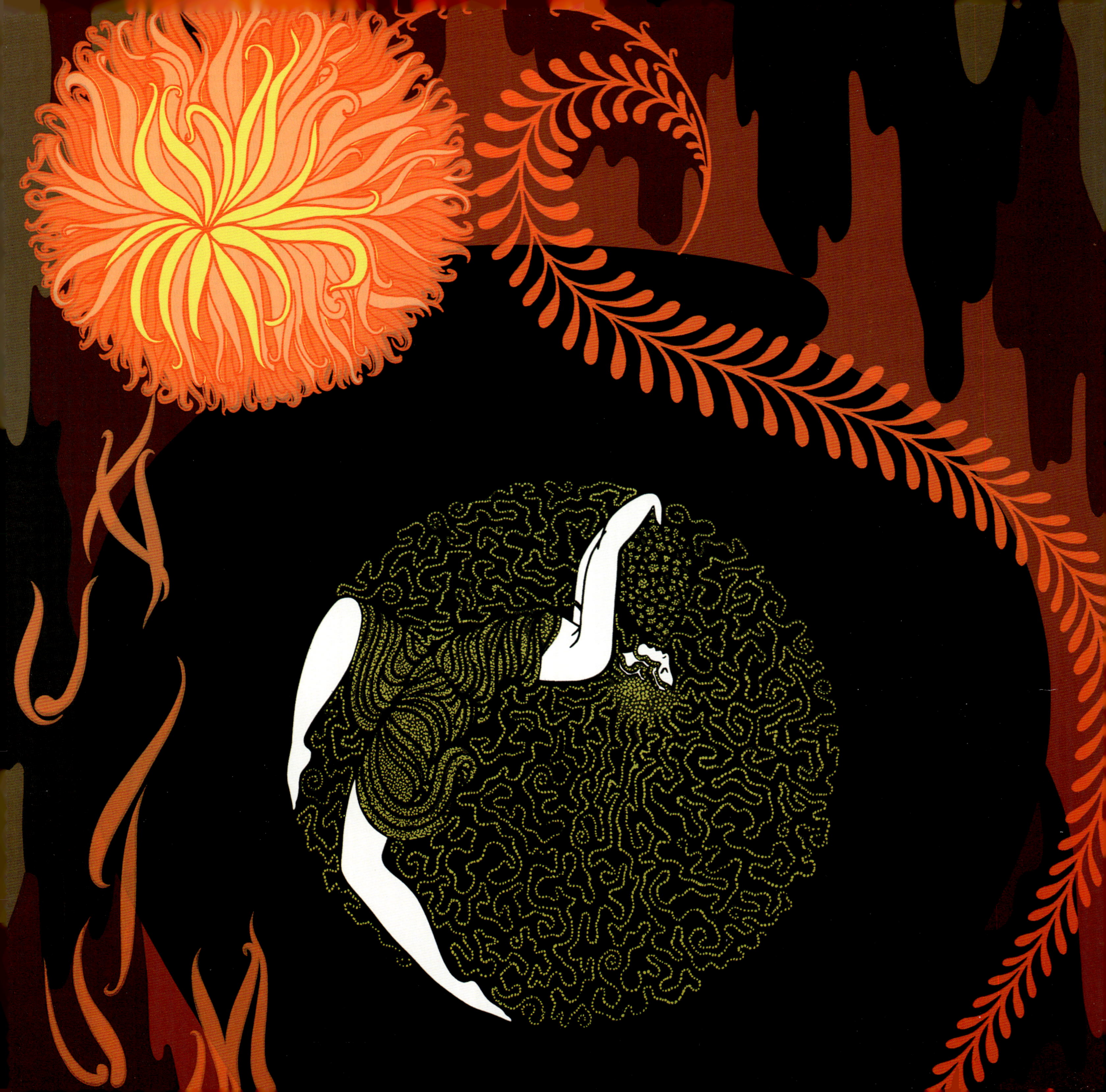

Chantilly lace laid over pink taffeta and decorated with fresh roses along the décolletage neckline. He recalled the scent of the roses as she kissed him goodnight. Erté said that even as a young child he loved to invent, and he 'couldn't live without drawing'. At five years of age, immersed in sketching, drawing and painting, he designed an evening dress for his mother styled on the traditional Russian sarafan. She was so impressed with the design that her dressmaker copied it and made the dress for her, which she wore to a reception at the Winter Palace. It was his first design creation to be made into a garment. These early drawings are sadly no longer extant. Erté cited the upheaval of the 1917 Russian Revolution for the loss of his drawings and paintings, and much of the family's possessions.

BABA LOLA

For Erté, his maternal grandmother Elena was a favourite whom he called 'Baba Lola'. Her three rules of life included eating very slowly (which he maintained throughout his life), washing her face in rainwater only, and eating carrots every morning. She lived to be 102 years of age. From the age of seven Erté was allowed to visit the Mariinsky Theatre with Baba Lola to sit with her in a private box. The first ballet he saw was *The Hunchback Horse*, based on a Russian fairy tale by Pyotr Yershaw (1815–69). It was such an experience for him that he pleaded with his parents to let him have lessons in choreography and ballet. They agreed, and he studied ballet with the noted Russian dancer Maria Mariusovna Petipa (1857–1930), daughter of a famous French dancer and choreographer Victor Marius Petipa (1818–1910).

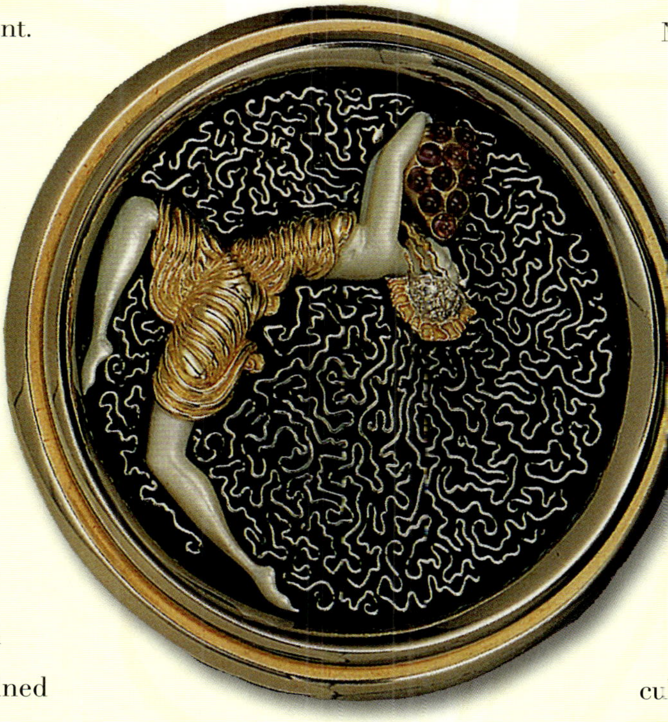

A LOVE OF OPERA

The first opera Erté saw in his grandmother's private box was *Sadko*, composed in 1896 and premiered at the Solodovnikov Theatre, Moscow in 1898 by Russian composer Nicolai Rimsky-Korsakov (1844–1908), a friend of the family. The opera had its St Petersburg premiere at the Mariinsky in January 1901. The music, the live orchestra, the singers, as well as staging, lighting and the costumes all had a great effect on Erté. He was passionate about opera and later would create many stage sets and costumes for operas and operettas, a highlight of which would include *Der Rosenkavalier* at Glyndebourne, England in 1980. For now, in childhood, his introduction to the rich cultural life of St Petersburg, in music, ballet, opera and art, found him to be a willing participant.

SCHOOL

At twelve years of age Erté was sent to school, the Eighth Gymnasium on Deviataia Linia Street, to receive a formal education. He relates that he disliked the all-black uniform, so

Autumn Song, *1977, serigraph, 46 x 34 cm (18 x 13½ in)*
This serigraph is based on Erté's painting for the November 1921 *Harper's Bazaar* cover.

Autumn Song *necklace pendant, c.1979–90, gold, silver, diamonds, amethysts, mother-of-pearl*

unlike the sailor suits and colourful velvets suits and hats he normally wore. He found school a visually dull place with grey walls and black desks, and too noisy for him. He disliked it but made some good friends. His favourite subject was Russian literature, due to a kind teacher who praised his poetry readings; but after returning home each day he immersed himself again in drawing, painting and design.

RICH CULTURAL HERITAGE

The high standing of the de Tirtoff family in the St Petersburg community meant many important visitors were entertained at their home. Apart from naval and political friends, the family welcomed composers, actors, opera singers, and both Russian and visiting performers, who were regular guests when in St Petersburg to play at the Mariinsky Theatre and other venues in the city, the Alexandrinsky and the Michailovsky. Erté's attendance at performances exposed him to theatre design, which inspired his later work. He recalled that his first exposure to modern art used for theatre design was at a performance of *Ruslan and Lyudmila* by the Russian composer Mikhail Glinka (1804–57), often called the 'father of Russian classical music'. Erté noted that the costumes and sets were by the Russian modernist artist and stage designer Alexander Golovine (1863–1930). He became familiar with the music of

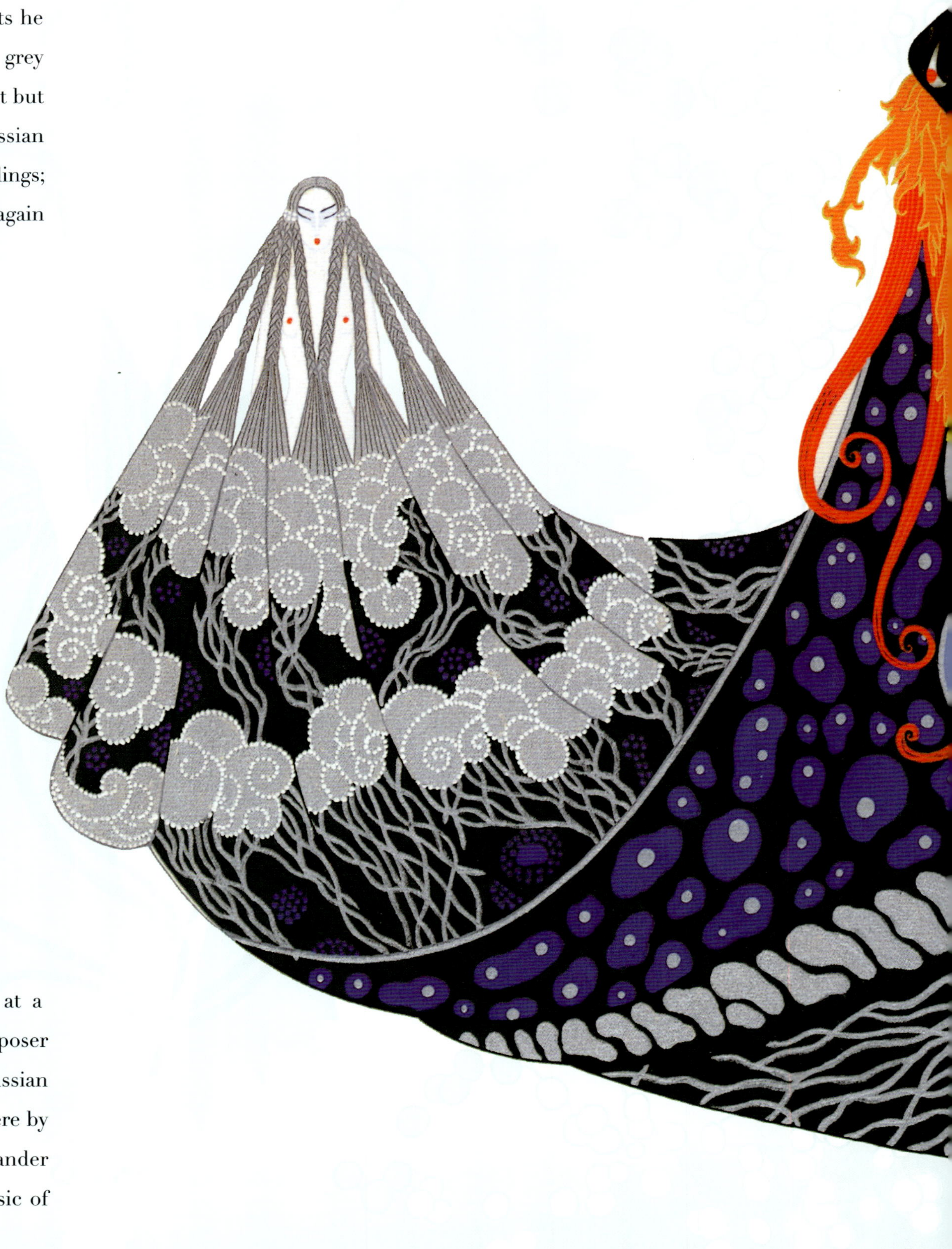

Triple costume design for the Ocean, **Les Mers**, *George White's 'Scandals', New York, 1923, gouache, 34 x 47 cm (13⅜ x 18½ in)*

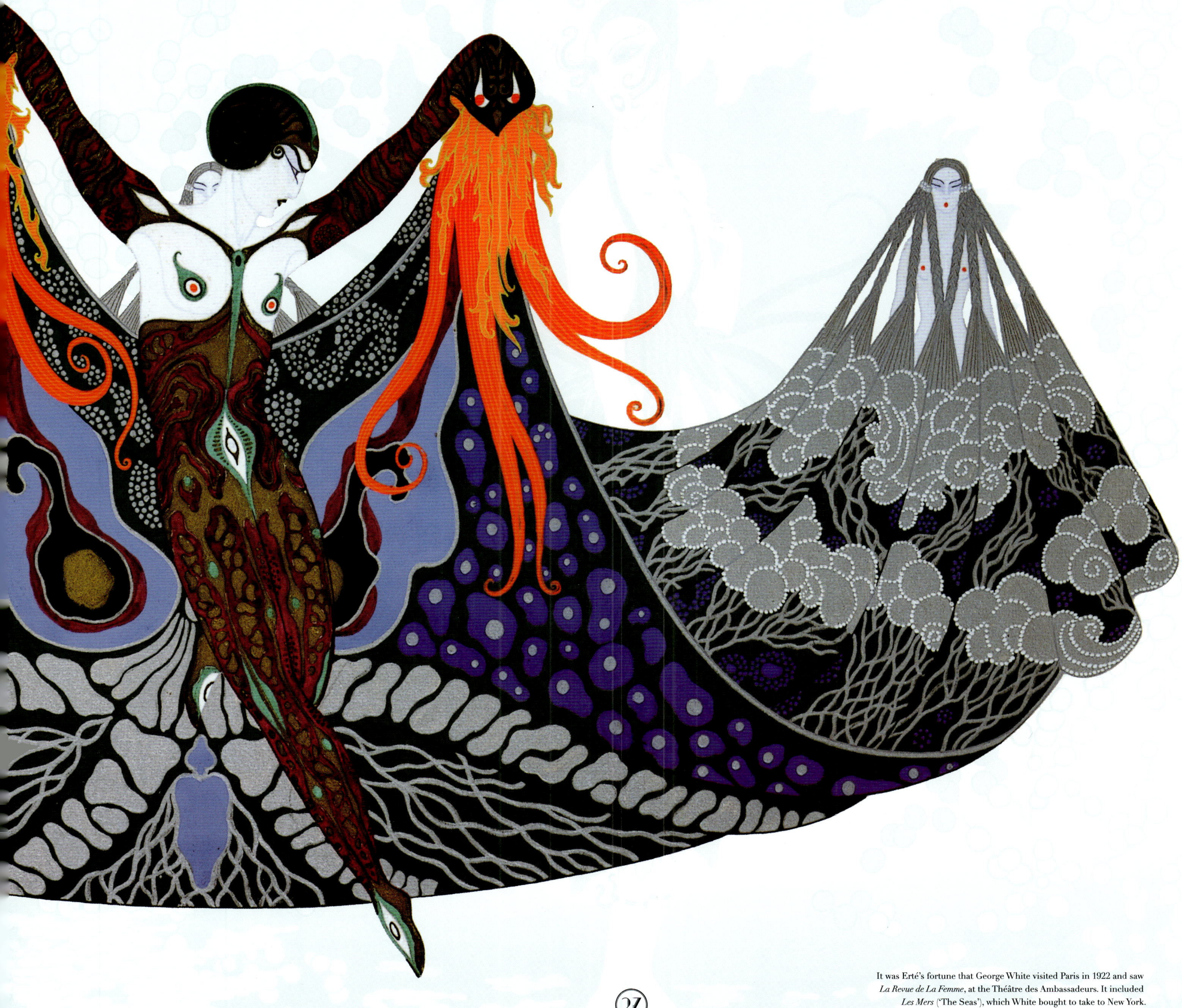

It was Erté's fortune that George White visited Paris in 1922 and saw *La Revue de La Femme*, at the Théâtre des Ambassadeurs. It included *Les Mers* ('The Seas'), which White bought to take to New York.

Russian composers and foreign singers. His first autobiography (1975) lists the dancers, the stars of Moscow's Bolshoi Ballet and the Australian operatic soprano Dame Nellie Melba (1861–1931), amongst many others, as guests at the de Tirtoff home. With the de Tirtoff house full of notable names from art, music, opera and ballet, and his regular visits to cultural institutes in St Petersburg, Erté had laid down the foundation of his future career as artist, fashion illustrator and theatre set designer.

ST PETERSBURG ACADEMY

Following his reluctance to enlist for a military career in order to concentrate on art and design, Erté's mother arranged for him to have art lessons with the famed Ukrainian artist Ilya Repin (1844–1930). In 1906, when Erté was 14, he was given several lessons with Repin at St Petersburg's Académie des Beaux Arts. After this, the artist Dmitri Lossevsky, a student at the Academy and one of Repin's pupils took over. Lossevsky gave Erté lessons on perspective, the use of light and shade, anatomy and academic instruction in landscape and portrait painting. However, Erté recalled that Lossevsky recognized the free spirit in him and gave him freedom to paint in his own style. After this early practical foundation in art, Erté painted many portraits of his family members and family pets.

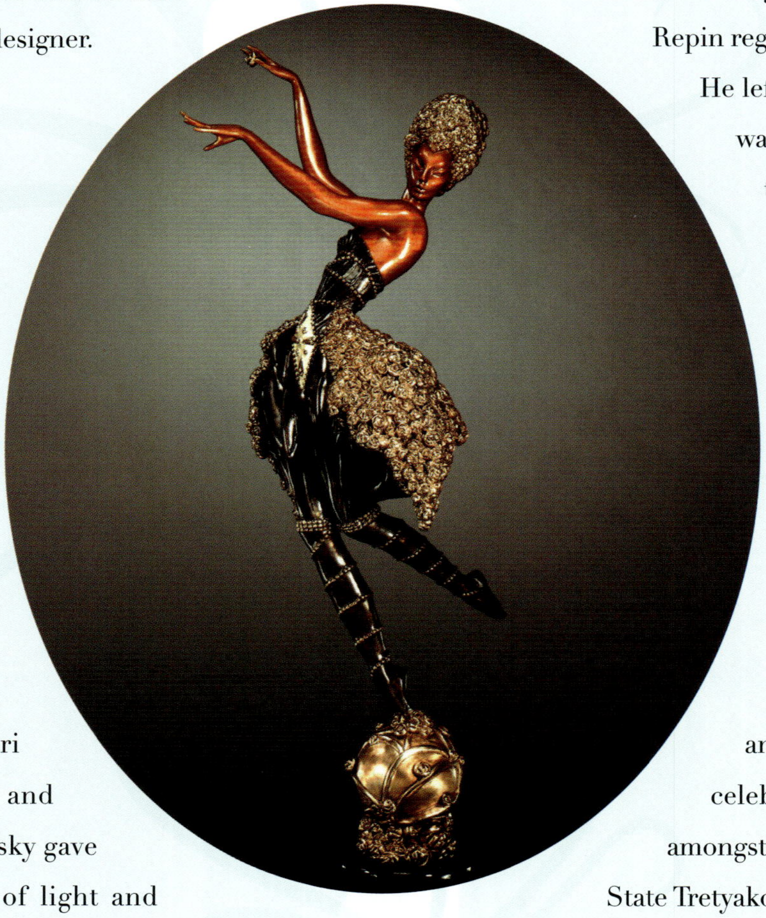

RUSSIAN ARTISTS

The renowned Russian artist of Erté's day was Ilya Repin, a member of the avant-garde Peredvizhniki ('itinerants' or 'wanderers'), a group of travelling artists who put on art exhibitions beyond Moscow and St Petersburg. They focused on Russian history, its peasantry, people and landscape. Repin regularly exhibited his work with the group. He left Moscow for St Petersburg in 1882 and was made Professor of History Painting at the Académie des Beaux Arts in the city in 1894. Erté, taught by Repin, would have been familiar with the artist's superb portraiture and vast history paintings full of colour and vibrancy. *Reply of the Zaporozhian Cossacks to Sultan Mehmed IV of the Ottoman Empire* (1880–91), currently in the State Museum of St Petersburg, took Repin over ten years to complete. Isaak Levitan (1860–1900), another member of the Peredvizhniki was celebrated as a landscape painter, noted amongst many works is *Evening Bells* (1892) in the State Tretyakov Gallery, Moscow.

THE RUSSIAN AVANT-GARDE

Younger artists were following in the path of the Peredvizhniki, who had broken away from the formality of

Rose Dancer *sculpture, 1988, bronze, 64.8 x 19.1 x 17.8 cm (25½ x 7½ x 7 in)*

Rose Dancer, *1984, embossed serigraph with foil stamping, 67.6 x 49.8 cm (26½ x 19½ in)*

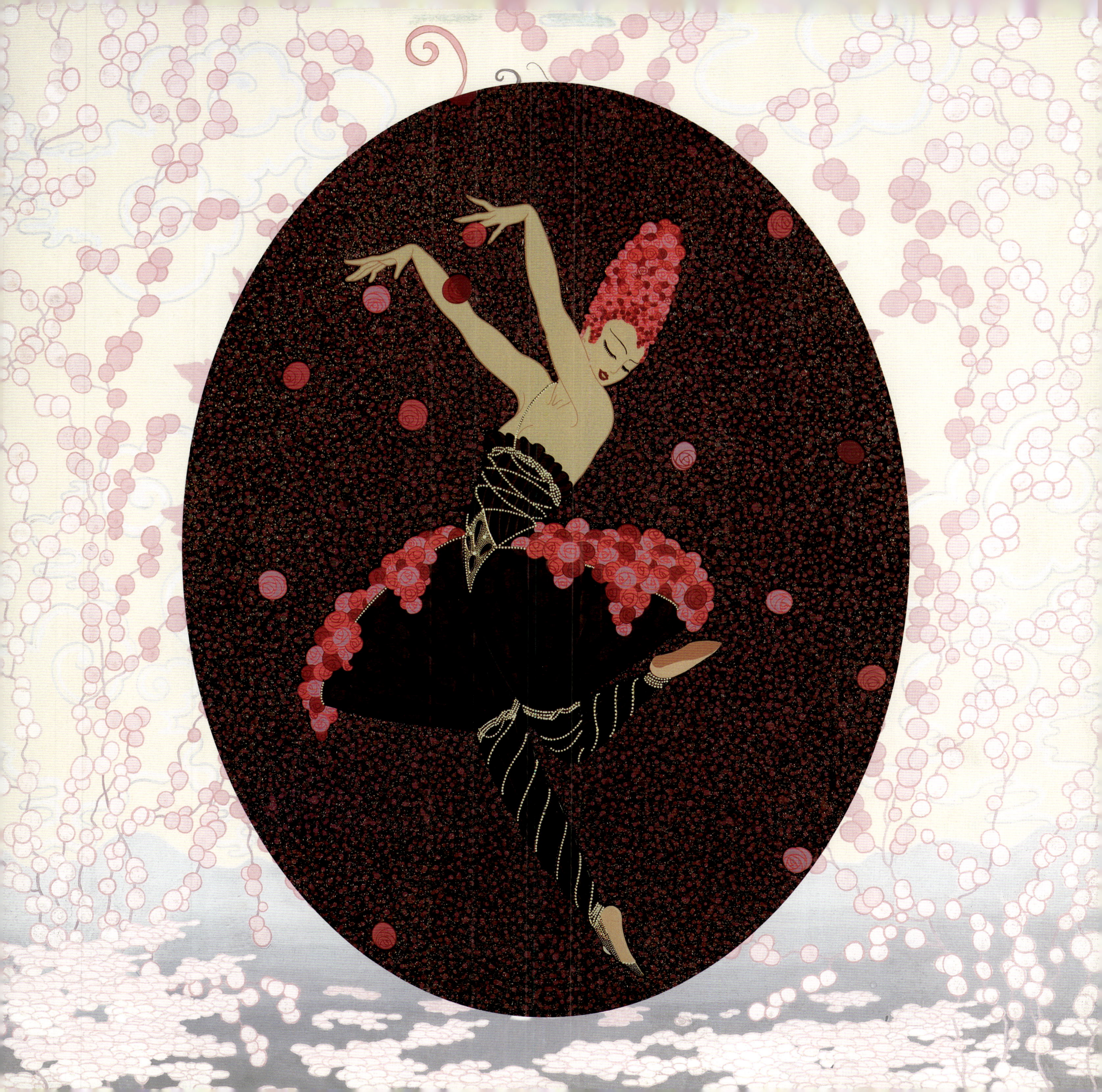

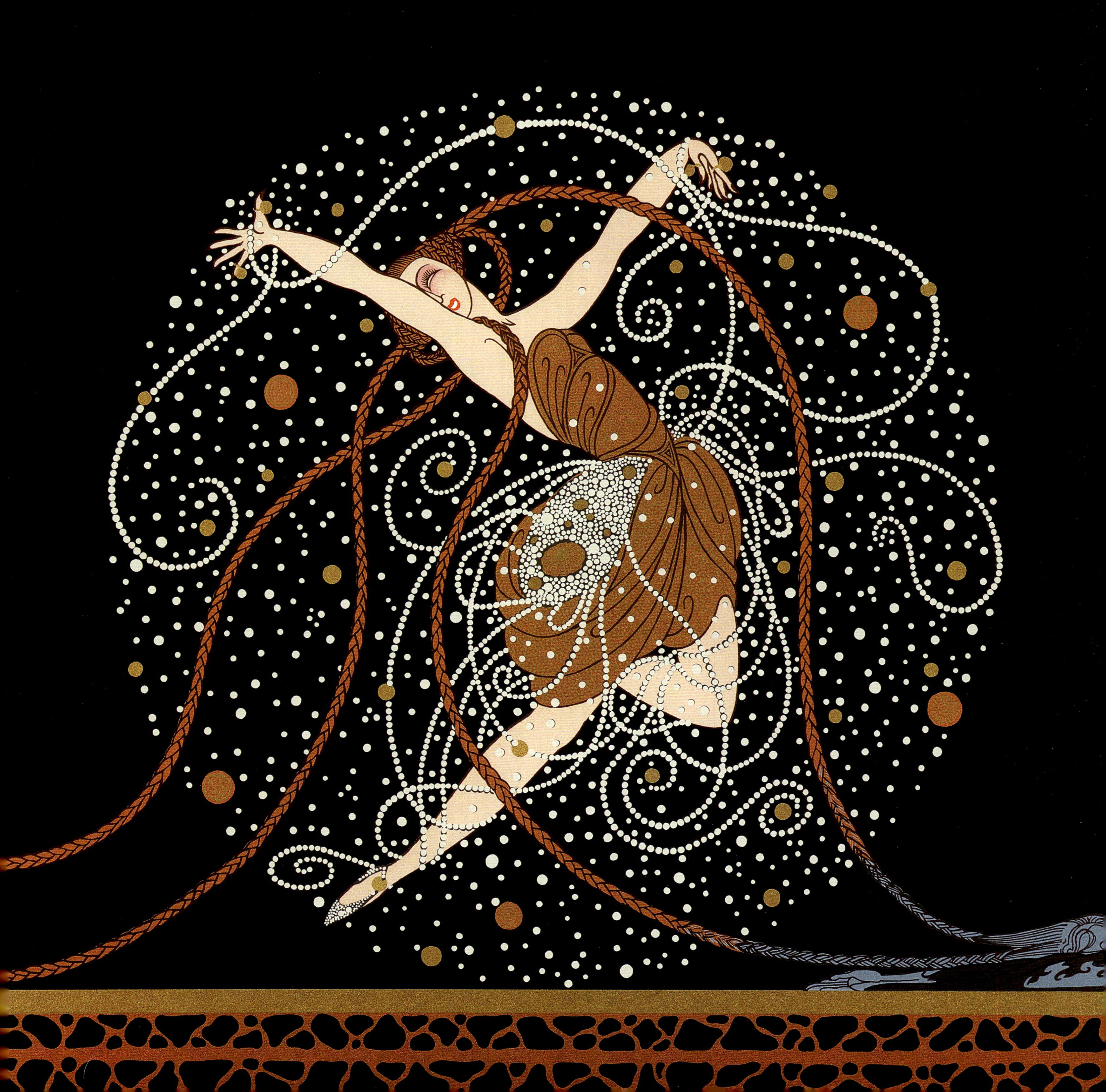

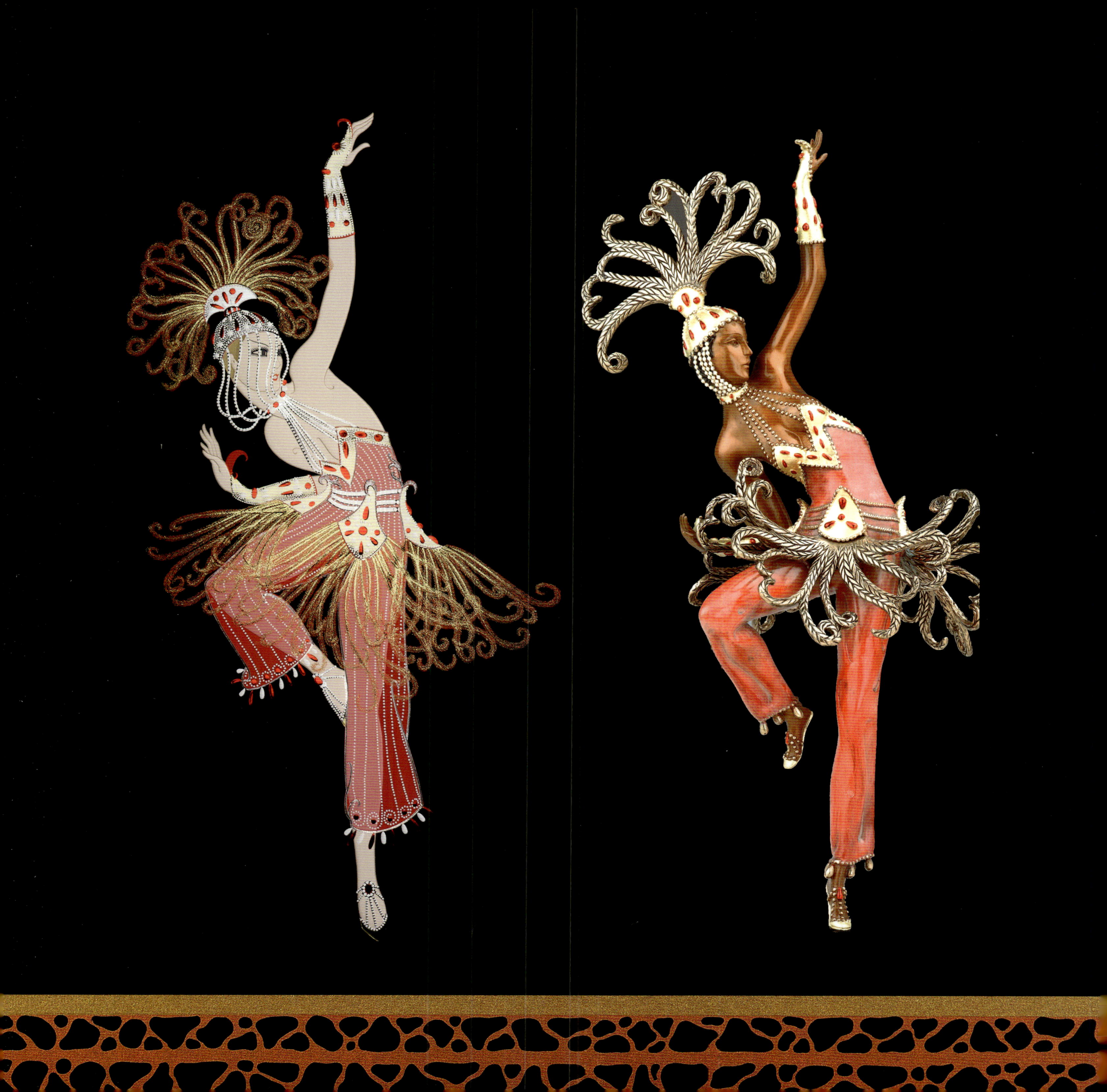

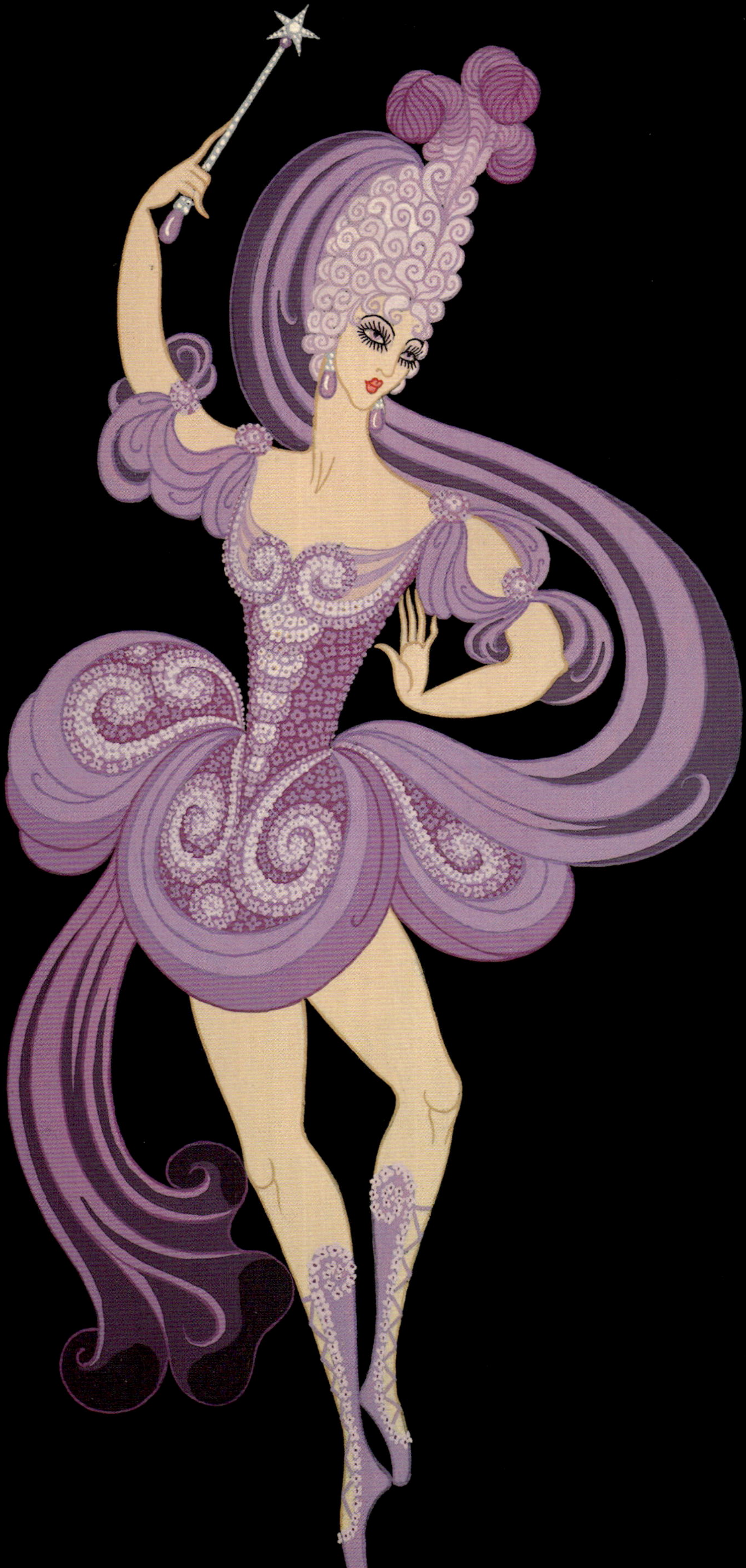

academic art teaching. Although preferring to work at his art solo, and in his own style, Erté would have been aware of avant-garde developments. St Petersburg was the Russian 'Paris' for culture. Of whom would he have been aware? Born in Moscow, Vassily Kandinsky (1866–1944) is credited as the first artist to paint a purely abstract work. His works, rich in colour, were inspired by Russian fairy tales, folk art and landscape. Kiev-born Kasimir Malevich (1878–1935), a pioneer of abstraction, stands out for his painting *Black Suprematic Square* (1915) in the Tretyakov Gallery, Moscow. Vitebsk-born Marc Chagall (1887–1985), a near-age contemporary to Erté, studied art in St Petersburg from 1907–10 before moving to Paris, living there from 1910–14. The rich dynamic of colours in Chagall's art, as in *I and the Village* (1911, Museum of Modern Art, New York), reflect his interest in the Fauves.

Russian artists in Paris included Mikhail Larionov (1881–1964), founder of art groups Jack of Diamonds (1909–11), and the Donkey's Tail (1912–13), who moved to Paris in 1915, and Natalia Goncharova (1881–1962), a painter, set designer, costume designer and illustrator noted for her interest in Russian folk art and Byzantine art. Both worked for Sergei Diaghilev's Ballets Russes, and their work would have been known to Erté in St Petersburg and Paris.

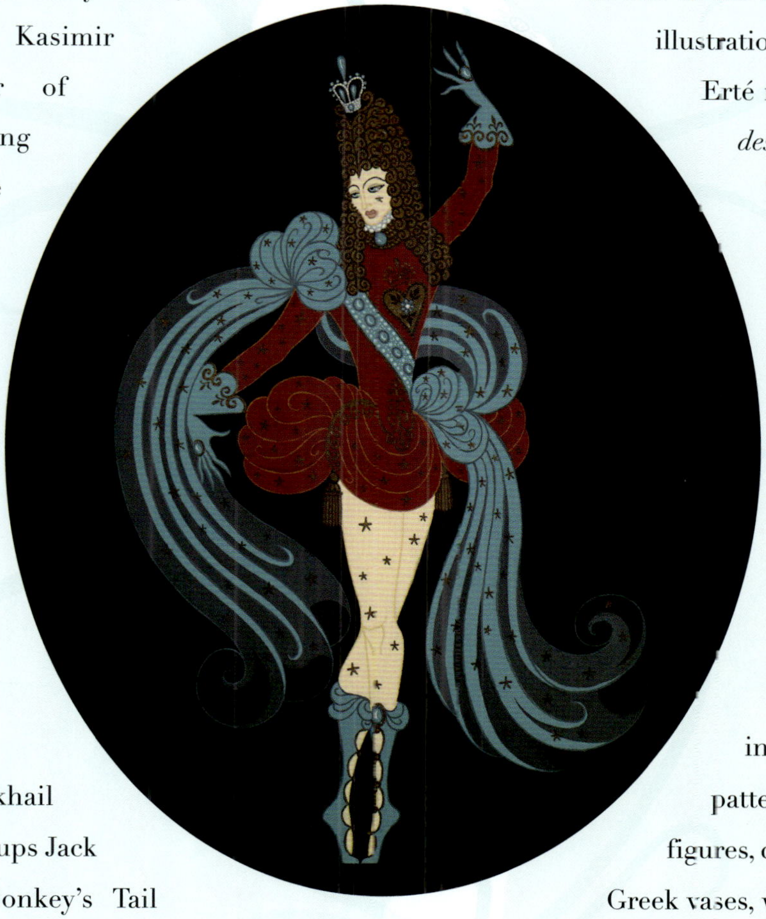

EARLY INFLUENCES ON COLOUR & DESIGN

Writing in his autobiographies about his earliest memories of inspiration for design, Erté referred back to his studies of Indian and Persian miniatures. His first exposure to this art form was in one of his father's books which contained colour illustrations of this type of rich, visual illustration. Erté refers to the 'exotic feminine eyes' and *des yeux de biche* ('ascending eyebrows'). They riveted his attention. The art inspired him. The Persian love of richness of colour and pattern can be seen in his works, including the *Triple costume design for 'the Ocean'* (1923) for the musical revue *Les Mers* (*see* pages 26–27); in the *Curtain design for Phantasm* (1928), *see* page 164); and stage sets and costumes for *Scheherazade* (1929), just three of so many examples. Erté spent much time in the Hermitage Museum too, studying pattern and visual content, for example the figures, clothing and style of painting on ancient Greek vases, which is evident in his illustrations and sculptures. At home he would try to recreate what he had seen at the Hermitage in his own works. The museum's rich collections from ancient Egypt to contemporary Russia, the decorative arts and costumes, and the design of the building itself, must have seeped into Erté's consciousness, like osmosis. The many types of art and design from Egyptian motifs to

(Previous left) **Ondée**, *1983, serigraph, 76.2 x 55.9 cm (30 x 22 in)*
(Previous centre) **Firebird** , *1987, serigraph, 108.6 x 72.4 cm (42¾ x 28½ in)*
(Previous right) **Fire Dancer** *sculpture, 1989, bronze, 60 x 27 x 17 cm (25½ x 10½ x 6½ in)*

(Left) **Costume design for the Lilac Fairy in The Sleeping Beauty,** *Diaghilev Ballet, 1921, gouache, 51.4 x 41.3 cm (20¼ x 16¼ in)*
(Above) **Costume design for Prince Charming in The Sleeping Beauty,** *Diaghilev Ballet, 1921, gouache, 51.4 x 41.3 cm (20¼ x 16¼ in)*

Russian icons, Byzantine mosaics and European Orientalism all feature in his professional work, many elements of which were formed in these early years of historical study in St Petersburg.

AT THE BALLET

Erté's introduction to the ballet in St Petersburg created a lasting passion. Unfortunately, his costume drawings from that period are lost. However, one of his earliest extant illustrations, dated 1911, is *Design for an Imaginary Ballet*. Erté continued to patronize Russian performances that were in demand in Paris. In 1912 he attended the Ballets Russes performance of *L'Apres-Midi d'un Faune* ('The Afternoon of the Faun'), choreographed by the principal dancer, the young Ukrainian-born Russian Vaslav Nijinsky (1890–1954). *Loge de Théâtre* (1912, *see* page 17) gives a flavour of the fun to be had attending the ballet, plays, operas or a ball. Erté encapsulated it in early works and later echoes of it can be found in the serigraphs *The Balcony* (1989, *see* page 11), *Ready for the Ball* (1981), and *Opening Night* (1985, *see* page 12). They summarize the culture of St Petersburg and Paris at the beginning of the twentieth century, where the richly dressed audience were part of the spectacle, to be seen and commented on in the newspapers.

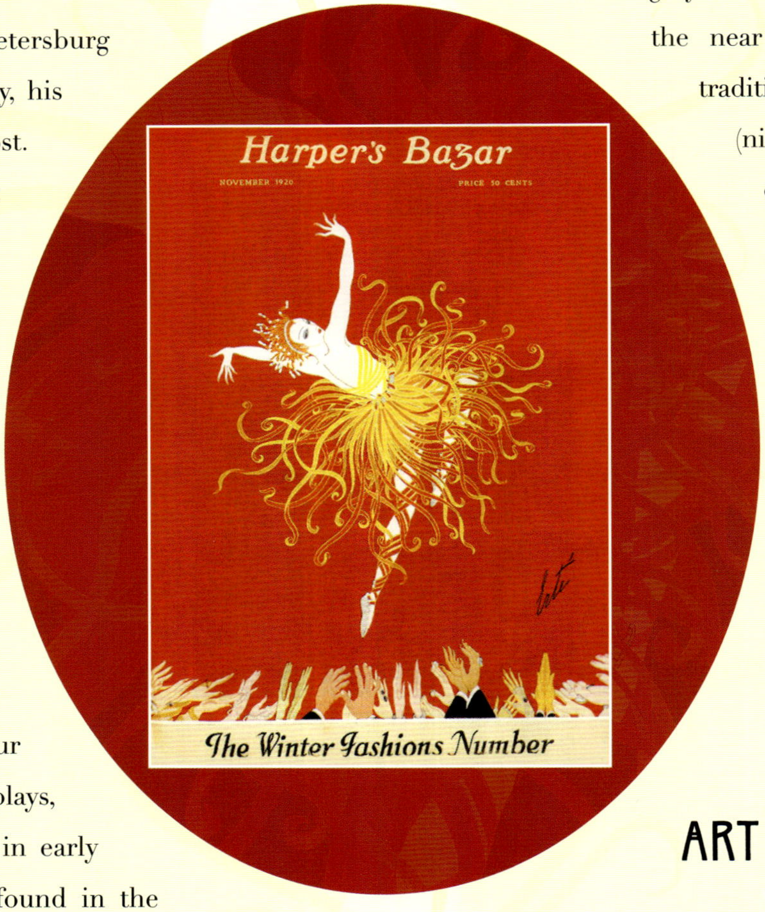

1900: EXPOSITION UNIVERSELLE, PARIS

Erté and his family visited the 1900 *Exposition Universelle* in Paris, held from April to November. At its centre was the Eiffel Tower. Many of the temporary buildings and pavilions surrounding it were in the decorative style of Art Nouveau with historicist references mixing styles and eras from the Orient, Indo-China, Japan, the near East, Egypt and European folklore tradition. The Porte Monumentale entrance (nicknamed *La Salamandre*), near the Place de la Concorde was a fantasy combination of many decorative styles. In the streets the de Tirtoff family would have seen public entrances to the new Metropolitan Line 'Metro', created by Hector Guimard (1867–1942), from 1898–1901, each station with its distinctive cast iron frames in green, decorated with Guimard's trademark curling, curving plant tendrils synonymous with Art Nouveau.

ART NOUVEAU ON SALE

Siegfried Bing (1838–1905), owner of the Paris shop 'Salon de L'Art Nouveau' at 22 rue de Provence, had his own pavilion at the 1900 *Exposition Universelle* displaying decorative art, graphics and fine art. Notable names in his collection were Louis Comfort Tiffany (1848–1933), René Lalique (1860–1945), Henri de Toulouse-Lautrec (1864–1901) and Alphonse Mucha (1860–1939).

Harper's Bazar *cover, November 1920*

Applause, *1981, serigraph, 74 x 58 cm (29 x 23 in)*

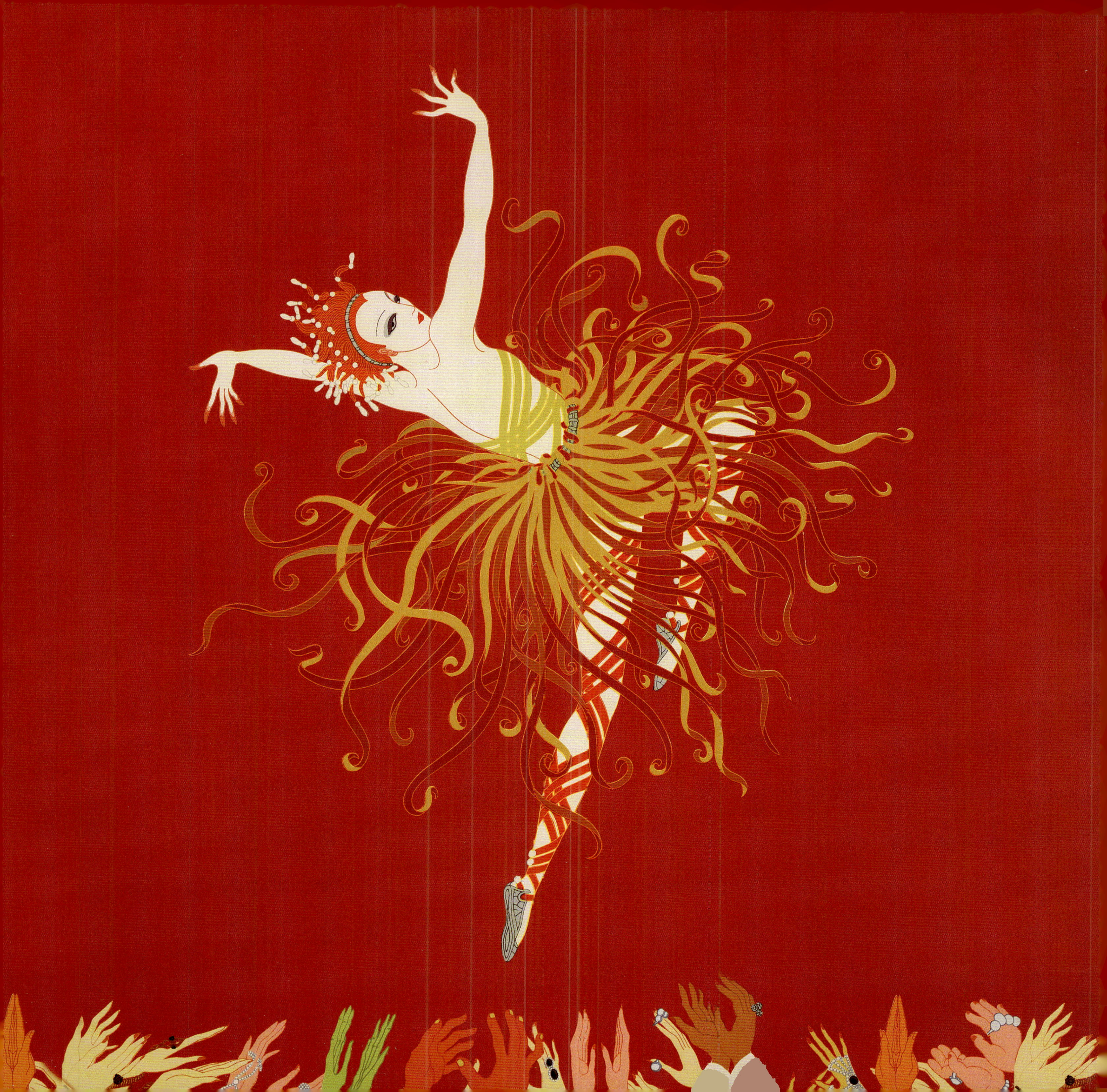

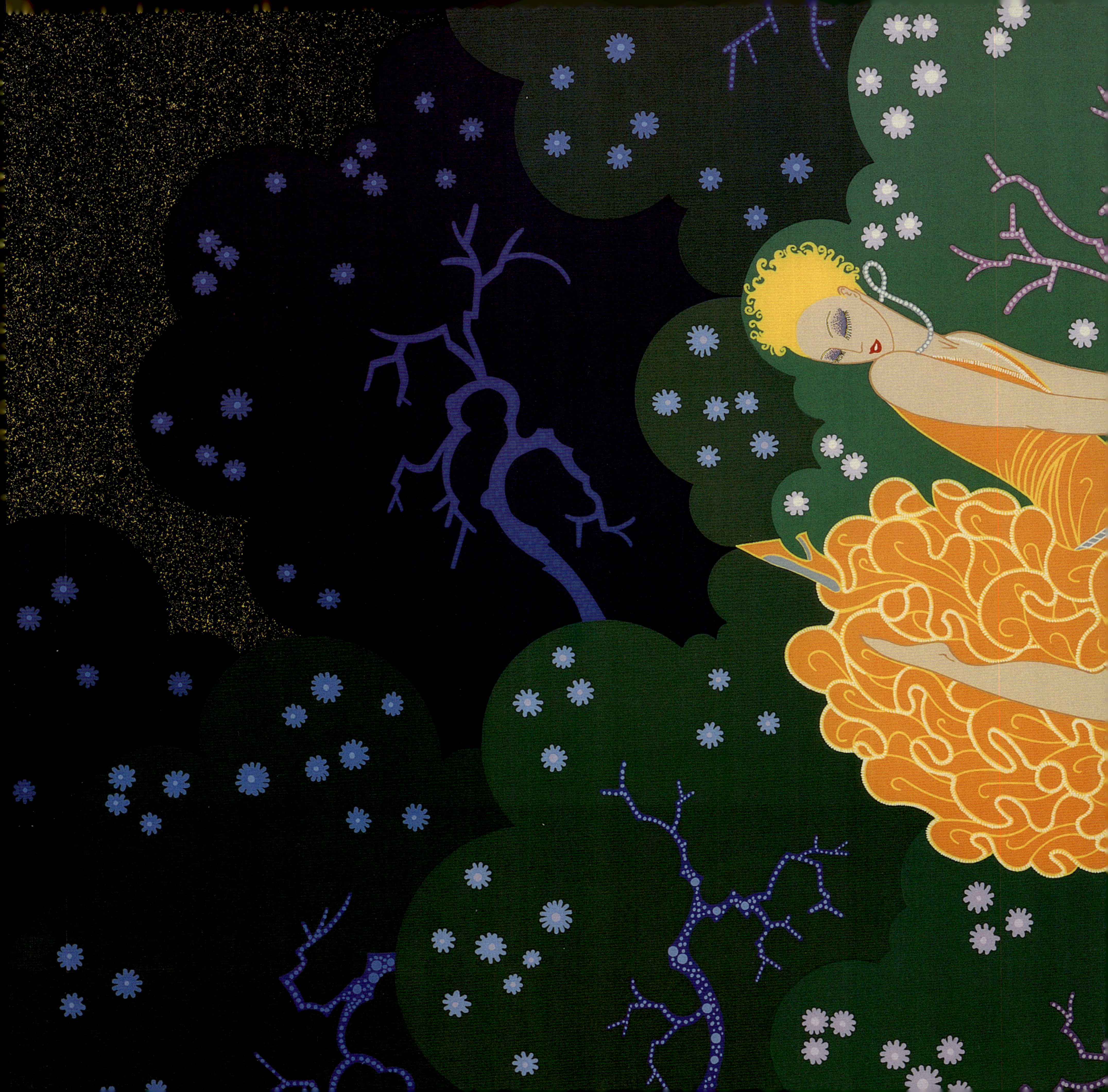

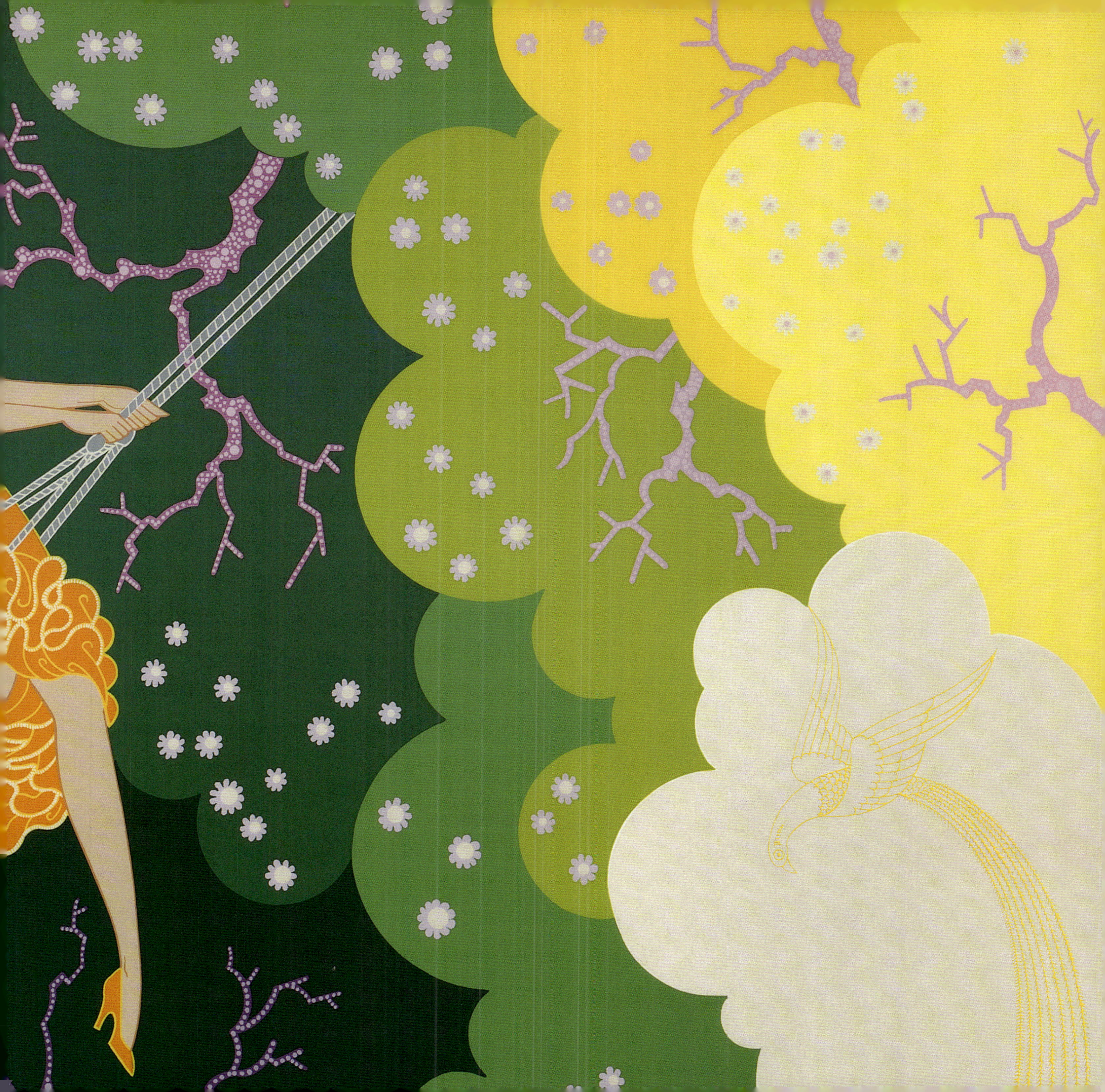

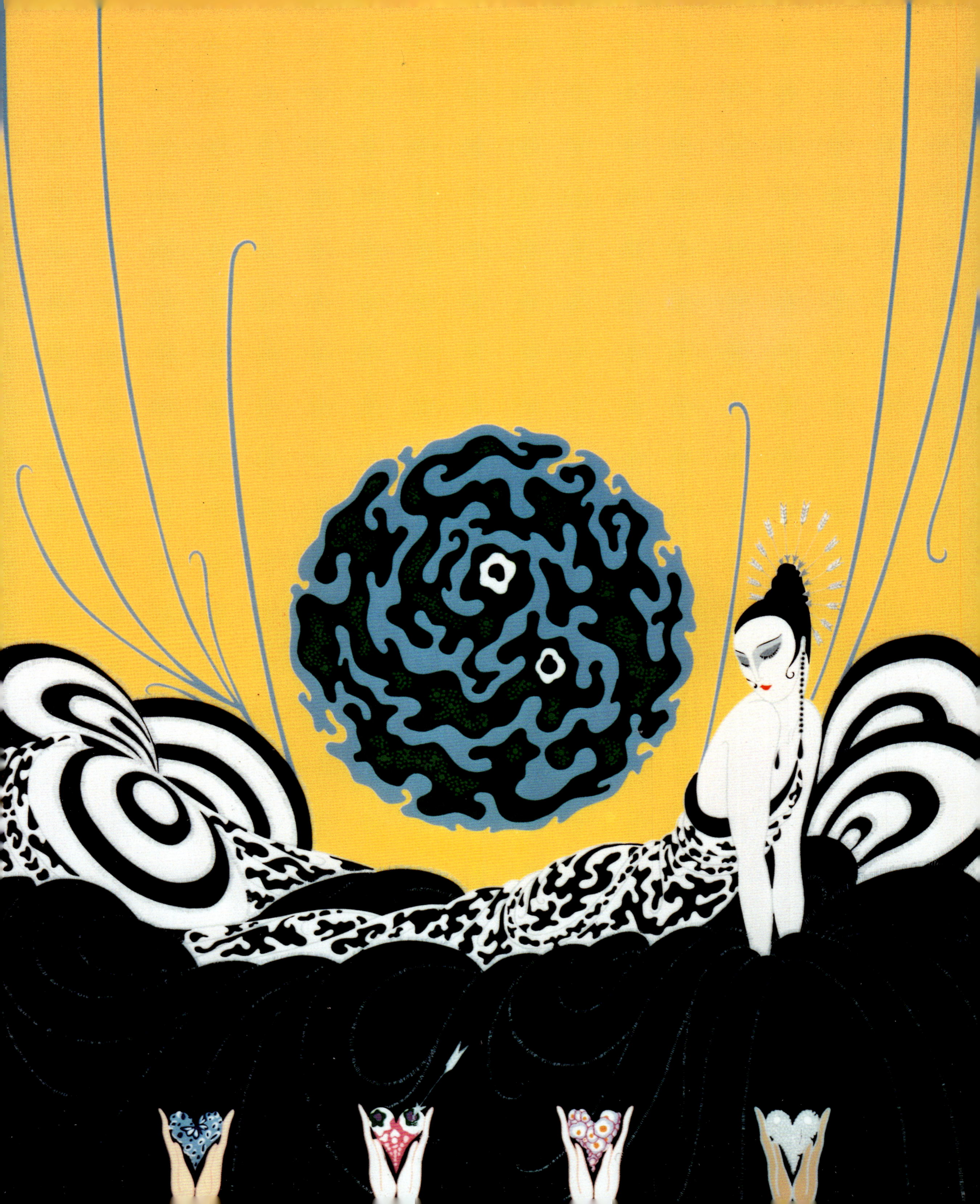

INSPIRED BY ART NOUVEAU

From the outset of his career in fashion, Erté's costume designs were always accessorized, often with pieces of jewellery. Limited edition jewellery would later become a lucrative addition to his commercial sales of prints and sculptures. What inspired his style? Who was influencing jewellery design in Erté's early years? Parisian jeweller Georges Fouquet (1862–1957) filled his Paris shop with decorative Art Nouveau jewellery. For his display at the 1900 *Exposition Universelle* he commissioned Alphonse Mucha, the Czech émigré artist living in Paris, to design jewellery pieces that were similar to creations originally invented by the artist in posters advertising the plays of the French actress Sarah Bernhardt. The Mucha jewellery sold with great success. The exposition also showcased the work of the St Petersburg jewellery designer to the nobility, Karl Fabergé (1846–1926), who displayed his fabulously jewelled Easter eggs. When one looks for influences on Erté for his creative designs, the 1900 *Exposition* was sure to have provided many that were to have a profound affect on him for the rest of his life. It must have been a thrilling starting point for the young artist. One needs only to look at the sinuous lines of some of Erté's designs (*see* pages 24–25 and 54–55 for example) to see the legacy of Art Nouveau.

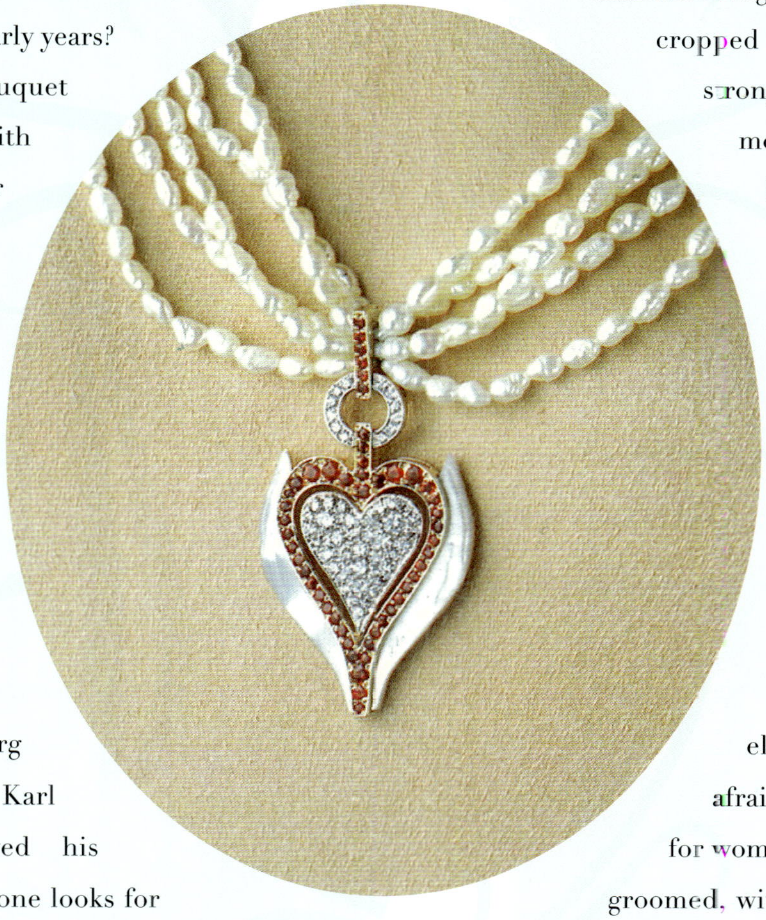

ERTÉ'S 'NARCISSUS' REFLECTION

Looking through Erté's early pen and ink drawings or gouache designs, dated to 1913–16, his female models wear their hair short, cropped or hidden by a turban or hat (*see*, for example, pages 118–19). One can see Erté making – rather than following – fashion in the later craze for short, cropped bobs or shingle cuts, which emerged strongly after the First World War. Looking more closely, and comparing the shape of his models' facial features and short hair, one can perhaps see a 'Narcissus' reflection of Erté himself. (In ancient Greek mythology Narcissus fell in love with his own image.) If one looks at early twentieth-century photographs of Erté in his formal hand-made suits, or flamboyant costumes for a ball or a masquerade, he was always immaculately groomed, elegant in his form of dress and not afraid to wear couturier costumes designed for women. His facial features were handsome, groomed, with soft dark eyes, an aquiline nose, a small rosebud mouth, and hair styled short and slicked; a twentieth-century refined dandy. Comparing his features to his models' one can see in his features a reflection of the ideal he portrayed in his drawings and gouaches: an elegant, slim body shape, with short, cropped hair. He was the inspiration for the recognizable Erté look.

(Previous) **The Swing**, *1984, serigraph with foil stamping, 57.4 x 80.6 cm (22½ x 31¾ in)*
This playful composition echoes an earlier famous painting, *The Swing*, 1767, by Jean-Honoré Fragonard (1732–1806), in the Wallace Collection, London. Erté may have seen it in person during visits to London.

(Left) **Selection of a Heart**, *1978, serigraph, 60 x 47 cm (23½ x 18⅜ in)*
(Above) **Selection of a Heart** *necklace, c. 1979–90, gold, diamonds, rubies, freshwater pearls, mother-of-pearl*

1912: PARIS

In Erté's own words, after an enthusiastic embarkation from St Petersburg in 1912, he found his first year in Paris 'rather difficult'. He had loved the city since his first visit with his parents and sister in 1900 to see the *Exposition Universelle*, a memory that remained with him for the rest of his childhood. Now, living in the city alone it would be a different Paris. Erté had insisted that his family did not continue to support him financially. He had money saved. After initial plans to rent lodgings recommended by friends – it was full – he found a modest room in a lodging house. He later realized it to be a *maison de passe* (brothel), a low-rental hotel frequented by prostitutes and clients in rooms paid for by the hour. Even so, Erté found the girls very polite to him as they passed by on the stairs, and he stayed.

ARCHITECTURE OR ART?

Piotr and Natalia de Tirtoff wanted their son to study architecture at the École des Beaux Arts in Paris, as they believed it to be a better profession than that of an artist. Erté had agreed but always planned to study art instead and enrolled at the sought-after private art school, the Académie Julian (established in 1868). It was *the* place to study art in Paris and a good primer for artists wanting to enter the École des Beaux-Arts. There were four locations in Paris (one solely for women artists), and the Académie had a roster of around 600 students. The list of its now-famous artists is dazzling. From Erté's era, French artists in Paris include Henri Matisse (1869–1954), André Derain (1880–1954) and Marcel Duchamp (1887–1968); and foreign students, the American Robert Henri (1865–1929), Czech artist and graphic designer Alphonse Mucha, and German-Danish artist Emil Nolde (1867–1956).

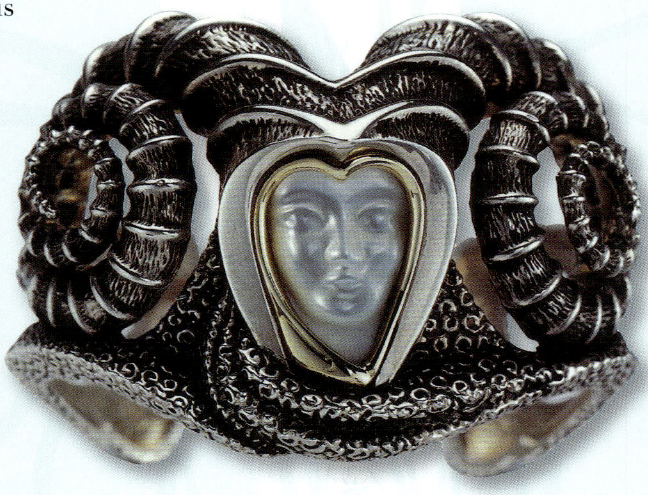

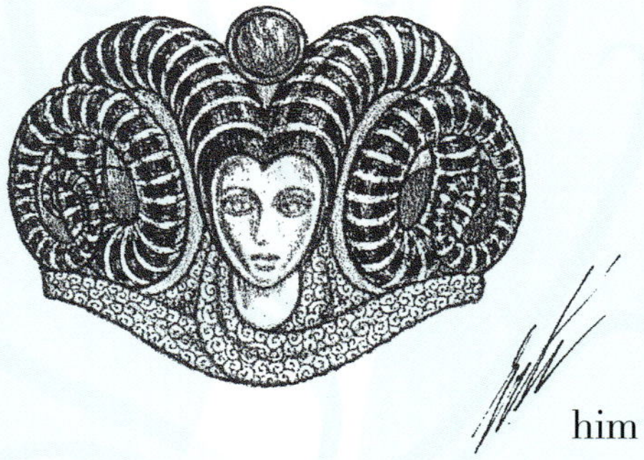

ACADÉMIE JULIAN

At the Académie Julian, Erté studied in a class taught by the French painter Jean-Paul Laurens (1838–1921), a noted artist of historical paintings in the classical academic tradition. However, perhaps due to his earlier dislike of attending school as a teenager, Erté preferred to work on his own rather than in a group of fellow artists. He did not want others to watch him at work, a habit that was formed in his childhood, closing his book or paint box if anyone stopped to study his drawings or paintings. He left the Académie after a three-month study period. Money was in short supply. It was a problem Erté suffered even through his most productive periods in the 1920s to 1940s when he was earning vast amounts, as his lifestyle at times overtook his income. In 1912 in Paris he recalled that

(Above) **La Courbe** *bracelet, c. 1979–90, silver, gold, mother-of-pearl*

(Right) **The Golden Fleece**, *1986, embossed serigraph with foil stamping, 90.2 x 74.9 cm (35½ x 29½ in)*

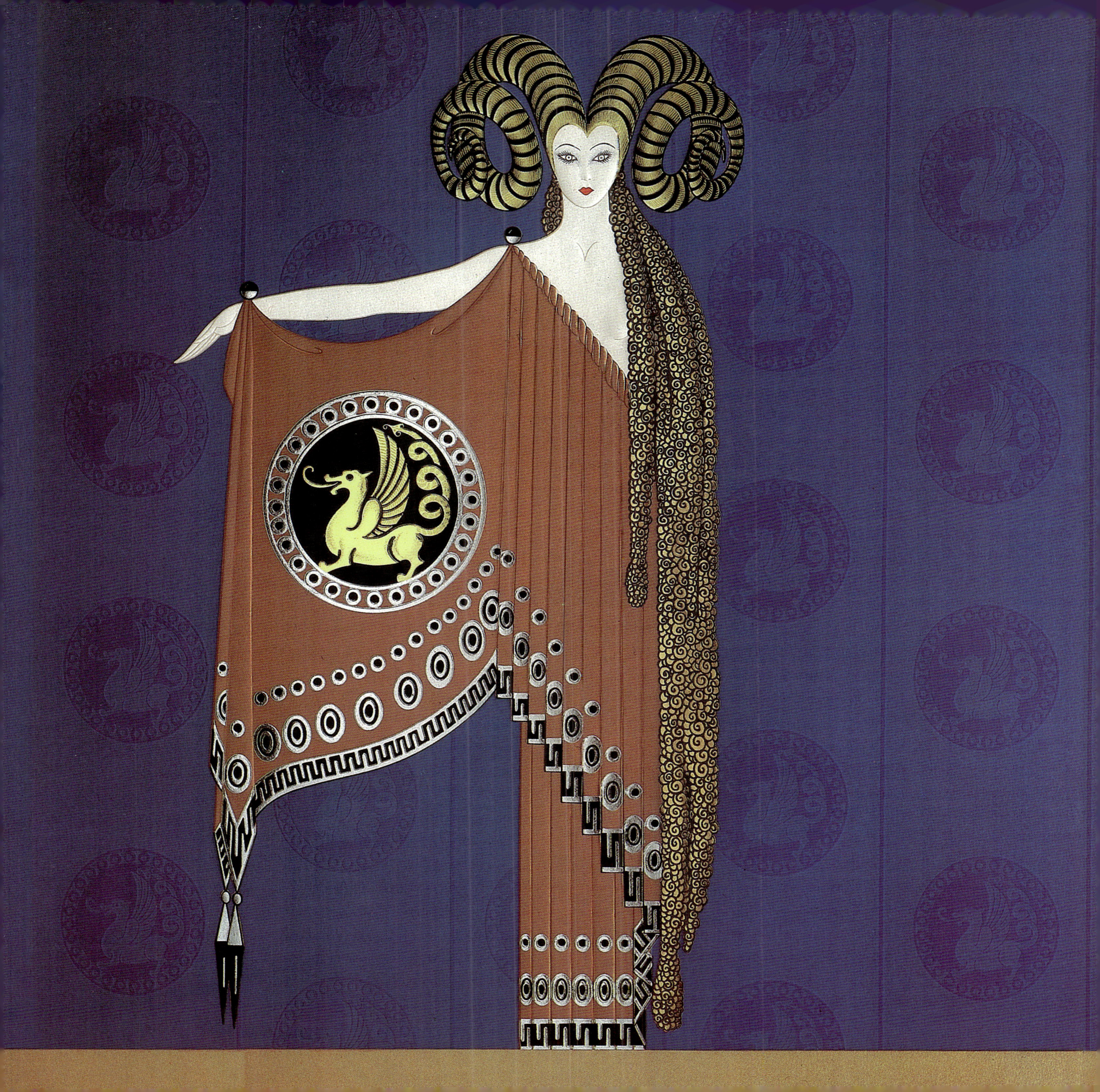

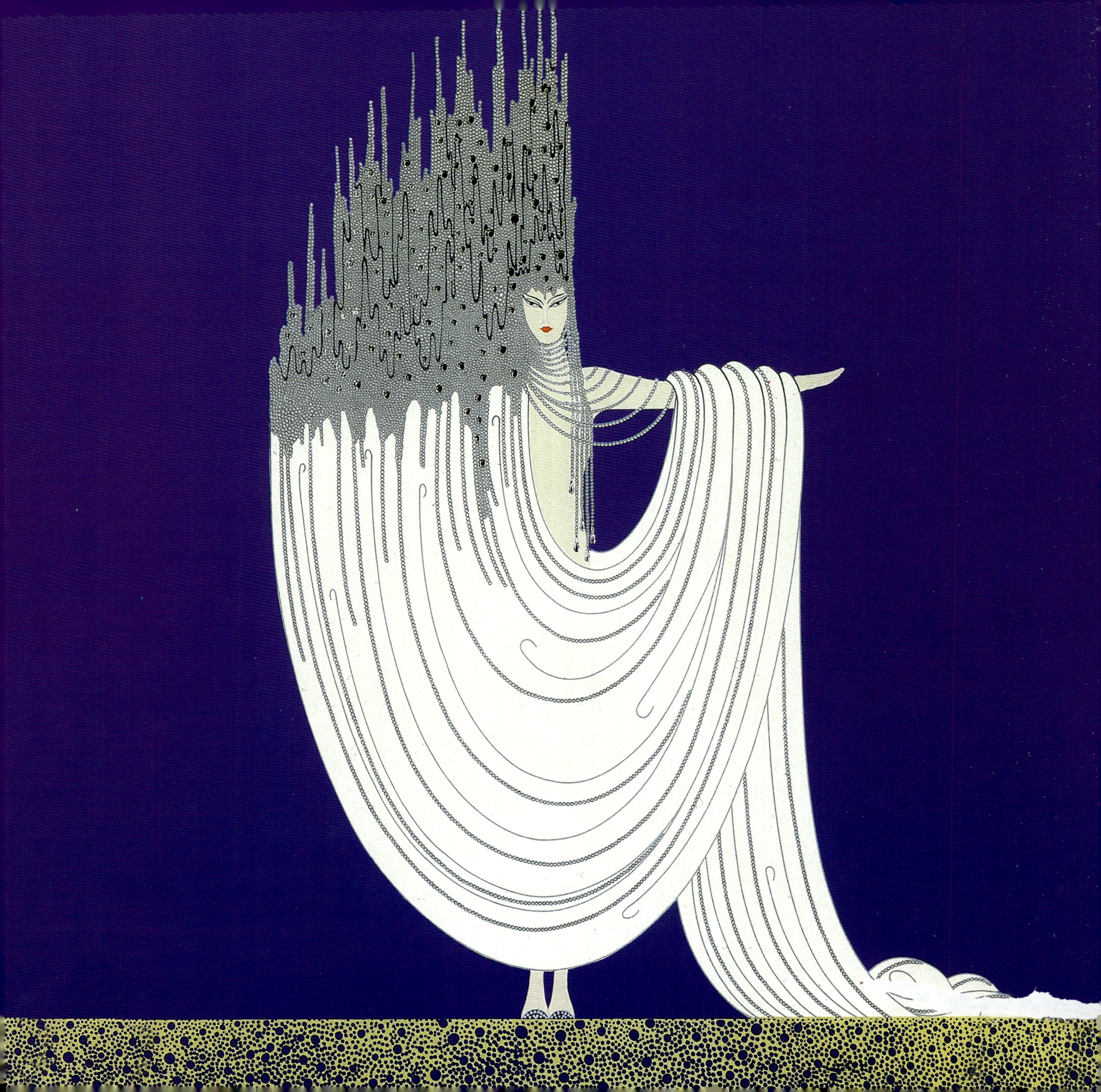

when he had little money he survived on hot chestnuts bought from street vendors and bowls of boiled beef broth from the Bouillon Duval restaurant. However, he did spend money on regular visits to the theatre, even when impoverished, as an essential cultural preference.

FROM ART NOUVEAU TO CUBISM

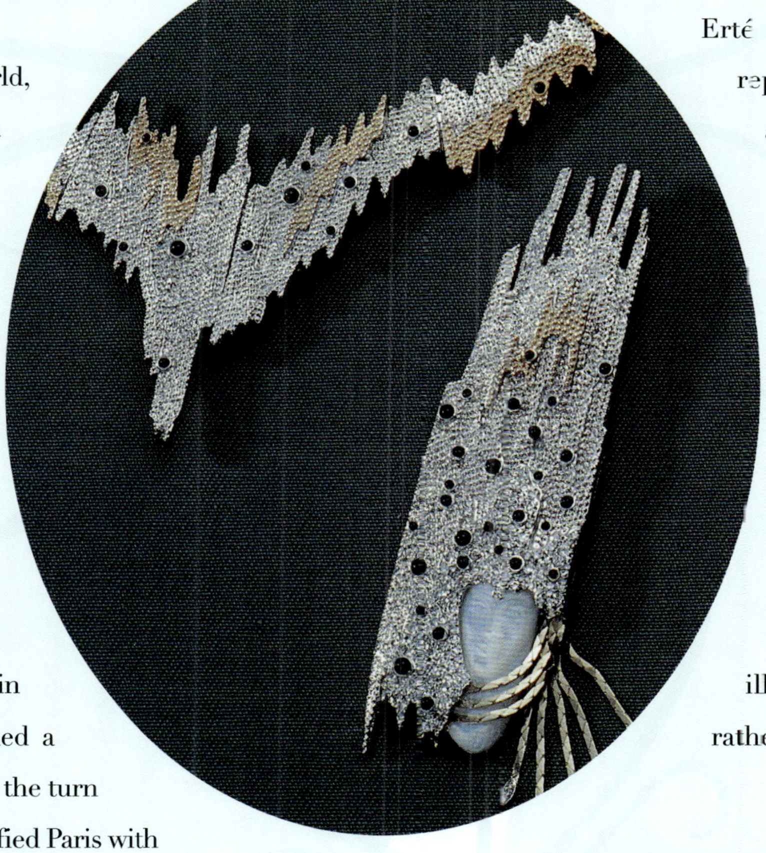

In 1912, Paris was the centre of the arts world, not only for traditional, modern and contemporary art but also for fashion, decorative art and graphic design. When Erté arrived in 1912, Cubism, first practised by Pablo Picasso (1881–1973) and Georges Braque (1882–1963), was at it is height of interest in avant-garde art circles. The Italian art movement Futurism was launched in Paris in 1909, and held its first exhibition in the city in 1912. Orphism, a colourful interpretation of Cubism, appeared around 1913. And in decorative art, Art Nouveau had remained a strong design style since the 1890s. Before the turn of the century Alphonse Mucha had electrified Paris with his graphic designs for posters in the Art Nouveau style, known as *Le Style Mucha*, for the French actress Sarah Bernhardt (1844–1923). Artists Henri Matisse, André Derain, and Maurice de Vlaminck (1876–1958), had created a sensation in 1905 at the Salon d'Automne, earning them the nickname *Les fauves* (wild beasts), for their vibrant non-naturalistic paintings full of pure colour. Erté recalled the 'boldness and daring' of Matisse, Picasso and Braque. He preferred visits to the Salon des Indépendants to see paintings by the Fauves more than the official Salon exhibition of art held at the Grand Palais.

REPRESENTATIONAL VS ABSTRACT

Erté stated that he appreciated representational art but had always been attracted to the abstract: 'I have never been able to understand the artist who reproduces faithfully what he sees, rather than the impression that a real object has made on his mind' (*Erté: Things I Remember*, 1975). To his art teacher who told him to paint what he saw, he responded 'Why should I paint something that already exists?' This argument may explain why Erté's illustrations were of idealized people rather than the reality.

THE BALLETS RUSSES

Parisians were in love with the Russian dance company Ballets Russes, the brainchild of ballet impresario Sergei Diaghilev. The vibrant costumes and spectacular stage designs created by contemporary Russian artists had stunned its

...ph, 41 x 56 cm (16 x 22 in)

(Above) **Sophistication** *necklace, c. 1981–90*

audiences since its debut at the Théâtre des Champs-Élysées in May 1909. Erté had attended performances in St Petersburg and was an avid fan of the artist, stage and costume designer Léon Bakst (1866–1924), who had revolutionized theatrical design with exotic costumes and modernistic sets. Erté said that he collected postcards of Bakst's work, particularly a production of *The Fairy Doll*, performed at the Mariinsky Theatre, St Petersburg in 1903. Bakst and the Ballets Russes must have influenced Erté's ideas for theatre stage design and costumes, although he stated his ideas were unique to him, his own invention.

ILLUSTRATION OR DESIGN?

The history of Erté's studies to be an artist and his subsequent choice of illustration over fine art show him to be more suited to the craft of graphic design. But what of a possible career as a fashion designer? His autobiography tells of his first forays into fashion design at the age of five, designing a dress for his mother from his own imagination. From an early age Erté would spend hour upon hour drawing with intensity to create the perfect work. Looking through his pen and ink sketches of original fashion designs for his first major employer, the French high-fashion couturier Paul Poiret, Erté had a great flare for design that was fashionable, stylish and wearable. The closing of Poiret's salon in 1914 at the outbreak of the First World War, stopped Erté's fledgling career in its tracks. From here he moved on to fashion illustration for *Harper's Bazaar*, creating chic aspirational designs that were not intended to be realized for wear. During the war period Erté concentrated on costumes for theatrical revues. He continued to submit fashion drawings and gouache fashion illustrations to *Harper's Bazaar* and to American *Vogue* but theatrical costume design took him further away from haute couture and into a different sphere of fashion. Today one notices the showiness of his theatrical costumes but had the war in Europe not intervened, Erté may have been noted as a fashion designer rather than illustrator.

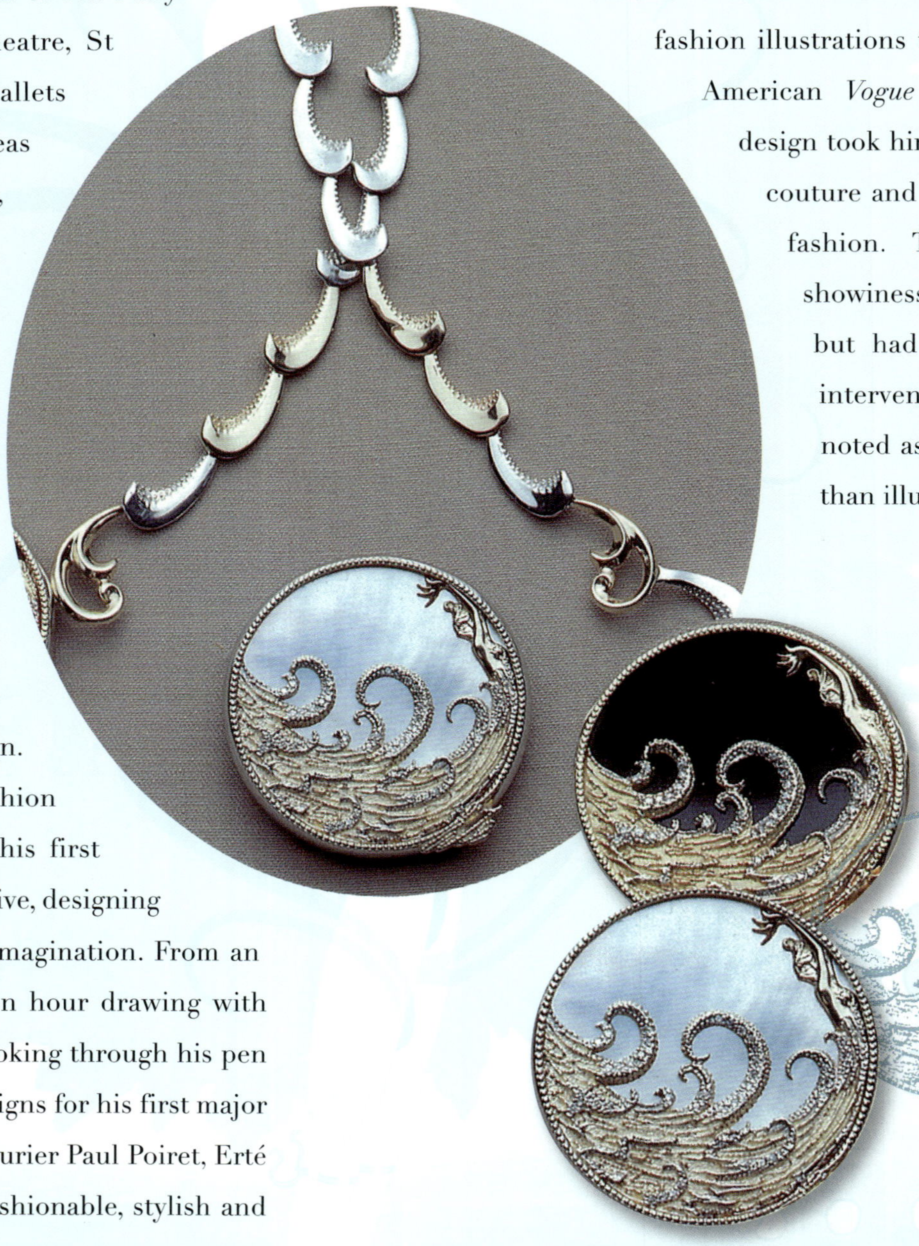

Aphrodite *necklace/brooch, c.1979–90, gold, silver, diamonds, black onyx/mother-of-pearl*

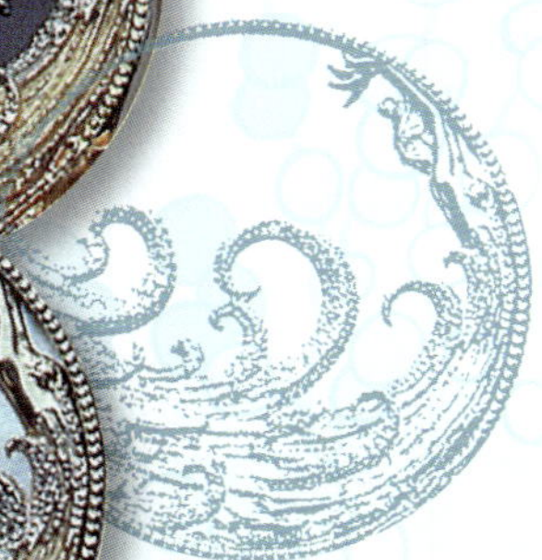

The Wave, *1980, embossed serigraph with foil stamping, 24.1 x 25.4 cm (9½ x 10 in)*

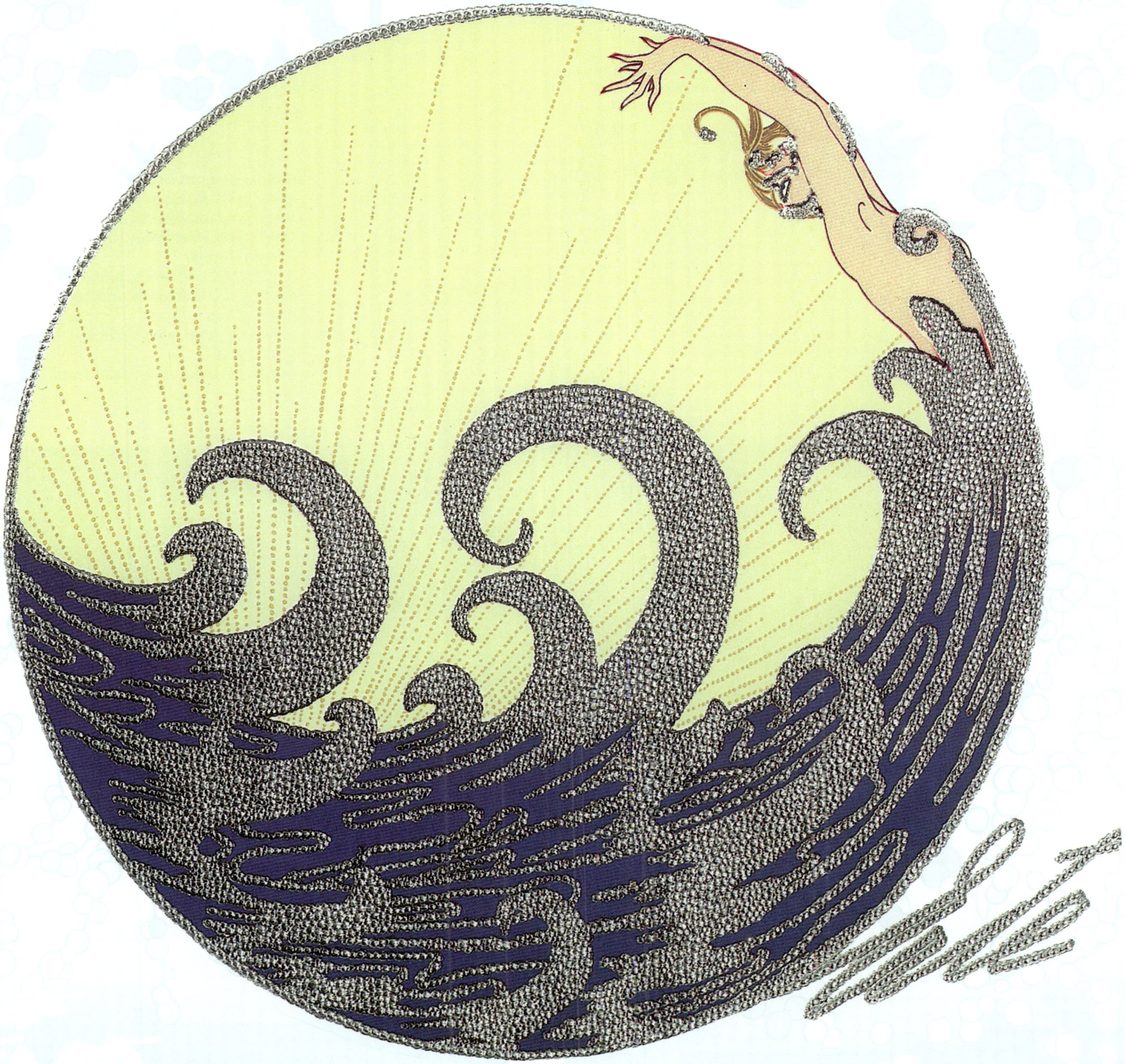

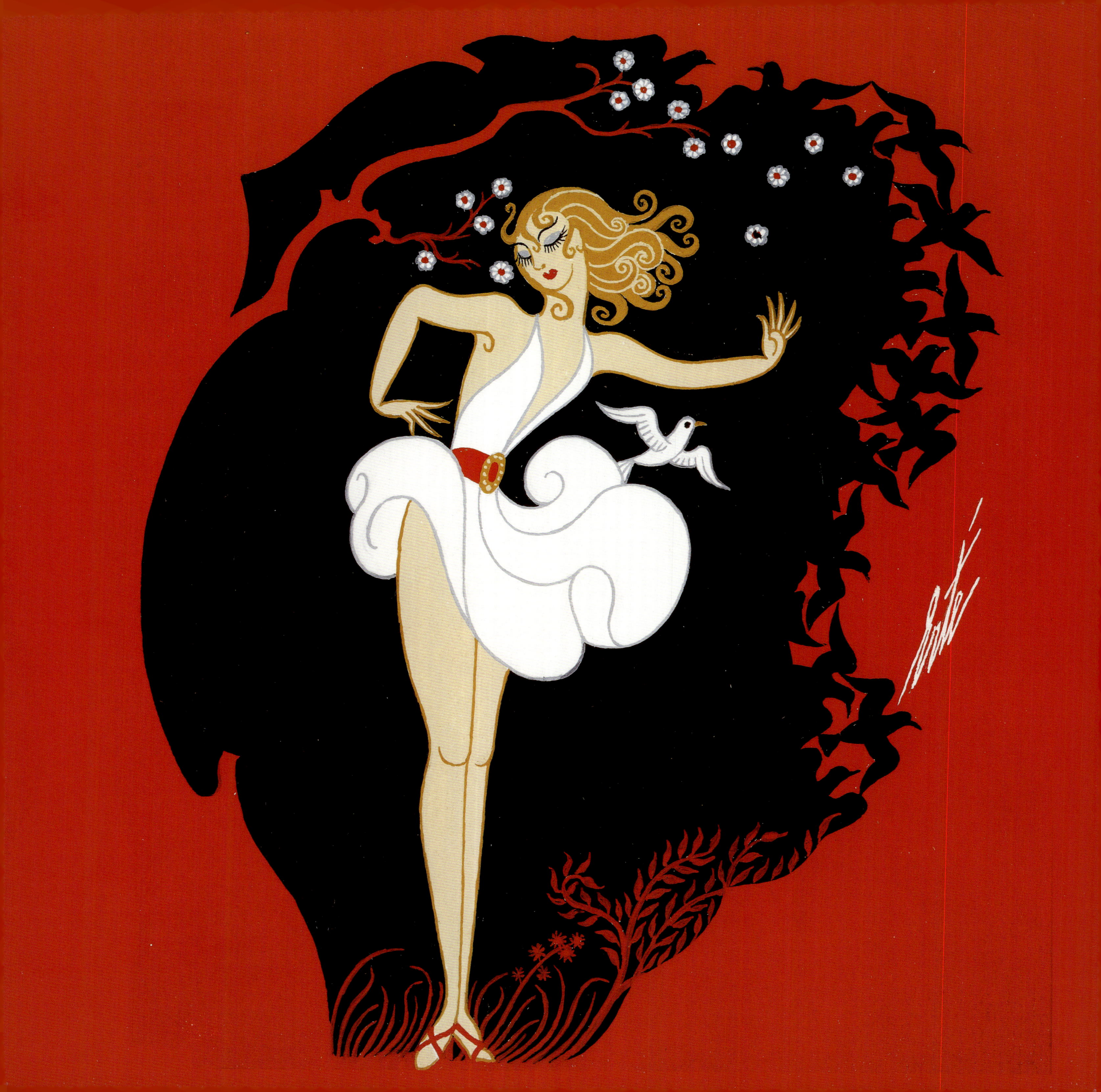

ART DECO ÉMIGRÉ

Erté lived a full life in Europe and later the USA, working constantly before, during and after the two World Wars. His career took him from the haute couture circle in Paris to America, working for *Harper's Bazaar*, and Metro-Goldwyn-Mayer in Hollywood; it took him on many paths, from fashion illustration and theatre set and costume design, to graphic printmaking and the challenge of jewellery and sculpture. Of course, as an émigré in Paris, his career took a little while to get off the ground. In 1912, after three months studying art at the Académie Julian, and funds always low, Erté looked for work. He expected to find a job quickly. However, he could not find the work he wanted and Paris was an expensive place to live without an income. His savings dwindled....

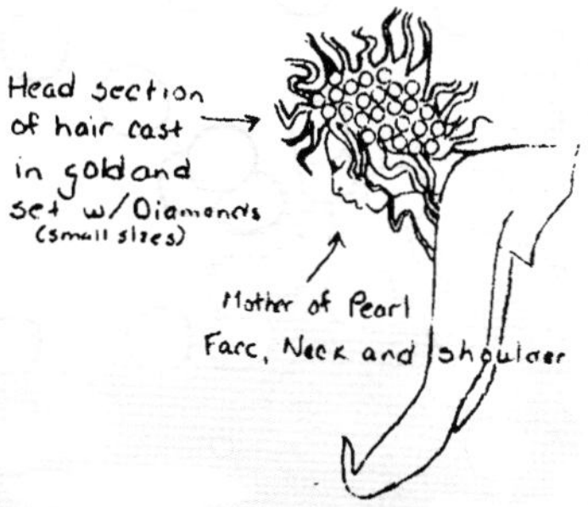

WORKING FOR RUSSIA IN PARIS

Fortunately, prior to leaving St Petersburg he had arranged with the Russian fashion magazine *Damsky Mir* ('Ladies' World') to send them pen and ink drawings of the latest Paris fashions on a monthly basis. It was an income, and his first published works. They were signed 'Romain' or 'Tir' or 'Pitch' (his sister Natalia's nickname for him). He used a nickname to avoid giving unwanted attention to his family at home. He survived on the regular fee and a small monetary supplement sent to him by his Uncle Nicolas. *Damsky Mir* would have paid him more for selling their advertising space but he was a failure in this venture.

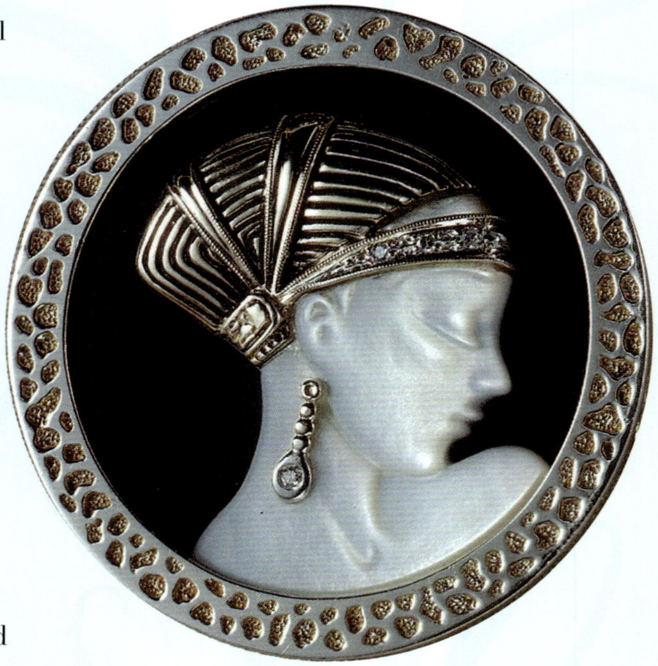

WORKING FOR CAROLINE

In December 1912, after nearly a year applying for jobs and searching for work suited to his aspiration to be a fashion artist, his first job in Paris was as a draughtsman for a fashion company called 'Caroline' in the Rue Royale. The promise of a regular income instigated his move to a small apartment in the Rue de Acacias. His memoirs refer to the fashion company as 'an obscure, second-class fashion house'. The feeling of disagreeability must have been mutual as it was not a successful venture. Erté discovered that his creative ideas and fashion drawings were not appreciated by everyone and he recalled that at the end of the month he was sacked. The owner Caroline's advice to him was short and sharp. 'I want to give you a mother's advice. Give up the idea of being an artist. You have no talent for it.'

A BOLD MOVE

Undeterred by Caroline's condemning opinion of his work, Erté had the forethought to ask if he could take some of his drawings with him, which he retrieved from the owner's waste bin. At the beginning of January 1913 he packed them in a parcel, added a card with his name and address and left the package with the concierge of the illustrious fashion house of the famous designer Paul Poiret, internationally heralded as the 'king of fashion'. One must admire Erté for aiming high. He was focused on how to achieve his ambition to be a top fashion illustrator and designer. It was a bold move and one that paid off. The very next day, which Erté recalled as 3 January 1913, he received a *pneumatique* (correspondence delivered by courier) from Poiret, requesting that Erté call in to see him as soon as possible. Poiret had found his drawings of worth. Erté ventured to Poiret's impressive fashion house on the Rue de Faubourg Saint-Honoré, where he was taken by Poiret to one of the studios to complete a test of his fashion drawing skills. On this occasion he met another young designer working for Poiret, José de Zamora (1889–1971).

(Previous page) **Design for Charnos Stocking package**, *1974, gouache, 51.4 x 41.3 cm (20¼ x 16¼ in)*
(Above) **Love's Enchantment** *pendant, c.1979–90, gold, silver, diamonds, black onyx, mother-of-pearl*

Flames of Love, *1978, serigraph, 68.6 x 53.3 cm (27 x 21 in)*

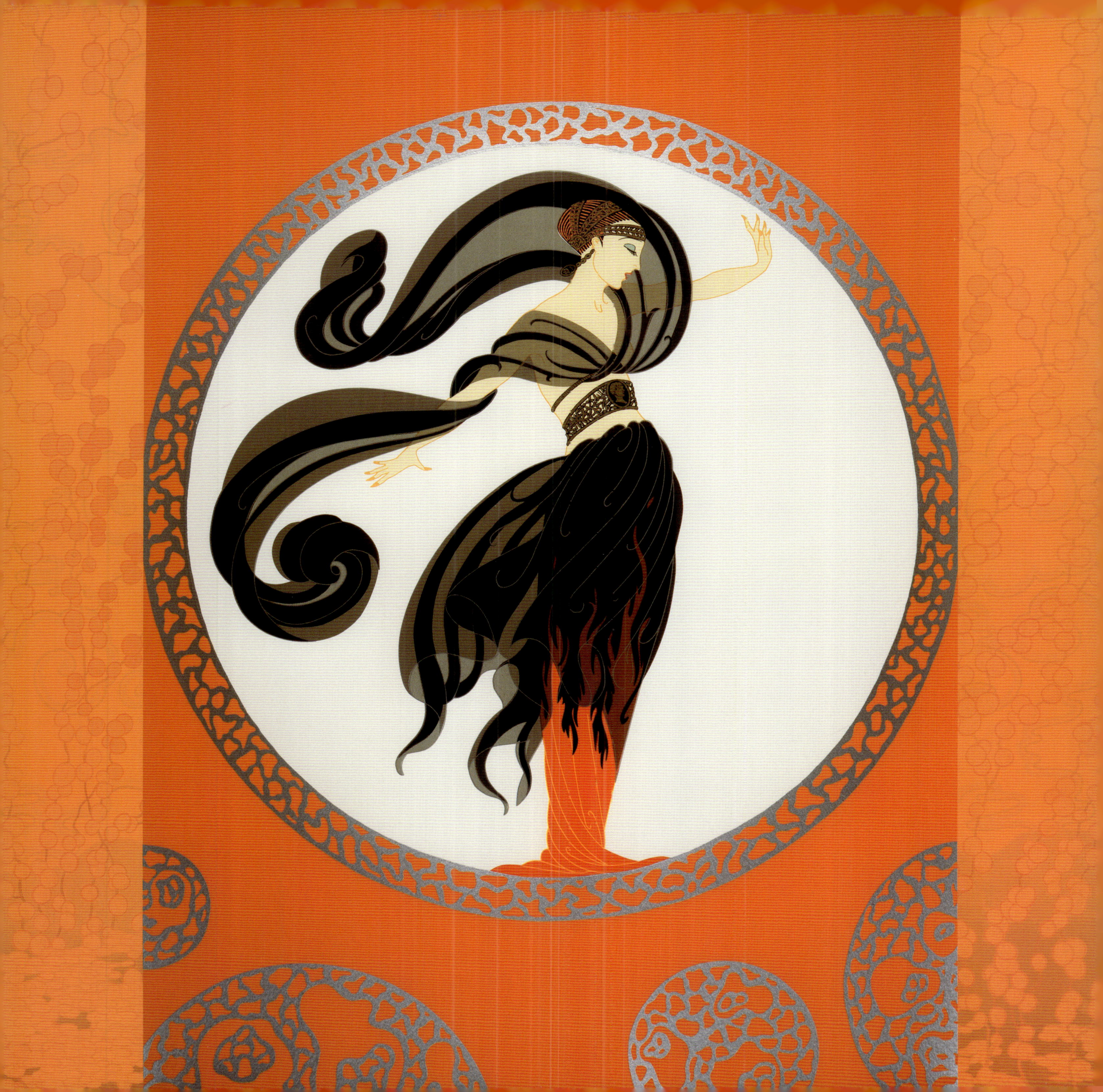

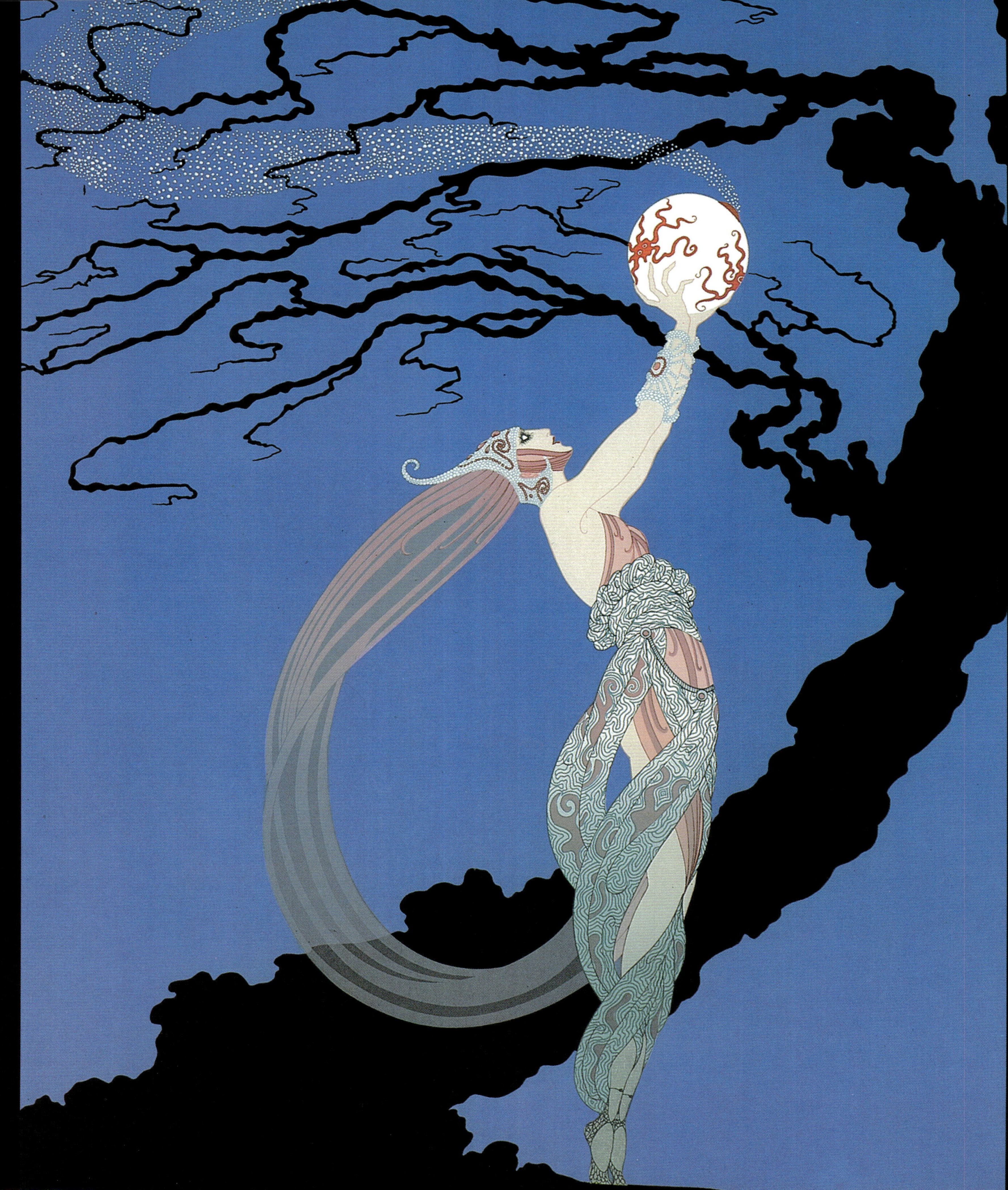

WORKING FOR PAUL POIRET

At the time of their first meeting in early January 1913, Poiret was at the peak of his career. It was possibly Poiret who suggested the pseudonym 'Erté'. Poiret had opened his fashion house in 1902 after first working for the elite couturier Jacques Doucet (1853–1921) from 1898–1900. Here Poiret created his famous costume 'Aiglon' (eagle), for the French stage and film actress Sarah Bernhardt. He moved to the House of Worth in 1901. During his time working for Charles Frederick Worth (1825–95) – considered the first French couturier – a notable success was a costume called 'Confucius' in a geometric Oriental kimono-style, which shocked his clientele but made his name. At his own fashion house, Poiret's designs were influenced by the slim body of his wife Denise, whom he married in 1905. He created radical designs of loose corset-less clothing that followed the contours of the body, prompting the successful revival of the Directoire style (*c.* 1795–99), which he launched in 1906. His abandonment of the corset, to alter the flow of the dress, and the introduction of the *soutien-gorge* (bra), liberated women's bodies from constricted clothing. However, Poiret is also noted for the 'hobble' skirt that restricted movement when walking. Into this establishment, at the heart of Parisian couture fashion, Erté, through his own initiative, had landed a fantastic job.

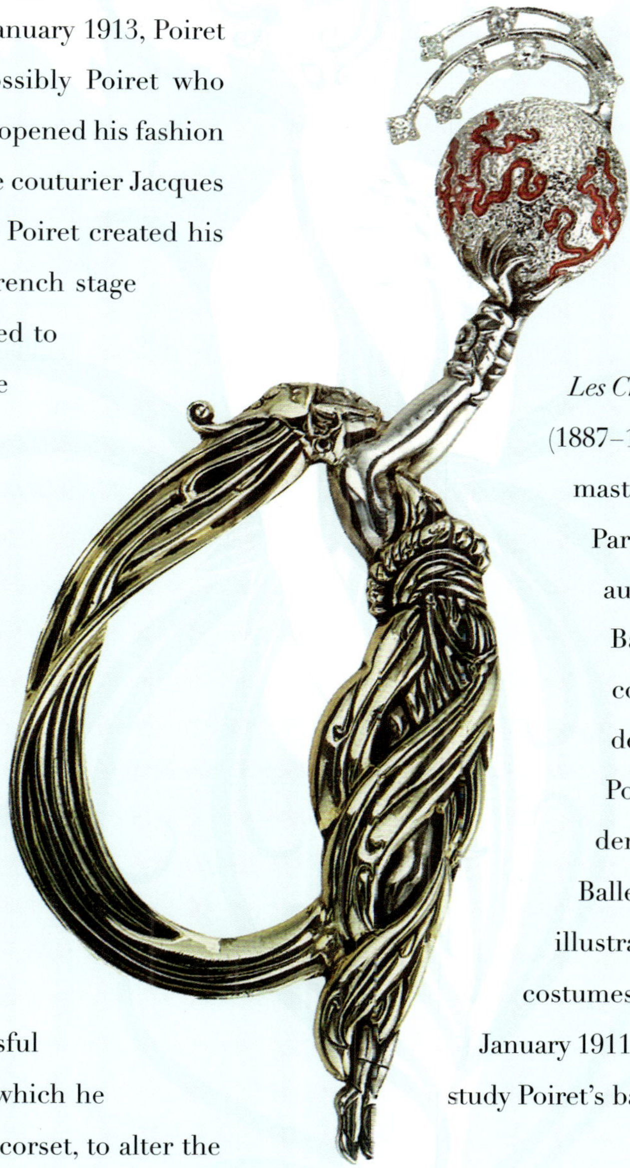

LES ROBES DE PAUL POIRET

Always looking for new ways to promote his name, in 1908 Poiret commissioned the French illustrator Paul Iribe (1883–1935) to create a limited edition fashion album, *Les Robes de Paul Poiret*, which was published in October 1908 and sent to special clients. He followed this with a further special album *Les Choses de Paul Poiret*, illustrated by Georges LePape (1887–1971), published in 1911 and considered LePape's masterpiece of illustration. The Ballets Russes' Parisian 1910 production of *Scheherazade* wowed audiences with Russian artist and designer Leon Bakst's sets and costumes. The exotic Oriental costumes greatly influenced fashion, interior design and fine art, particularly creations by Bakst. Poiret was asked if these had affected his work. He denied that it had but the exotic vibrancy of the Ballets Russes affected all of Paris, from designer to illustrator to artist. Notable are Poiret's theatre costumes for *Nabuchodonosor* in Paris, premiered in January 1911. Other theatrical successes followed. Erté would study Poiret's back-catalogue of work and learn from it.

POIRET ON TOUR

A successful tour of Vienna, Frankfurt, Budapest, Bucharest, Moscow and St Petersburg (where Erté saw Poiret's collection), consolidated Poiret's position as 'king of fashion'. He had an

Fireflies, *1980, serigraph, 67.3 x 47.6 cm (26½ x 18¾ in)*

Fireflies *brooch, c.1980–90 gold, silver, diamonds, red enamel*

outgoing personality, brilliant for marketing the Poiret brand. He was the first designer to produce his own perfume company *Parfums de Rosine*, in 1911, named after his eldest daughter. A decorative arts company *Martine*, named after his younger daughter, was opened the same year with three sections: an interior design business, a school to teach poor girls design to use in his own works, and the Atelier Martine. He opened a School of Decorative Art in 1912 and employed artists, including the French painter Raoul Dufy (1877–1953) to create his fabric designs. Dufy also set up a small factory to make the fabrics. Erté would become involved in aspects of these add-on businesses.

THE ONE THOUSAND AND SECOND NIGHT

When Erté moved to Paris in 1912, high society (of which he was a member though his Russian heritage), revelled in social entertainments of masked balls and extravagant fancy dress parties. Socially Poiret, a natural showman, was noted for throwing costume parties of pure spectacle, such as the One Thousand and Second Night party in June 1911, dubbed the first fashion show. Poiret played the Sultan. His wife Denise was on view as a 'concubine', kept in a gigantic gold-coloured birdcage at the centre of the attractions. She wore a gold tunic, a jewelled turban with a feather, and jewelled harem pantaloons. Poiret released her at the height of the festivities. The 300 guests were greeted by footmen wearing harem pantaloons. The invitation specified a Persian-style dress code. Those that did not conform were asked to change into the Eastern-style clothes provided by Poiret. During the evening he launched a spectacular fashion show that included his latest designs featuring harem pants and lampshade tunic dresses, which shocked and delighted his fashionista clientele. Poiret's extravaganza launched the hottest fashion look in Paris, swiftly spreading through Europe.

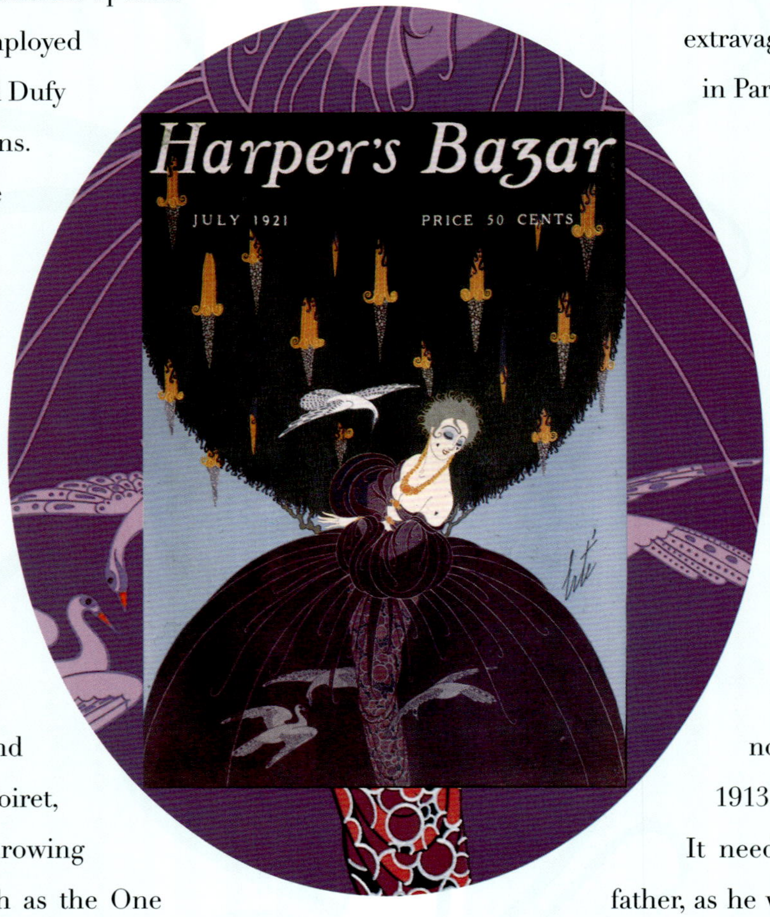

A CONTRACT SIGNED

In Paris, the couturiers patronized by the aristocracy were notably the Houses of Doucet, Paquin, Redfern and Worth. New couturiers to which clients flocked were Poiret, Lanvin, Chéruit and Beshoff-David. Erté was going to work at the heart of the fashion and theatre industry for the most noteworthy clients. By the end of January 1913 Poiret raised a contract to employ Erté. It needed the signature of the young man's father, as he was still not of age. His father was most reluctant to agree and Erté recalled that he was 'angry and humiliated' that his son should prefer to be a dressmaker rather than aspire to be an Admiral of the Russian Fleet. However, the contract was signed and a positive partnership between Poiret and Erté began. It would last until Poiret closed his fashion house at the outbreak of the First World War.

Harper's Bazar *cover, 1921*

Freedom and Captivity, *1982, serigraph with foil stamping, 83.2 x 62.2 cm (32¾ x 24⅜ in)*

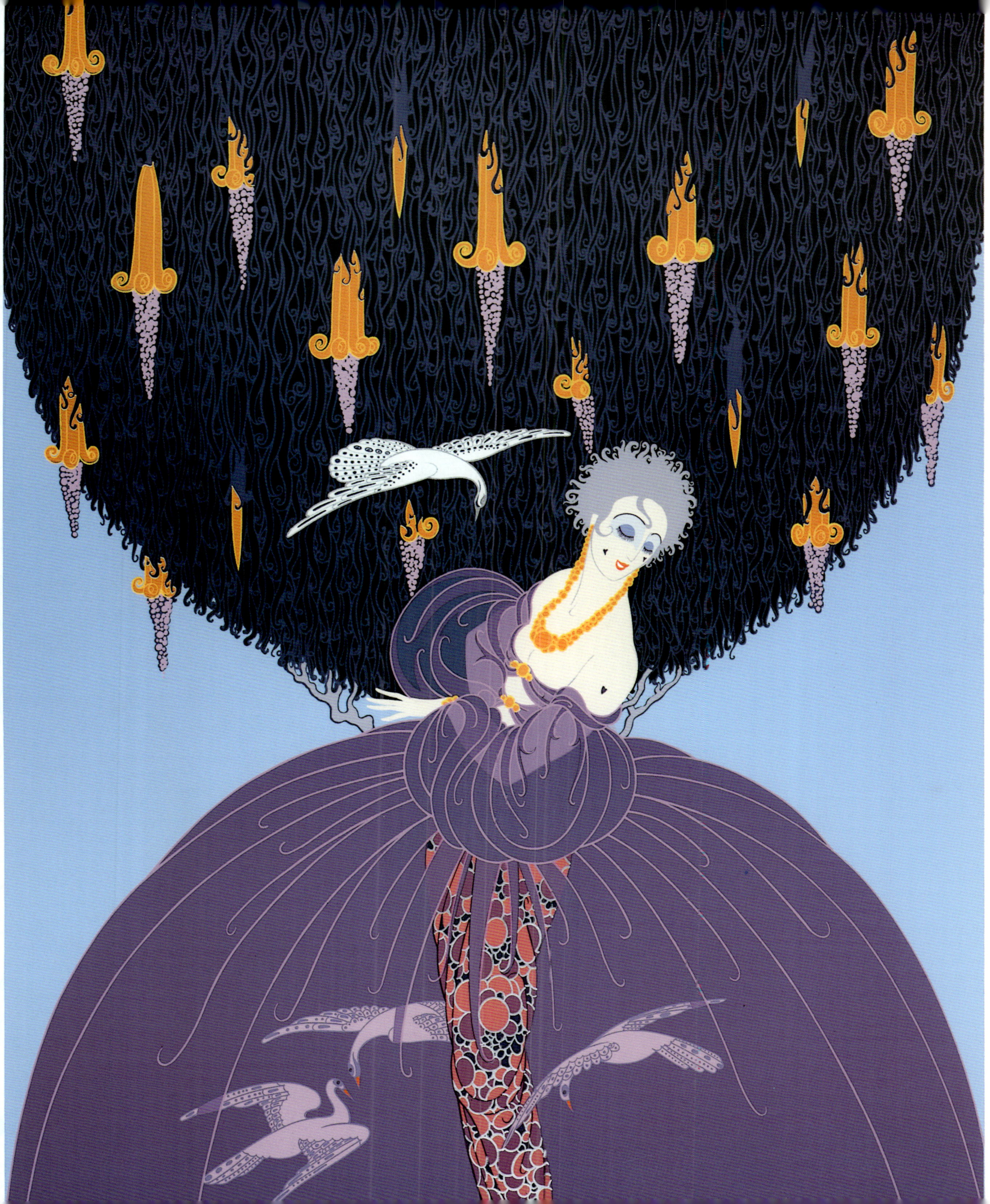

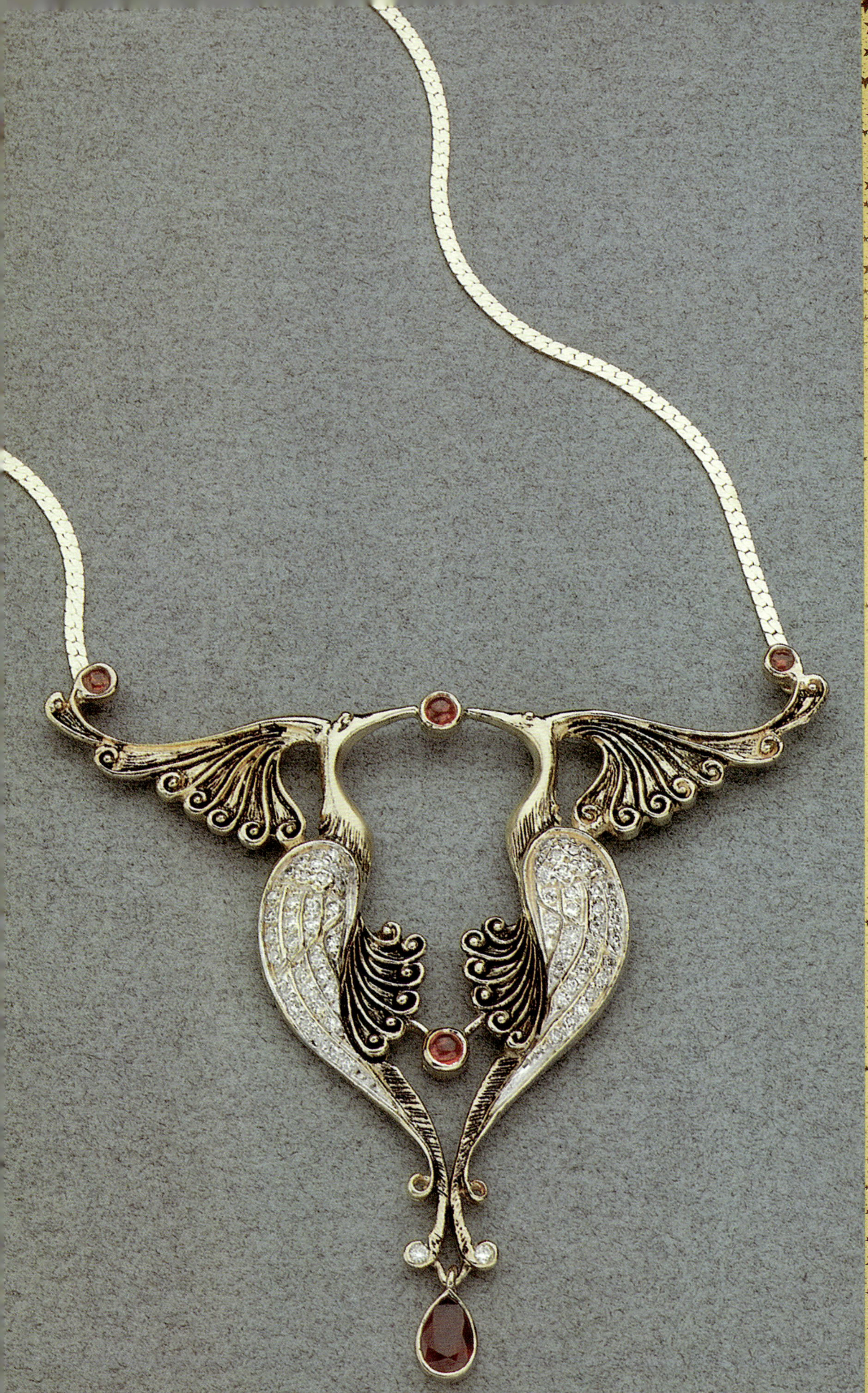

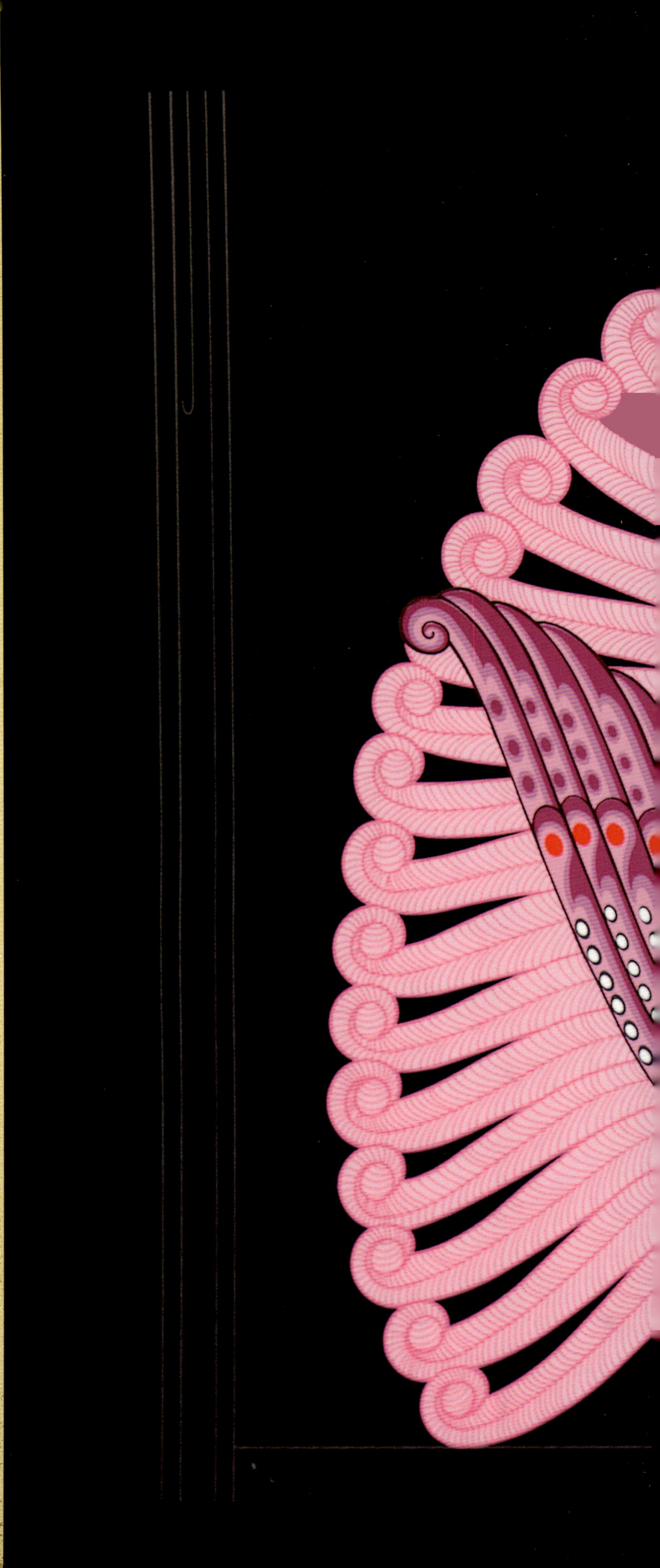

(Above) **Phoenix** *necklace, c.1979–90, gold, diamonds, rubies*
(Right) **Phoenix Triumphant**, *1983, serigraph, 71.1 x 101.6 cm (28 x 40 in)*

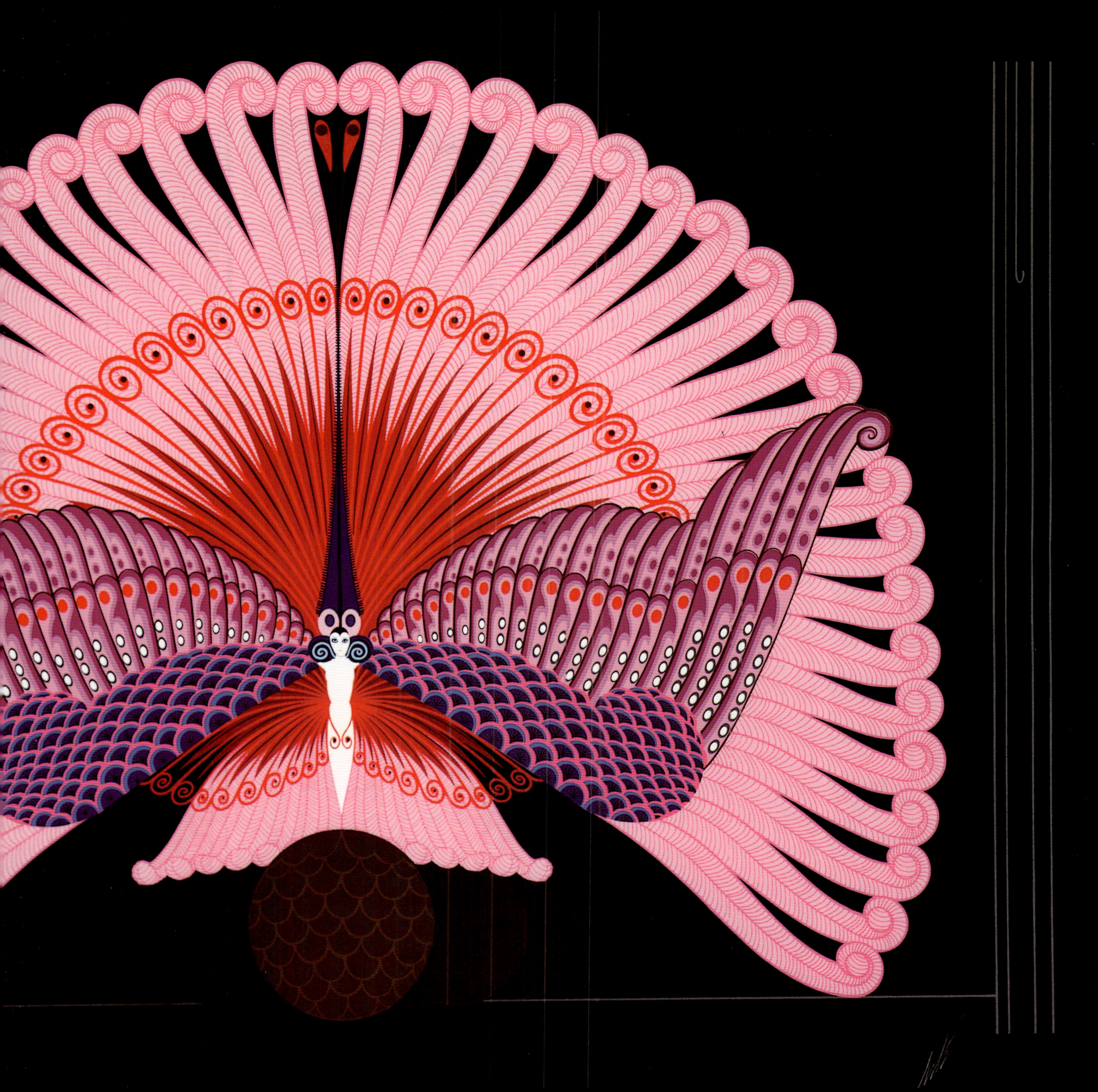

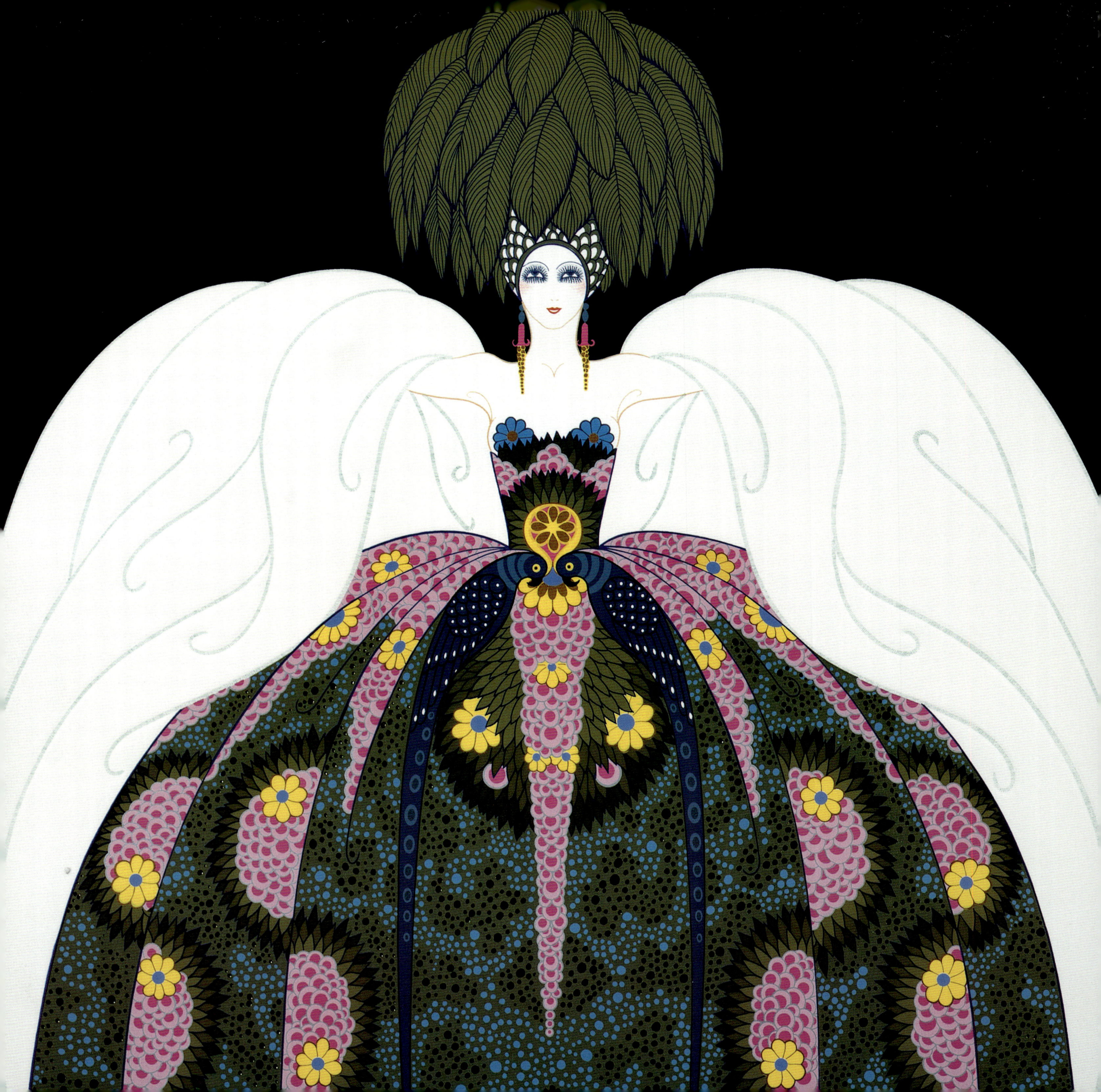

THE LUXURY OF THE THEATRE

Poiret, although noted for outbursts and a short-temper, nevertheless nurtured the social as well as professional needs of his newest recruit. He immediately included Erté alongside Zamora in his activities in the fashion house, and accompanied him to special nights at the theatre. Erté recalled the women's exquisite costumes and dazzling jewels, the headdresses, tiaras, turbans and birds-of-paradise plumes worn by guests to the prestigious gala opening of the new Théâtre des Champs-Élysees on Rue Montaigne, which he attended as a guest of Poiret. Erté's later bronze sculptures capture the opulence of guests, such as *Opening Night* (1989, *see* page 10), and, not to mention the performers, as seen in, for example, *Fedora Fan* (1990, *see* page 95) and *Fedora Butterfly* (1990, *see* page 99), all echoing this luxurious era. The building, which opened on 2 April 1913, was designed by the French architect-designer Auguste Perret (1874–1954), a specialist in the use of reinforced concrete construction. The stripped classicism of the building, coupled with monumental bas-reliefs in a contemporary frieze designed by French artist Antoine Bourdelle (1861–1929), is recognized as early Art Décoratif (Art Deco). The building stands as a visual sign of the gradual change from Art Nouveau towards Art Décoratif in the second decade of the twentieth century.

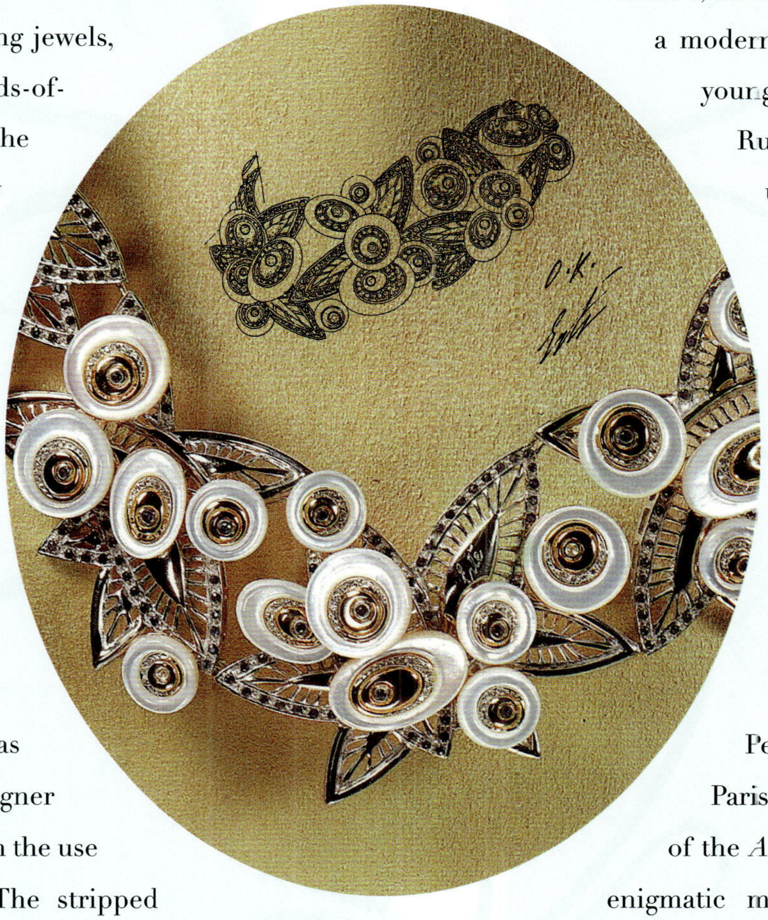

INFLUENCED BY STAGE PRODUCTIONS

The availability of many shows – from musical revues to opera and ballet – gave Erté exposure to the latest creativity in set design, costumes and stage production, as well as to the best actors and actresses. A notable influence on him was *La Pisanelle ou la Mort*, directed by Vsevolod Meyerhold (1874–1940), a modernist theatrical production starring the young Russian dancer, Ukrainian-born Ida Rubenstein (1885–1960) who studied under the dance choreographer Michel Fokine (1880–1942), shocking St Petersburg audiences with her near naked performance of 'The Dance of the Seven Veils' in a 1908 production of Oscar Wilde's *Salome*, which was immediately banned. It earned her a place in Diaghilev's Ballets Russes as the protégée of Léon Bakst. Erté may have seen her perform before he left St Petersburg. Splitting with Diaghilev in Paris she was dubbed by reviewer Alan Dale of the *American Examiner* in June 1912 as 'the enigmatic most mysterious actress-dancer', and 'probably the most interesting theatrical personality in Europe'. In the same year, two other Paris productions added to her celebrity status, *Hélène de Sparte* (Helen of Sparta), and Oscar Wilde's *Tale of Salome*, with costumes and sensational sets by Bakst. These productions gave Erté inspiration for his future theatre set and costume designs.

Copacabana, *1983, embossed serigraph with foil stamping, 86.9 x 74.2 cm (34⅛ x 29⅛ in)*
The *Copacabana* serigraph, although similar in its colour-ways, is vastly different to the female in the later patinated bronze sculpture *Copacabana* (1991), with its fishtail skirt.

Le Jardin *necklace, c. 1979–90, silver, gold, diamonds, blue sapphires, mother-of-pearl (with sketch)*

FIRST WORK

At the 'House of Poiret', Erté initially designed dresses, coats, hats and headdresses. The early designs from this first year confirm that he was completely in tune with the style demands of the period. Paris and Europe were in love with everything from the East. Orientalism was in demand. Poiret's lampshade skirts and wired-at-the-hem tunic tops worn over harem pants became must-have items. Erté confirmed that they were inspired by 'the transparent veil skirts of the Hindu miniatures, and by the pleated kilts of Greek folk costumes' (*Erté: Things I Remember*, 1975). The success of this initial collection led to an assignment to design all the costumes for a play, *The Minaret*, by Jacques Richepin (1880–1946), which opened in 1913 at the Théâtre de la Renaissance in Paris (Paul Poiret had been commissioned to design the theatre set and costumes). Erté noted how Poiret set about establishing the mood for each scene, changing colour schemes for each act. It was a new idea and one that established a design trend in theatre production.

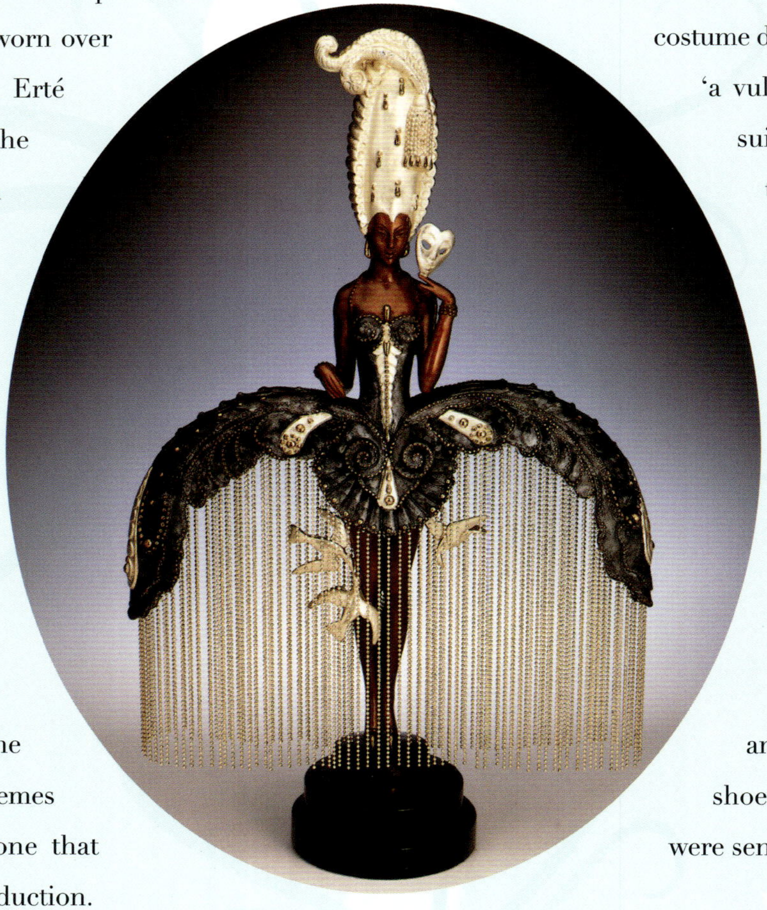

A COSTUME FOR MATA HARI

To mark the fiftieth performance of *The Minaret*, the lead actress Cora Laparceire, the director of the theatre and wife of the playwright Richepin, suggested hiring the Dutch exotic dancer Margarethe Geertruide Zelle MacLeod (1876–1917), better known as Mata Hari. She was contracted to dance in the third scene, the 'Nuptial Festival'. Poiret gave Erté the privilege of designing an exotic, Oriental costume for the celebrated performer. It was, Erté said, one of his first theatrical design commissions, and one that would launch his name into the mainstream of theatrical costume design. Erté described Mata Hari as having 'a vulgar beauty, but a superb body', better suited to wearing theatrical costumes than two-piece day suits. He found her agreeable if a little humdrum when offstage. 'She was not really beautiful. She had a sensuous body, but she lacked personality and there was even something a little vulgar about her.' The Mata Hari costume included a spectacular beaded stand-up shawl collar, a jewelled turban headdress, kimono-style wrap with sumptuous sash, Persian harem pants and Aladdin-style curled-toe jewelled shoes. On stage Mata Hari and the costume were sensational.

THE MINARET DRESS

Costumes for *The Minaret* were to influence the fashion seasons of 1913. One particular dress called 'The Minaret' (also known as the 'Sorbet' dress, and the 'Lampshade Tunic')

Her Secret Admirers *sculpture, 1990, bronze, 61 x 38 x 10 cm (24 x 15 x 4 in)*

Her Secret Admirers, *1982, serigraph, 83.8 x 61 cm (33 x 24 in)*
A costume drawing for *Harper's Bazaar*, frontispiece July 1922, was used for a costume in the 'Greenwich Village Follies' revue of 1922. A variation of it for a Holeproof Hosiery advertisement in 1934 later appeared as this serigraph and a sculpture (1990).

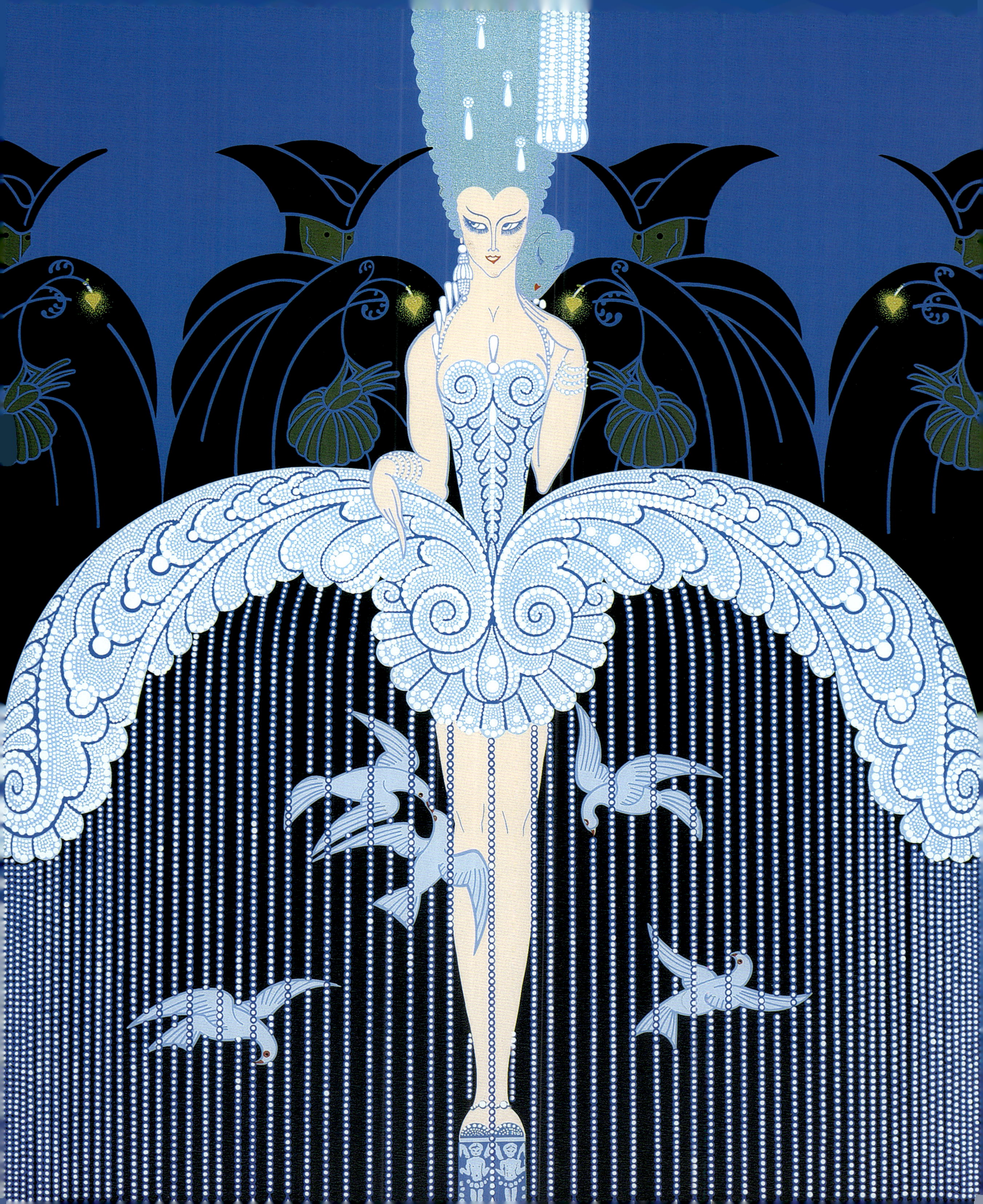

was an immediate hit. Erté described it as a *jupe-culotte*, a skirt wrapped around the legs, to form a culotte shape. The addition of a tunic with a wired hem, to make the fabric stand away from the body, gave the garment an Oriental-Eastern mystery and femininity. Copies of the design were in great demand and sold in large numbers. Erté worked on variations of the original design.

CRAZY FOR LE TANGO

Working for Poiret, Erté was in touch with all that Paris thought 'hot' and avant-garde, from art to dance. The sensuous tango dance, originating from Buenos Aires, Argentina in the 1890s crossed the Pacific to France, becoming a high society dance phenomenon by 1913. It is thought that the dance first appeared in a theatrical review in Paris in 1908. It was officially demonstrated at the Sorbonne in 1910 by the French actress, singer and comedienne Mistinguett (Jean Florentine Bourgeois, 1875–1956), dancing with Professor B.T. Botallo, director of the Academy of Dance and Deportment. It reached fever pitch by 1913 with tango dinner-dances, tango tea-dances, tango nights, a summertime 'tango-train' to dance from Paris to Deauville, and tango-on-ice at the Palais de Glace. Erté designed some of the costumes that Poiret produced for Jacques Richepin's play *Le Tango* at the Athenée Theatre in 1913. He created a special orange colour, or 'tango', as he called it, supporting the craze for 'Le Tango' fashions. The main leads were two actresses Spinelly (Elise Fournier, 1887–1966), playing the female lead, and Eve Lavalliére (1866–1929), playing her husband. Erté recalled that he created a dress solely of silver lamé for Spinelly's character, the first of its kind. He included shades of 'tango' to some of the costumes in the play, varying in shades from yellow to rust red.

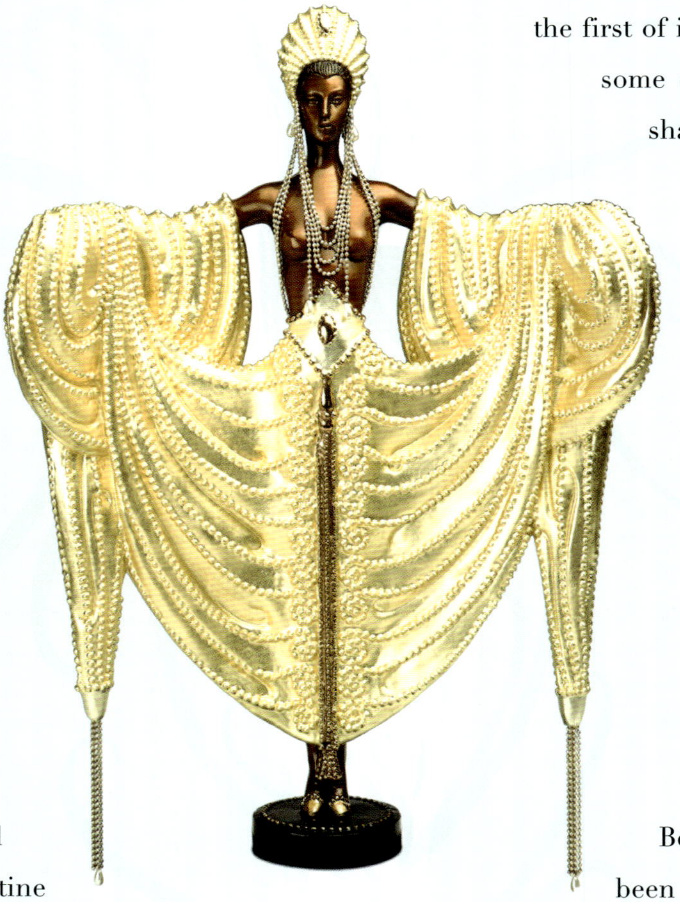

AUBREY BEARDSLEY

A close study of Erté's early fashion drawings reveal a similarity between his style and that of the young English aesthete Aubrey Beardsley (1872–98), an illustrator and co-founder of the London publication *The Yellow Book* (1894–97). Erté, however, refuted this association, reflecting that he first saw Beardsley's work in 1913, a year after he had been staying in Paris. Of course, the sensuous use of the elongated curvilinear line in Art Nouveau drawings, paintings and posters, accompanied by a femme fatale, a near-naked young woman, was associated with the Symbolist painters from this era. It was a signature of the period which Beardsley helped to stimulate through his sensational semi-erotic illustrations. He created illustrations for the one-act play *Salome* (1891), written by the English

Radiance *sculpture, 1988, bronze, 58 x 39.4 x 22 cm (22¾ x 15½ x 8½ in)*

Radiance, *from the* **Celestial Virtues** *suite, 1985, embossed serigraph with foil stamping, 86.4 x 67.3 cm (34 x 26½ in)*
Based on 1923 costume design, 'Le Luxe', for the Ziegfeld Follies production *L'Or*.

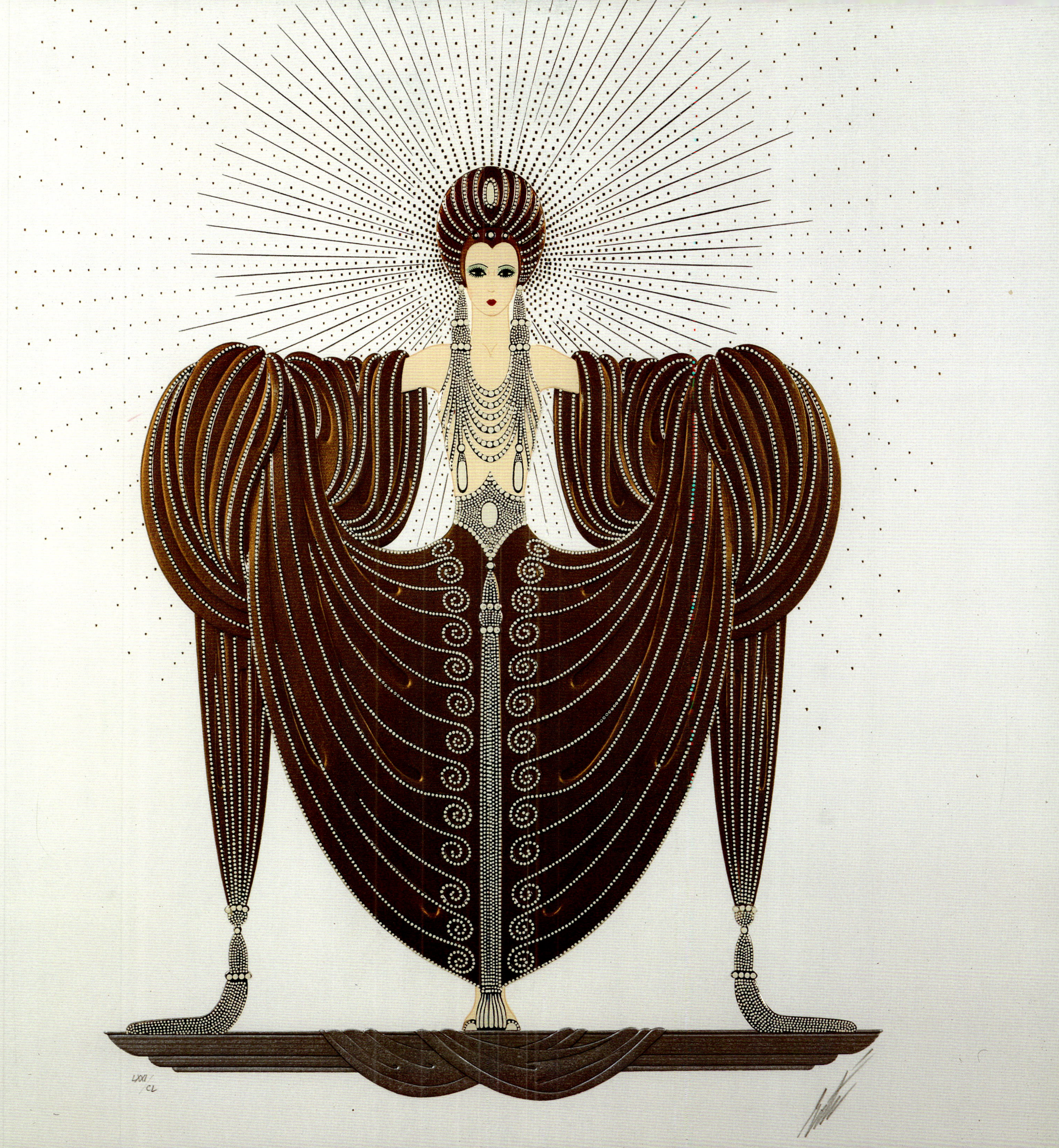

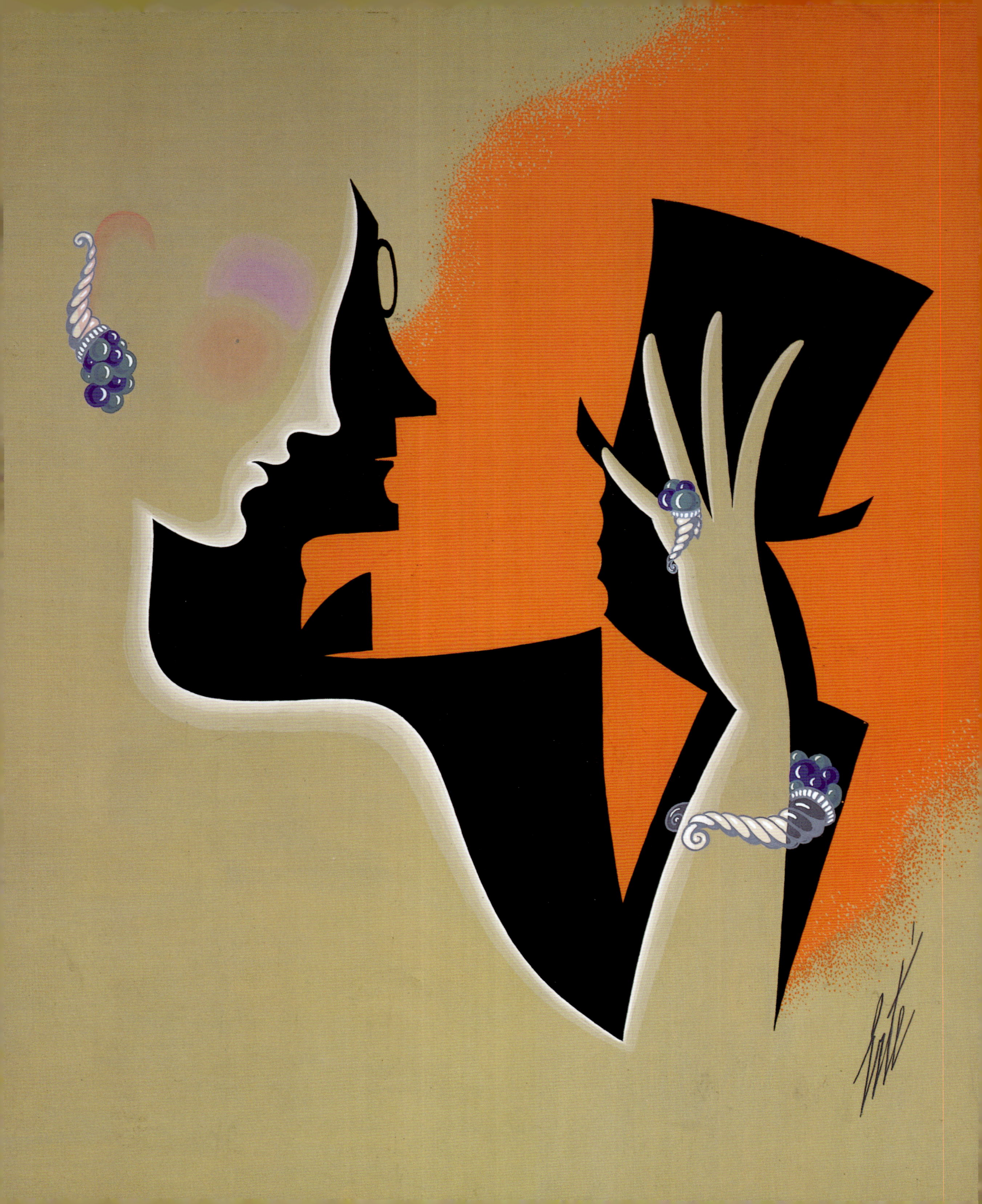
Erté

writer Oscar Wilde (1854–1900). They were published in *The Studio* magazine in 1893. The historical novel *Salammbô* (1862), by French writer Gustave Flaubert (1821–80), noted for its exoticism had a great effect on contemporary art (for example the Symbolist painters), and in decorative art and graphic design and fashion illustration from its publication through to the 1920s. Salome became an ever-popular character in Erté's work.

SUMMER IN BIARRITZ

In the summer of 1913 Erté, now established in a wonderful job and living in a new apartment, went with his sister Natalia on holiday to Biarritz, a place that was part of the social season for Parisian society (particularly in late-autumn and winter). His memoirs recall whom they met and where they went. One woman, who he first saw walking on the beach, stood out for her chic appearance. She was tall and thin and, as Erté described, 'when the breeze blew along the beach she swayed like a reed in the wind'. With her was a Borzoi dog whose collar and lead always matched its owner's clothing. She was a high-class courtesan named Dolly Canada (also recorded as Cavoda). Thus, high society mingled with the *demi-monde* world, and dressed alike.

A SPECIAL FRIENDSHIP

1913 was a special year for Erté in many ways. It began with a prestigious appointment by Paul Poiret, which led to his status rising as a designer and a move to a new apartment. In the summer a meeting with a distant cousin Prince Nicolas Ouroussoff, thirteen years his senior, was eventful. Theirs was to become a very close relationship, 'one of the most important of my entire life', Erté said, that lasted until the prince's death in 1933. When Ouroussoff met Erté he was in Paris on his way to London. His personal plans included marriage to an American millionairess but he called it off and instead moved to Paris in 1914. He became Erté's companion, patron and mentor, and a brilliant advisor who created fortunes for the fashion illustrator. Nicolas was made welcome by Erté's mother and father but with regret his sister Natalia did not warm to the new relationship. Erté later put this down to Prince Nicolas usurping somewhat the close relationship and 'control' that his older sister had previously had over her much younger sibling.

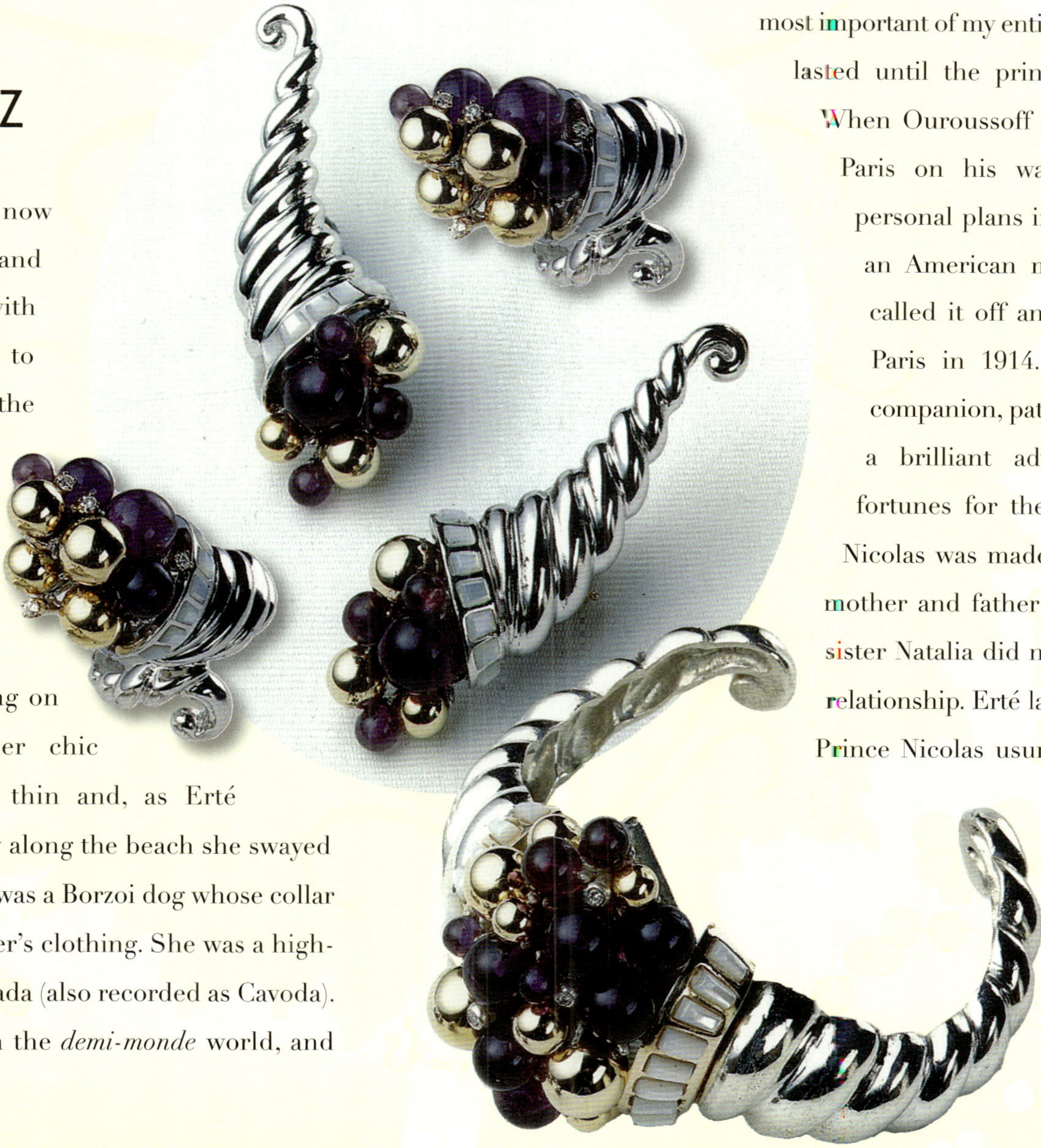

Fashion design with Ceres bracelet, *1920s, gouache*
Erté was often influenced by classical mythology, such as the Greek goddess of the harvest, Ceres, who was frequently represented with cornucopia of fruits and vegetables. Erté first used this motif in this fashion design.

Ceres *bracelet, earrings and ring, c. 1979–90, silver, diamonds, mother-of-pearl, amethyst beads, gold beads*

DRESSING UP

By now Erté could afford to live in a better apartment. He moved to 9 rue de Civry in Auteuil, Paris, which he kept in his possession until 1923. He decorated the reception rooms with low divans and lots of cushions, no doubt covered with fabrics of his own design. He spent nights out at the theatres. It was the fashion for socialites of high society to attend the dress rehearsal of a new play. *La Phalène* ('The Moth'), by Henry Bataille (1872–1922), at the Théâtre de Vaudeville, was to premiere on 22 October 1913. For the dress rehearsal Erté decided that he would dress up more than usual. He invited a Poiret model to accompany him and three other friends. Models were allowed to borrow dresses from the collection to special events and Erté wore the ensemble his guest had borrowed, a stunning Poiret dress with an ermine and red velvet coat and a red velvet turban, accessorized with long red gloves and large earrings. His friends were dressed in evening tailcoats with red camellia buttonholes. When they arrived and took their places in a private box, the audience turned to look, astonished. The following day the papers were full of the mystery girl in red, 'wearing her remarkable ensemble with an air and a sense of style that few models are lucky enough to possess'. Poiret guessed immediately that it was Erté and, perhaps tongue-in-cheek, offered to design dresses for Erté that he could model. Erté swiftly declined.

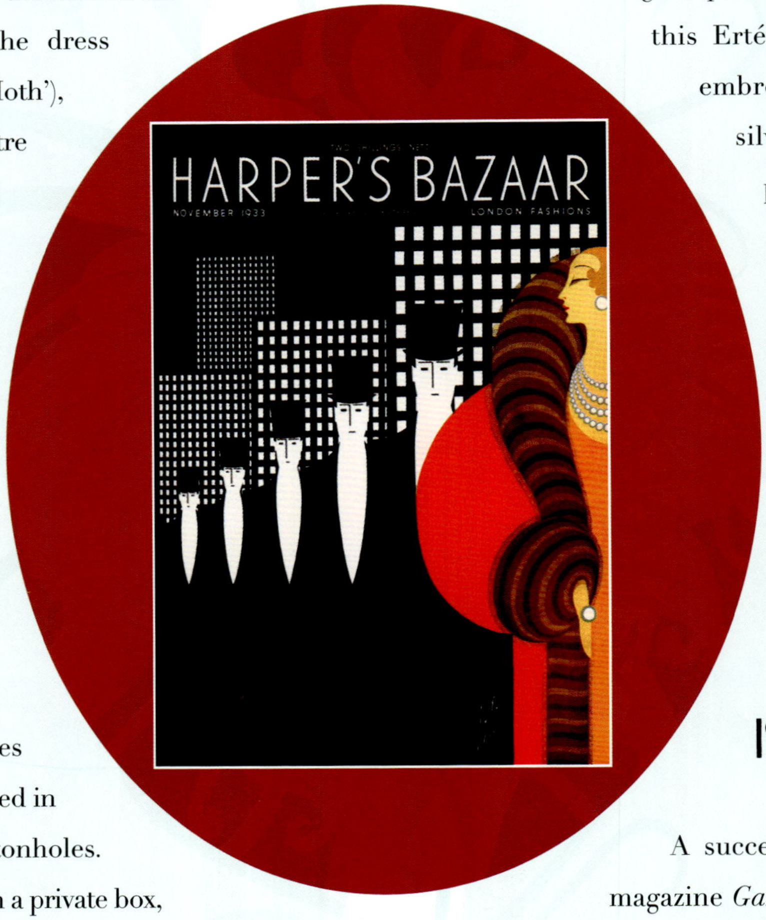

Harper's Bazaar *cover, November 1933*

GRAND PRIX BAL D'OPERA

Erté did not borrow further clothes from Poiret's couture collection but designed his own. Notable is a stunning creation he wore to the Grand Prix Bal d'Opera in 1914, a close-fitting body costume in silver lamé with hundreds of strings of pearls linking arms to legs, like wings. Over this Erté wore a black chiffon cape with an embroidered train. His headdress was a silver and pearl helmet with long black plumes attached. In his own words, 'My arrival caused a sensation'. He was a sensational advertisement for his theatrical fashion designs. And he loved to dress up. One extravagant outfit was a body-hugging costume studded with diamonds, worn with a gold lamé cape lined with 300 fresh red roses.

1914: GAZETTE DU BON TON

A successful liaison with the French fashion magazine *Gazette du bon ton* (Journal of Good Taste) began for Erté in 1914. The magazine, printed in colour, had been launched in November 1912 by the French publisher Lucien Vogel (1886–1954). It was an expensive subscription magazine, 100 francs per annum, covering 'Arts, Modes & Frivolité'. The fashion, lifestyle and beauty pages were aimed at high society readers. Vogel made contracts with France's top

Top Hats, *1975, lithograph, 61 x 49 cm (24 x 19¼ in)*
This serigraph is based on a 1933 gouache created for *Harper's Bazaar*. In 1981 the image was used again as a limited edition lithograph poster to celebrate Erté's 89th birthday, and as a bronze bas-relief wall sculpture in 1991.

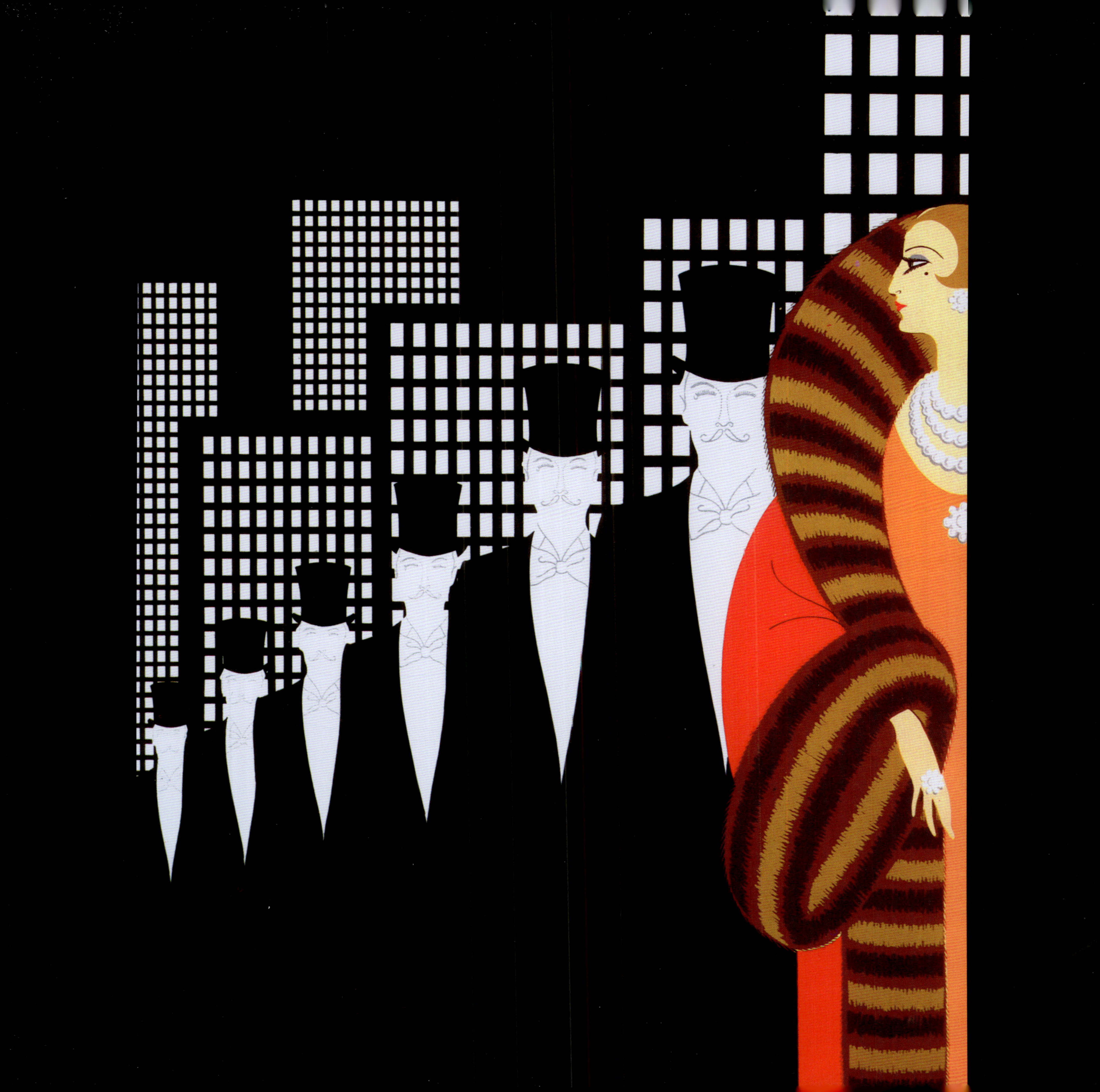

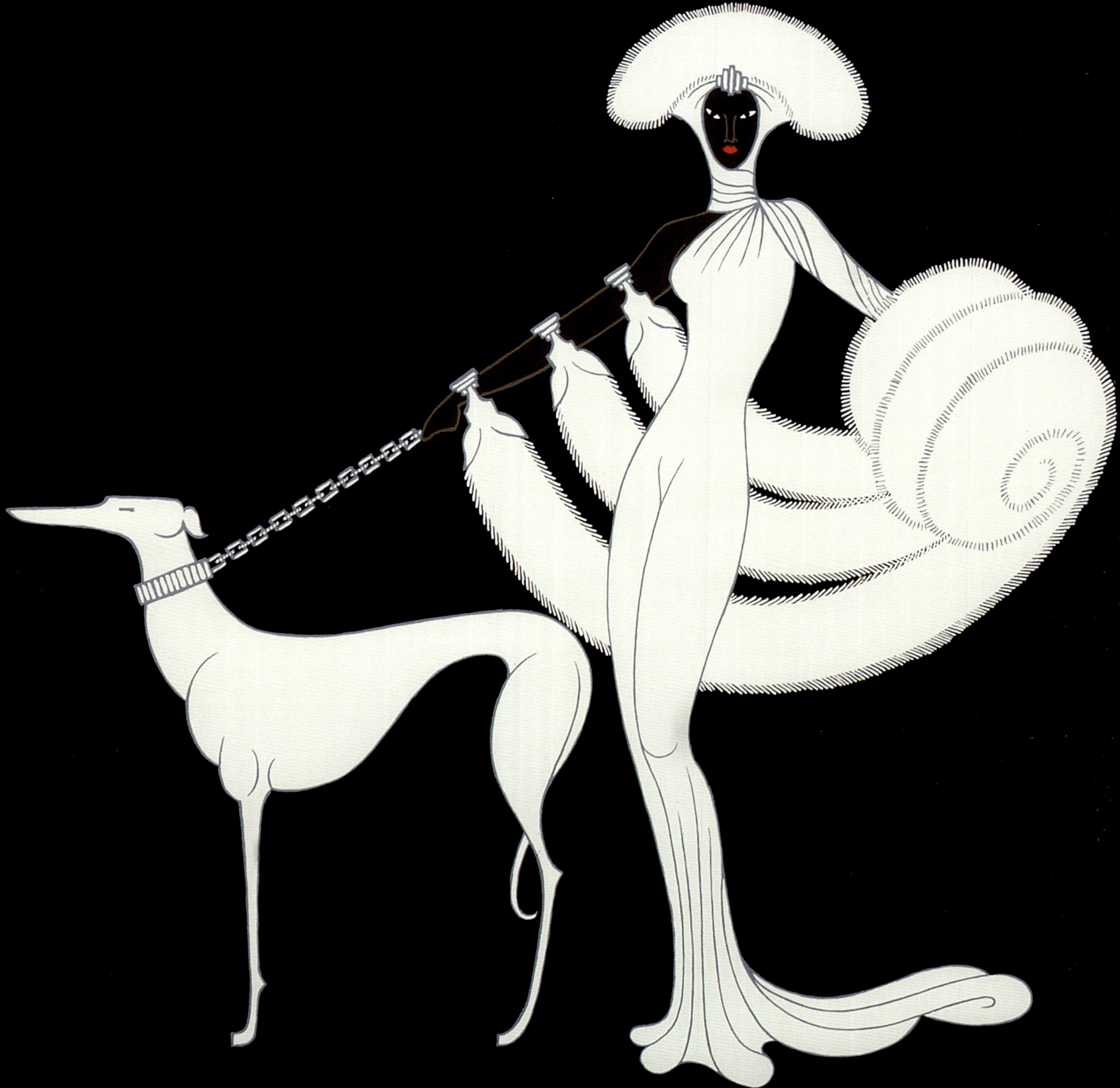

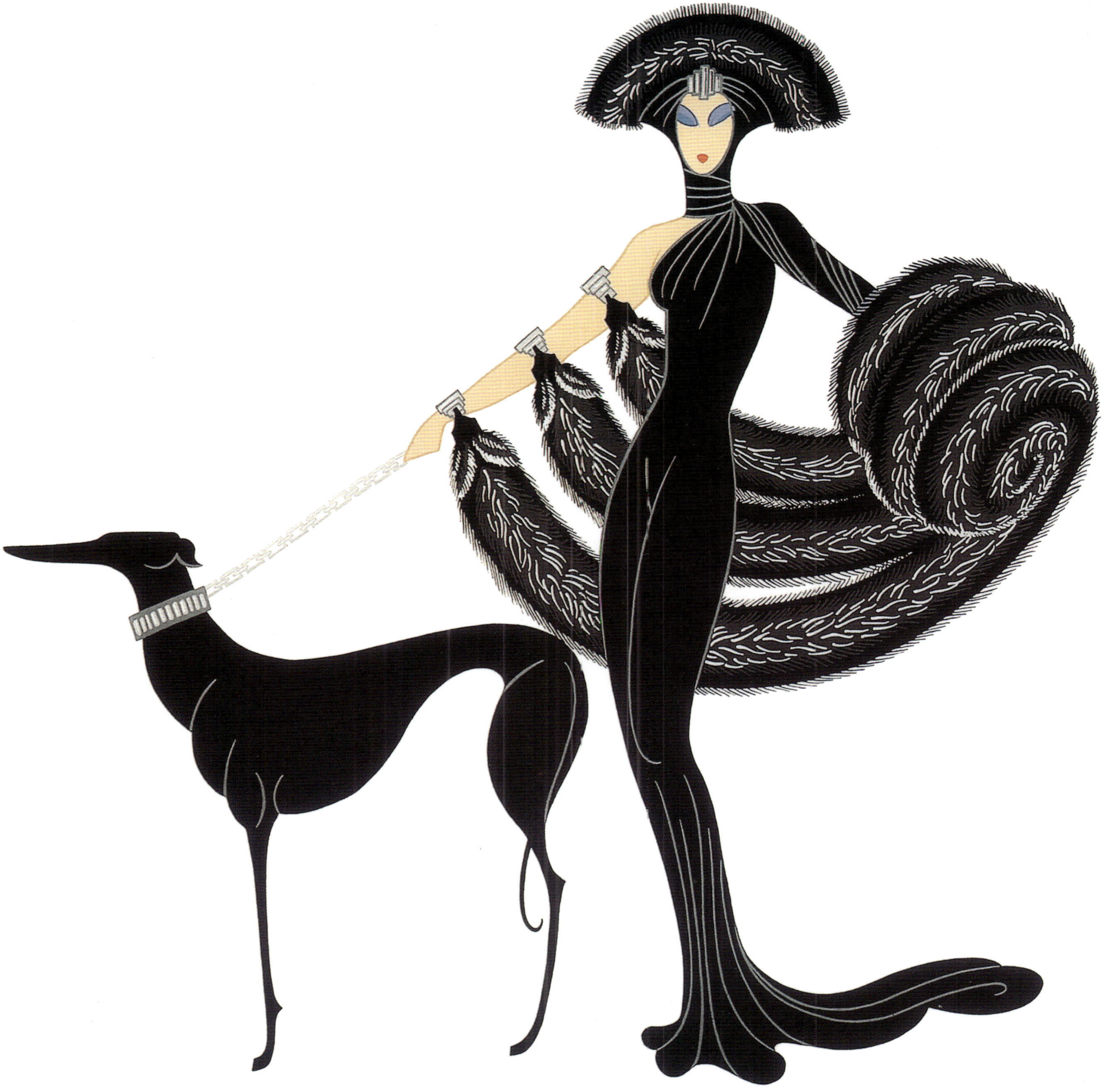

couturiers to deliver monthly fashion spreads, which he interspersed with illustrated articles on fashion and lifestyle. The American edition (published in French) was titled *Gazette du bon genre* (Journal of Good Style). It was in the *Gazette du bon ton* May 1913 edition that the first designs with an Erté signature appeared in print. His name appeared under two hat designs, although a further six designs by him were left unsigned.

ERTÉ'S CONTEMPORARIES

Working for Paul Poiret, one of the most sought-after fashion labels in Paris, Europe and America, placed Erté at the centre of fashion illustration, to learn from the best practitioners. His commission from *Gazette du bon ton* furthered the public's knowledge of his name, and he made a life-long friend of one of the magazine's chief contributors, the exceptional French illustrator Georges Barbier (1882–1932). It would lead to work for *Harper's Bazaar*, *Vogue* and the Philadelphia-based magazine *Ladies' Home Journal* (from 1923), and *The Sketch*, London (1924–29). But who were his contemporaries in this field of illustration? Top favourites at *Gazette du bon ton* were Georges Barbier, André Édouard Marty (1882–1974), and Georges LePape, who had illustrated a special album, *Les Choses de Paul Poiret*, for Poiret in 1911. All three worked constantly for the magazine and other publications. Other fashion illustrators were Paul Iribe (who also produced a fashion album for Poiret), 'Thayaht' Ernesto Michahelles (1893–1959), Léon Bénigni (1892–1948), Umberto Brunelleschi (1879–1949), Pierre Brissaud (1885–1964), and Maurice Leroy.

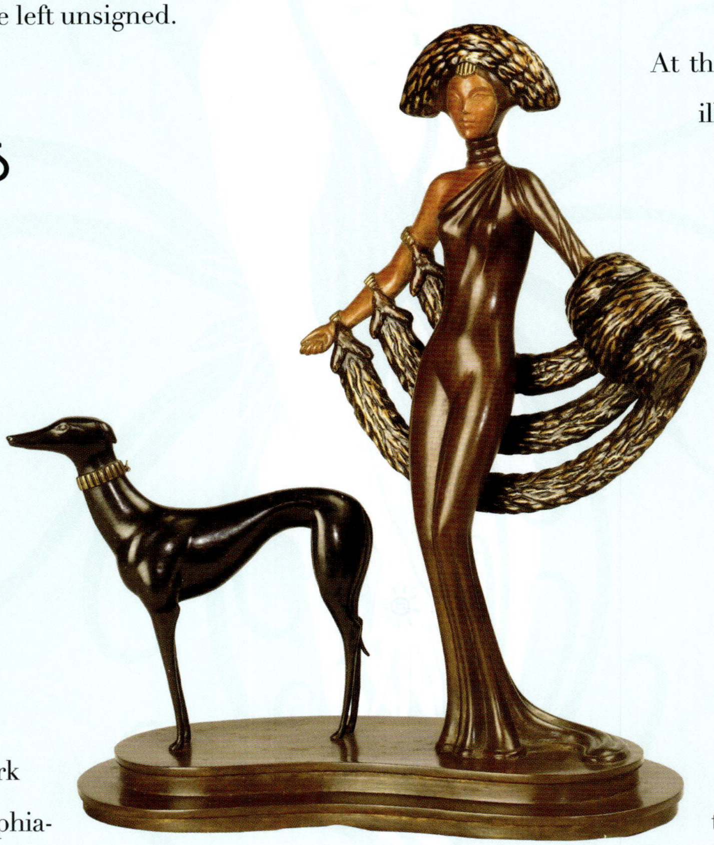

ILLNESS AND ANXIETY

At the age of 21 Erté contracted the debilitating illness scarlet fever. It was so severe – Erté called it 'critical' – that his parents travelled to Paris to be with him. But the First World War was imminent and his father, a serving officer in the Russian navy, needed to return to St Petersburg. Germany declared war on Russia on 1 August 1914, and invaded France the following day. Erté, his mother and Nicolas Ouroussoff stayed in Paris until he was fit enough to travel and then, like many Parisian citizens, embarked on a long train journey far away from the city. Erté's doctor advised moving to the south where the warmer climate would improve his health, so the decision was made to move to Monte Carlo.

PRISONER OF WAR

Erté's father had not crossed the French border before war was declared and he was taken as a prisoner-of-war. The family would

(Previous left) **Ebony and White**, *1982, serigraph, 55.9 x 76.2 cm (22 x 30 in)*
(Previous right) **Symphony in Black**, *1983, serigraph, 55.9 x 76.2 cm (22 x 30 in).*

(Above) **Elegance** (**Symphony in Black**) *sculpture, 1980, bronze, 41 x 31.5 x 16.5 cm (16¼ x 15½ x 6½ in)*

not hear from him for over three months. Erté was very close to his family and it was an anxious period. For him, his illness had made him infirm for military duty. In his autobiography *Erté: Things I Remember* (1975), he also made the point that, as a Russian citizen, and the eldest son of the family, he would have been ineligible for military call-up in Russia. Later Erté's mother met up with her daughter Natalia, returning to Russia via Scandinavia. The family would not be reunited until 1923 when Erté's parents moved from Russia to France.

1915: HARPER'S BAZAAR

In 1914, at the beginning of what would become known as the Great War, Erté's employer Paul Poiret was enlisted for military service (he was utilized as a designer of military uniforms). Poiret closed his fashion house in August 1914 for the duration of the war. Erté moved to Monte Carlo where he needed to find work, and he decided to offer original designs to an upmarket American fashion magazine. This may have been on the advice of Prince Nicolas, residing with Erté in Monte Carlo. It is recorded that Erté flipped a coin to choose between *Harper's Bazaar* (initially spelt '*Bazar*' until the extra 'a' was added in November 1929), owned by William Randolph Hearst, and *Vogue*, owned by Condé Montrose Nast (1873–1972). The coin chose the former. Erté recalled that on his twenty-second birthday, 23 November 1914, he received a cheque from *Harper's Bazaar*, enclosed with a letter requesting a set of drawings on a monthly basis. His first cover for the magazine appeared on the 1 January 1915 edition. The illustration was of 'Scheherazade'. It was probably an omen of a spectacular year ahead. For the March 1915 edition, Erté produced a range of original design illustrations of dresses, coats and accessories under the heading *Les Modes Creées à Paris* ('Paris Fashions'), which became a regular feature. A second front cover followed in November 1915. The exposure greatly increased his presence in the American fashion industry.

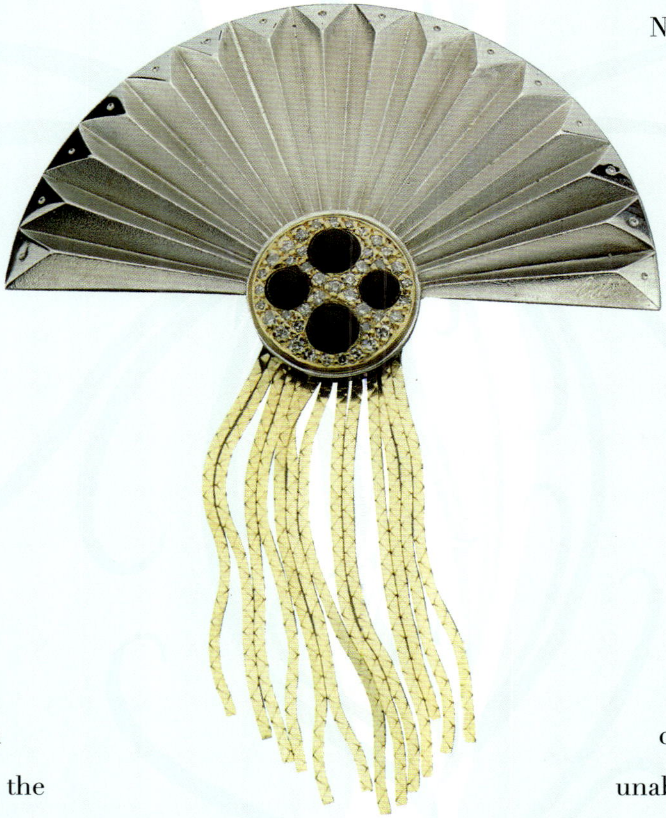

ERTÉ AND ADRIENNE

Around the same time that *Harper's Bazaar* offered him work, Erté visited Paris to meet Adrienne Ridou, a former leading dressmaker at Paul Poiret's fashion house. They teamed up to create 'Erté et Adrienne' fashions for the American market, haute couture dresses for society women now unable to travel to Paris. He would design the clothes and she would make dresses from his designs. However, unusually for a person of Erté's sensibility he created a fashion faux-pas that resulted in Paul Poiret taking legal action, severing all ties. Erté's business card, sent to prospective buyers, noted Adrienne as formerly *première de Poiret* ('best dressmaker to Poiret'). When Poiret discovered that his name had been used without his permission (or commission), to promote the new

(Above) **Très Chic** *brooch, c. 1979–90, gold, silver, black onyx, diamonds, 6.4cm (2½ in)*
An earlier *Très Chic* was a 1975 serigraph, which featured a typically elegant Erté woman wrapped in fur stoles over a heavy drape coat.

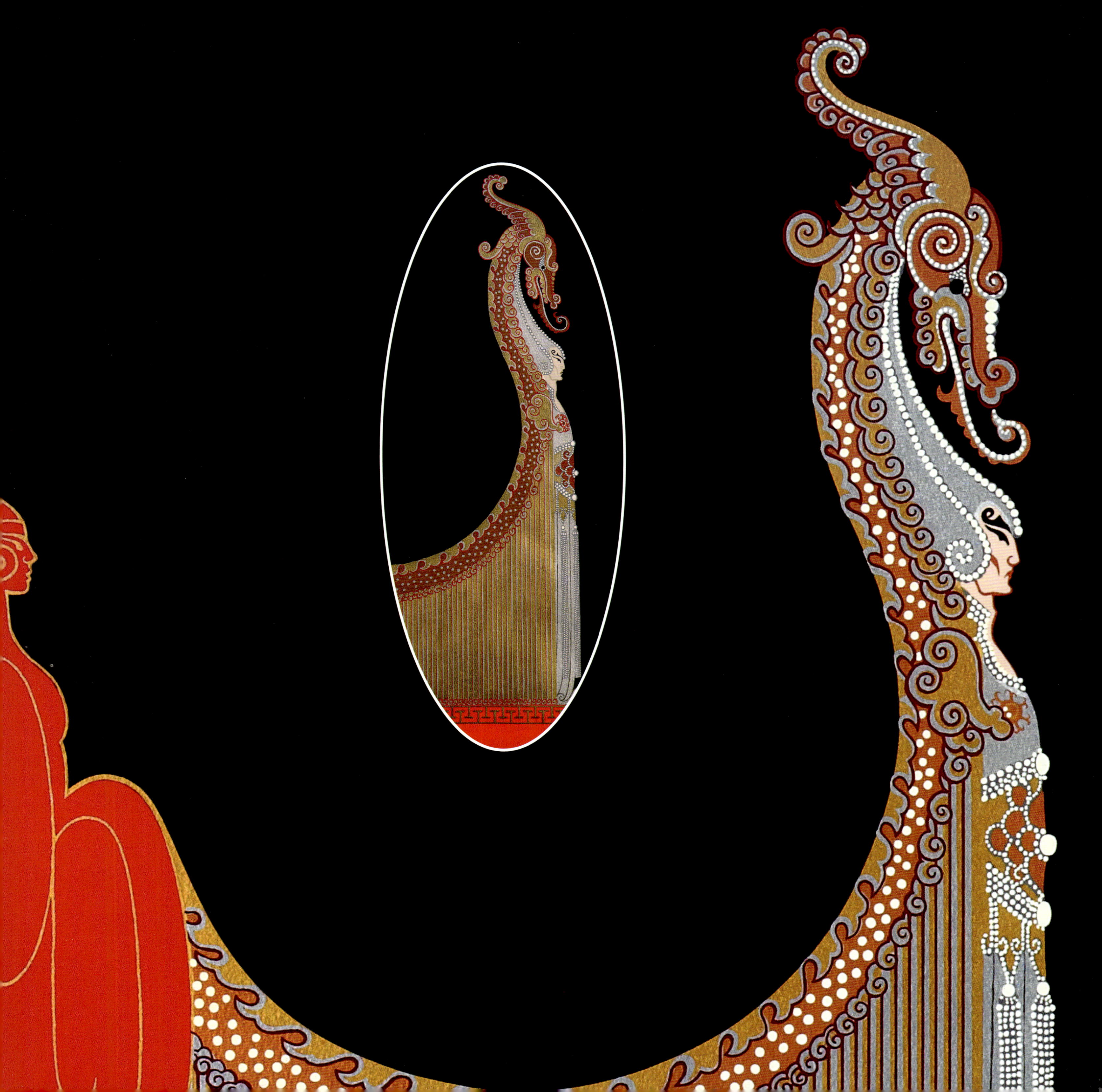

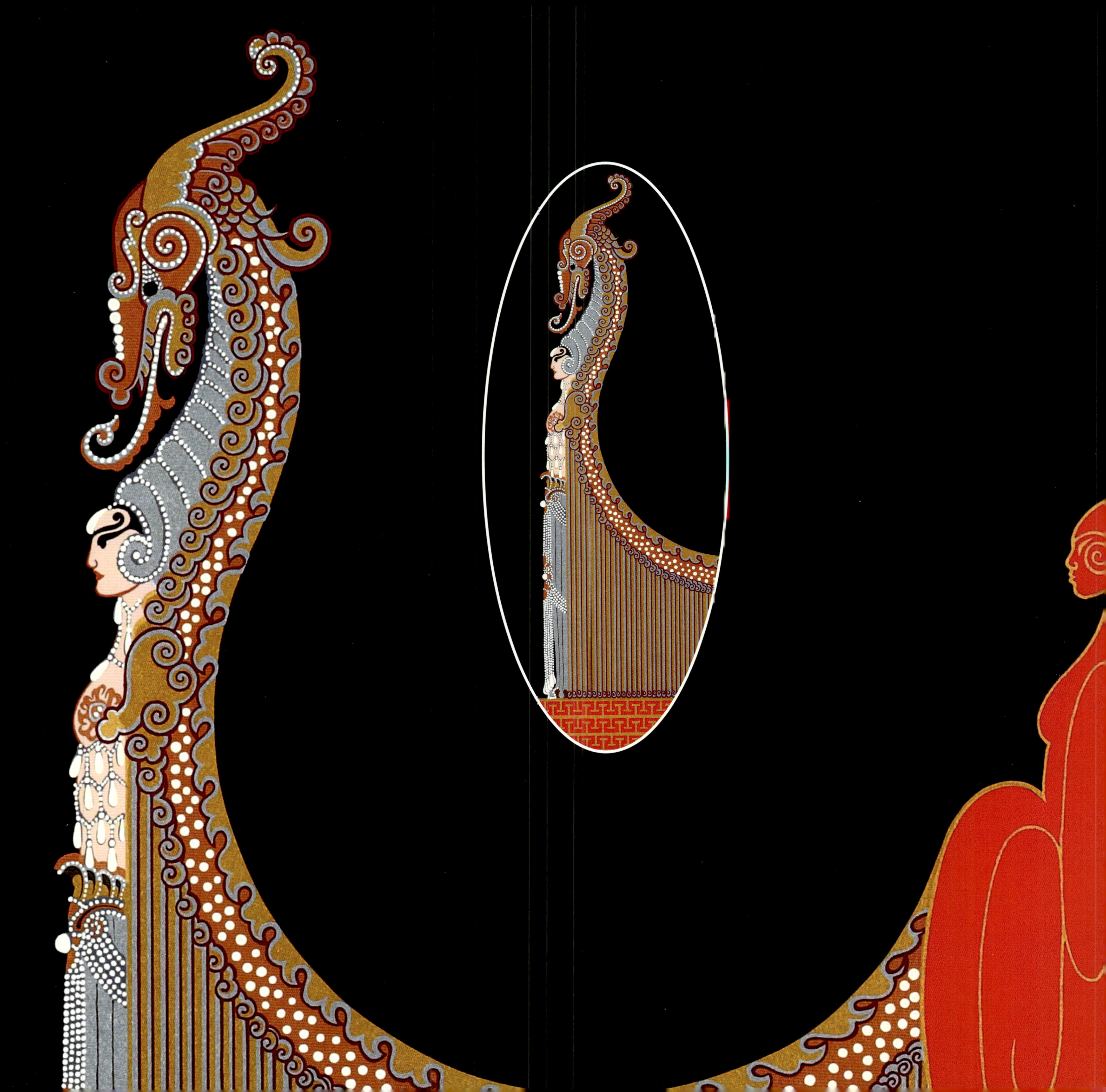

business he promptly sued Erté and won the case. Erté had to pay damages. It created a rift that would never be fixed.

HENRI BENDEL

On the plus side of Erté and Adrienne's agreement in 1915, the New York high-fashion company Henri Bendel (*see* pages 118–19) placed an initial order for 35 dresses and coats. It led to two collections per year from 'Erté and Adrienne' for the H. Bendel store, noted for its French flair from superb fabrics to fashion design. The design was in the immaculate workmanship of Adrienne and the design expertise of Erté. Clients loved the fabrics and the fashion details, such as dresses with empire line drawstring fastenings, high collar, balloon sleeves, and contrasting pinafore overlays with patch pockets. Erté created daywear, sportswear and evening wear for an appreciative clientele. And later, the department store B. Altman & Company contracted the team for a range of clothing.

WORKING FOR VOGUE

In 1916 the New York society and fashion magazine *Vogue* invited Erté to create a set of designs for their pages each month. Not contracted to *Harper's Bazaar*, he was free to accept. Erté stated that he needed the money, and the exposure aided his American status as fashion illustrator and designer. His drawings first appeared in the 15 June 1916 issue of *Vogue*. Further issues, on 1 August and 15 August, carried his illustrations.

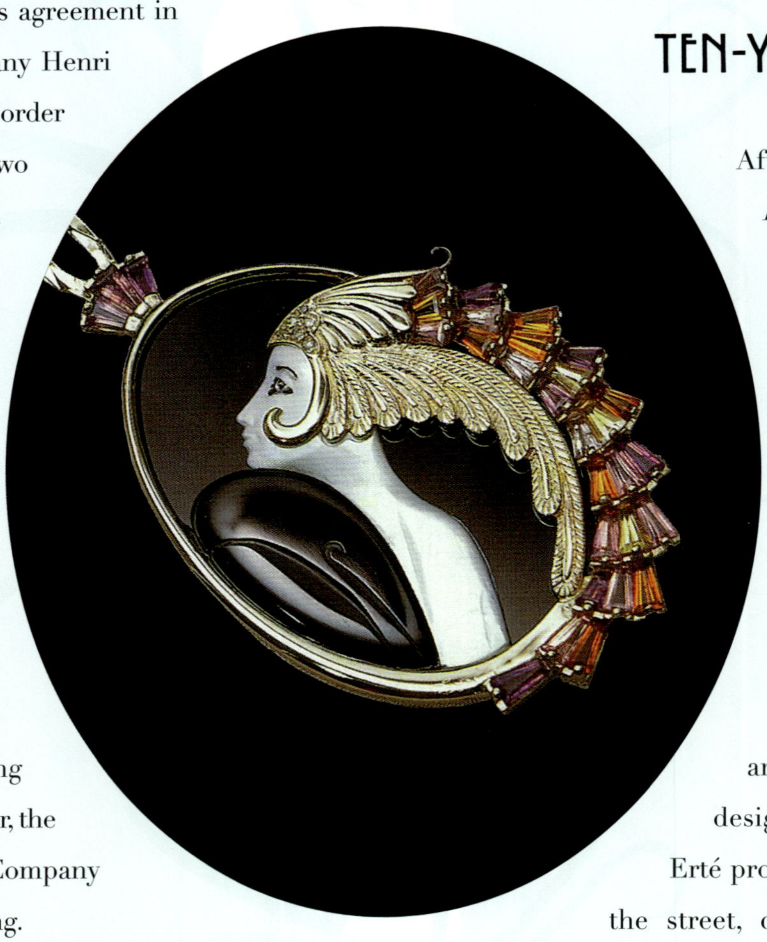

TEN-YEAR CONTRACT

After Erté's first success with *Harper's Bazaar* in 1915, followed by equally successful illustrations for *Vogue* in 1916, Hearst, the publisher and owner of *Harper's Bazaar*, offered him a ten-year contract for exclusivity. Erté accepted and his six-month involvement with *Vogue* was concluded. A contract was drawn up by Hearst. In addition to producing each cover design, Erté created hundreds of fashion drawings and illustrations, including interior designs. The front cover of each issue gave Erté prominent exposure at the news kiosks on the street, creating a strong brand identity for *Harper's Bazaar* in America. *New Bridges for the Seven Seas* (March 1919, *see* page 104), a reference to new-world horizons post-First World War, was a particularly successful cover edition. It was later adapted for the serigraph *Wings of Victory* (1978, *see* page 106), and used for a pendant design 'Aventurine' in 1979 (*see* pages 105 and 107).

(Previous page inset on left) **Wedding costume design for the Groom, Aladdin,** *Folies Bergère, 1929, gouache, 69.2 x 52.7 cm (27¼ x 20¾ in)*
(Previous page full spread and inset on right) **Aladdin and His Bride,** *1984, serigraph, 78.7 x 94 cm (31 x 37 in)*

(Right) **Beauty and the Beast,** *1977, serigraph, 45.7 x 34.6 cm (18 x 13⅝ in)*
(Above) **Beauty of the Beast** *pendant, c. 1979–90, gold, diamonds, black onyx, amethysts, mother-of-pearl, pink tourmaline, madeira citrines, champagne citrines*

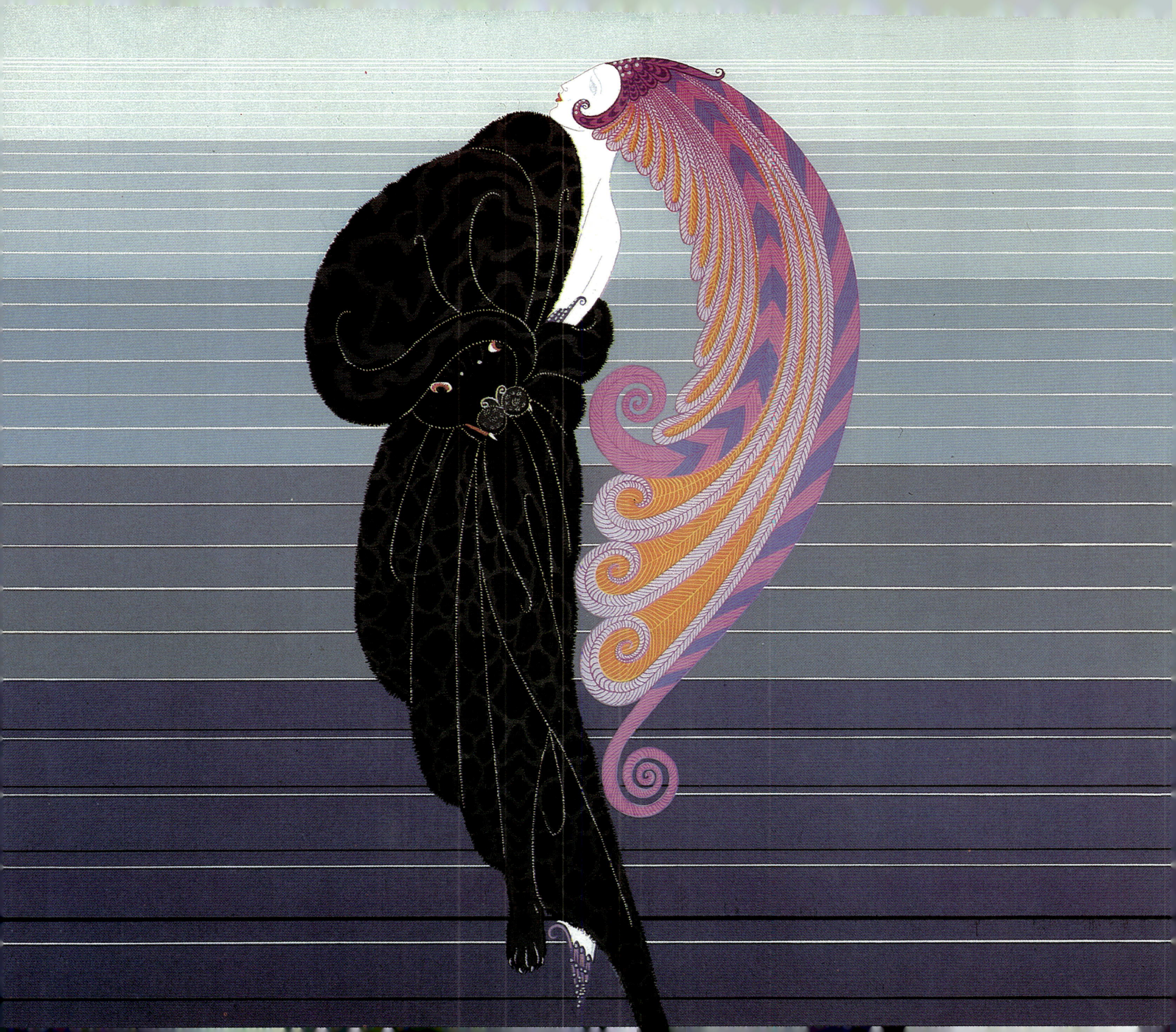

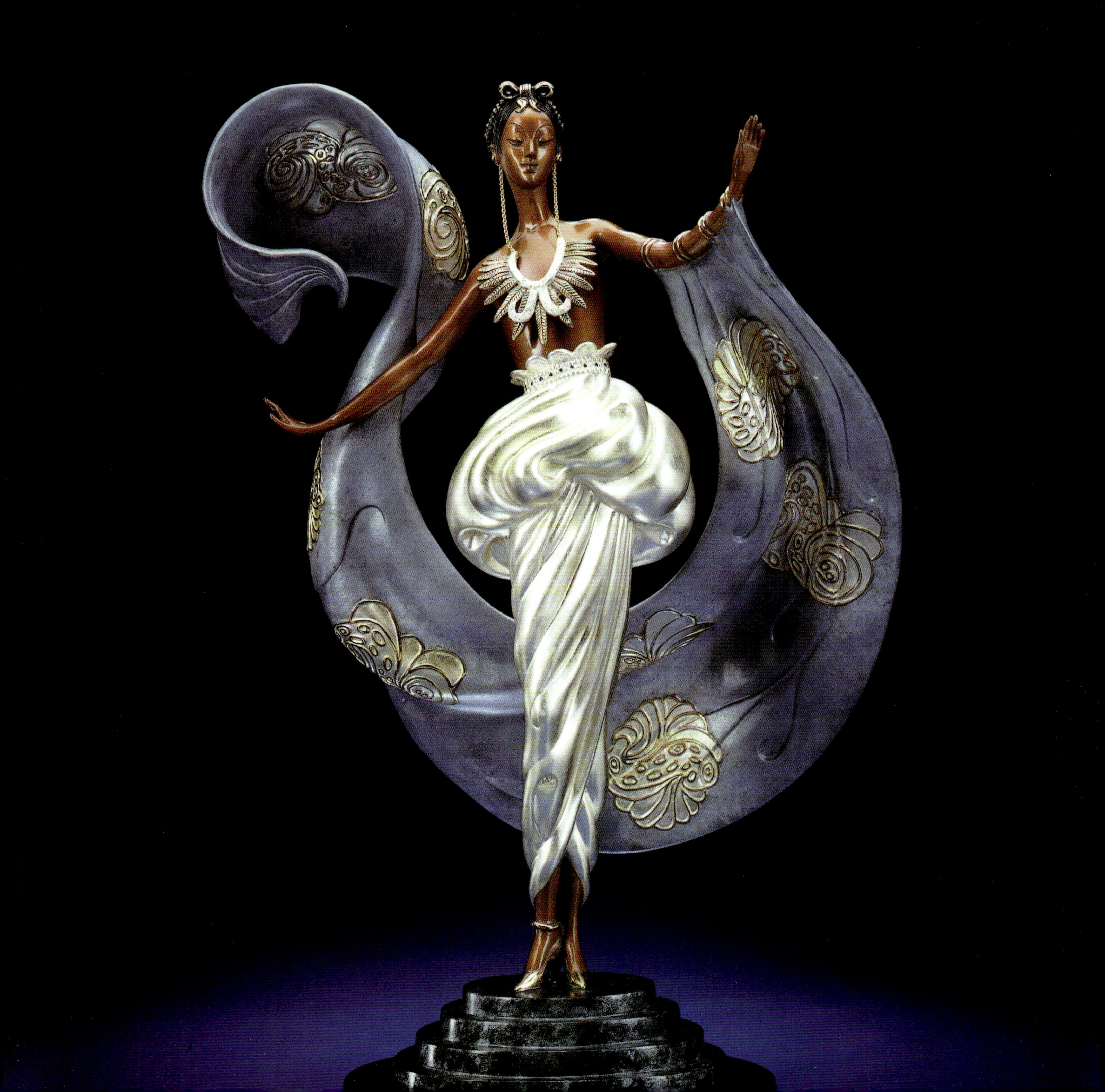

ESSENTIALLY ERTÉ

The characteristic Erté illustration that pleased *Harper's Bazaar* was the 'Winter Fashions Number', for the November 1920 cover (*see* page 34), later to be recreated as *Applause* (*see* page 35). He often started an illustration with an arabesque shape. Here, a young dancer stretches her body in an arabesque arc. She is dressed only in a starburst of swirling ribbons of red and gold. She turns her head to accept the applause of the audience (only their hands are visible). It is set on a scarlet background. Erté used the shape over and again throughout his career. Each cover was original in concept, *Souvenirs* (1922, *see* page 167), *Aquarium* (1923, *see* page 152) and *The Heat and the Clouds* (July 1926, *see* page 150), are a few examples of Erté's diversity and creativity. It was such a successful arrangement for Hearst that Erté's contract was renewed on expiry. By 1927 Erté was famous enough to include a reference to himself on the Christmas cover *Riviera*, 'Christmas Number' (1927, *see* page 160). The relationship with *Harper's Bazaar* lasted a total of 22 years. In that time Erté produced 240 covers for the magazine.

VILLA EXCELSIOR

In 1916 Erté and Nicolas moved house in Monte Carlo to a grand terraced apartment in the Villa Excelsior. In his autobiography (*Erté: Things I Remember*, 1975), he recalled the thrill of designing the interior and the soft furnishings, as well as choosing the antique furniture, bought locally, to create their home. He chose a plain oak worktable (which could be adapted to serve as an easel) to work on and to store his pencils and paints. He used it throughout his working life.

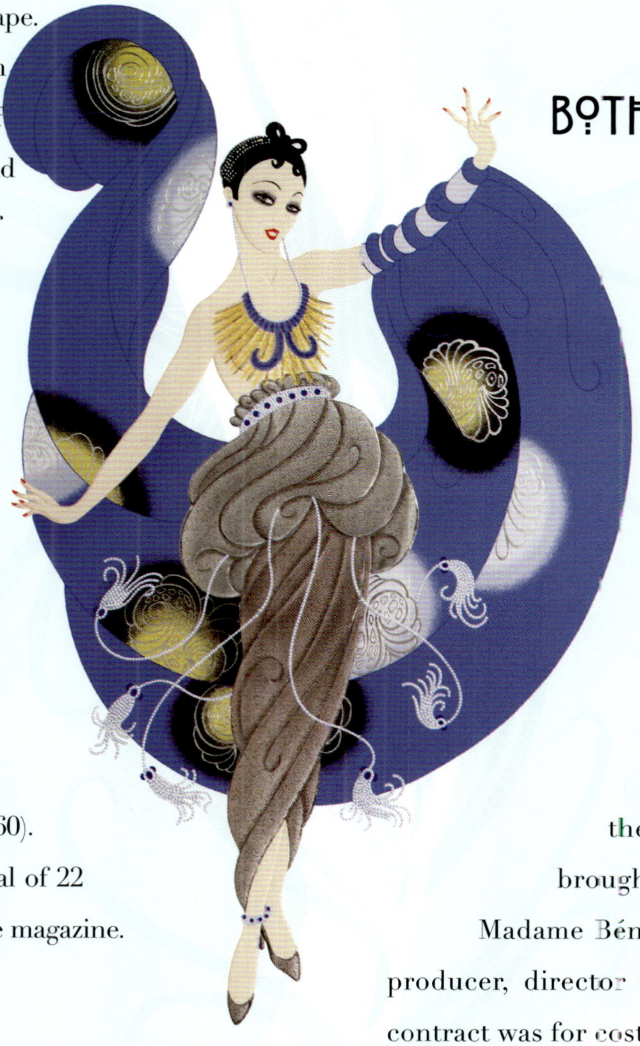

BOTH SIDES OF THE ATLANTIC

In addition to American commissions, Erté was working again in Europe designing stage and music hall costumes for theatrical contacts. Established as a fashion designer in America, he was better known for stage costumes at home. In 1916 'Rip' (George-Gabriel Thenon, 1884–1941) a revue writer and stage comic, commissioned Erté for designs for 'Revue de Saint-Cyr'. They had worked together before on the review *Aphrodite* in 1914. Its success brought further work from Rip. As it did from Madame Bénédicte Rasimi (1874–1954), a theatrical producer, director and successful costumier. Erté's first contract was for costume designs for *Panachot the Dictator* at the Bataclan Theatre, 50 Boulevard Voltaire, Paris, which Madame Rasimi owned. It was followed up in 1917 with costumes for the leading actors Maurice Chevalier (1888–1972) and Mistinguett, performing in *Gobette of Paris*. Individual singers and actors called on him, too, to

Dream Girl *sculpture, 1991, bronze, 54 x 36 x 24 cm (211/4 x 14 x 9½ in)*

A Dream, *1992, embossed serigraph with foil stamping, 101.6 x 75.5 cm (40 x 29¾ in)*

create spectacular costumes for their revue shows. The beautiful French actress, music hall chanteuse and dancer Gaby Deslys (1881–1920), mistress of King Manuel of Portugal, contracted him for a whole series of dresses (*see* page 171). In 1919 Erté designed all the costumes and sets for *La Marche à l'Etoile* at the Théâtre Fémina, Paris, in which she starred. In addition, Erté worked for the Alcazar Theatre in Marseilles.

Folies Bergère

The first music hall cabaret to open in Paris was the Folies Bergère, at 32 rue Richer, near Montmartre, founded in 1869. It was first called Folies Trevise after a nearby street but the name was changed in 1872. The Folies Bergère offered raucous cabaret, ballet, operettas, pantomime, acrobatics and nudity. It was part of the gaiety of the Parisian *fin de siècle*. French painter Édouard Manet (1832–83), the 'painter of modern life', immortalized its clientele in his work *Un Bar aux Folies Bergère* (1881, Courtauld Gallery, London). Posters for its shows were created by the artist-illustrators Jules Cheret (1836–1932) and Henri de Toulouse-Lautrec, amongst others. The exuberance and decadence of 'La Belle Époque' and the Folies Bergère ceased at the outbreak of the First World War. The music hall closed its doors from 3 August 1914 until February 1915. But back in business it pulled in new audiences. Erté was one of many designers called upon to create costumes for the performers. It was here that he first met Max Weldy (*c.* 1895–1983), the chief set designer and costumier at the Folies Bergère.

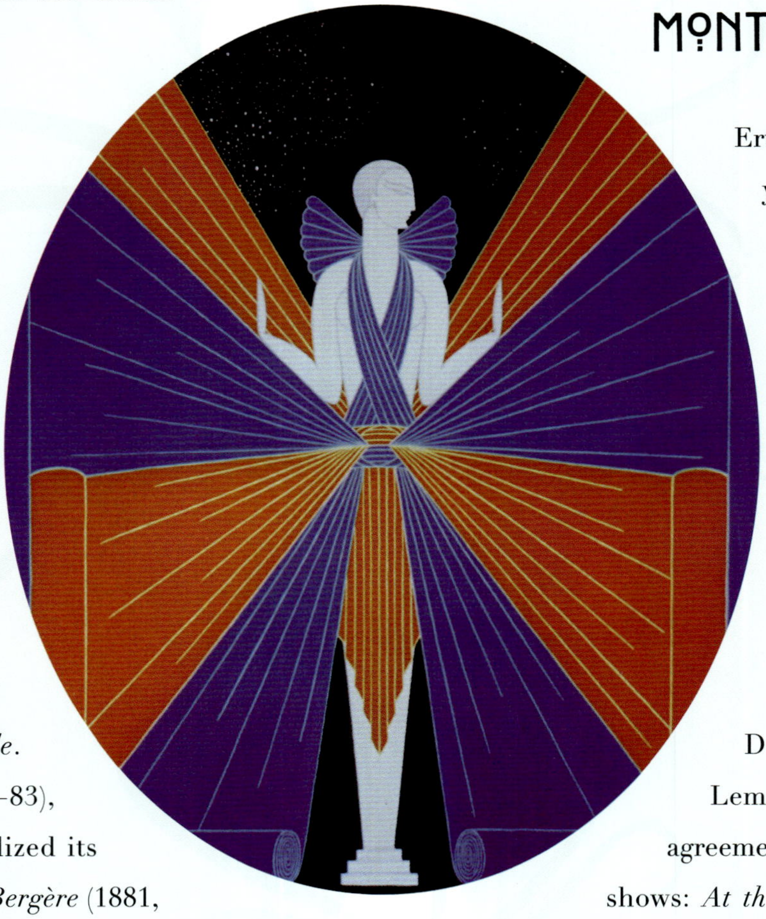

Monte Carlo Paris

Erté made three or four trips to Paris each year from 1914 for the next eight years, whilst living in Monte Carlo. Apart from his dress design partnership with Adrienne Ridou, he was in demand for theatrical costumes. It kept his name as a designer noted. In 1919 Max Weldy wrote to Erté to offer him work as a set designer. After a meeting in Paris between Erté, Nicolas (his partner and manager) and Weldy, as well as Paul Derval (the owner) and Louis Lemarchand (the shows' producer), an agreement was made. Erté would design for two shows: *At the Bottom of the Sea* and *Venice in the Eighteenth Century*. Both were successful. On the strength of this, Weldy and Erté forged a long working relationship at the Folies Bergère and for productions elsewhere, as well as a good friendship. Weldy facilitated Erté in his creation of set designs and taught him much about the mechanical workings of stage production.

Robes Nouvelles, No. 127, *cover design for* Harper's Bazaar, *October 1927, gouache, 40 x 29.8 cm (15¾ x 11¾ in)*

Summer Breeze, *1978, serigraph, 77.7 x 59 cm (301/2 x 231/8 in)*

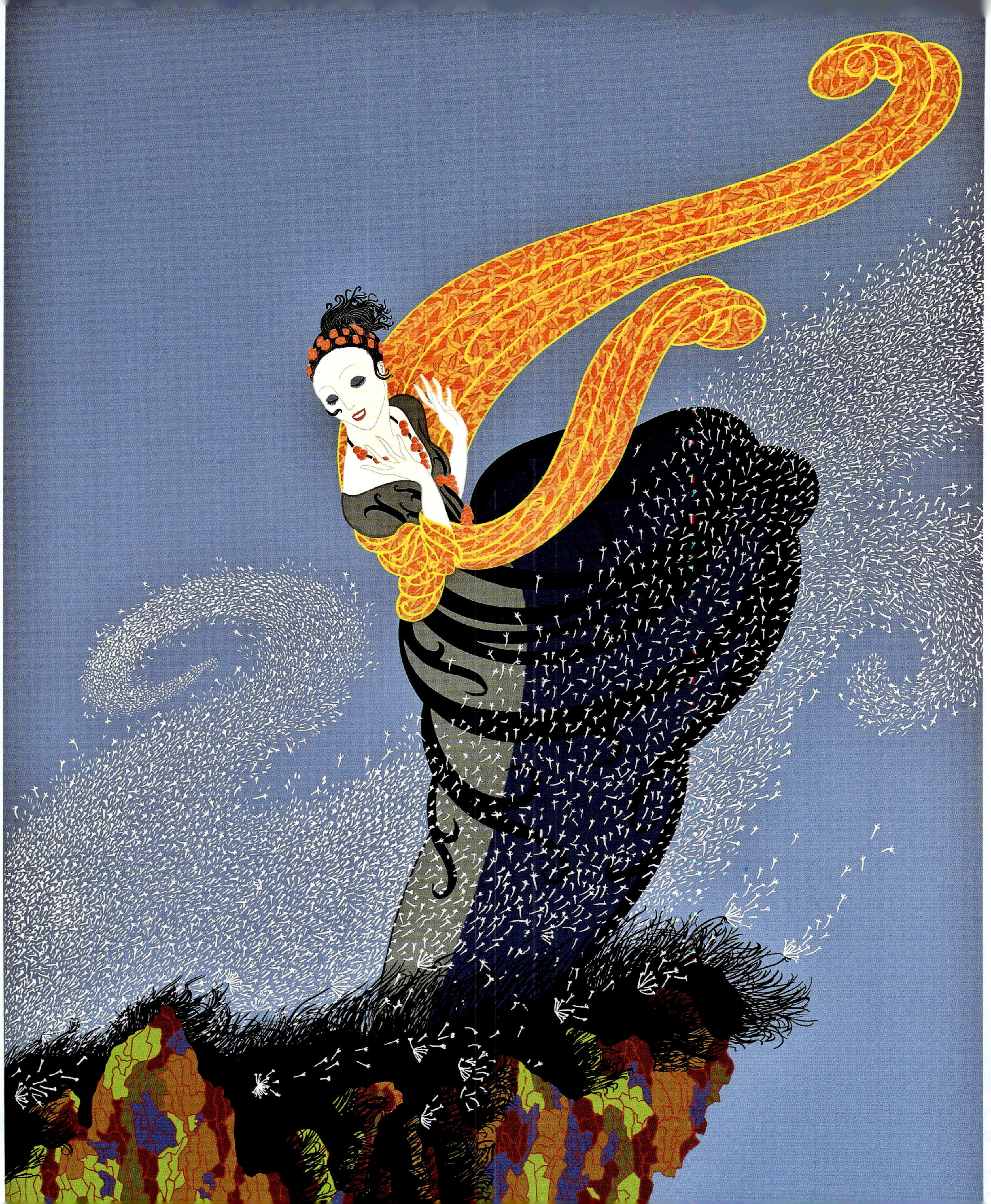

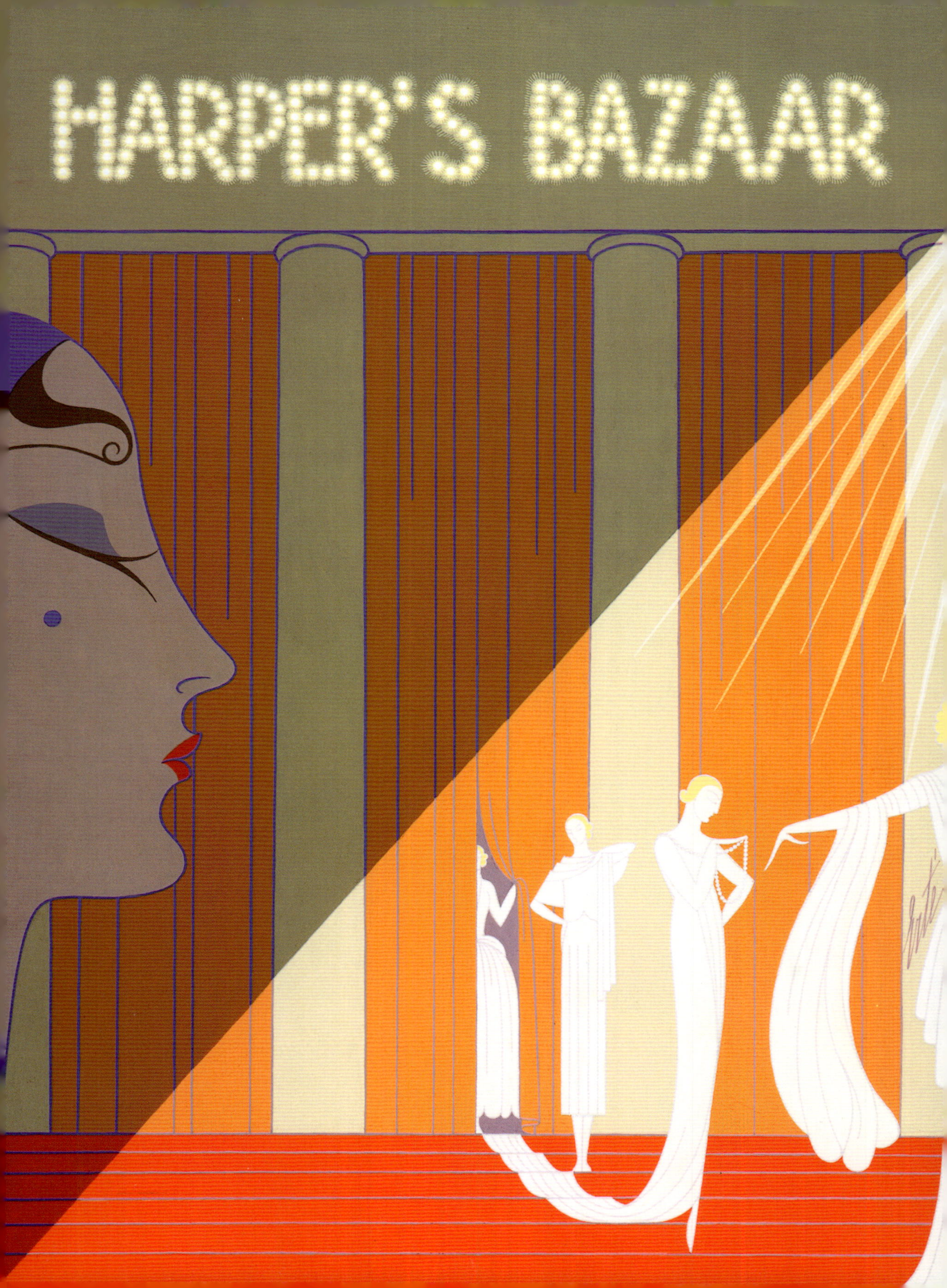
HARPER'S BAZAAR

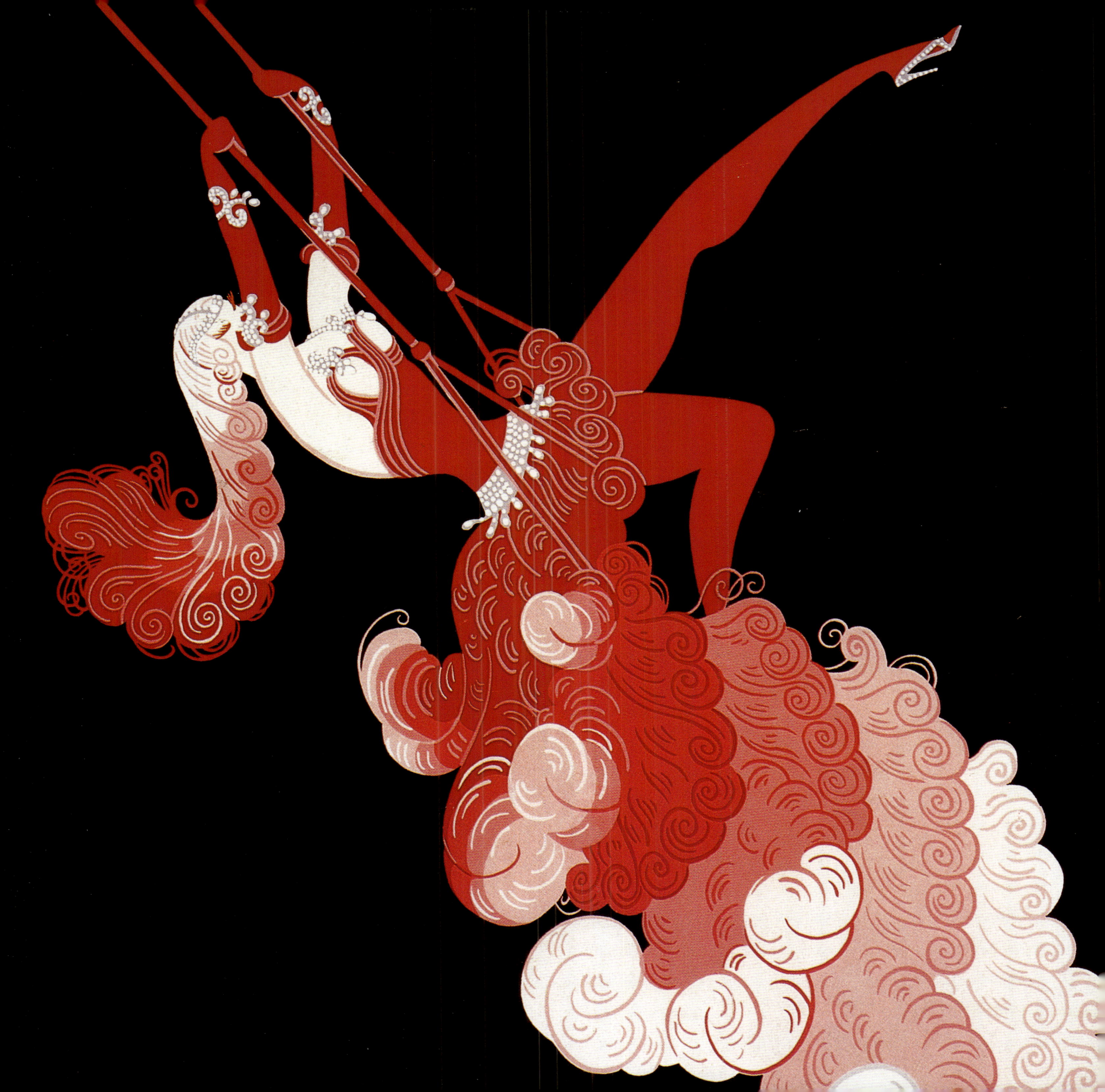

ERTÉ'S PRIVATE STUDIO

In 1920 a young American, Howard Greer (1896–1974), got an introduction to Erté through the daughter of Erté's friend, Madame Bénédicte Rasimi, the theatrical producer, director and costumier. Greer wanted to become one of Erté's copyists (he would later become a Hollywood fashion and costume designer) and an interview was arranged. Later, Greer recalled the event and it is a fascinating insight into Erté's private life at home. Greer recalled that Erté's villa was perched high on a hill overlooking the Monte Carlo Casino. 'A fiacre [a small four-wheeled horse-drawn carriage] met me at the station'. The door to the villa was opened by a servant wearing a green and white vest with black satin sleeves, and Greer was shown into a large, well-lit room. Erté's vast desk and a chair were positioned in the centre of the squared black and white marble floor. Along the walls a grey and white striped curtain covered a framed collection of hundreds of Erté's original works. Greer described Erté wearing lounge pyjamas, possibly made of ermine. Coming into the room behind Erté was a Persian cat, and Prince Nicolas Ouroussoff, Erté's companion. The description of Erté's desk and its contents enlightens our view of him. On the desk a large bowl held hundreds of different types of paintbrushes of varying widths, lengths and thicknesses. The top drawer of the desk, which Erté opened to show Greer, contained a plethora of tempera paint jars all red in tones. The drawer below it contained blue jars, below that, yellow, purple and so on, each drawer holding a different colour. Unfortunately for Greer, returning soon after with the copy he had made of the drawing Erté had loaned him was not good enough. He did not get the job.

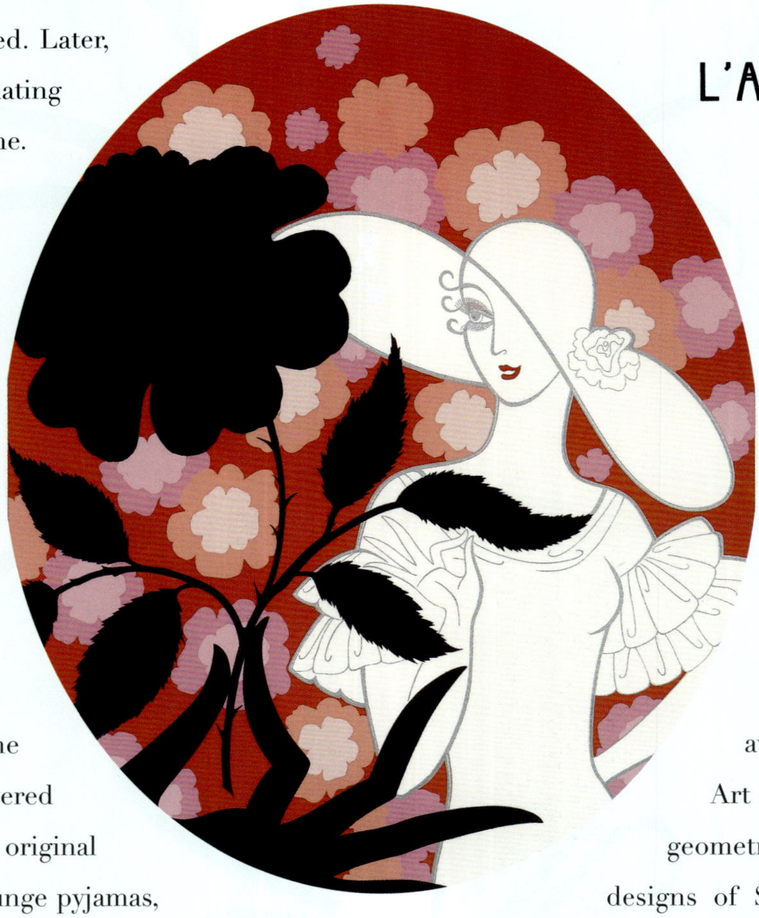

L'ART DÉCORATIF

At the turn of the nineteenth century in Paris and in other cities in Europe such as Vienna, Brussels and Barcelona, the Art Nouveau style was at its zenith (from 1895–1905). However, the new century saw artists and designers looking for new forms of art, away from historicism and towards a modernity sparer in design line. Picasso and Braque's 'Cubism', from *c.* 1908, pushed away the sinuous whiplash curves of the Art Nouveau style with more emphasis on geometric form, visible in the architecture and designs of Scotsman Charles Rennie Mackintosh (1868–1928), the Belgian Henry van der Velde (1863–1957), the Austrian Josef Hofmann (1870–1956), the American Frank Lloyd Wright (1867–1959), and the Frenchman Charles-Édouard Jeanneret-Gris (1887–1965), known as Le Corbusier. Erté admired Le Corbusier's architecture and design. Art, architecture and decorative art returned to classical lines with

(Previous page, left) **Paris Openings**, *cover design for* Harper's Bazaar, *March 1931, gouache, 40.6 x 30.5 cm (16 x 12 in)*
(Previous page, right) **The Trapeze** *(detail), 1983, serigraph, 76.2 x 55.9 cm (30 x 22 in)*

(Above) **Black Rose**, *1975, serigraph, 64 x 51 cm (25 x 20 in)*
(Right) **Make-up**, *1978, serigraph, 46 x 33 cm (18 x 13 in)*
Advances in the creation of cosmetics and perfumes in the 1920s, particularly by French companies, made the topic popular in fashion and style magazines. Erté designed several make-up gouaches for *Harper's Bazaar*.

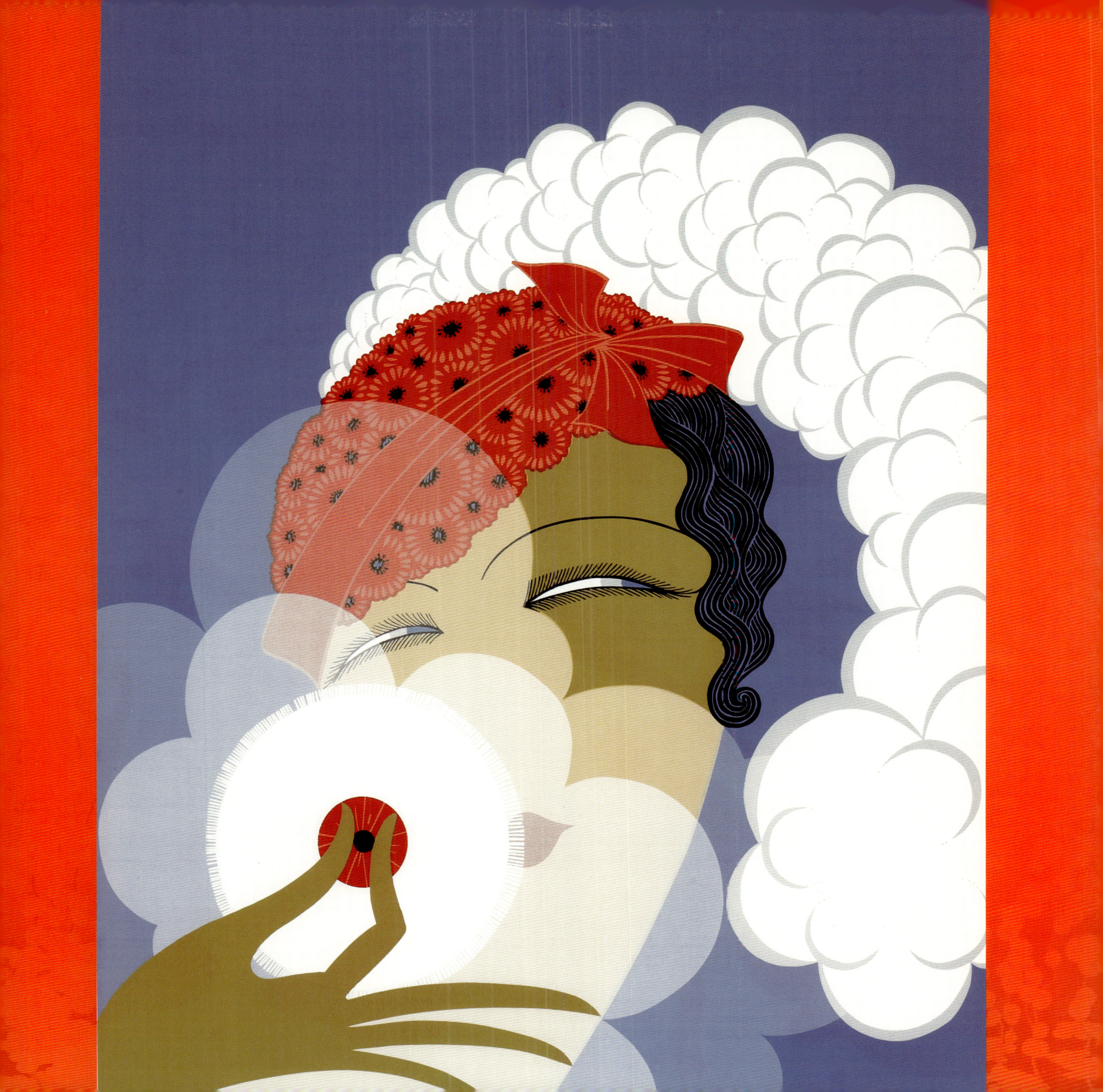

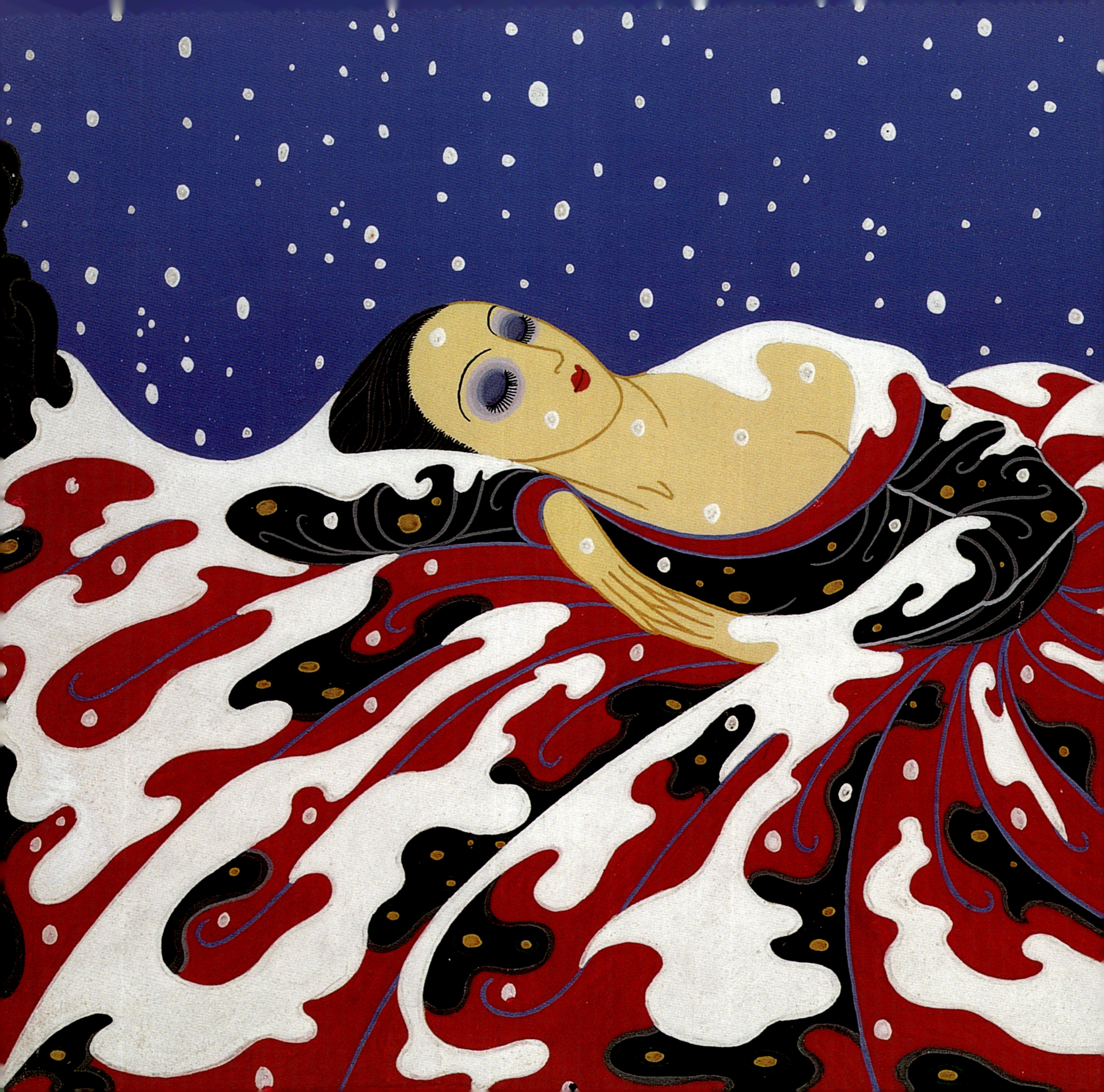

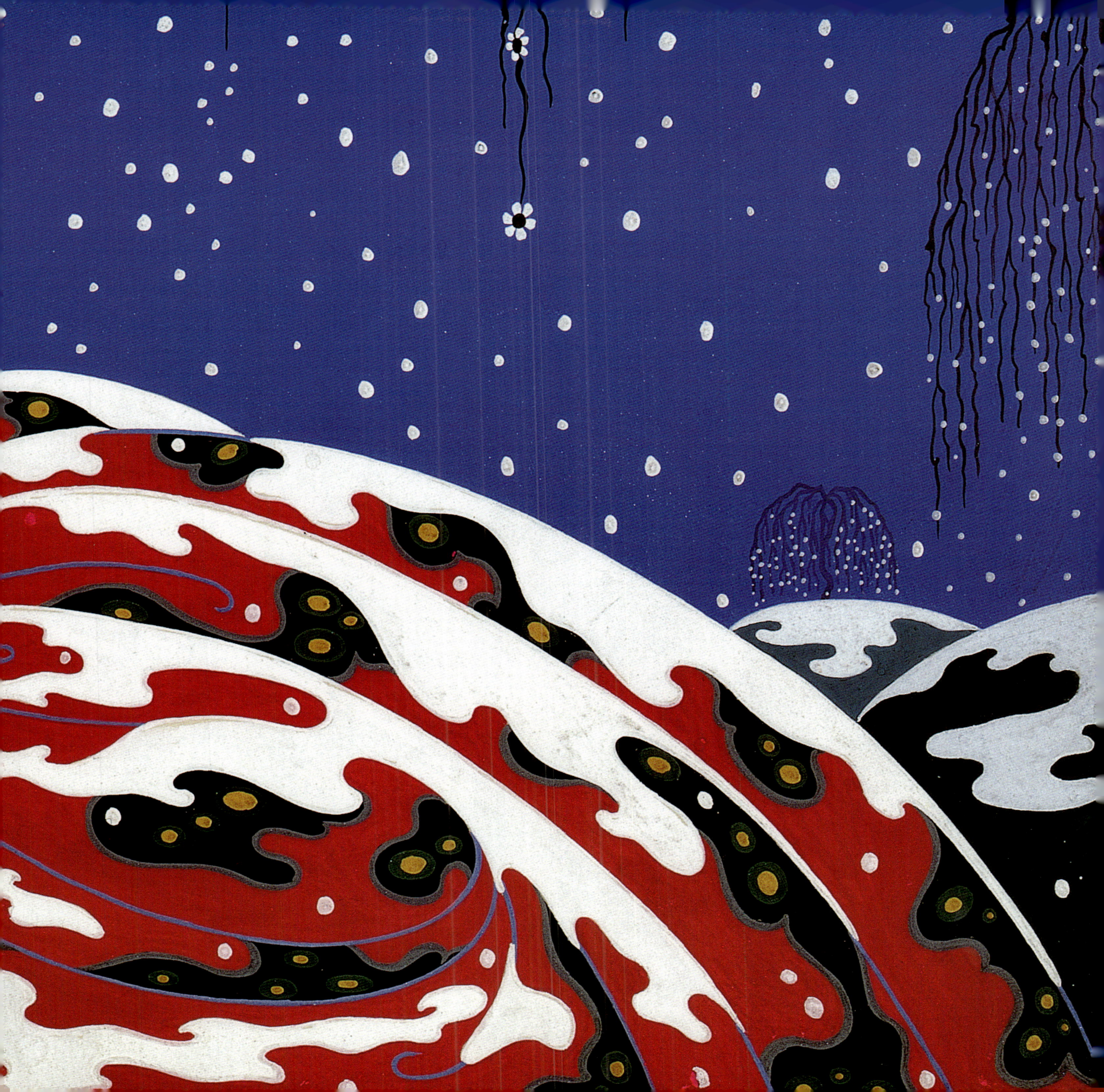

decorative detail, which Erté embraced, but only if it was the right style for each new commission. And, gradually, through the years prior to the First World War, the style known as Art Décoratif was forming. Post-war, from 1918, it flourished. It was associated with luxury and modernity during the 1920s–30s interwar years.

COSTUMING 'GANNA WALSKA'

Ganna Walska (1887–1984), born Hanna Puacz, was a Polish opera singer who became a regular client of Erté. He recalled that in 1920 she wrote to him with her plan to travel from New York to Europe, to meet him, 'the most imaginative man in the world'. His first costume designs were for her roles in Jules Massenet's *Fédora* (1919, *see* page 97) and *Thaïs* (1920, *see* page 178), by Umberto Giordano (1867–1948). Erté sent them to her in America. Walska was delighted, and sent him a cheque and a note stating that she was coming to Monte Carlo to meet him in person, which she did. They agreed that he would design all her costumes for her forthcoming performances with the Chicago Opera Company. Erté produced a diverse range of simply beautiful designs for *La Tosca* (1920, *see* page 189) and *Manon* (1922, *see* page 165). Other roles for which he made Walska costumes were *Martha*, and *Faust*, both in 1920, and roles in *Rigoletto*, *Monna Vanna*, *Madame Butterfly*, and *Aphrodite* (*see* page 144), *La Bohème*, *Zaza*, *Louise*, and *I Pagliaci*. The costumes were made up by the fashion house Redfern.

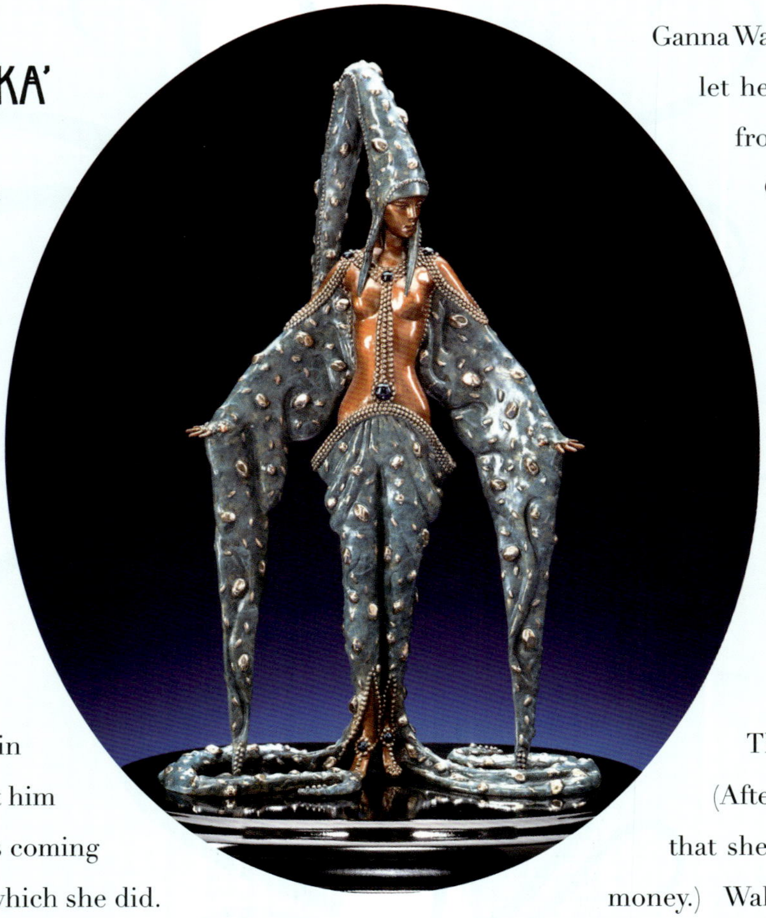

THÉÂTRE DES CHAMPS-ÉLYSÉES

Ganna Walska often did not sing well as her nerves let her down. In 1920 she had walked away from the first rehearsal of *Zaza* at the Chicago Opera Company due to a very poor performance. Erté's costumes for future productions would be unused as all her imminent performances at the Chicago Opera Company were cancelled. She retrieved her standing, although perhaps not respect for her voice, by marrying American businessman Harold Fowler McCormick (1872–1941), in 1922. As a present he bought her the Théâtre des Champs-Élysées in Paris. (After their divorce in 1931,Walska insisted that she had bought the theatre with her own money.) Walska could sing here in her own productions and Erté created further costumes: for her role of Mélisande in *Pelléas et Mélisande*, the Countess in *The Marriage of Figaro*, and Donna Elvira in *Don Giovanni*, all performed at the Théâtre des Champs-Élysées. Erté also recalled a very special costume created for her when she sang soprano in a performance of Beethoven's *Ninth Symphony*. He made sure her

(Previous page) **Neige de Printemps** *(detail), cover design for* Harper's Bazaar, *1923, gouache on cardboard, whole sheet 35.2 x 26 cm (137/8 x 10¼ in)*
This design was later recreated as a *Sleeping Beauty* serigraph in 1983.

(Above) **Starfish** *sculpture, 1988, bronze, 50.8 x 38.1 x 25.4 cm (20 x 15 x 10 in)*
(Right) **Starfish**, *1986, embossed serigraph with foil stamping, 100.3 x 74.4 cm (39½ x 29¼ in)*

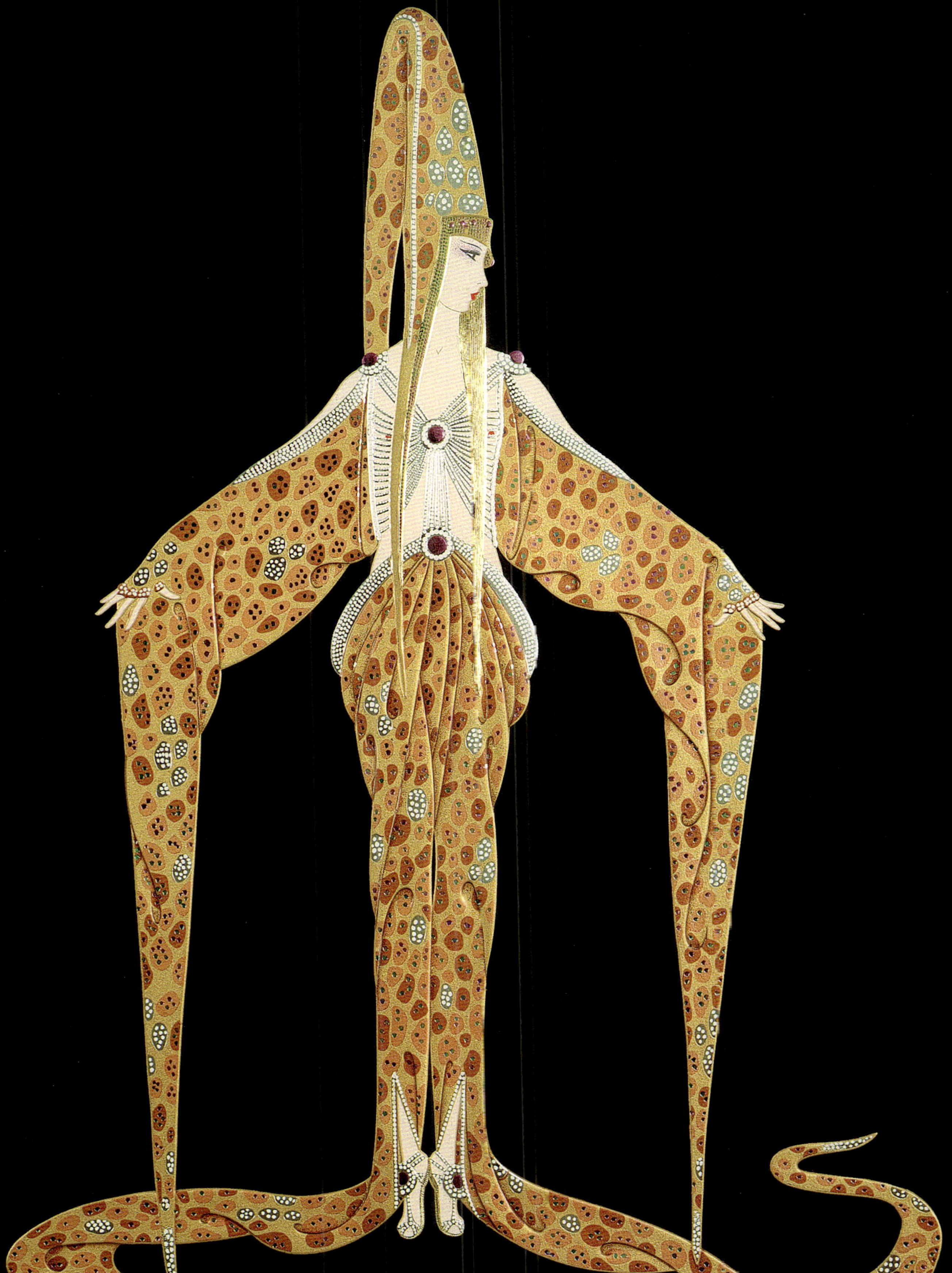

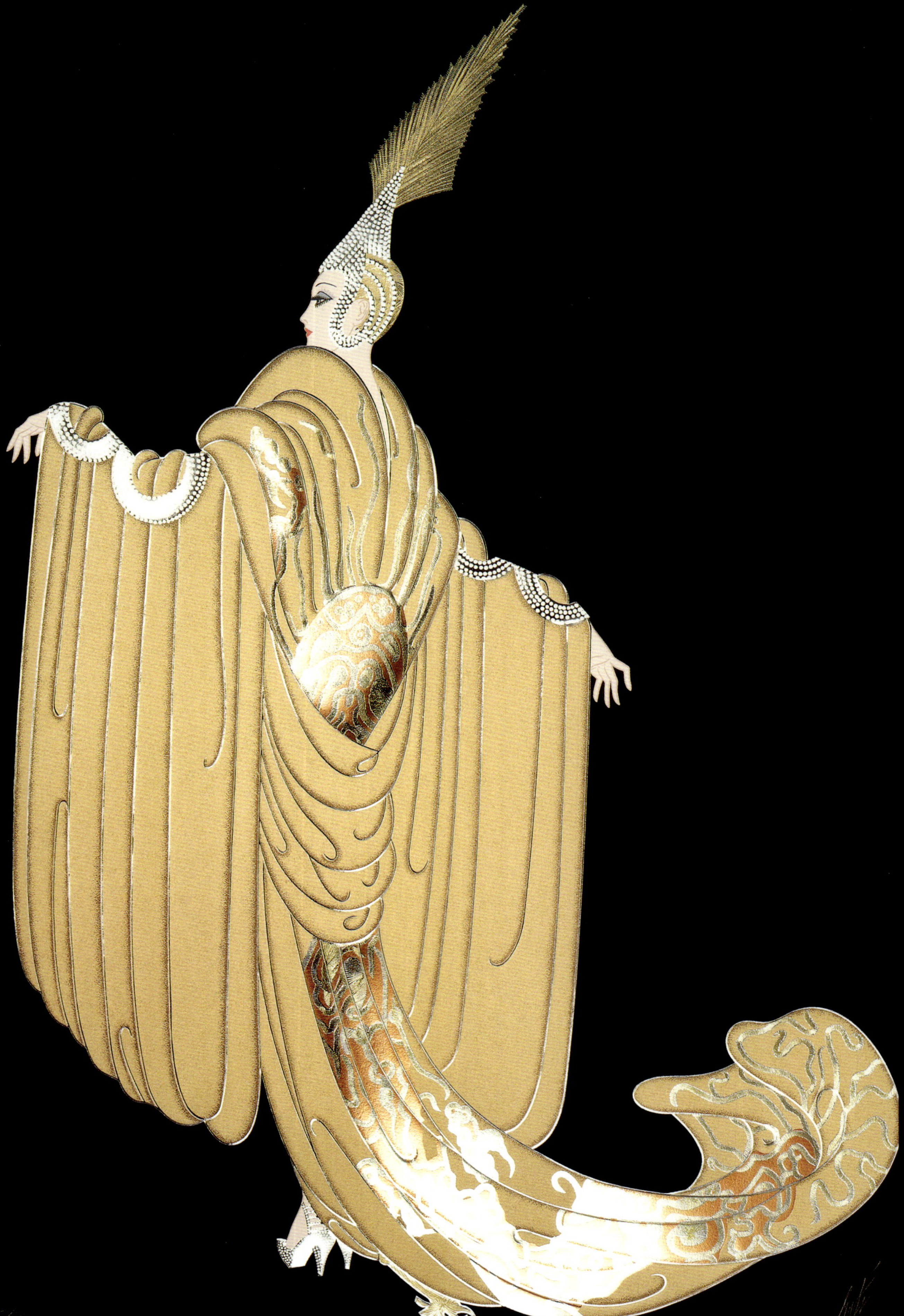

costumes included accessories for her hands to hold, to lessen her nerves. For *Don Giovanni*, Erté created a jewelled mink wristband which he said was in shreds by the time Walska's performance ended.

A CHANCE TO WORK FOR DIAGHILEV

What must have been a dream job for Erté, influenced so much by Sergei Diaghilev's Ballets Russes as a teenager, was a commission to design costumes for Diaghilev's ballet *The Sleeping Beauty* in 1921. The original stage sets and costumes created by Russian artist, stage and costume designer Leon Bakst (1866–1924), had been confiscated in London by Sir Oswald Stoll, director of the London Coliseum, as a result of a monetary disagreement with Diaghilev. Diaghilev therefore needed new sets and costumes quickly. Erté began work, with the *Lilac Fairy* (1921, *see* page 32), and the costume for *Prince Charming* (1921, *see* page 33). The arrangement was then put on hold, and then cancelled due to Erté receiving a better financial offer from his friend, the theatrical costumier Max Weldy, who needed help with sets and costumes for the musical revue *Greenwich Village Follies* (1922). The fee was too good, and Erté needed it to maintain his fashionable lifestyle. Diaghilev understood. They remained friends.

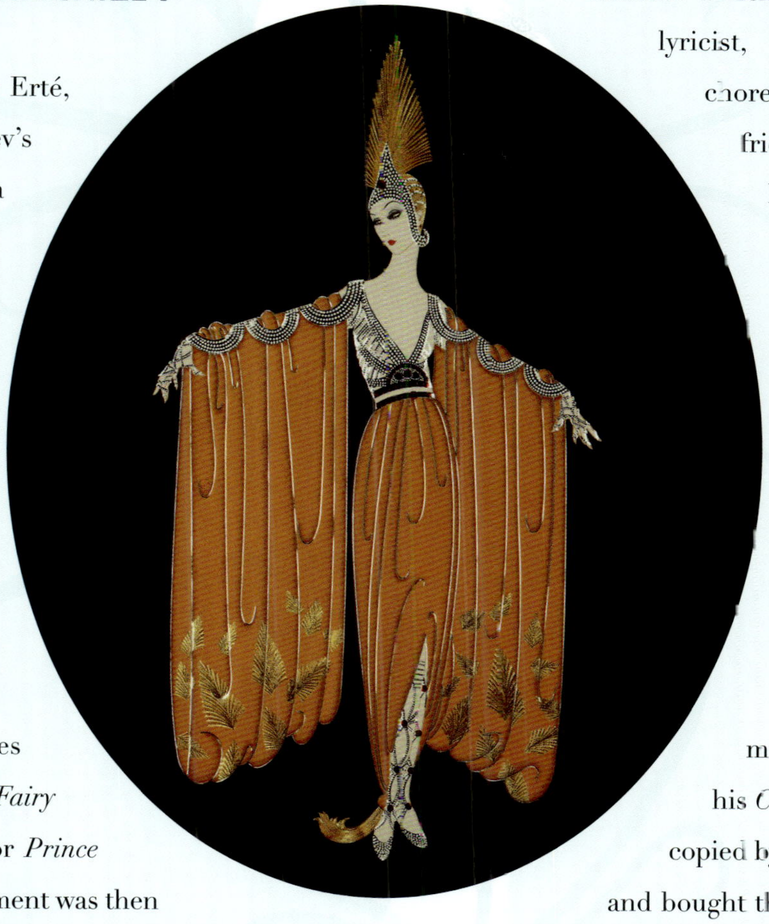

MEETING GEORGE WHITE

George White (1892–1968) – birth name Eassy Whites – was an Austrian-born American impresario, one of nine siblings. His parents emigrated to New York *c.* 1901. He skipped school, got a job as a boot boy and earned money by street dancing. He would become a rich Broadway and Hollywood producer, lyricist, composer, writer, theatre owner, choreographer and director, and a very good friend to Erté. In 1922, on a visit to Paris he watched a performance of *La Revue de La Femme* at the Théâtre des Ambassadeurs – just off the Champs-Élysées – which included the scene *Les Mers* ('The Seas'). The sets and costumes by Erté were fantasy creations symbolizing the Mediterranean, the Black Sea, the Red Sea and more. They were designed as a collective group, each costume and setting relating to the main character of the group. Erté called it his *Costume Collectif*, originated by him, later copied by others. White liked *Les Mers* very much and bought the show to take to America for his own revue 'Scandals'. The triple costume design for the 'Ocean', *Les Mers* (1923, *see* page 26–27), was produced for White's 1923 'Scandals' revue. It highlights Erté's originality in his application of sumptuous colour, extravagant costume design and theatricality. One can see here Erté's progression of ideas from the colours of Persian miniature paintings to Paul Poiret's

Cape à la Russe, *'Ensemble du Soir Suite', 1989, embossed serigraph with foil stamping, 102.4 x 74.4 cm (40¼ x 29¼ in)*

Gown Orientale, *'Ensemble du Soir Suite', 1989, embossed serigraph with foil stamping, 102.4 x 74.4 cm (40¼ x 29¼ in)*

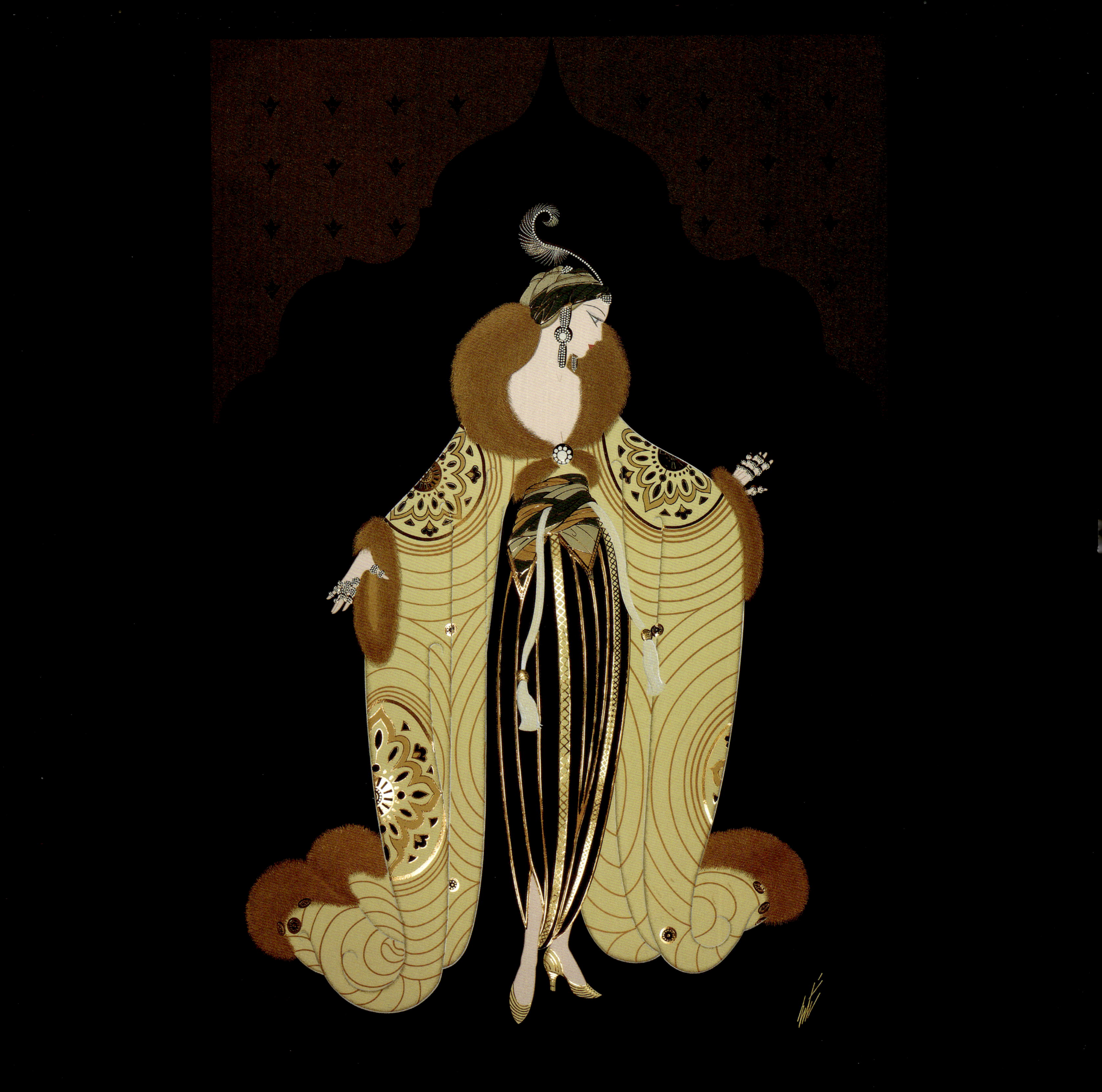

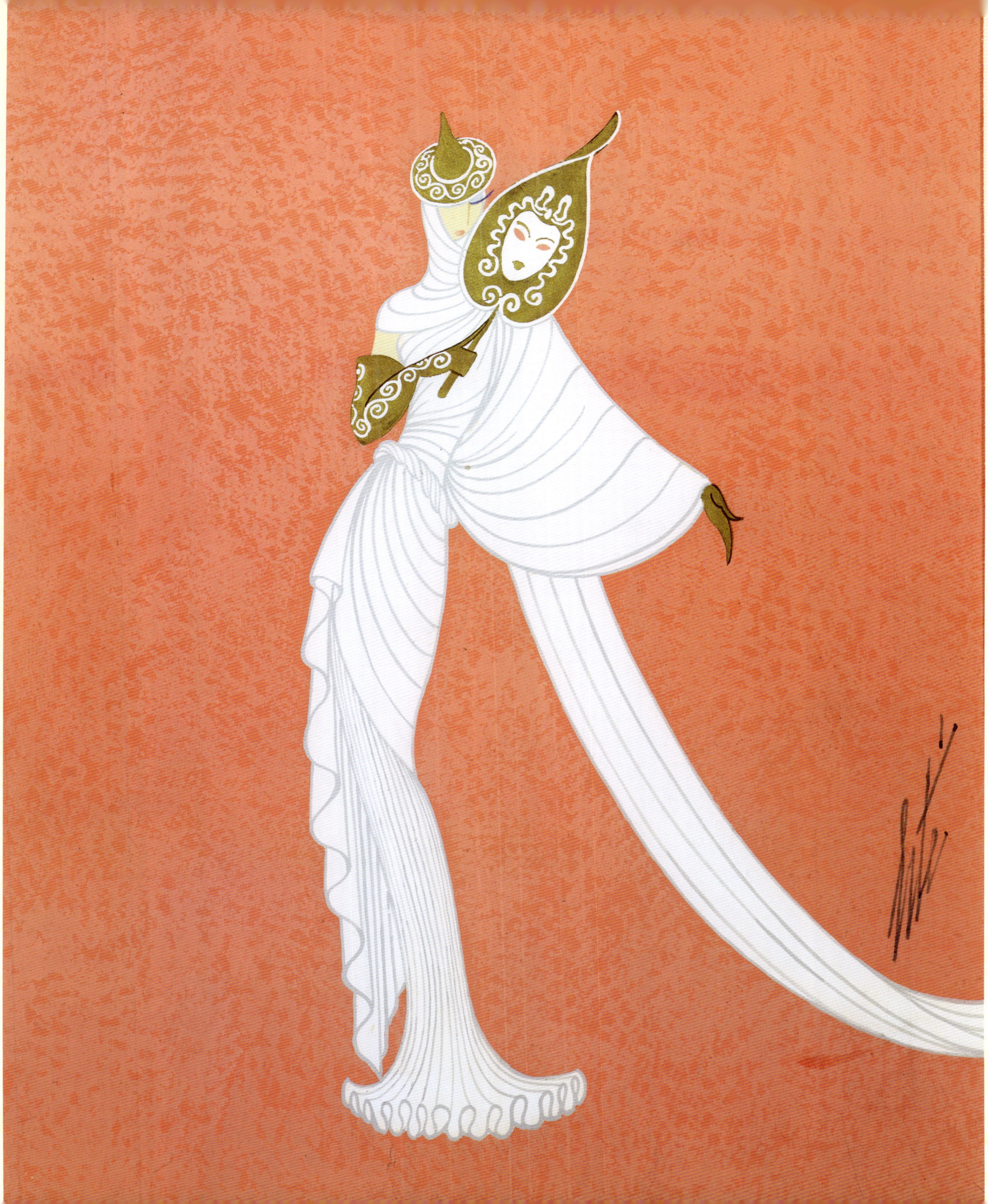

innovative colour set designs for the theatre, where the colours changed with each scene to symbolize mood, tone and location.

GEORGE WHITE'S 'SCANDALS'

The year following the sale of *Les Mers*, a productive partnership sprang up between White, Erté and Weldy. 'Scandals' was a successful series of musical revues with songs, music, sketches and beautiful women. Erté's sets and costumes for each show were made in Weldy's Paris workshop at 18 rue Saulnier, close to the Folies Bergère. They were then dispatched to New York. Erté's sets and costumes featured in 'Scandals' revues in theatres on Broadway from 1922 until 1929, appearing in seven productions. The lavish Oriental style of the 'Golden Wedding' triple costume for the 'Scandals' 1924 production *Les Mariages* (*see* page 131) was complemented by the near-naked triple costume for 'Marriage' (*see* page 130). One can see why the costumes – some little more than combinations of jewellery and spangles on bare skin – were so popular in White's music hall revues. The set (*see* page 173) and costume design for *The Golden Fables* in 'Scandals' (1926) and the exotic and semi-erotic design for *The Nile* (*see* pages 14–15), for 'Scandals' in the same year, show the richness in originality and colour of Erté's productions.

BIRTH OF THE BLUES

Erté's design for the finalé of White's highly popular production *The Blues*, featured his signature-style 'living curtains' with a vast cast of 'angels' playing harps, trumpets and lyres. His gouache illustration *Angel Harpist*, a costume design for *The Blues* (1926, *see* page 103), reflects the opulence associated with the Art Décoratif period in the use of black, gold, grey and white. The angel's costume hints at ancient Greece, the wings and halo perhaps a reference to Renaissance 'Annunciation' paintings. The 'angel' with a fashionable bobbed haircut plays the strings of a female harp. Another gouache *Ange Harpiste* (1926), in the collection of the Metropolitan Museum, New York, illustrates only the angel in gold metallic paint on a white background. It was in this show that the now-famous song, 'The Birth of the Blues', was first performed. It also included the music 'Rhapsody in Blue' by American composer George Gershwin (1898–1937). When Erté created *Angel* in bronze in 1985, the pale blue colour of the angel's costume and wings was inspired by his 1925 costume design for a scene called 'Rhapsody in Blue'.

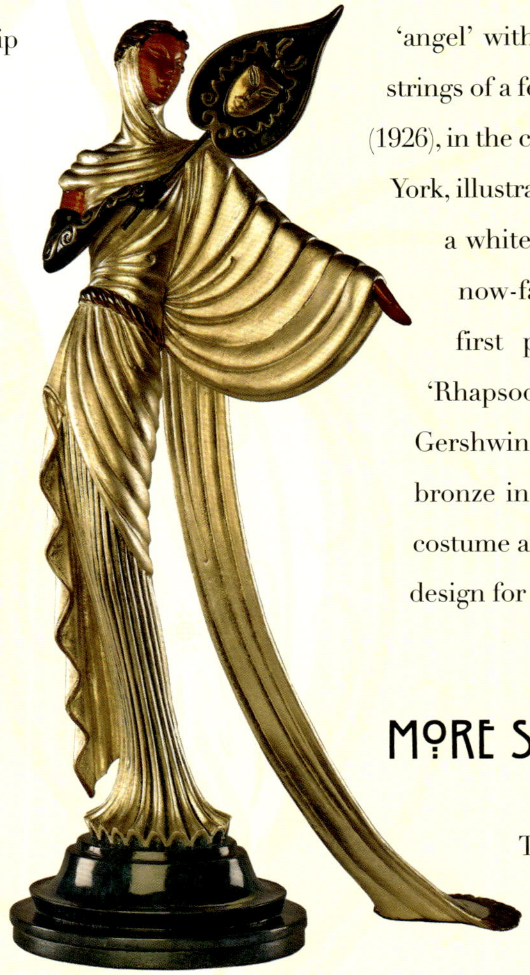

MORE SUCCESS ON BROADWAY

The following year George White, with Erté designing sets and costumes, put on a highly successful revue about the 'Scandals' shows, a musical comedy titled *Manhattan Mary*, running from 26 September 1927 to 12 May 1928. The design for the opening curtain hailed the modernity of New York's skyscraper skyline (*see* page 120), and the costumes (*see* pages 121, 123–27) related to chic contemporary daywear, creating new interest in Erté as a fashion designer.

(Previous left) **Le Harem Moderne I**, *1990, serigraph, 105.4 x 76.2 cm (41½ x 30 in)*
(Previous right) **Costume design for Madame Phidias in Phi-phi**, *1940, gouache*
This design was later reworked by Erté to create the sculpture above and the serigraph opposite, which was also created in turquoise and in red.

(Above) **Tanagra** *sculpture, 1988, bronze, 53 x 28 x 23 cm (21 x 11 x 9 in)*
(Right) **Tanagra (Blue)**, *1989, serigraph, 104 x 76 cm (41 x 30 in)*

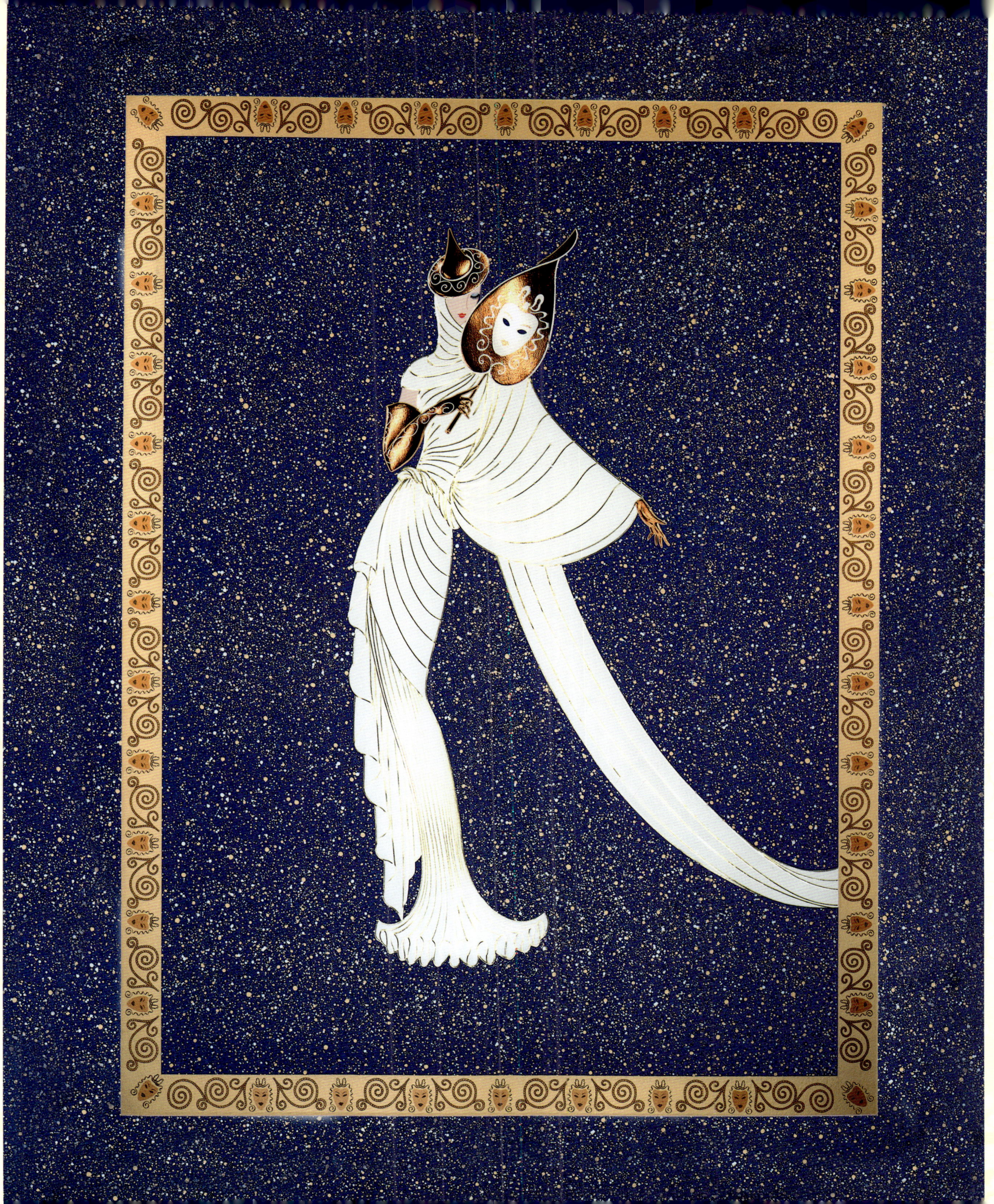

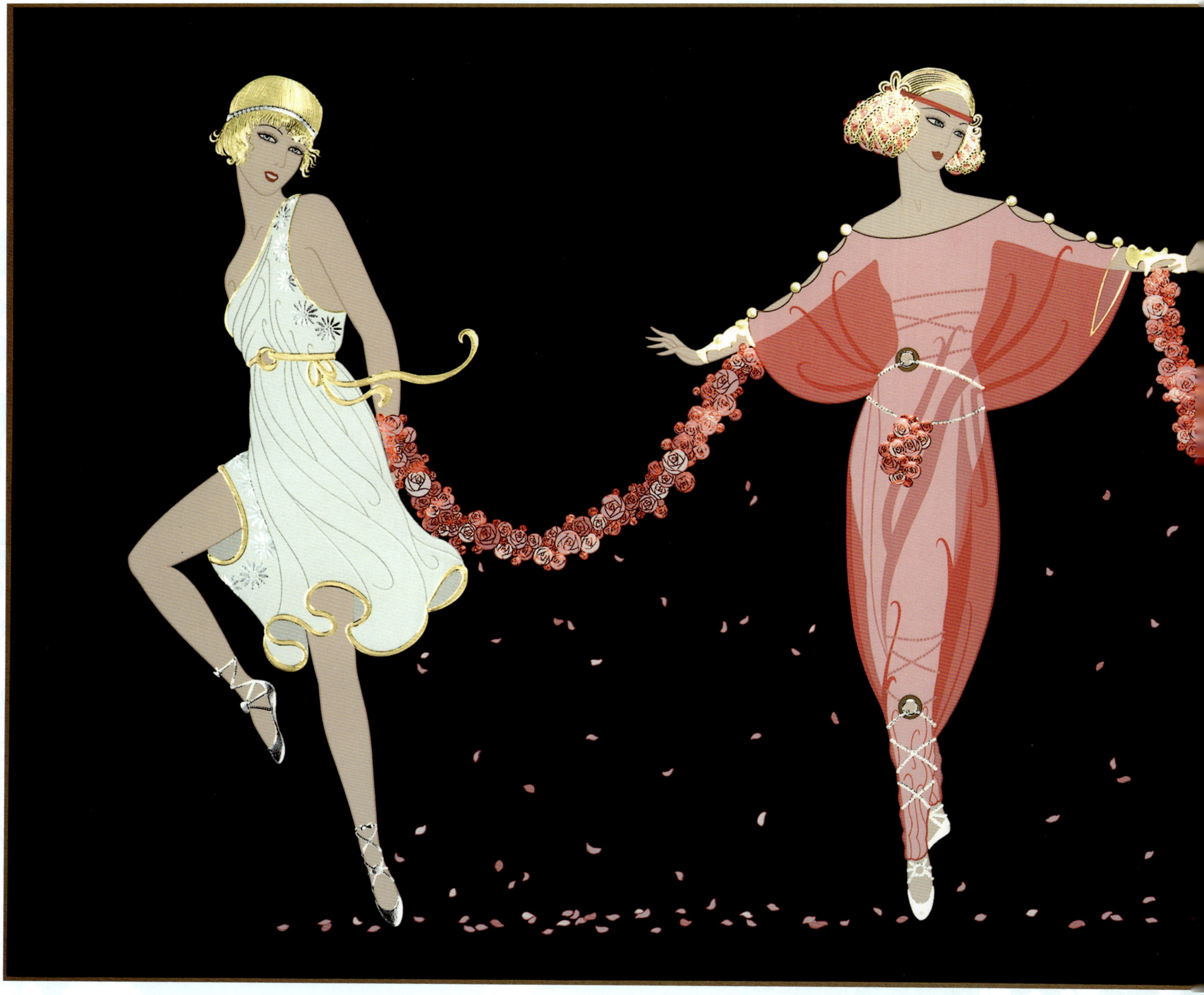

Printemps, *1990, embossed serigraph with foil stamping, 47.6 x 59.2 cm (18¾ x 23¼ in)*

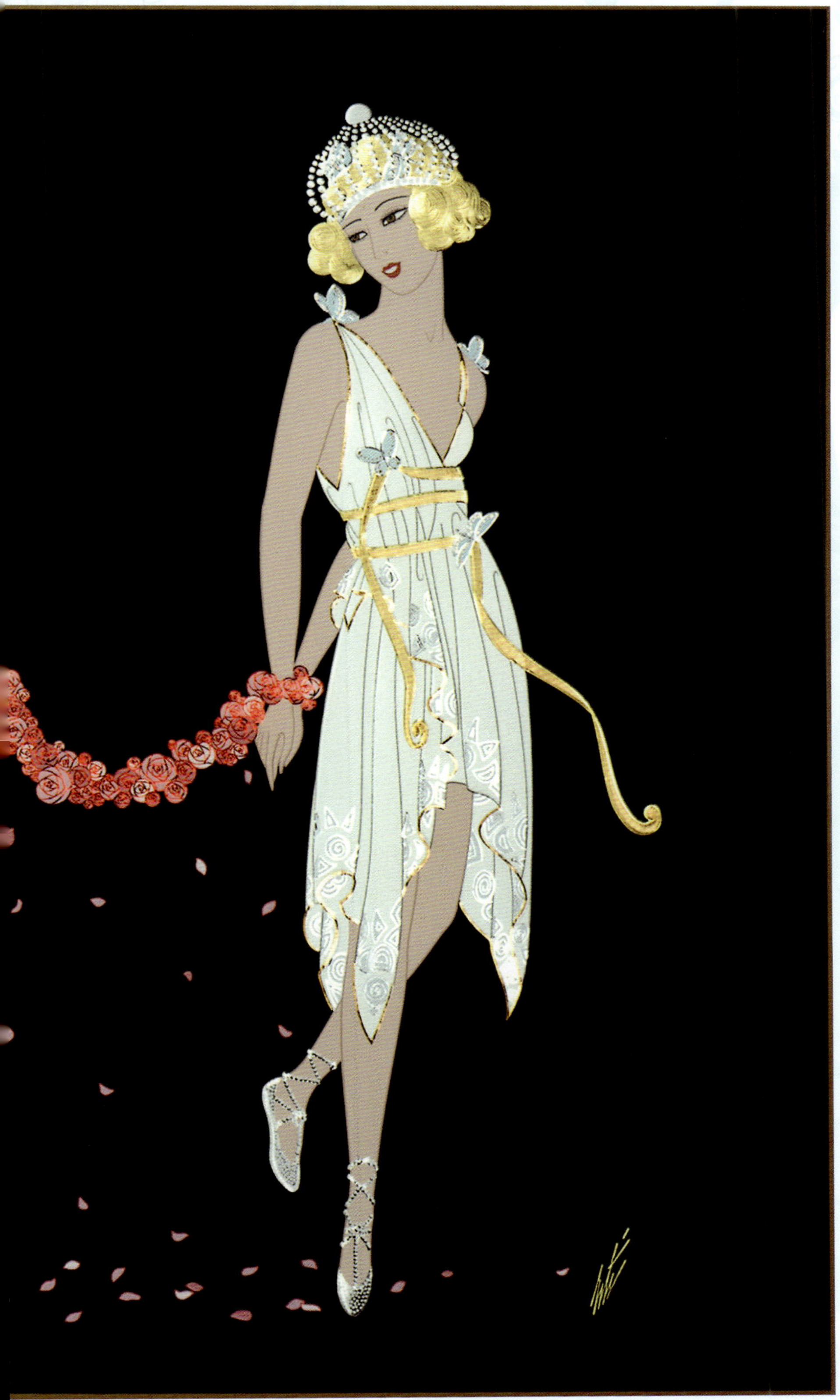

THE ZIEGFELD FOLLIES

Working with George White for Broadway shows in New York brought Erté attention from American producers and filmmakers. The Impresario Florenz Ziegfeld Jr. (1867–1932) had based his glamorous musical revue *Ziegfeld Follies* in New York (1907–31), on the Folies Bergère in Paris. Erté was commissioned for two shows. He recalled that one costume for a Ziegfeld set called *Gold* required six-and-a-half miles of gold lamé, made for Erté in Lyons. The show transferred to the Folies Bergère in Paris at a later date. Erté and Weldy now had a set-up that made money. Each revue set created for Paris or New York was reproduced and sold again individually. It was thus possible to have the same set and costume reproduction in many countries, from Berlin and Brussels to Buenos Aires, London and Amsterdam to Madrid and Rio de Janeiro. Erté's fame had reached nearly all parts of the world.

BACK TO PARIS

The amount of theatrical work contracted to Erté via Weldy increased. Erté designed sets for two American productions of *Music Box Review* for the composer Irving Berlin (1888–1989), and more for the *Greenwich Village Follies*. This was additional to working for *Harper's Bazaar* and other American magazines that Hearst, the publisher, was putting his way through recommendation. It left little time for socializing in Monte Carlo and after eight years in Monaco Erté and Nicolas moved back to Paris. Erté kept the Villa Excelsior in Monte Carlo, gave up his Paris apartment in rue de Civry and bought a country house in Sèvres on the outskirts of Paris. With the First World War over,

Paris was returning to its full Parisian gaiety. Socialites and nobility moved comfortably through the salons once again. But it was a different Paris. Modern life included new dance crazes such as the American charleston and hemlines had moved up since the pre-war era. It was a good time to be a fashion designer, theatre costumier and fashion illustrator on both sides of the Atlantic. Erté was entering his prime years.

CECIL B. DEMILLE

Erté was a man with many friends and a vast network of acquaintances, which greatly helped his business and social life. In Monte Carlo he was visited by fellow Russian Alexandra Baldina-Kozloff (1885–1977), a former ballerina at the Mariinsky Theatre, St Petersburg. She now lived in Hollywood with her Russian husband, Theodor Kozloff (1882–1956), owner of a ballet school and a filmmaker. She offered Erté an introduction to the noted American director and producer Cecil B. DeMille, at Metro-Goldwyn-Mayer, the most successful Hollywood studio. After an encouraging introduction, DeMille wanted Erté to design sets and costumes for a film based on the biblical 'Prodigal Son'. In 1921 DeMille, looking for the best Art Deco set and costume designers in Europe, had signed, amongst others, the innovative Paul Iribe, for a drama *The Affairs of Anatol* (released 1921). Erté was excited about the prospect and DeMille was keen but the deal floundered. In a bid to stop Erté working for Metro-Goldwyn-Mayer, Hearst, the owner of *Harper's Bazaar*, offered him a generously paid three-year contract with Hearst's production company, Cosmopolitan Films.

THE RESTLESS SEX

In the silent movie *The Restless Sex*, starring Marion Davies (1897–1961), Erté's only assignment was to design costumes for a 'fancy-dress Arts Ball'. Having spent his professional life creating fantasy costumes, either for society balls or for the theatre, it was a gift to him. Some of the costume designs were published in the April 1920 edition of *Harper's Bazaar*. The costumes for the Arts Ball were to represent gods from different nationalities and religions: Aztecs, Chinese, Egyptians, Greeks and Hindus. To give one example, the costume for *Athena* (1919), was a fair interpretation of ancient Greek female dress. Erté chose an Assyrian background for the set and was able to draw on his wide knowledge of costume history. The film was released on 20 September 1920. But it was the only film work that Hearst offered him. Erté realized that the generous contract had been a ruse to keep him solely in the employ of the Hearst Corporation in America. However, the illustrations for the film's costumes, such as *Femme Scandinave* (1919, *see* page 179), remained part of Erté's collection.

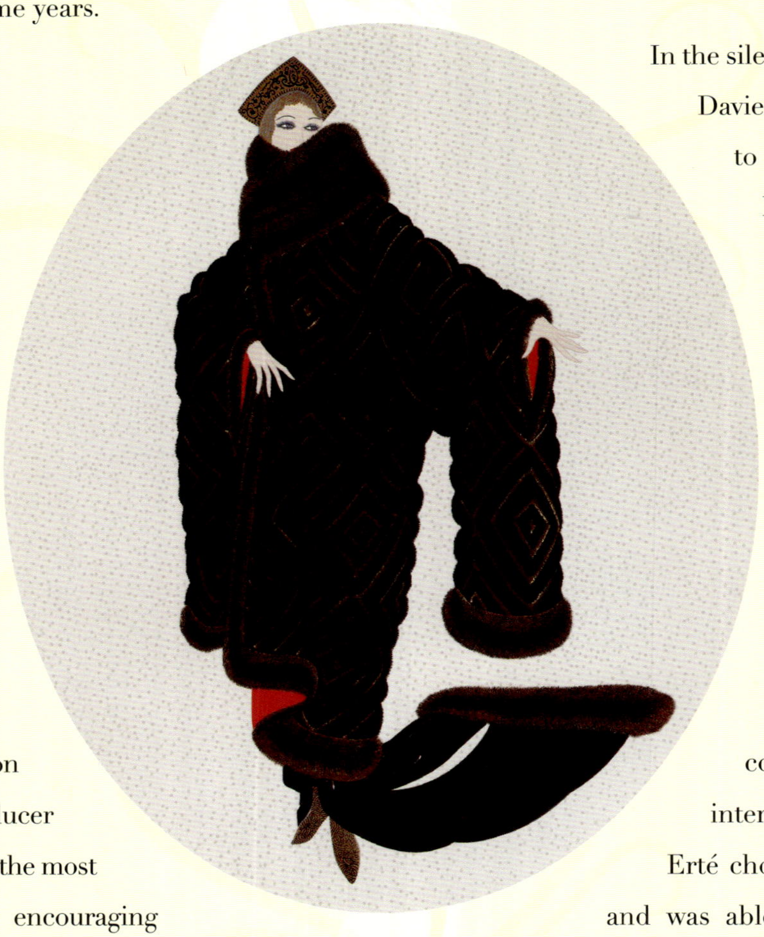

Fedora Fur, *1990, embossed serigraph with foil stamping, 100.6 x 77.7cm (39½ x 30½ in)*

Fedora Fan, *1990, embossed serigraph with foil stamping, 100.6 cm x 77.7 cm (39½ x 30½ in)*

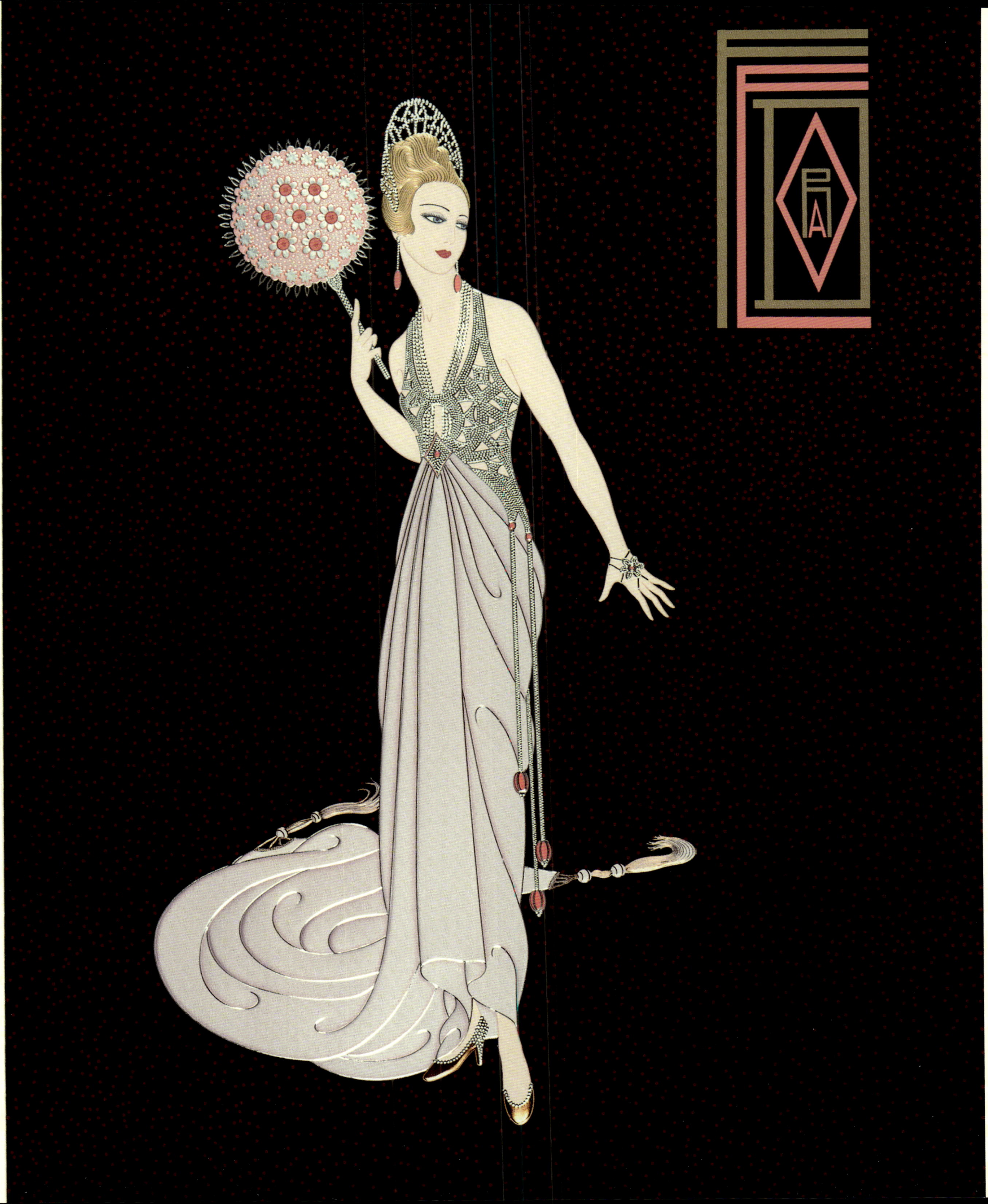

It was reworked 70 years later for Erté's graphic design print, *Scandinavian Princess* (1990, *see* page 179), one of his last works.

HOLLYWOOD CALLS

At the end of 1924 Erté received the invitation that many lesser costumiers waited for indefinitely, an offer of a six-month contract from Metro-Goldwyn-Mayer, Hollywood, to design sets and costumes for two films: *Paris* and *Monte Carlo*. He would spend nearly a year in America. The salary was 'highly satisfactory', as Erté recalled, and he was able to take his partner-manager Nicolas, his secretary M. Gallois, and his own valet. Erté must have felt highly flattered as he was sucked into the vortex of Hollywood. The group departed on 25 February 1925 on the steamship *France*, bound for New York where Erté planned to stay before travelling on to Los Angeles. His memoirs recall staying at the Ritz Hotel. America was in the early years of alcohol prohibition (1920–33), so during dinner each evening the party's champagne was stowed under the table and served in a teapot with teacups. Metro-Goldwyn-Mayer's representative in New York looked after Erté, taking him to all their cinemas in the city. At one, Erté recalled that as he made his entrance to the private box the orchestra played the Tsarist National Anthem. It was, he pointed out, eight years after the Russian Revolution and thus no longer played but it underlines how well known Erté was and the esteem in which he was held in America.

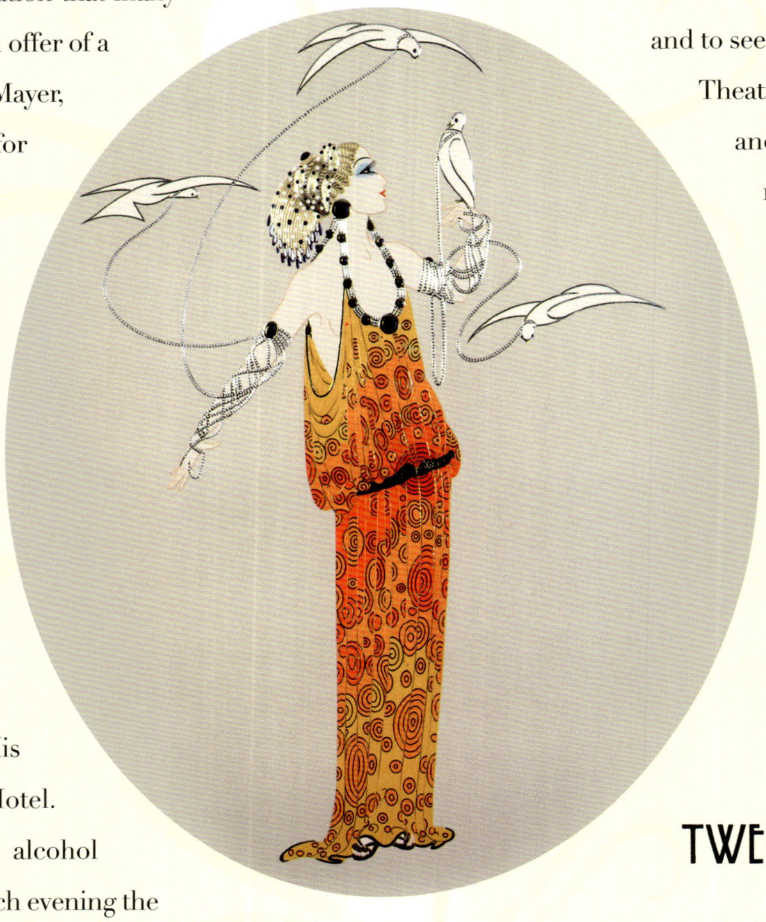

ERTÉ EXHIBITION IN MANHATTAN

Erté also used his time in New York to visit George White and to see one of the 'Scandals' revues at the Apollo Theatre. It was the first time he had seen his sets and costumes on an American stage. This revue ran from June to November 1925. In addition to this, the Ziegfeld Follies' 1924 revue show was still running, which he was able to see as well. In his honour a friend, Henry Sell, had organized an exhibition of Erté's work at the Madison Hotel. It received excellent newspaper and magazine reviews, a public comment on Erté and how much was known about his work as a fashion illustrator and costume designer.

TWENTIETH CENTURY LIMITED

The trip from New York to Los Angeles was undertaken in the comfort of the 'Twentieth Century Limited' train, a four-and-a-half day journey. From there it was on to an apartment at the Beverley Hills Hotel and a round of interviews, press conferences and parties in Erté's honour. At one he recalled that the room and tables had been decorated in orange and green,

Aphrodite, *1985, embossed serigraph with foil stamping, 101.6 x 78.1 cm (40 x 30¾ in)*

Costume design for Ganna Walska in Fédora *(last act), 1919, gouache*

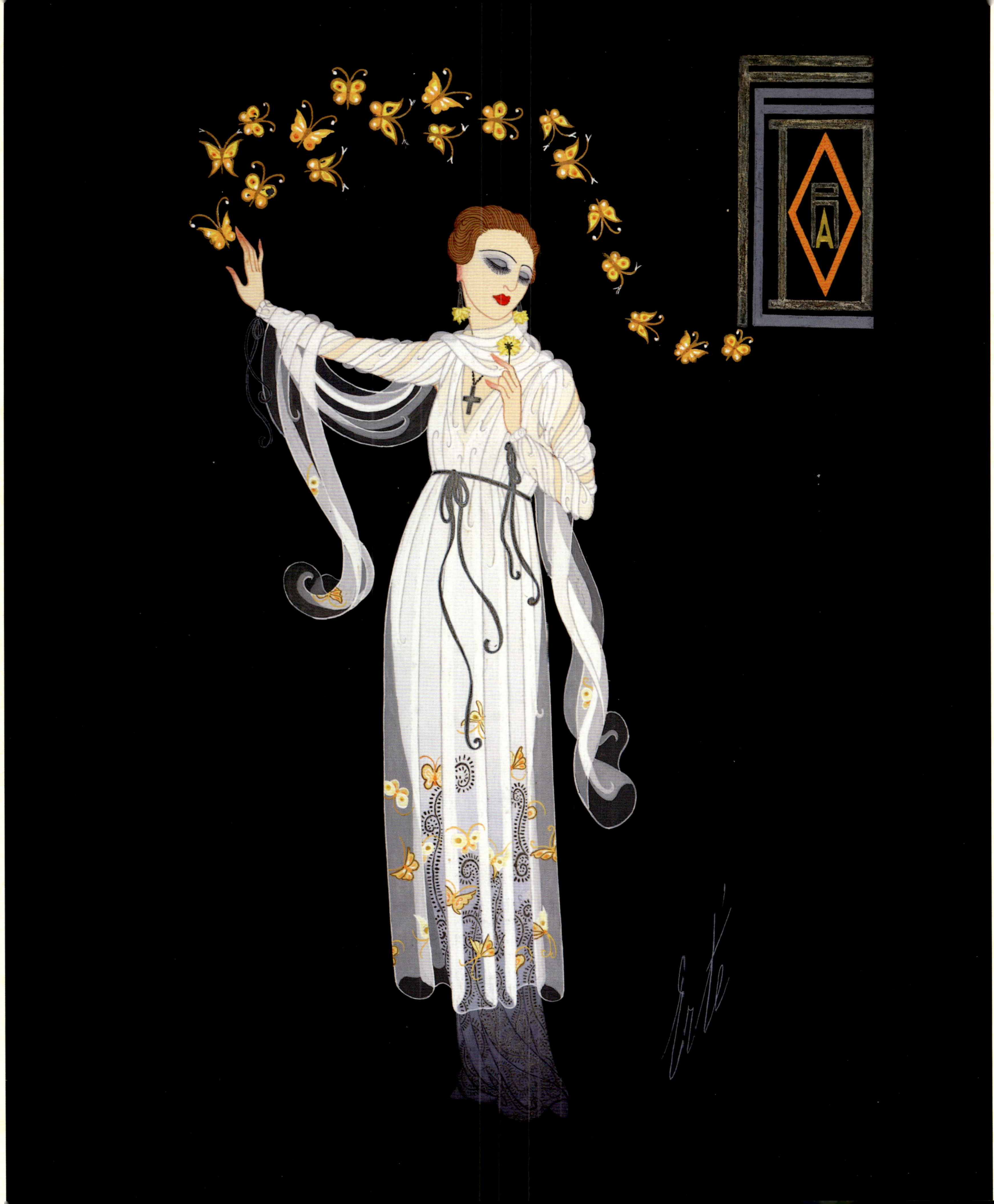
Erté

due to a previous remark he made that these were his favourite colours. *Harper's Bazaar* acknowledged his first visit to America in a tongue-in-cheek editorial published in February 1925.

Welcome to Erté in America! At last Erté has consented to come to America to serve and to work. Erté has left the seclusion of his monastic villa in Sèvres for the rough and tumble of a trip to Movieland. What will be the effect on our precise and gracious friend who always draws the curtains across closed windows before he begins drawing because he fears the intrusion of ideas from without? It is hard to imagine what will happen to Erté, whose servants never make a sound and whose gorgeous cat Mischa, sleeps all day on a black cushion. What will become of Erté in the city of backless houses in the wilderness, on the lot?

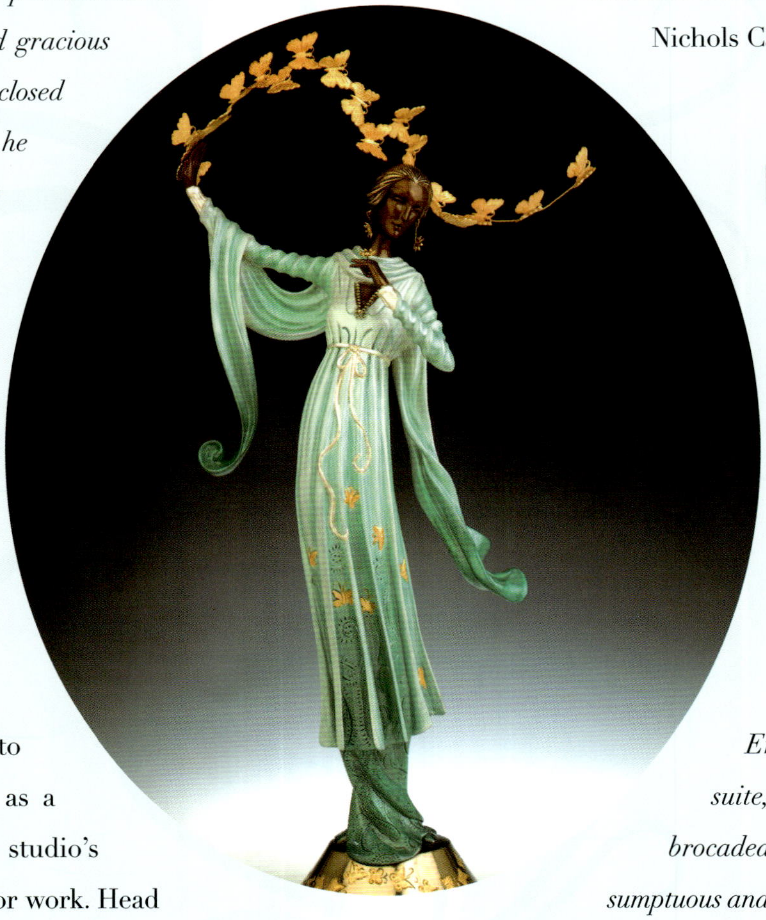

GETTING SETTLED IN

After the razzmatazz of Erté's welcome to Hollywood, afforded to all major stars as a publicity drive to focus attention on the studio's forthcoming films, he prepared himself for work. Head of Production, Belarus-born American Louis B. Mayer (1884–1957), was gracious to him, inviting him for family lunches. In addition, he recreated Erté's studio in Sèvres by referring to photographs, duplicating its size and interior design of cream and black. It was a warm gesture to help make Erté feel at home whilst working in Hollywood. A pleasant house was soon found on Beechwood Drive close to the mountains. Erté lived here with Nicolas and his French secretary-copyist. He bought a collie dog, naming it Chéri, and soon had a black cat too, abandoned and in need of a home. This set-up worked well. He used the studio as an office with his secretary-copyist in attendance, and worked from the quiet of his home. At the end of the six-month contract – with it extended a further three months – Erté moved house to Nichols Canyon Road in the Hollywood Hills.

IN HIS OWN FASHION

Erté was interviewed many times during the months he spent in America. The questions beyond his fashion looks for women centred on his choice of clothes and his view of men's fashion. The *Brooklyn Daily Eagle* (25 February 1925), reported a meeting with him:

Erté who is 32 years old, sat in his rose damask suite, wearing a gorgeous crimson and black brocaded coat over his pyjamas of pongee. The coat, sumptuous and silken enough for an Eastern potentate, was lined with cloth of gold and sashed with the same; his pumps were inlaid with crimson leather.

It is an accurate summation of Erté's lifestyle. In the year Erté spent in America he undertook 197 interviews. His opinions were sought on all matters, including hair colour preference for women

Joie de vivre *sculpture, 1989, bronze, 59.7 x 26.7 x 21 cm (23½ x 10½ x 8¼ in)*

Fedora Butterfly, *1990, embossed serigraph with foil stamping, 100.6 x 77.7 cm (39⅝ x 30⅝ in)*

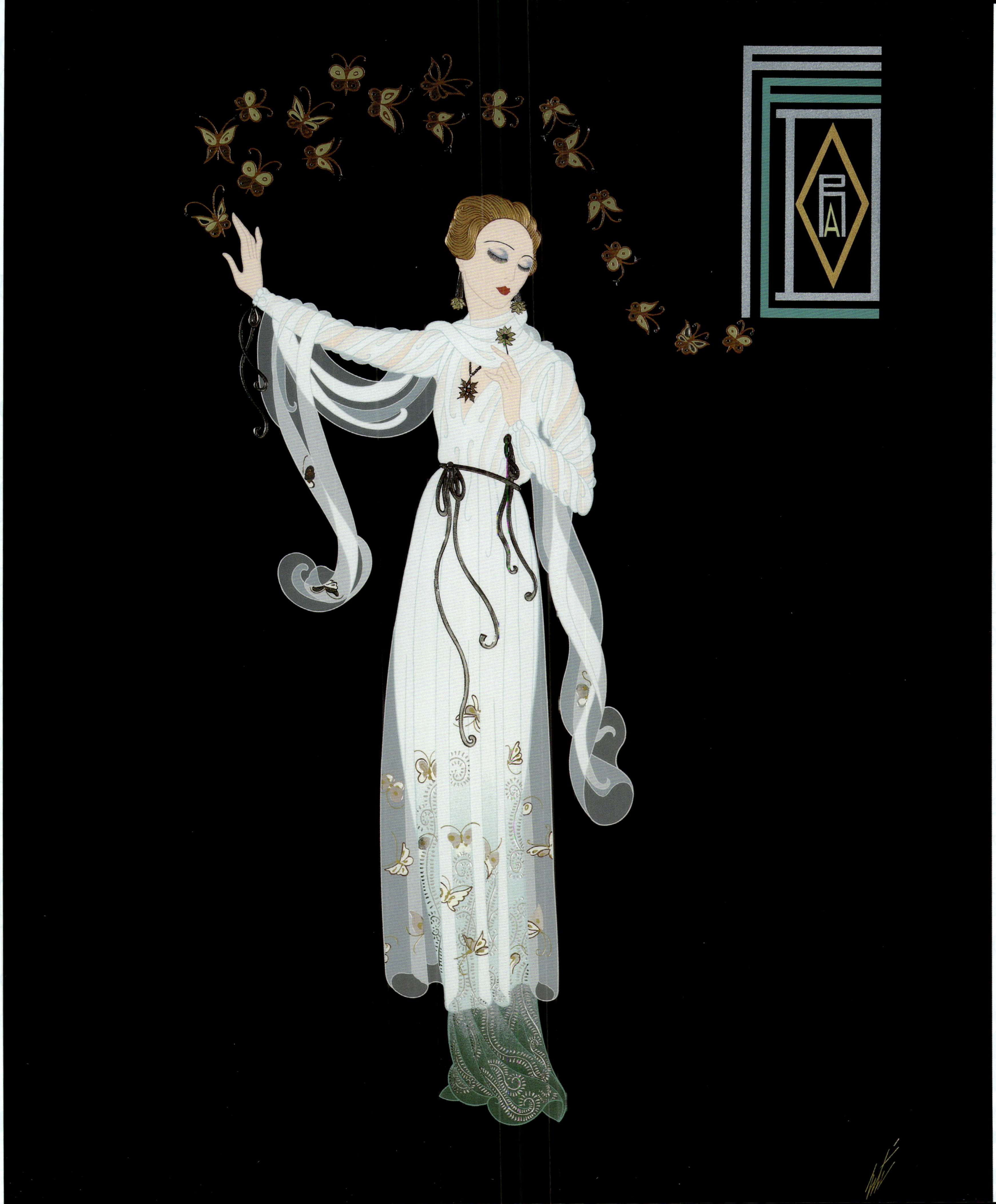

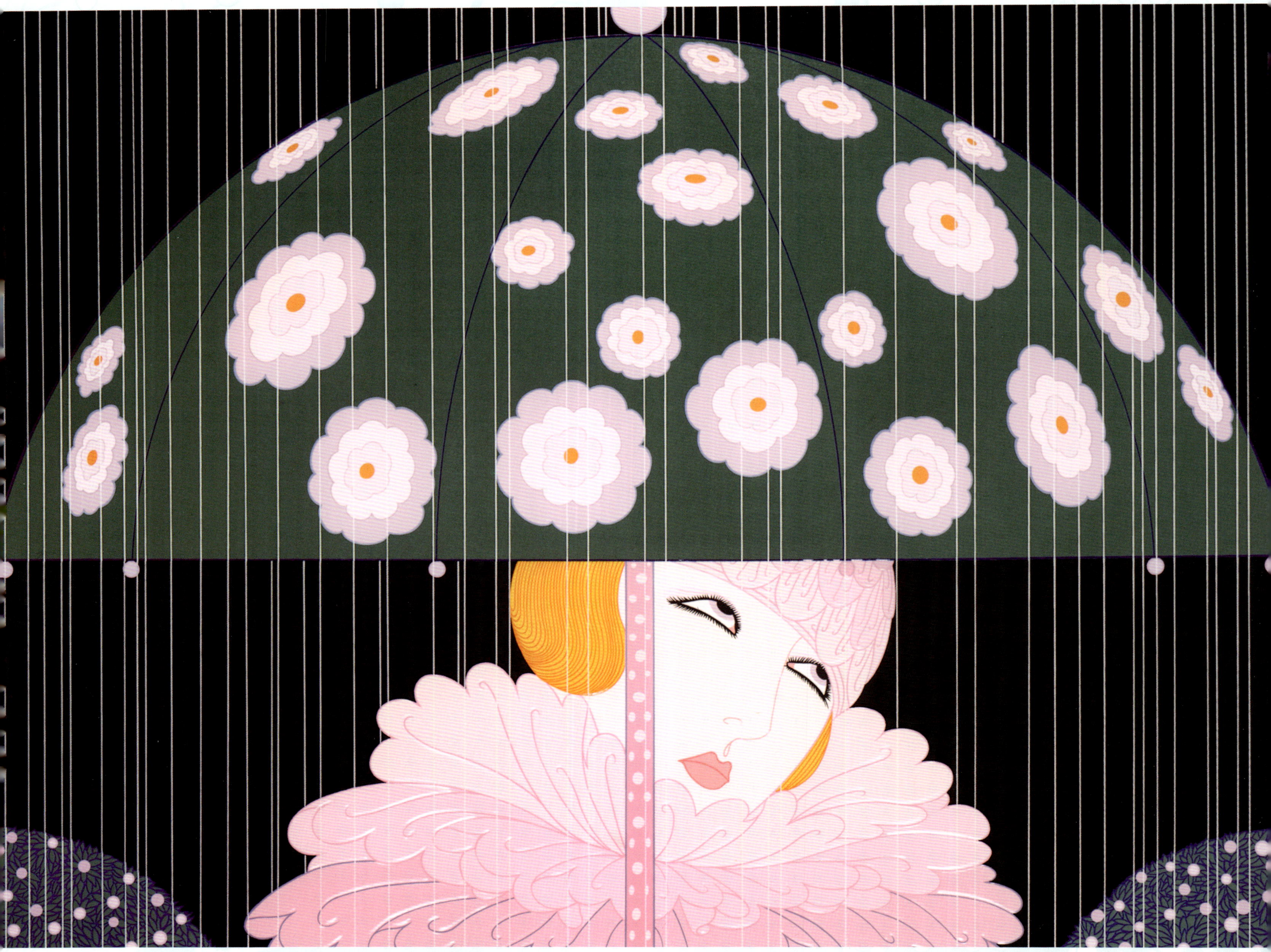

Spring Showers, *1984, embossed serigraph, 78.7 x 93.3 cm (31 x 36¾ in)*
A striking image that recalls the decorative *Harper's Bazaar* illustrations that Erté created from 1915.

(it was brunette) to whether he liked short hair on women (the answer was 'yes'). The current high fashion was the cropped bob. And, the most beautiful woman he had ever met? His answer was the dark-haired Italian opera singer Lina Cavalieri (1874–1944). In 1912 on Erté's life-changing departure by train from St Petersburg to Paris, the soprano, his idol, had been sharing his carriage.

WORKING FOR METRO-GOLDWYN-MAYER

The scripts for his contract films *Paris* and *Monte Carlo* were not finished but Erté was asked to start work on making sketches for the sets. He was troubled. How to design for a film set without knowing what was in the script? He was told to create what he wanted and the script would be altered to fit it. He recalled: 'Never mind. We'll adapt the script to your décor.' He knew the basic features: a nightclub, a highly modern house with garden, and an open-air theatre. There would be a ballet scene and Erté costumes from a previous production *Ballet de Perles* at the Folies Bergère would be used. Max Weldy, his business partner in Paris, was charged with organizing it. (The costumes sent over were not used; they later appeared in the film *Hollywood Revue* of 1929.) Erté designed the décor and costumes but the script was still delayed. Metro-Goldwyn-Mayer asked to extend his contract by three months, to which he agreed but he was bound by it not to work for anyone else, other than his on-going contract with *Harper's Bazaar* which was already in place.

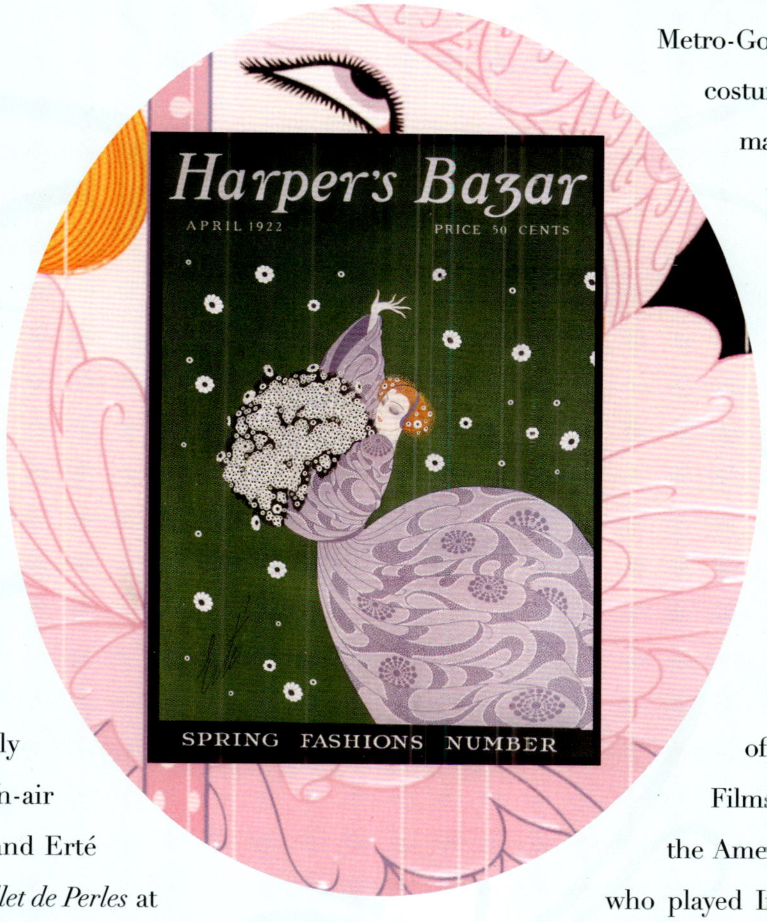

DRESSING THE STARS

To ensure Erté's time and their money was not wasted, Metro-Goldwyn-Mayer suggested that Erté design costumes for the stars of other films. The majority of silent films were shot in black and white, which made it difficult for him to see how the clothes would look. His choice was to design them in black, cream, white and grey but the actors wanted colour, even though it would not be visible on-screen. To get the right depth of shading Erté used a small blue glass lens. Looking through it at the coloured designs it successfully reflected the depth of monotone shading. He designed costumes for many of the leading actresses and actors of the day. Films included *Ben Hur*, in which Erté dressed the American actress Carmel Myers (1899–1980) who played Iras opposite the Mexican actor Ramon Novarro (1899–1968) as Ben Hur. The movie was released in December 1925. More followed. However, when designing costumes for Aileen Pringle (1895–1989) in *The Misfit*, Erté was vocally unhappy about the low quality of the MGM seamstresses' work. To keep him content, he was given his own custom-built workshop complete with a top French dressmaker. Following this, he designed

Harper's Bazar, 'Spring Fashions' *cover, April 1922*

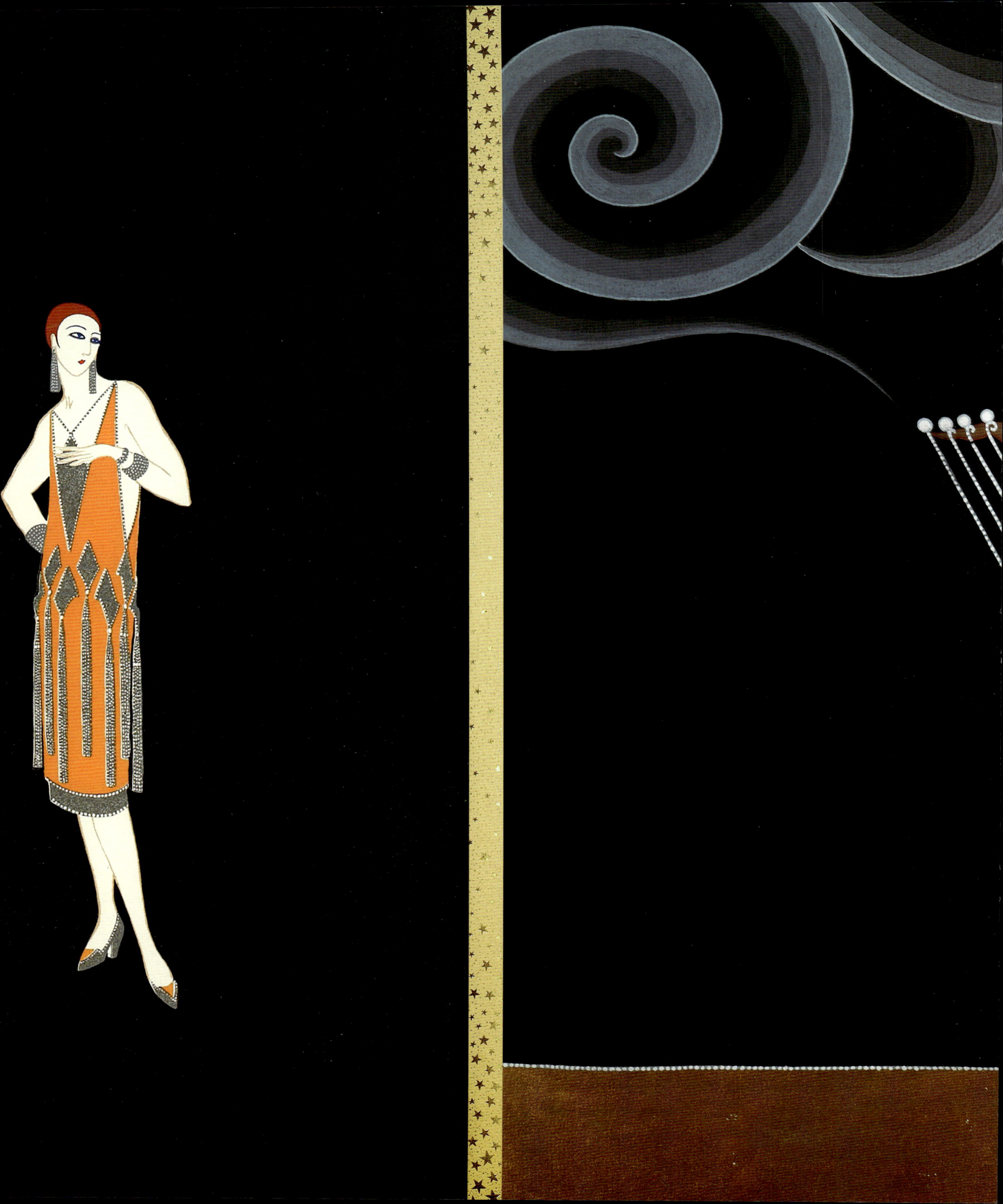

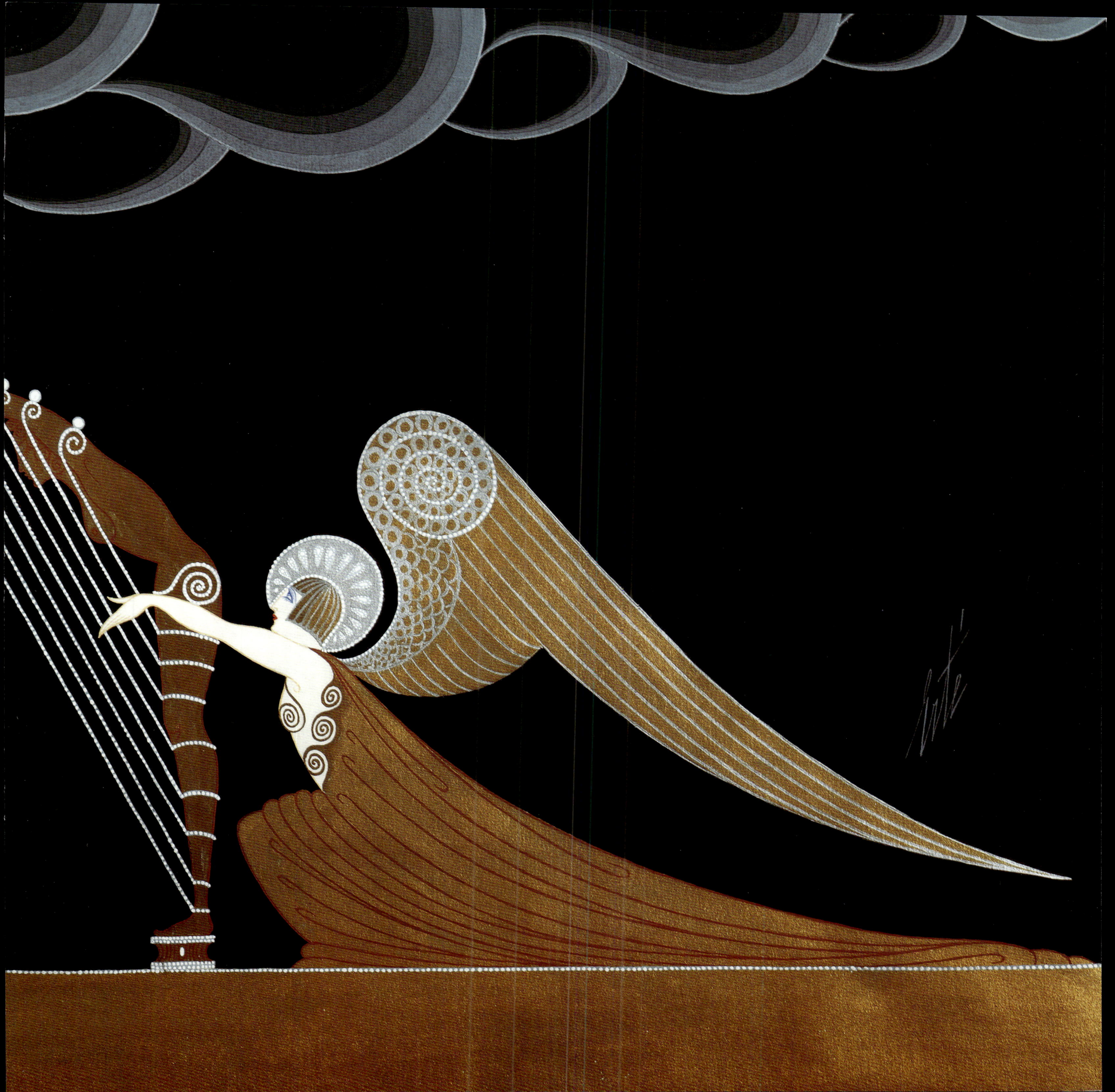
Erté

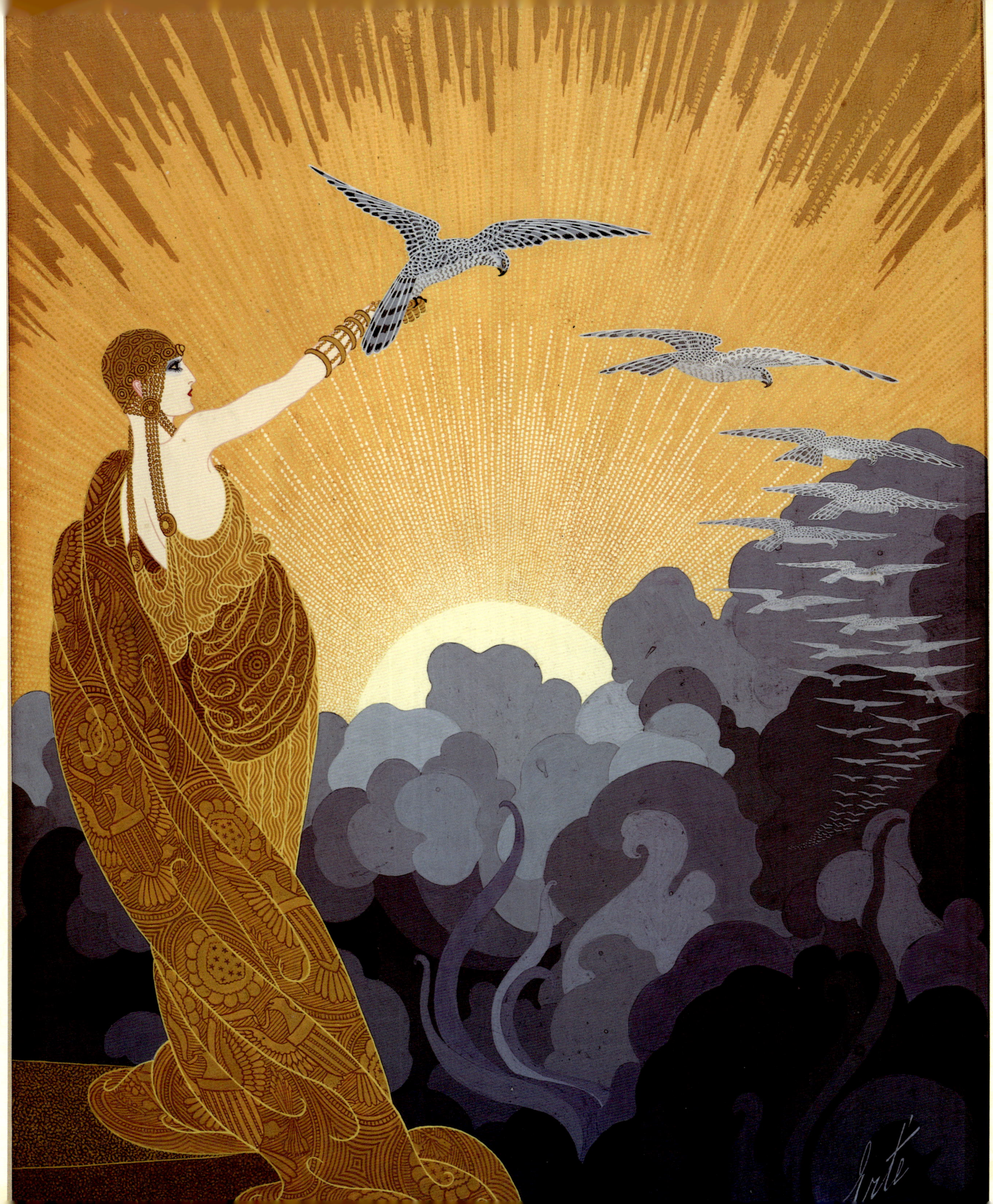
Erté

costumes for *Dance Madness* (1926), which included a ballet *The Masks*. Erté's set design and costumes were sensational. The production was so successful that he later adapted it for a 'Scandals' revue (and designed a pair of serigraphs, *The Masks*.)

'HER DAY'

A special fashion show, 'Her Day', featuring costumes by Erté created for Metro-Goldwyn-Mayer films was displayed at the Ambassador Hotel in Los Angeles in 1925. Many of the actresses Erté had dressed in films took part, including Pringle, Myers, Norma Shearer (1902–1983), Claire Windsor (1892–1972), Eleanor Boardman (1898–1991) and Pauline Stark (1901–77). Erté recalled it being talked of as 'one of the most brilliant events of the season'. However, there were dissenting voices from some women who thought the clothes too revealing. Erté disagreed.

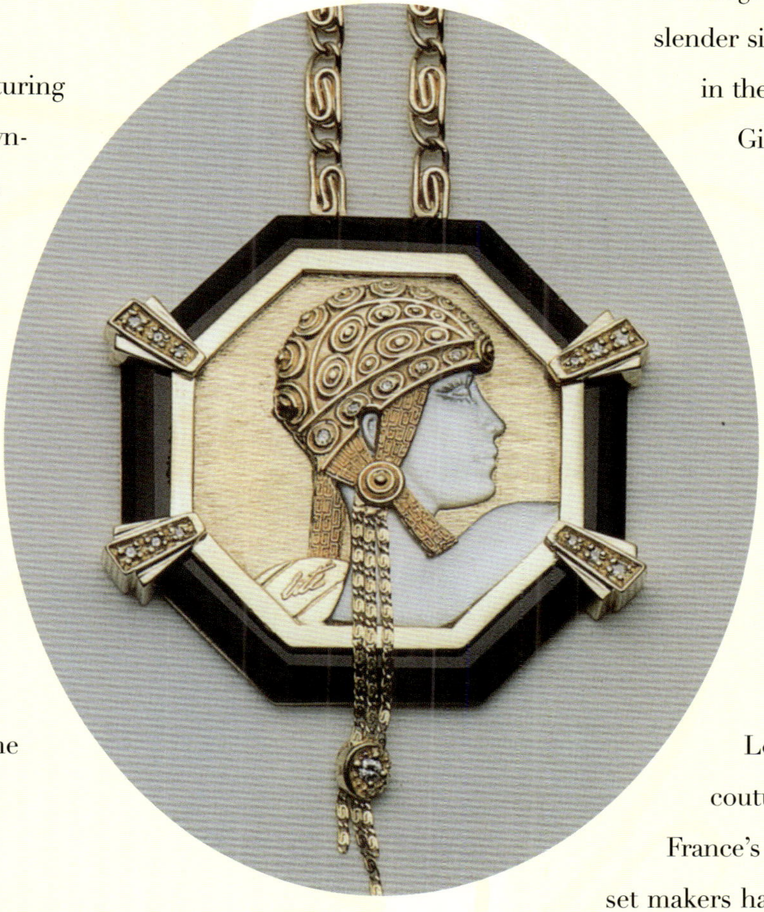

DISAGREEMENTS WITH ACTRESSES

Erté's designs in other films released in 1925 included *Time the Comedian*, *Bright Lights* (from the book *A Little Bit of Broadway*), *Sally, Irene and Mary*, and in 1926 *La Bohème* and *Paris*, both uncredited. A falling-out with the lead actress Lillian Gish (1893–1993) in *La Bohème*, set off a train of events that eventually sent Erté back to Paris. Gish, playing the role of a seamstress, did not approve of the materials chosen by Erté. He wanted to use poor-looking but not cheap fabrics for her costumes. She wanted him to use old silk. The heated disagreement led to him asking her to leave his studio. It is interesting to compare photographs of the actresses that Erté fitted with his design sketches. Not all suited his tall, gamine, slender silhouettes. Costumes for the other actress in the film *Renée Adorée* fared little better than Gish when he found the corseting removed.

PARIS

Erté reluctantly signed another three-month contract, in the hope that the *Paris* script would be finished. When it was eventually given to him he was appalled. The storyline of the silent film centred on a famous French couturier, Morand, living in Paris in the Louvre. Erté was incensed. How could a couturier have his house in the Louvre, France's most important building? And worse, the set makers had incorporated all Erté's designs for an ultra-modern interior into a mock-up of the Louvre. The open-air theatre was placed in the Place du Carrousel. What Erté may have expected was a film based on his life, and it was, but in a bizarre manner. His reasons for cancelling his contract were that he did not want the city of Paris caricatured in such a way. Perhaps it was his own character that he worried would be diminished.

(Previous page, left) **Manhattan Mary I**, *1979, lithograph, 55.2 x 43.9 cm (21¾ x 17½ in)*
(Previous page, right) **Angel Harpist** *(or* **Rhapsody in Blue**), *costume design for* The Blues, *George White's 'Scandals', New York, 1926, gouache, 54 x 69.9 cm (21½ x 27½ in)*

(Above) **Aventurine** *pendant, 1979, gold, diamonds, mother-of-pearl, black onyx, gold chain*
(Left) **New Bridges for the Seven Seas**, *cover design for* Harper's Bazaar, *March 1919, gouache, 55.9 x 38.1 cm (22 x 15 in)*

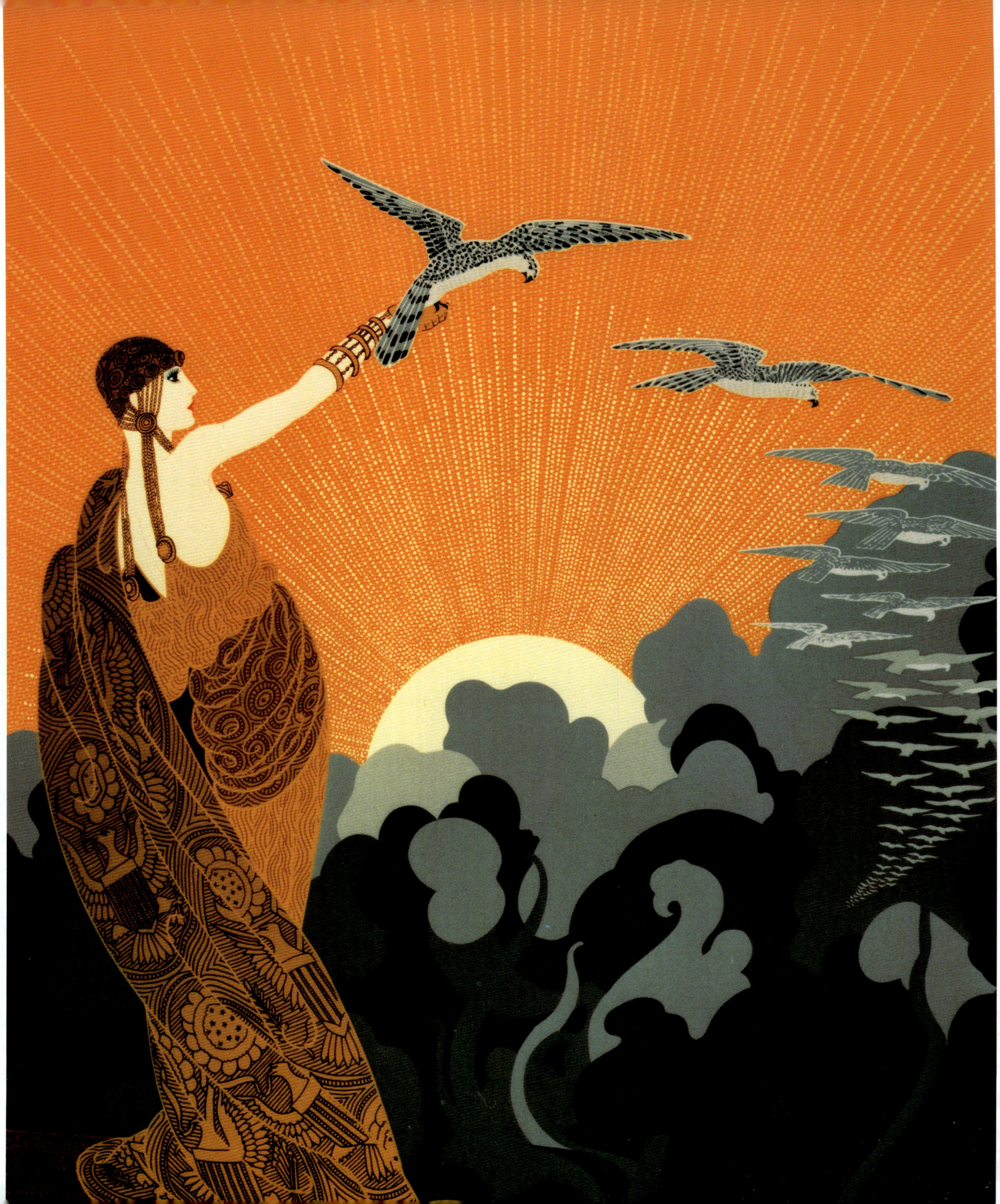

L'ART DÉCORATIF INTERNATIONAL EXHIBITION, PARIS, 1925

During Erté's sojourn in Hollywood, Paris hosted a spectacular exposition. From April to October 1925, a global exhibition took place that would confirm L'Art Décoratif (Art Deco), as more than just a passing fashion. The Exposition Internationale des Arts Décoratif et Industriels Modernes, a display of modern decorative art dedicated to luxury goods was intended to boost the industry after the Great War. Sixteen million visitors came. The overall aim was to show the most modern, contemporary design in furniture, fabrics, fashions, jewellery, architecture, art, graphic design, interior design, industrial machinery, gadgets, tools, and much more. Four department stores anchored the event, which focused displays on the newest, most modern consumer goods. The most noted designer of furniture and interior design was Émile-Jacques Ruhlmann (1879–1933), who was fêted at the Expo. One pavilion that received hostile reaction was Le Corbusier's *Pavilion de L'Esprit Nouveau,* a building constructed within the Exposition des Arts Décoratif. He displayed a new type of house, 'a machine for living in'. It fitted the post-war industrial aesthetic, using modern materials, minimal decoration and mass-production. It was the antithesis of what the Expo was intended to promote. But it was the future. Erté had friends who lived in an apartment designed by Le Corbusier, which he loved. On the 1925 Paris Expo, Erté said that 'missing this apotheosis of the style that is now known as Art Deco has been the greatest regret of my life', adding, 'especially as I made a considerable contribution to its development' (*Erté: Things I Remember*, 1975). It is an interesting summation of the effect the 1925 exhibition had on the recognition of the Art Deco style.

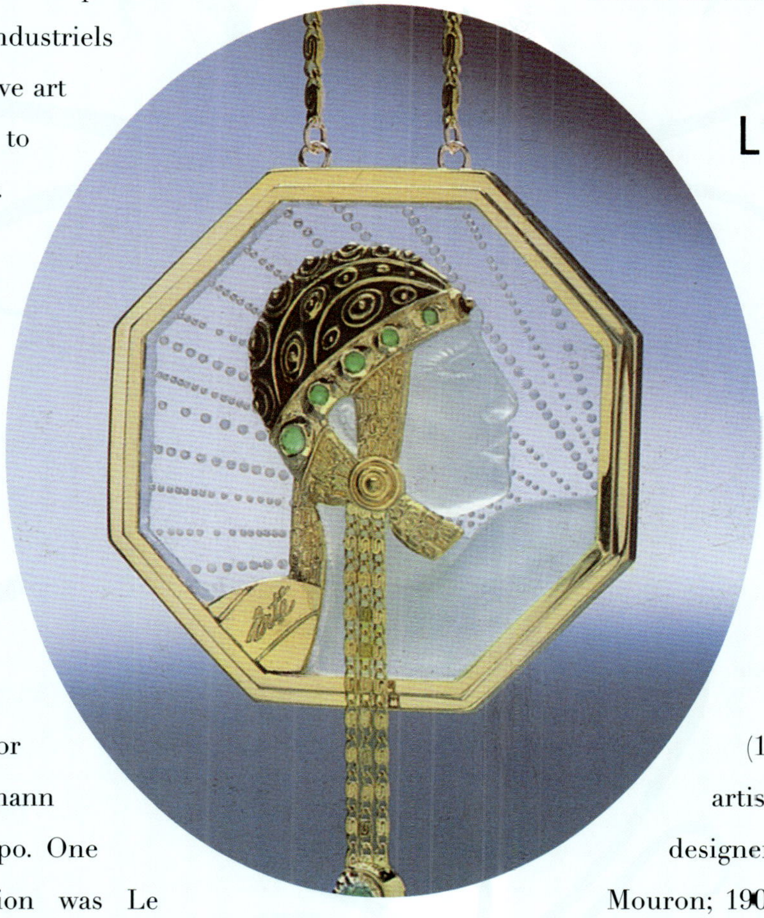

L'ART DECO

Today, Erté is often called the 'Father of Art Deco' but who were his contemporaries in this field? Erté's *Harper's Bazaar* cover *L'Arc en Ciel* (1929, *see* page 154), is a fine example of the Art Deco style with its geometric shapes and strong colour definition. Others succeeding in this arena were the Polish artist Tamara de Lempicka (1896–1980) and Ukrainian-born French artist, illustrator, typeface- and graphic designer Cassandre (born Adolphe Jean-Marie Mouron; 1901–68). De Lempicka's aim was to be original in a post-cubist use of shape, bright colour and light. *Self-Portrait* (*Tamara in the Green Bugatti*) of 1929 typifies her art and a 1920s lifestyle of speed, glamour, luxury and independence. She is depicted at the wheel of an open-top sports car wearing a Hermès leather helmet and gauntlets with a draped scarf blowing in the wind. It was commissioned for

Wings of Victory, *1978, serigraph, 68.6 x 48.3 cm (27 x 19 in)*
An echo of the 1919 *Harper's Bazaar* cover, *New Bridges for Seven Seas*. An adorned woman depicting 'Civilization' symbolized freedom 'from the cruel yoke of war' (Erté).

Aventurine *pendant, 1979, gold, emeralds, crystal, gold chain*

the German women's magazine *Die Dame*, who defined her as 'a symbol of women's liberation'. Cassandre, hailed as the greatest poster designer of his era, ousted Erté from his contract at *Harper's Bazaar*. He studied art in Paris and was a follower of Cubism. He is noted for bold, dynamic images, such as the poster for the newspaper *L'Intransigeant* (1925), with a stream of words in a bold typeface, sharp imagery and dramatic use of colour. Cassandre created a memorable series of travel posters too, including *Étoile du Nord* (1927) and Normandie (1935).

GALERIE CHARPENTIER

Erté was back in Paris in 1926, after nearly a year in America. Jean Charpentier (1891–1976), owner of the prestigious Galerie Jean Charpentier on the Rue de Faubourg St Honoré, offered to stage an exhibition of Erté works in April, to coincide with an exhibition of paintings by Jean-Gabriel Domergue (1889–1962), known for his glamorous paintings of Parisian women. The show was successful financially – nearly all the works sold – and professionally, with favourable reviews in the national newspapers. The French government bought *Le Reve et la réalité*, which had been a cover for *Harper's Bazaar*. Charpentier, delighted with such a successful show, offered Erté a follow-up exhibition for 1928–29.

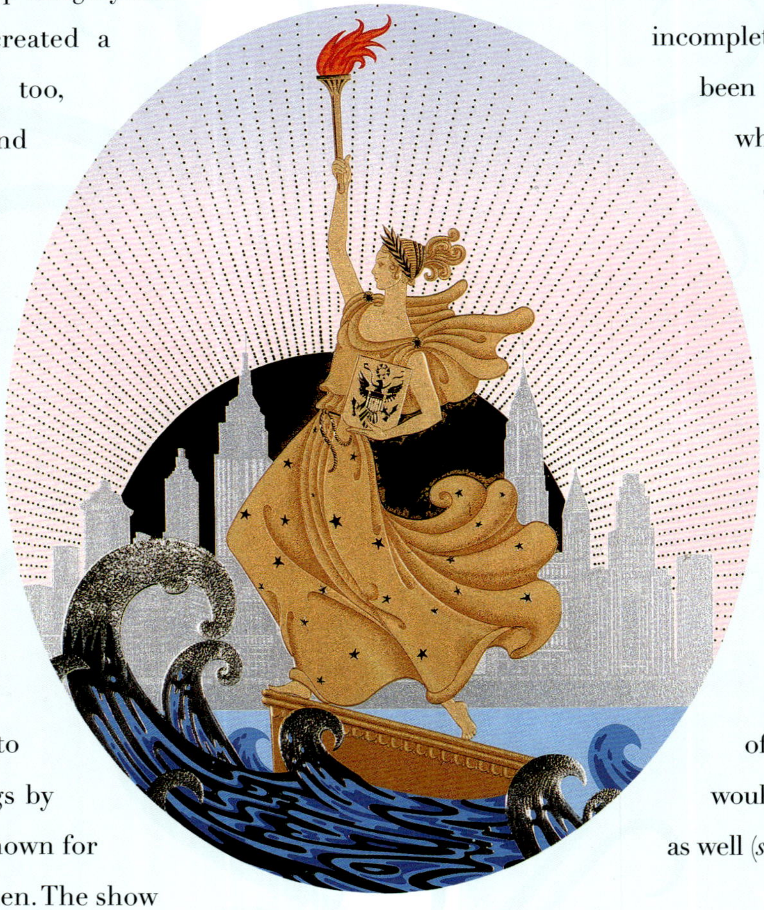

THE ALPHABET SERIES

A concept that had been fermenting in Erté's mind since 1926 to design a series of 'human figure' alphabet letters was underway by 1927 (*see* pages 7, 185–87 for the lithograph versions). He planned to show it at the second Charpentier exhibition. He had visualized it all at once but his full workload meant it remained incomplete until 1967. Erté stated that it had not been inspired by 'medieval, decorated uncials', which would have been a natural comparison. The origins of his scheme can, in fact, be traced back to his childhood when he learnt not only the letters of the alphabet but also the drawing and painting of their shapes. This, combined with his love of the movements of the human body in dance, brought two ideas together. On the 26 compositions Erté stated, 'I have closely associated the human body, exalted by dance, with the graphic features of the letters.' Much later, in the 1960s, he would create a complementary numbers series as well (*see* pages 182–83).

THE JAZZ AGE

The Jazz Age or Jazz Era as it is also called, synonymous with jazz music, flourished from 1918 until the end of the Great Depression in America, *c.* 1933. For high society it can be summed up in the

Statue of Liberty Day, *1986, embossed serigraph with foil stamping, 88.6 x 66.5 cm (34⅞ x 26⅛ in)*

Statue of Liberty Night, *1986, embossed serigraph with foil stamping, 88.6 x 66.5 cm (34⅞ x 26⅛ in)*

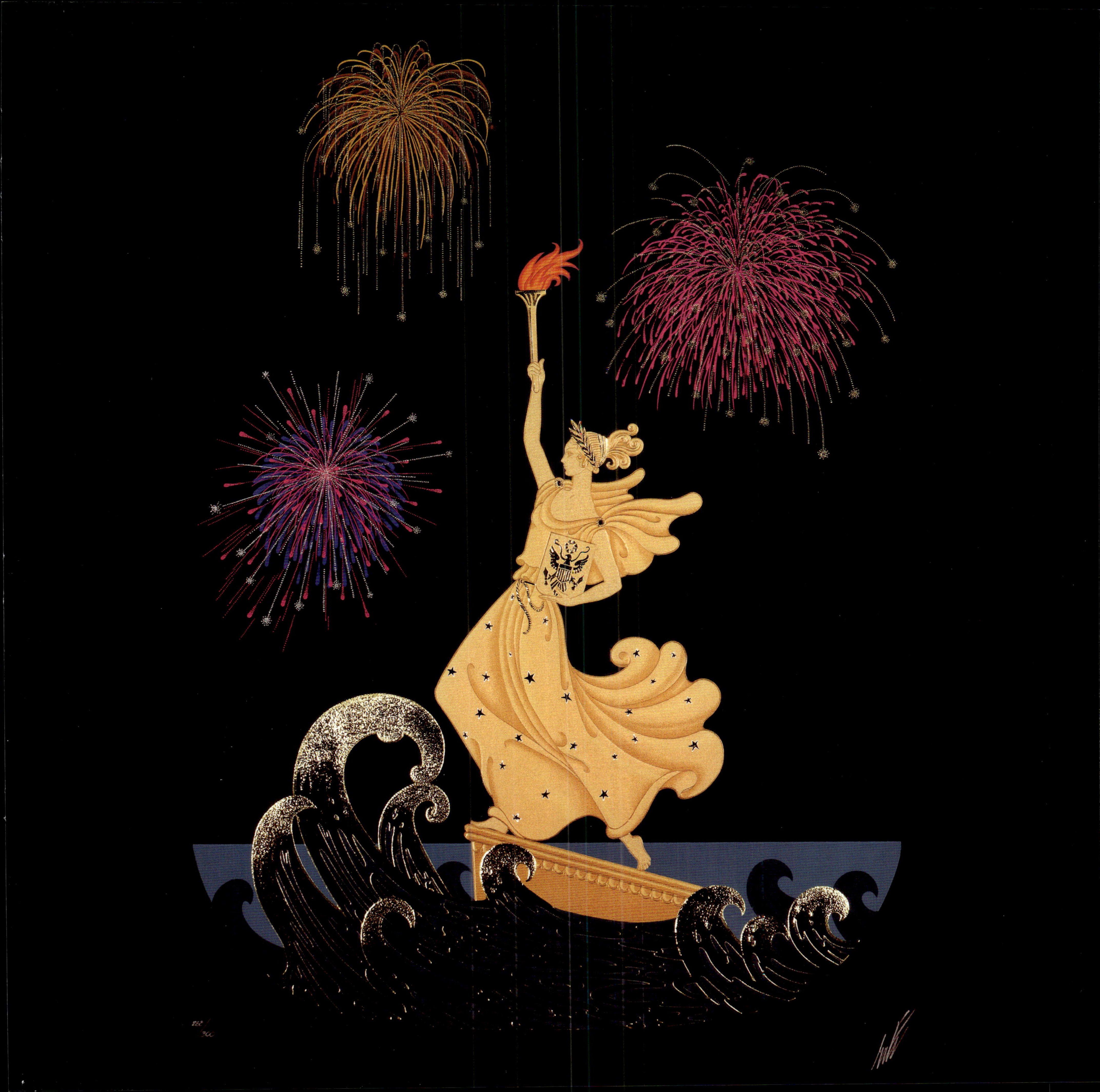

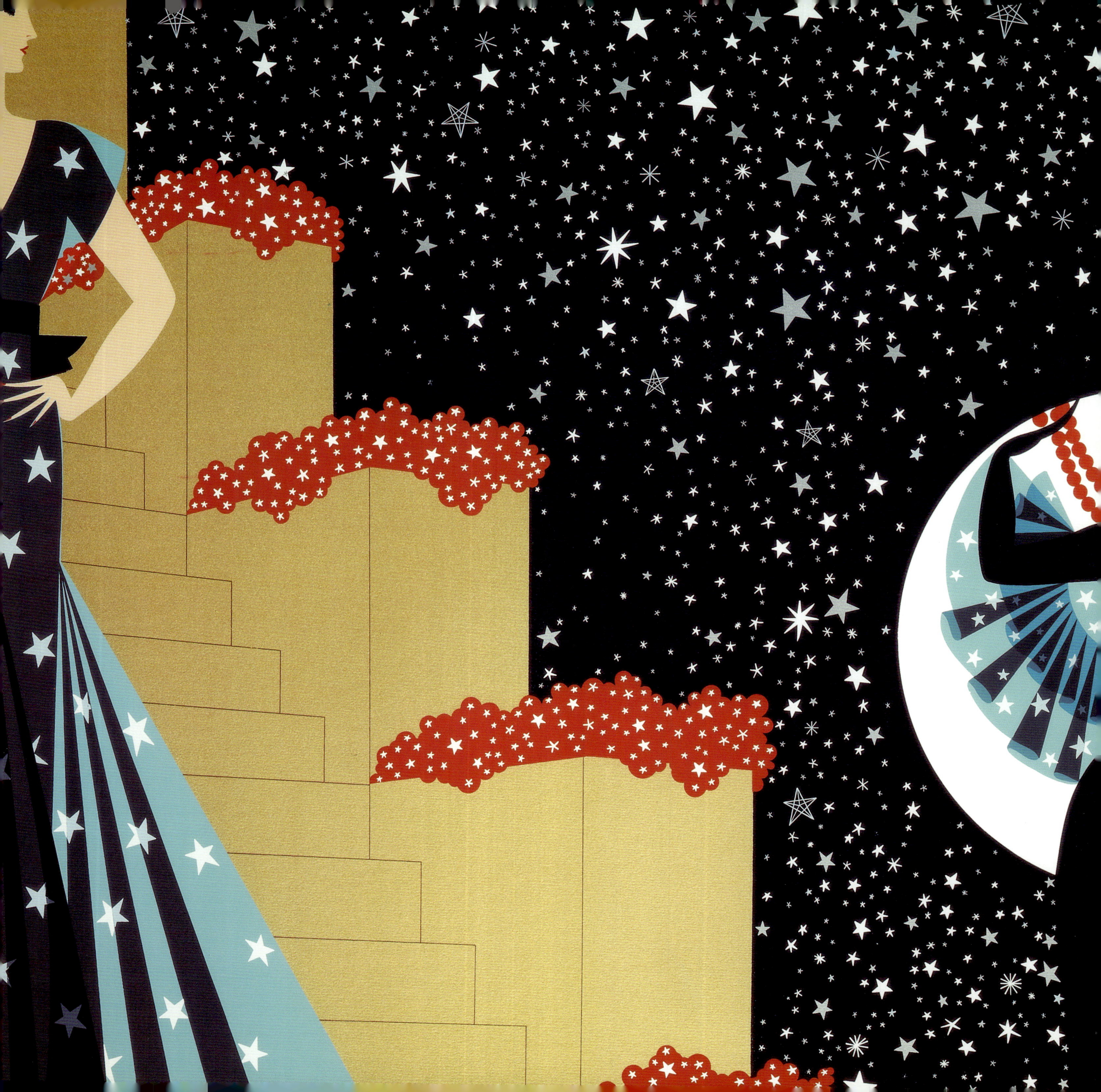

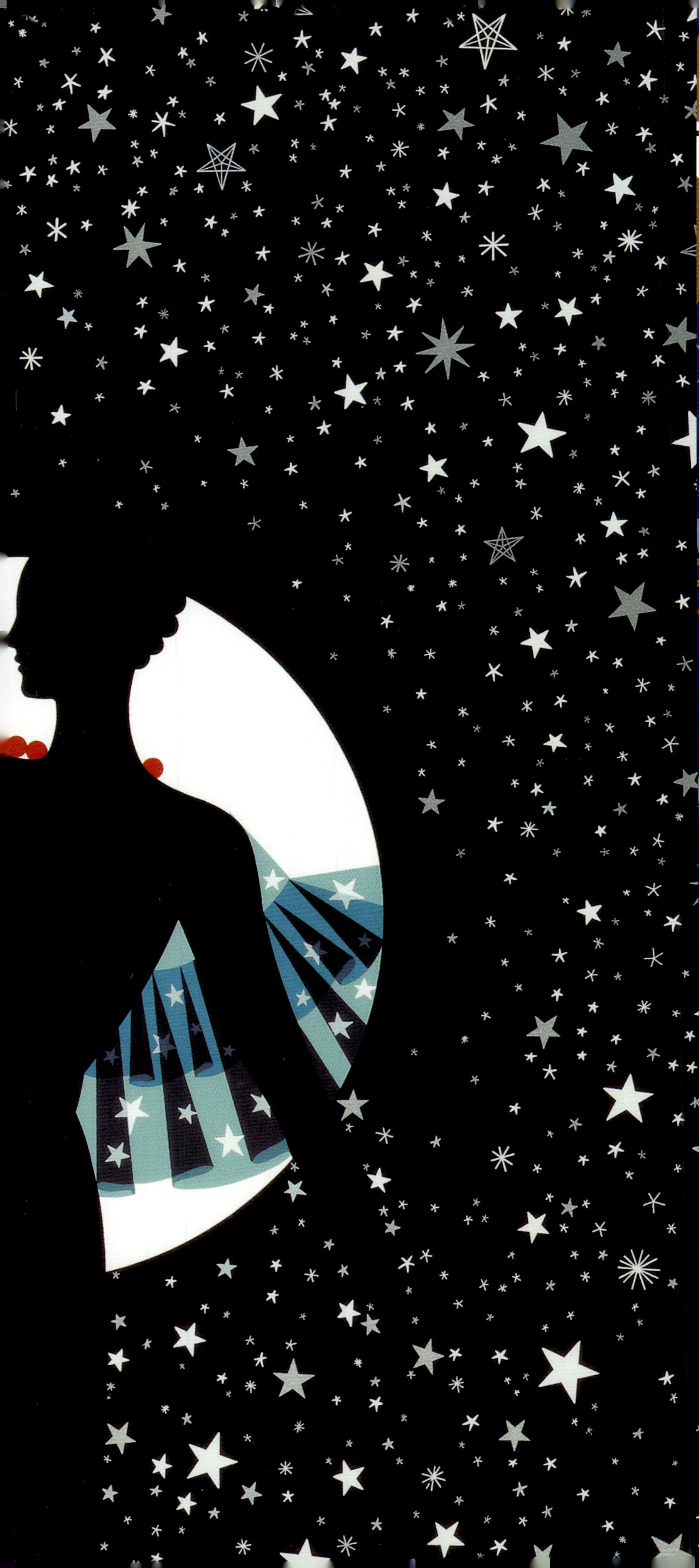

novel *The Great Gatsby* (published 1925), by American author F. Scott Fitzgerald (1896–1940). In the first 'talkie', the American musical *The Jazz Singer*, released on 6 October 1927, the costumes, sets and music were infused with the fashions, décor and lifestyle of the 1920s. This was the period that Erté spent in America and it informed his work. Many jazz orchestras were touring in Europe. In Paris in 1925, American-born French dancer Josephine Baker (1906–75) brought her *Revue Nègre* to Paris, combining jazz syncopation with exoticism. It is indelibly linked to Art Deco, reaching its zenith in Europe *c.* 1925–30.

EMANCIPATION THROUGH FASHION

The 'flapper' fashion for slim silhouette low-waisted, hipline dresses with shorter hemlines moved women's fashion from the pre-war ankle-sweeping hemline to knee-level and above. It was a boyish look; long hair was chopped and bobbed. Haute-couture designer Gabrielle 'Coco' Chanel (1883–1971) developed the 'sack' style in Paris, she 'let go of the waistline', calling the look 'La Garçonne' (little boy). Women bound their chests with strips of fabric to flatten their breasts. The 'garçonne' or 'flapper' dress was perfect for dancing the free-movement charleston. It represented, to a certain extent, emancipation for women. American women had won the right to vote in 1920. In Britain from 1918 only women over 30 years of age, with property, could vote but this was amended in 1928 to include all women from 21 years of age.

Star Spangled Night, *1990, serigraph,* ©
101 x 105.4 cm (39 7/8 x 41 1/2 in)

THE 'MODERNE' MACHINE AGE

A gradual change from the pre-First World War 'Orientalism' and 'Symbolism' of Art Nouveau progressed and transformed the Belle Époque into the sleek modernity of Art Décoratif (the term 'Art Deco' was coined in the 1960s to differentiate the revival Art Deco from the original Art Décoratif). Paul Poiret certainly kick-started a change in fashion design with his uncorsetted slim-line dresses. Architects, designers and industrial designers embraced the Machine Age, paring down excessive decoration, using industrial materials and removing colour to create a sophisticated *moderne* design. The Bauhaus collective begun at Weimar, Germany in 1919 under the directorship of Walter Gropius (1883–1969), was a force for change, embracing the 'machine age' and industrial design. Gropius's craftsmen and women set out to create 'total works of art' in design, art, sculpture, decorative art and, later, architecture.

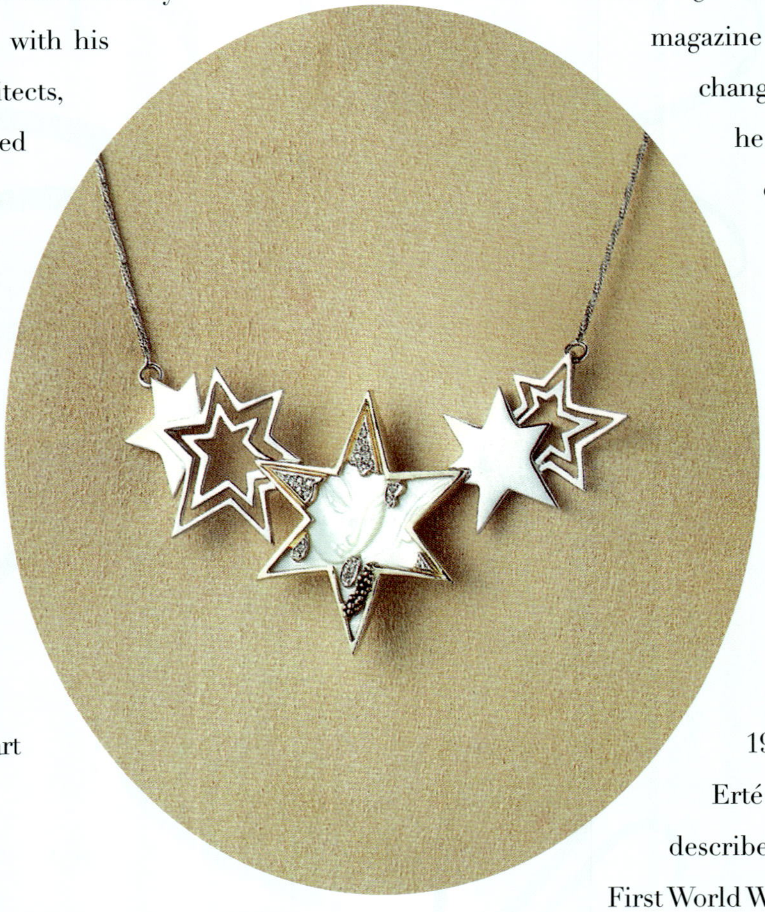

1926: ART ET INDUSTRIE, PARIS

A new phase of Erté's design career was triggered in 1926, with a commission to work for a new monthly magazine *Art et Industrie*. Its editor was Victor de la Fortelle. Erté said of the magazine that it was 'a perfect expression of one of the basic principles of Art Deco – the marriage of pure and applied art' (*Erté: Things I Remember*, 1975). Previously for *Harper's Bazaar* Erté had created designs for interior décor such as tables, lamps, lighting, cushions and more. For *Art et Industrie* he was to focus on designed interiors and applied arts, chairs, lamps, tables, mirrors, soft furnishings and decorative objects. As he recalled, it was a refreshing change from fashion design. He created magazine cover illustrations too. Erté embraced change, although not all changes in fashion – he said he was 'rather bored' with the 'sack' dresses created by French fashion designer Coco Chanel at this time. Was he now out of step with fashion?

A VISION OF HISTORY

Commissioned to write an illustrated article on modern fashion dress for the 14th edition of the *Encyclopaedia Britannica*, published in 1929 (entry to be found on pages 656–58), Erté chose to write about 'Modern Dress'. He described the years 1914 to 1920, the years of the First World War and its aftermath, as the 'least notable in the history of fashion'. Many French fashion houses had closed during the war through lack of clientele. In that period Erté had plied his genius for fashion illustration in the USA. His costume design focused on European musical revues. He made reference to the craze for the boyish 'flapper' dresses *c.* 1924, and commented wryly that:

Les Étoiles *necklace, c. 1979–90, gold, silver, diamonds, mother-of-pearl*

New York, New York, *1987, embossed serigraph with foil stamping, 84.6 x 75.2 cm (331/4 x 291/2 in)*

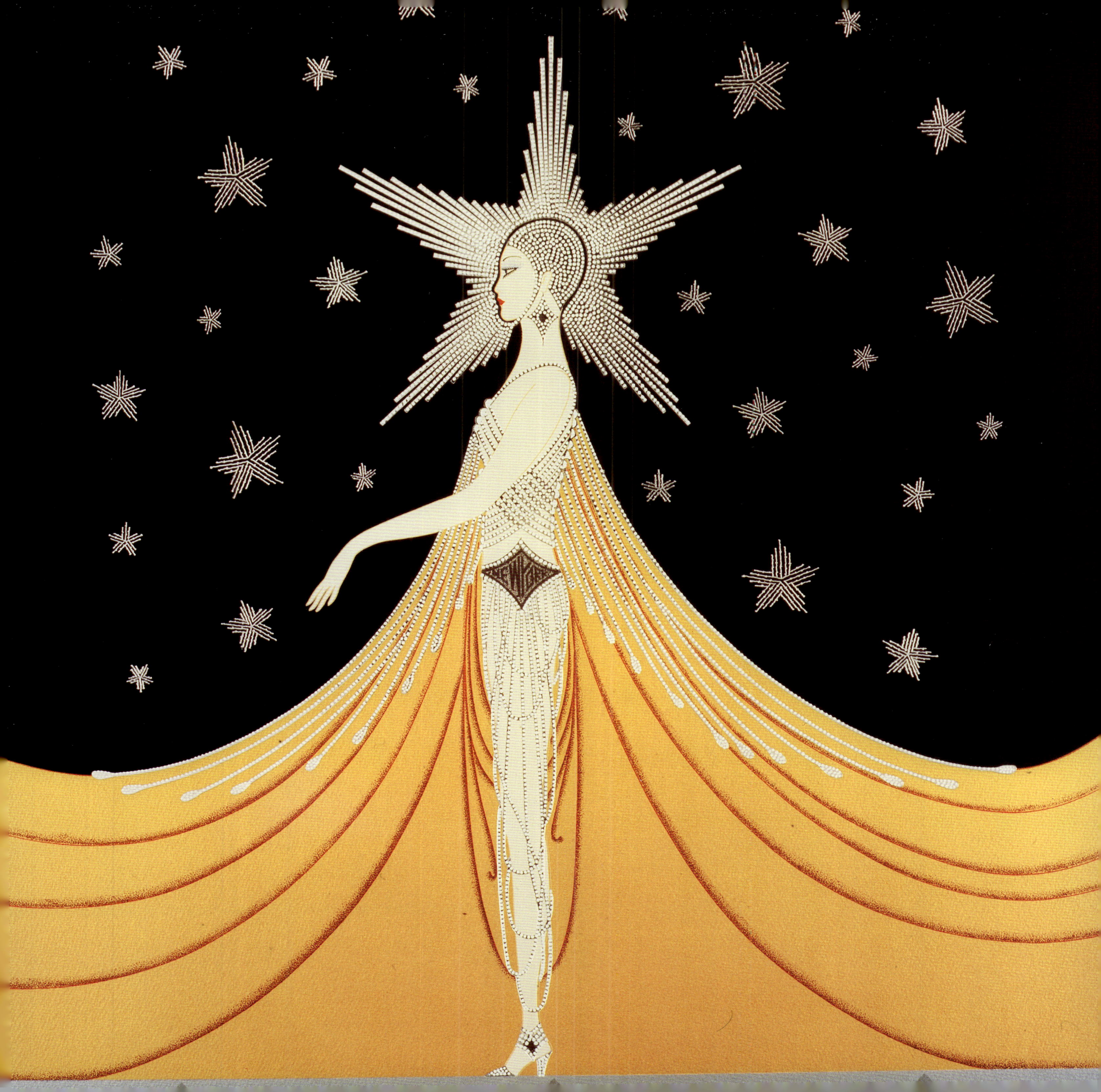

Traces of the masculine image will remain in feminine costume for a long time since woman has adopted two articles from man's wardrobe – the sweater, and the pyjama.

There was no reference to the enormous success of his younger rival Gabrielle 'Coco' Chanel's 'Garçonne' look and 'sack' dresses. Erté included an illustration to show four years of women's fashion from 1925–28 in silhouette, finishing with the popular drop-waist dress. He included a discussion on unisex dressing, a fashion style that would become the norm in future decades. Many of his own fashion creations were ambiguous in male–female definition. Erté stated that it was the first time that unisex fashion had been debated in an academic publication.

LA PRINCESSE LOINTAINE

In 1929 Erté was commissioned to design sets and costumes (such as that for Mélissinde, *see* page 133) for a revised version of the play *La Princess Lointaine* by Edmond Rostand, originally written for the actress Sarah Bernhardt in 1895. He was pleased with the casting of Vera Sergine (1884–1946), Henri Rolland and Paul Bernard (1898–1958). However, one of his costumes for Sergine as Princess Mélissinde caused the actress discomfort. Her cloak for the final scene weighed around 22 lbs (ten kilos). Erté had made it in gold and silver encrusted with 'jewels'. It looked as though his masterpiece of theatricality would be discarded until the director suggested one of Sergine's entourage could wear it instead.

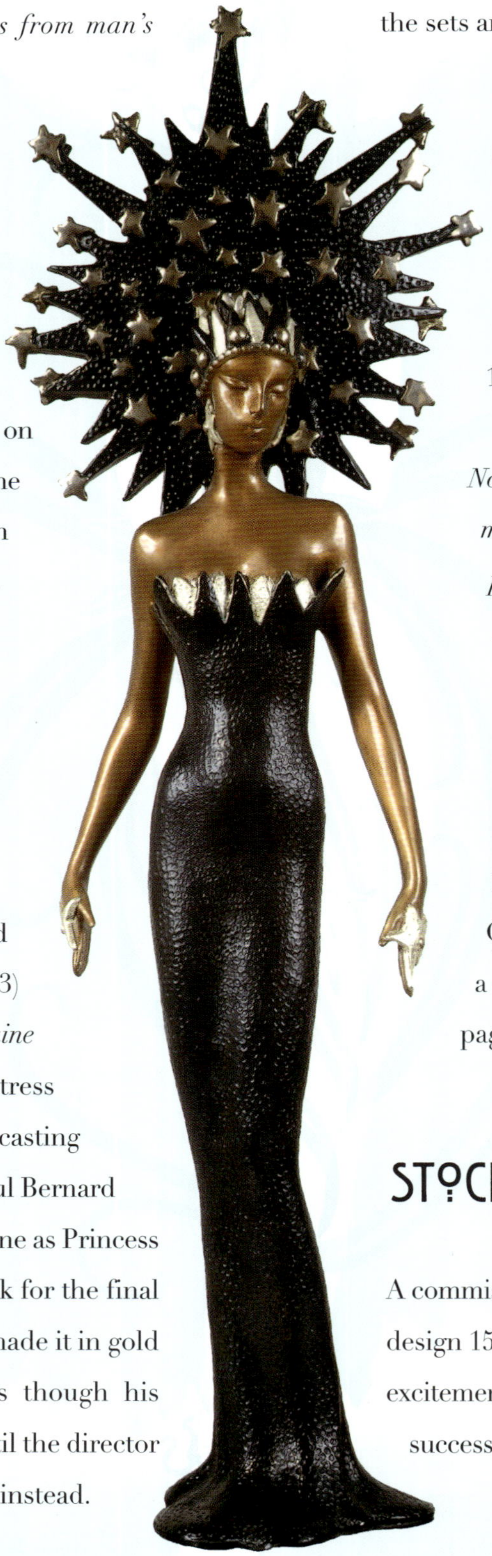

Sergine duly put up with the weight of it. When the play opened, the sets and costumes were hailed as triumphs by reviewers.

ERTÉ'S POETIC VISION

For *La Princesse Lointaine*, one design in particular, for the galley, was hailed a 'masterpiece'. On 9 November 1929, *L'Illustration* reported that:

No one could surpass Erté in translating the poet's vision into material terms in designs which are not tied to a particular period yet manage to combine East and West, the Christian Middle Ages and Byzantium in a composite synthesis….

The writer had succinctly summed up Erté's genius in his mastery of historicism, combining elements of national cultures in a fusion of styles, rich colours, luxury and fantasy, enough to give a magical taste of the Orient or the Byzantine. Erté revisited this success with a serigraph of Mélissinde's costume, *Byzantine* (1985, *see* page 133), and a bronze sculpture *Byzantine* (1988).

STOCKINGS AND SHOES

A commission from the Amalgamated Silk Corporation in 1929 to design 15 printed textile patterns was another new venture. Erté's excitement lay in the chance to create abstract forms. The resulting success of the commission led to Erté creating a series of fashion designs using his materials, although he found it difficult

(Above) **Starstruck** *sculpture, 1988, bronze, 55.9 x 16.5 x 13.3cm (22 x 6½ x 5¼ in)*
(Right) **Starstruck**, *1985, embossed serigraph with foil stamping, 83.8 x 61 cm (33 x 24 in)*

(Next page, left) **Angel Melody**, *1919, embossed serigraph with foil stamping, 142.9 x 74.3 cm (56¼ x 29¼ in)*
(Next page, right) **Diana**, *from the* **Myths** *suite, 1985, embossed serigraph with foil stamping, 85.1 x 62.2 cm (33½ x 24½ in)*
Diana accompanies another serigraph, *Circe* (1985), and is based on a 1923 costume design, 'Le Gloire', for the Ziegfeld Follies production *L'Or*.

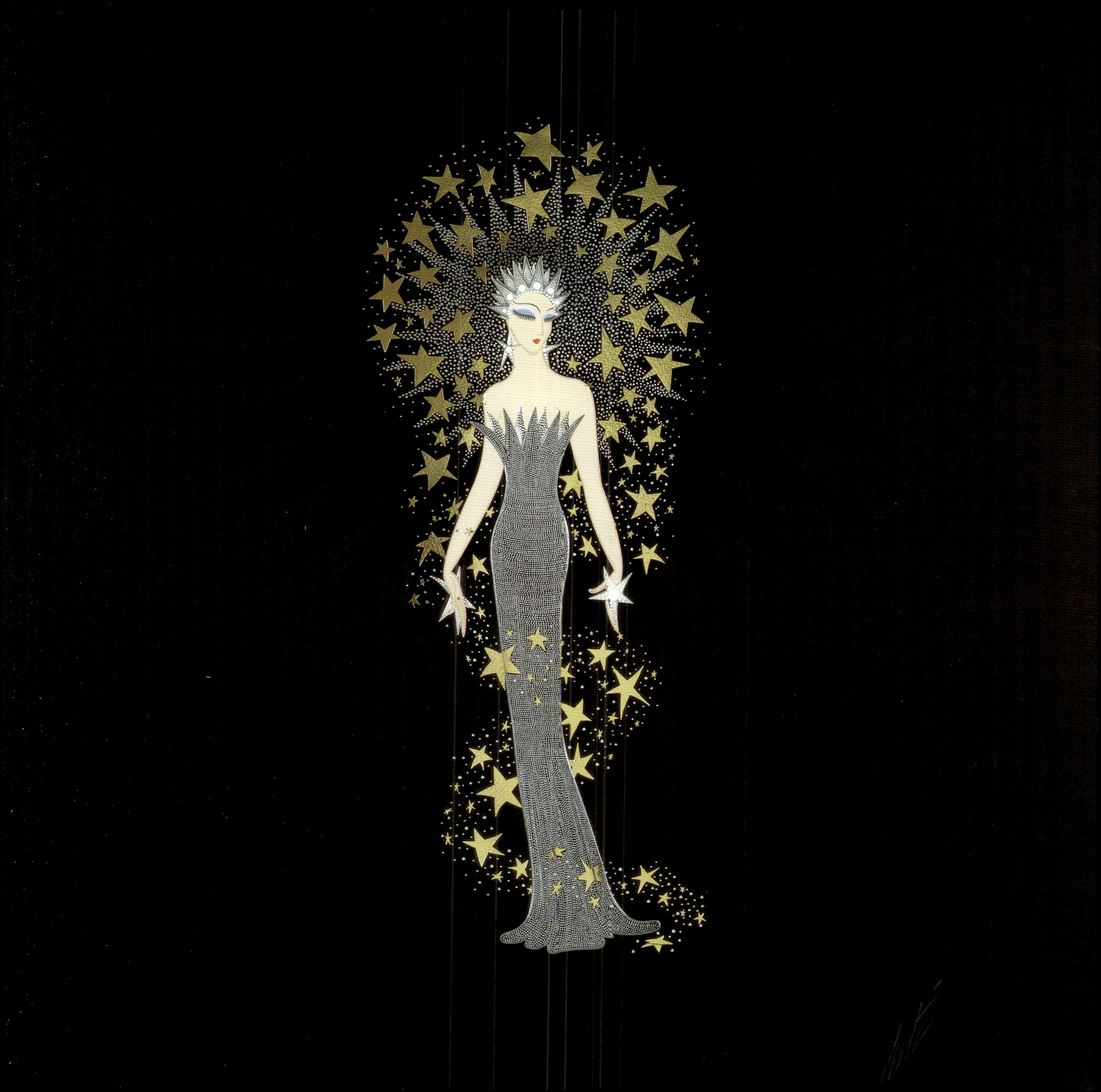

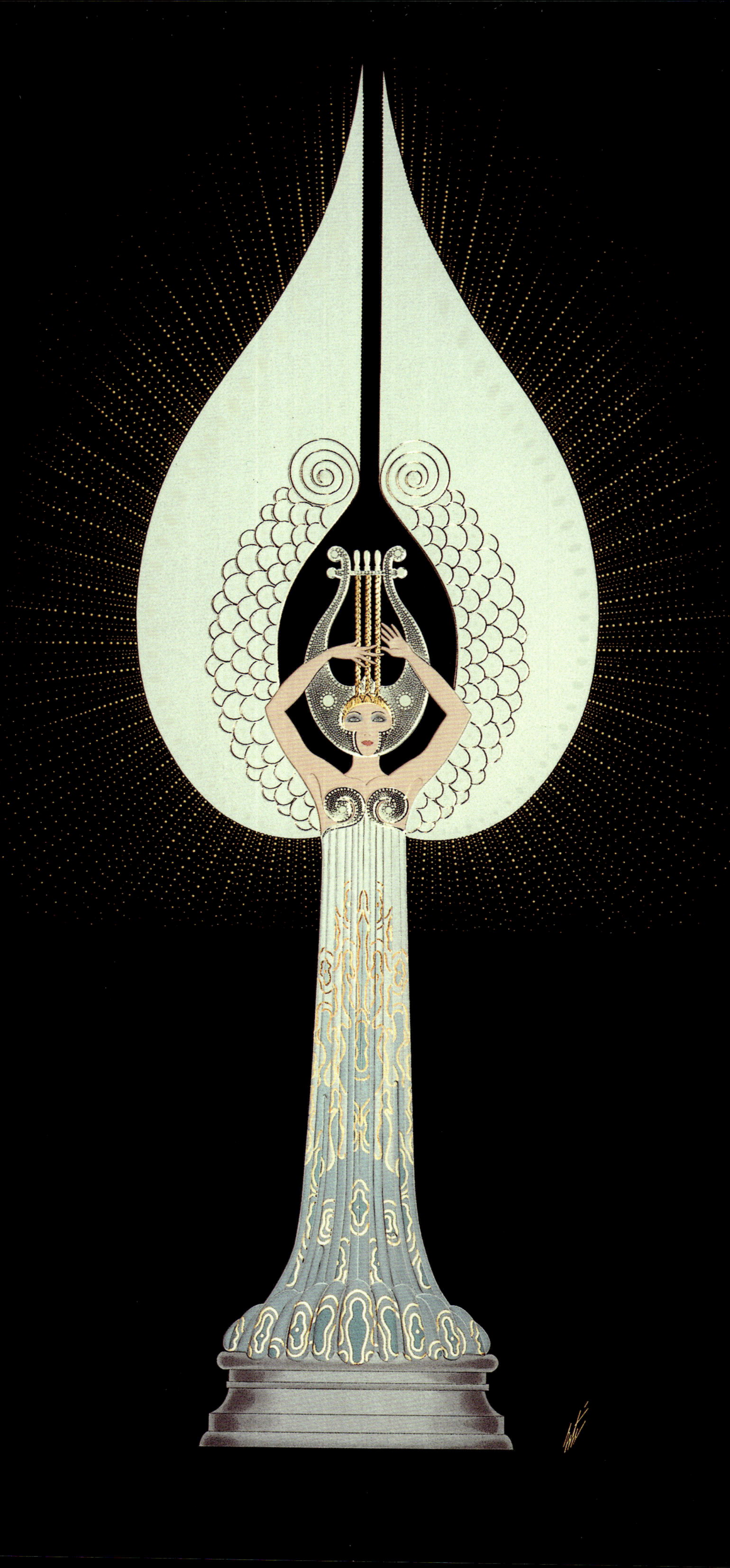

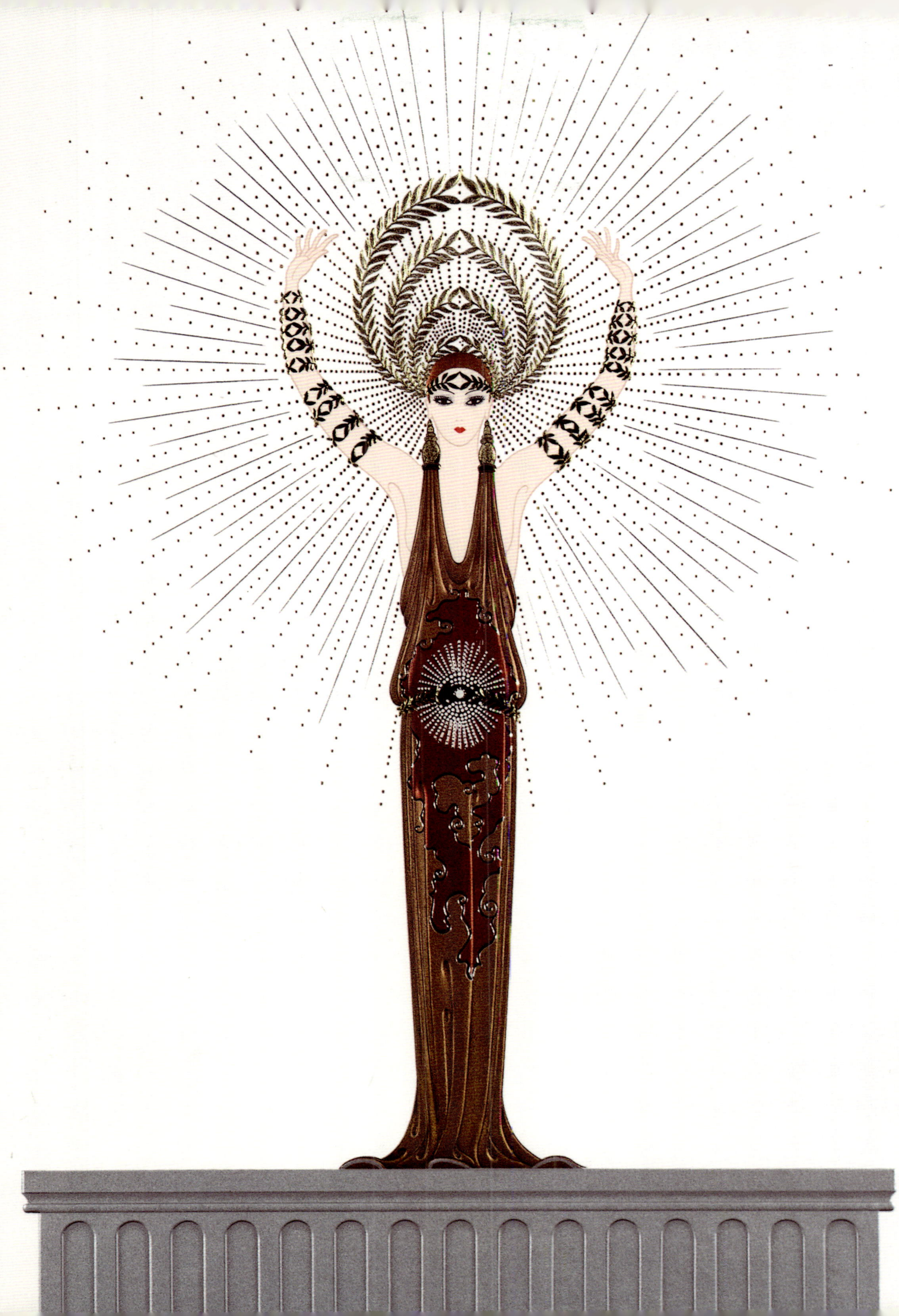

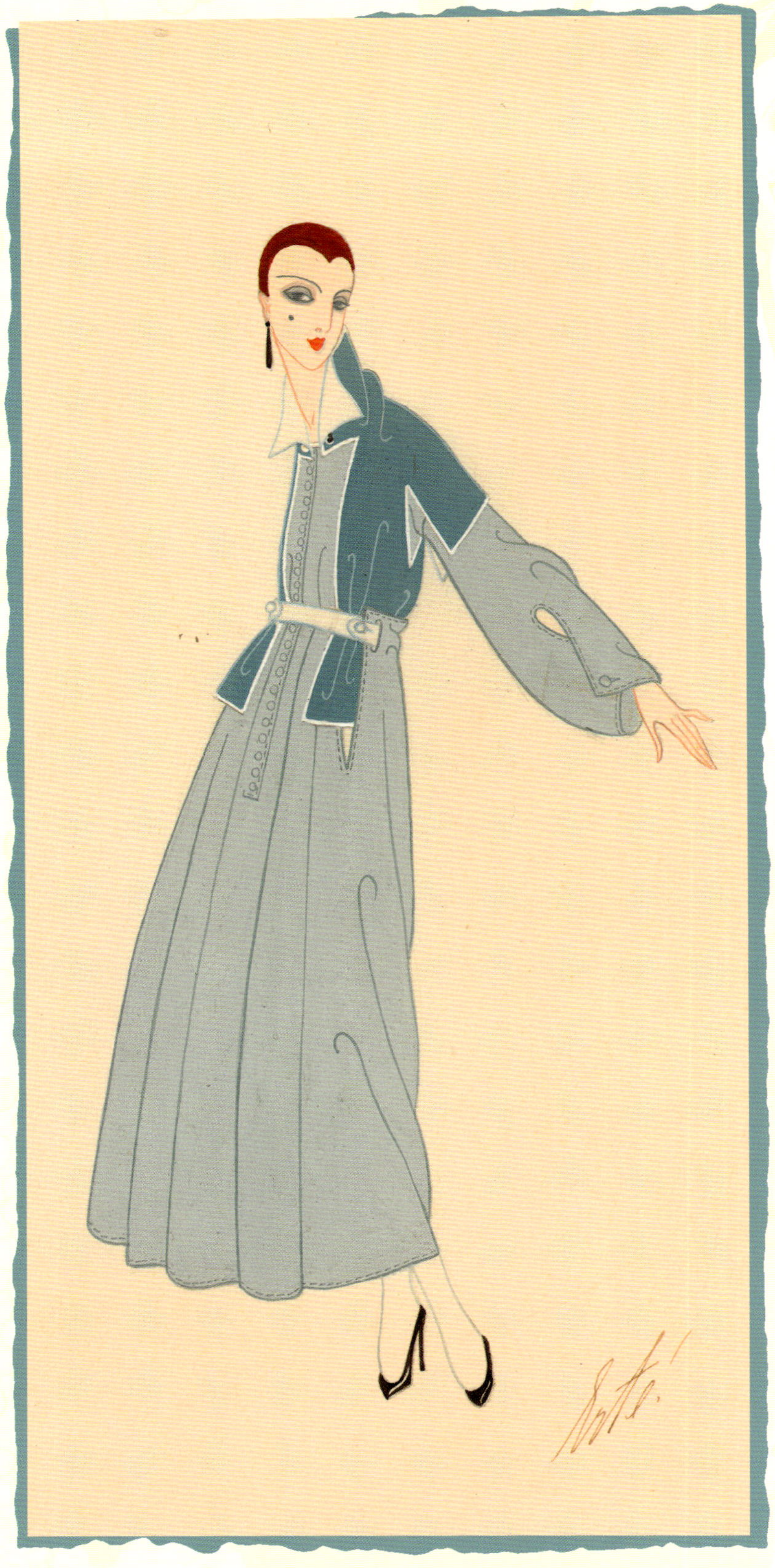

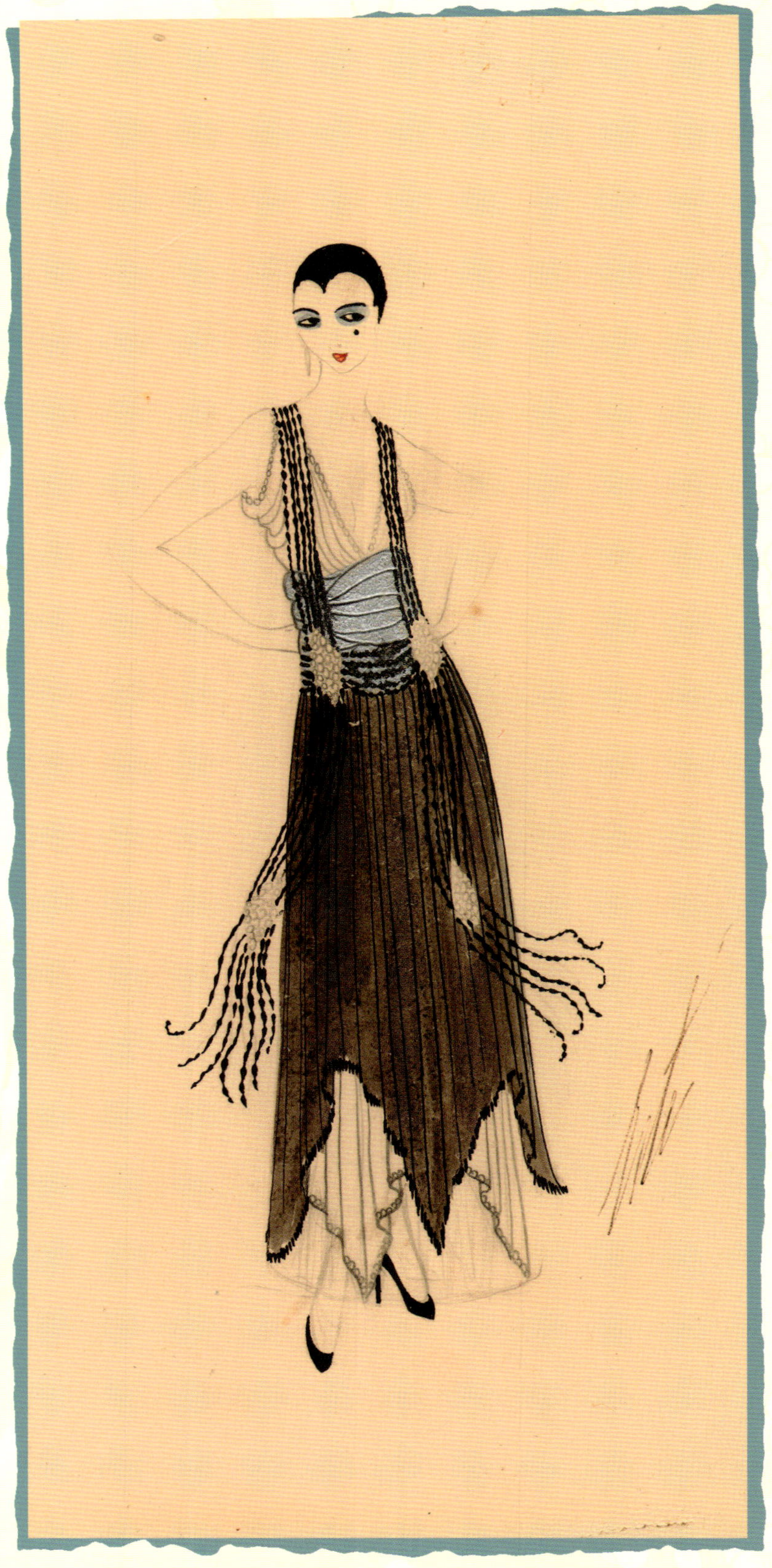

Designs for Henri Bendel, *1916, gouache, 16 x 24.8 cm (6¼ x 9¾ in))*
Erté's early fashion designs are complemented by his later designs and serigraphs – the fluidity of line is maintained, whether the designs are practical or full of fancy.

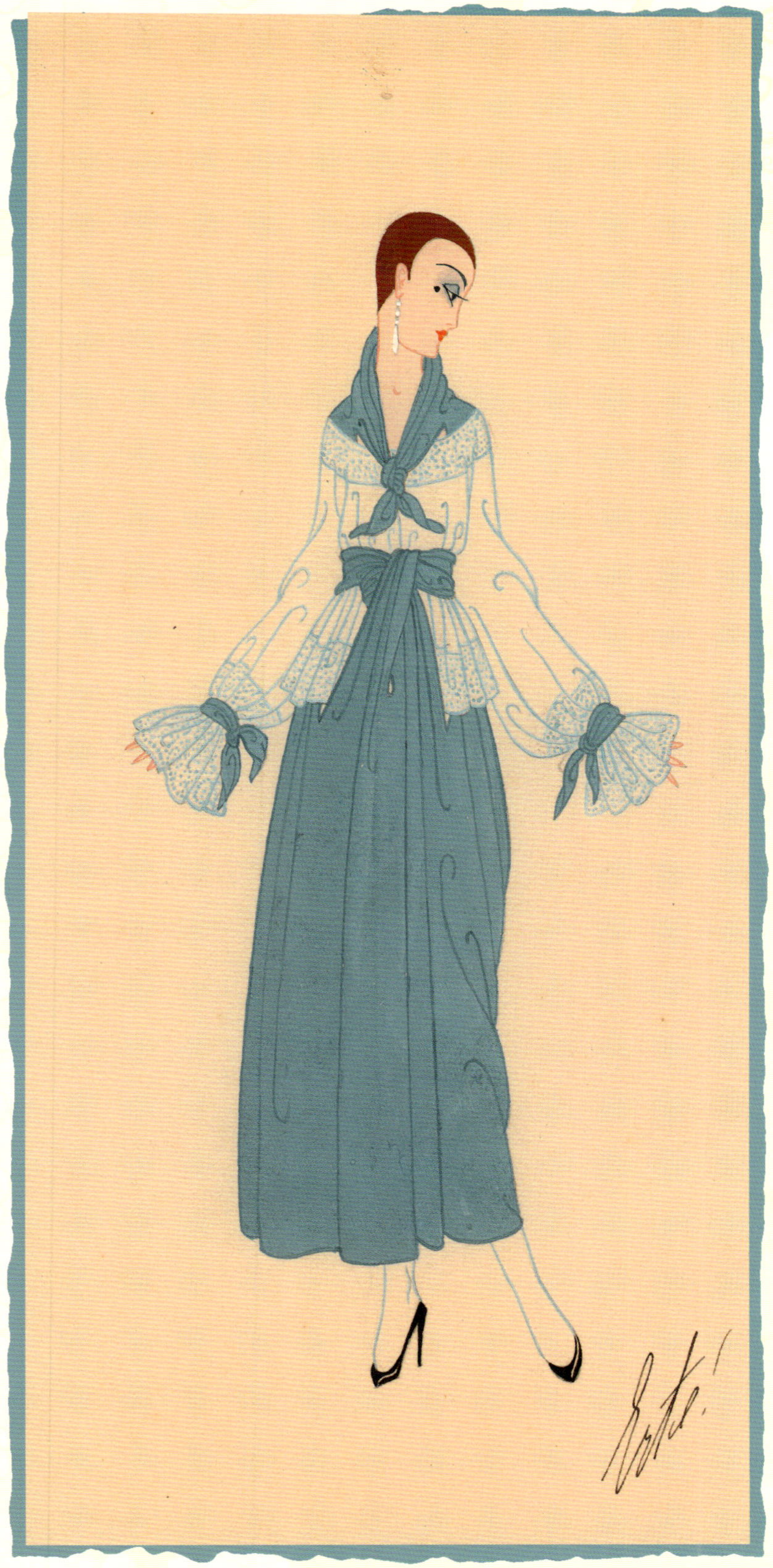
Erté

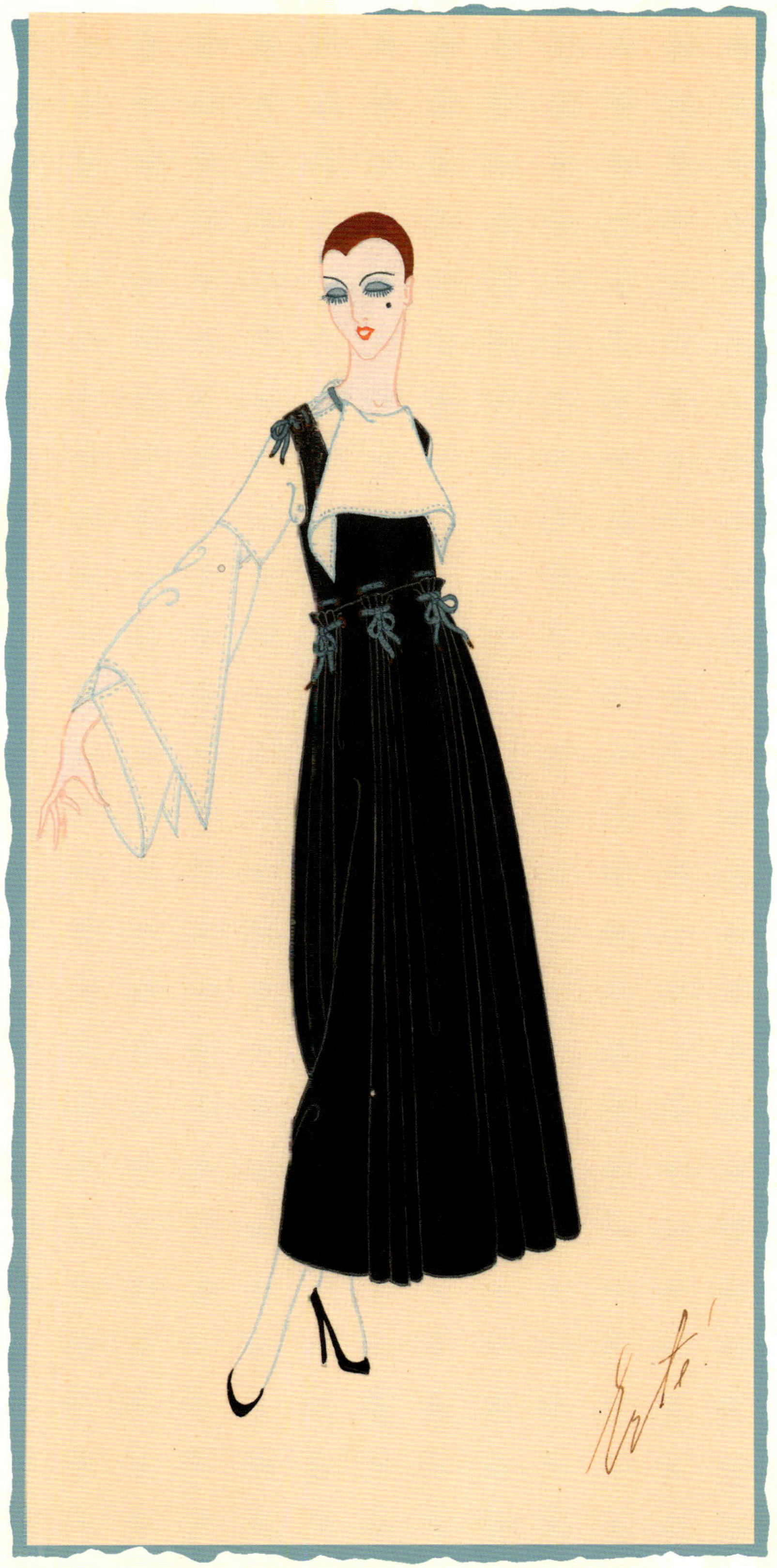
Erté

to make interesting shapes in printed fabric. This step led to lucrative contracts with the American company Holeproof Hosiery (*see* page 59), creating advertisements for them (1930–34). A further advertising contract was offered by Hermann Delman for Delman Shoes from 1931 to 1939, resuming post-war. In addition, Erté designed special edition shoes, which became part of each Delman shoe collection. The gouache *Red Pump* (1934) for Delman shoes is a stunning example of Erté's understanding of brand advertising. The shoe is prominent in red, with the backdrop an Art Deco 'staircase'. Later in his career he would return to hosiery stocking package illustration for Charnos in 1974 (*see* page 46). An energetic image, Erté knew how to brand the stockings to match the personality of the wearer: young, fashionable and fun.

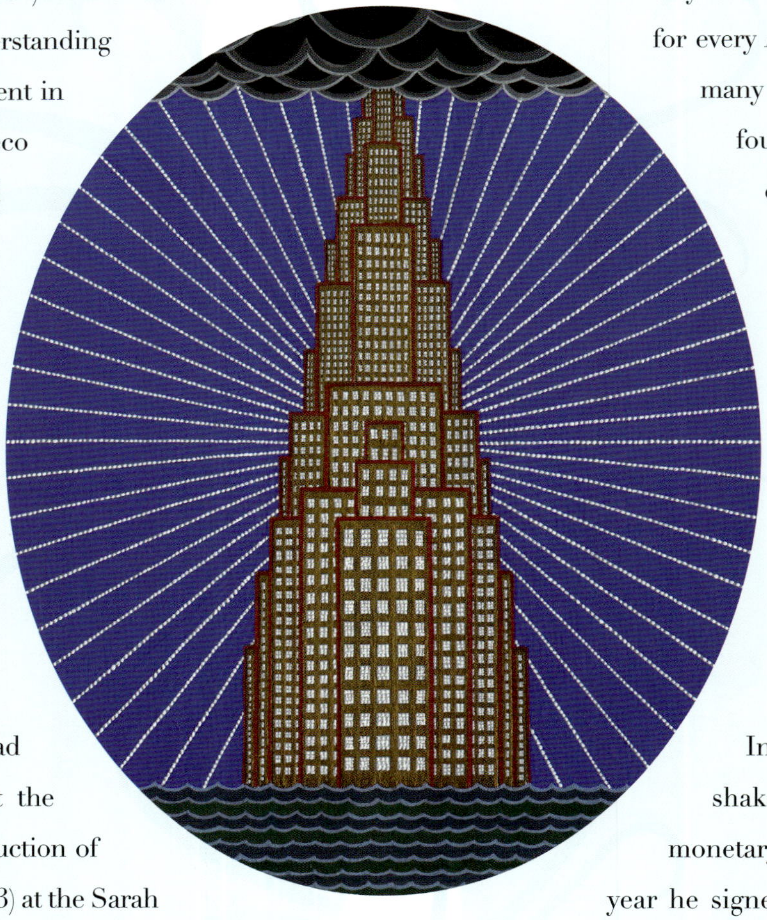

WALL STREET CRASH

1929 had been a good year for Erté. He had success with an exhibition of works at the Gallerie Jean Charpentier, the stage production of *La Princesse Lointaine* (*see* pages 114 and 133) at the Sarah Bernhardt Theatre in Paris, and his American advertising contracts were underway, plus the *Harper's Bazaar* (now spelt with a second 'a'), contract. An exhibition at the Warren Cox Gallery in New York resulted in nearly all the works being sold. Then the United States suffered the Wall Street Crash, having a devastating effect on all businesses; and for Erté it was an immense blow because all his money was invested in American stock markets. He collapsed financially and his workload was severely reduced. *Harper's Bazaar*, having recently published his superb gouache *Optimism and Pessimism* on its May 1929 cover (*see* page 156), now wanted fewer drawings. George White's 'Scandals' revues temporarily ceased. The works that had 'sold' at the Warren Cox exhibition became unsold as the buyers had no money to invest. It was a bleak period for every American citizen. And Erté, who had so many contracts with American companies, found his work cancelled or restricted or delayed. Fortunately he had work in Europe too, but he recalled having very little money. Work on a new house at Brunoy, south-east Paris, was stopped and his occupation of the Villa Excelsior in Monte Carlo ended, as Erté could no longer afford it.

BAL TABARIN, PARIS

In 1933 Erté emerged, alongside others, shaken but not bowed by the traumatic monetary effects of the Wall Street Crash. In that year he signed a lucrative contract in Europe with Pierre Sandrini, son of prima ballerina Emma Sandrini and owner of the Bal Tabarin club at 36 rue Victor-Massé, Paris. The club had speciality acts intermixed with ballet extracts and dance sequences. Erté provided designs for costumes. The good relationship and business contract between Pierre and Erté would last until Sandrini's accidental death in 1952.

Opening curtain for Manhattan Mary *(detail), 1927, gouache with metallic paint, 28.7 x 39.4 cm (111/4 x 151/2 in)*

Manhattan Mary III, *1989, embossed serigraph, 69.9 x 50.8 cm (27½ x 20 in)*

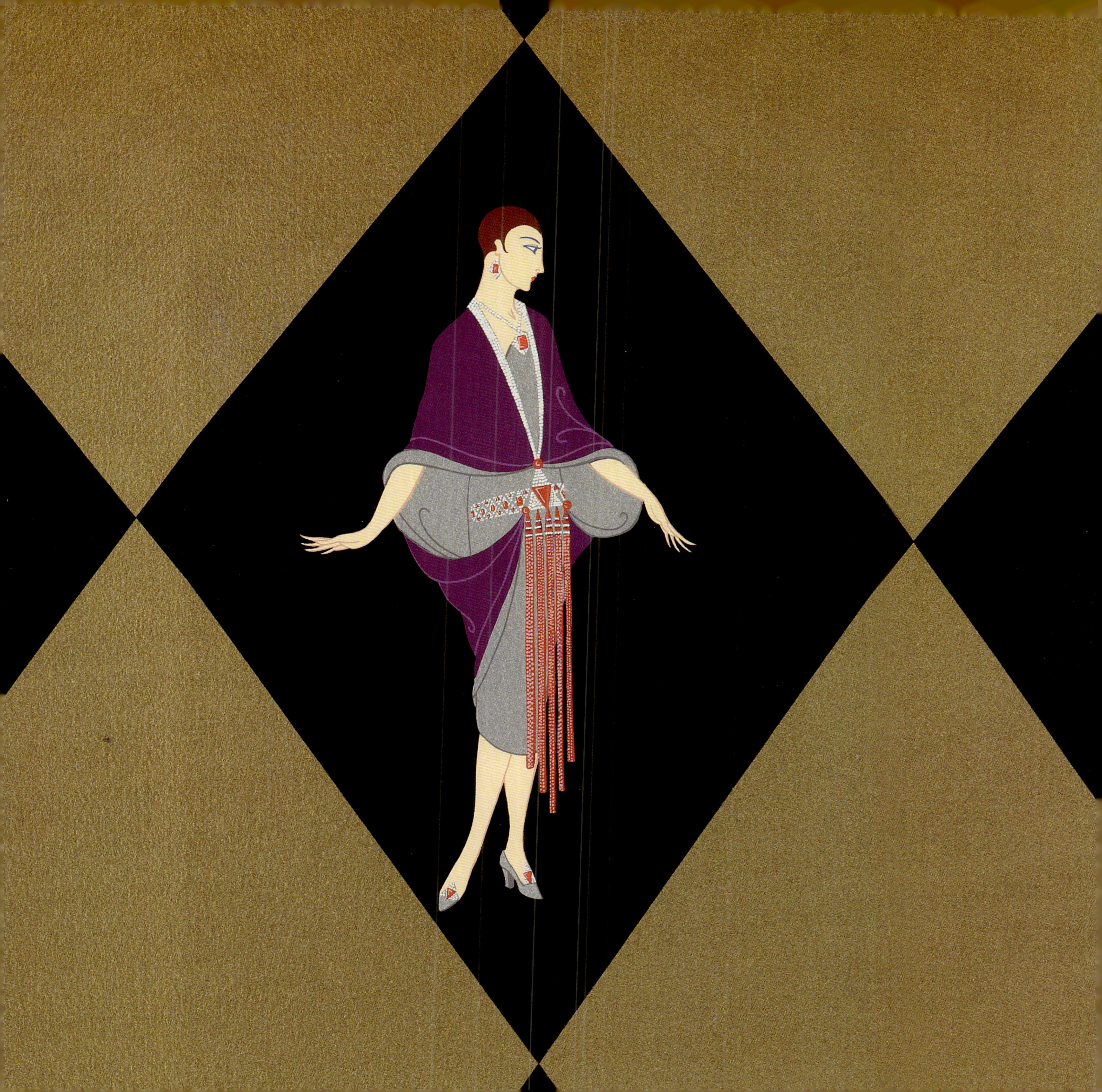

A SPLIT WITH HARPER'S BAZAAR

Dublin-born Carmel Snow (1887–1961), editor of American *Vogue* from 1929, moved to *Harper's Bazaar* as editor in 1933. She immediately changed the typeface, the fonts, the layouts and made it a 14-times per year publication. Reports of the Paris fashion shows were written on the spot by her and sent with sketches via the quickest transport links to London and the USA. Her aim was to modernize the magazine, and that included the front cover. Her preferred artist was Cassandre, the pseudonym of Adolphe Jean-Marie Mouron. His first cover appeared in March 1937, entitled *The Keys to Paris Openings*, and quite different to Erté's earlier *Paris Openings* cover of March 1931 (*see* page 78). Cassandre's illustration was Surrealist in content with a nod of recognition to the Belgian artist Henri Magritte (1898–1967), a master of Surrealism. Hearst, although unsure of what the illustration was intended to mean – a large key facing right, wrapped in a ribbon bow, which poked through a black background to reveal the blue sky – approved the editor's choice. He was reluctant to lose Erté but Snow did not want to work with him. Hearst reluctantly supported her decision as editor.

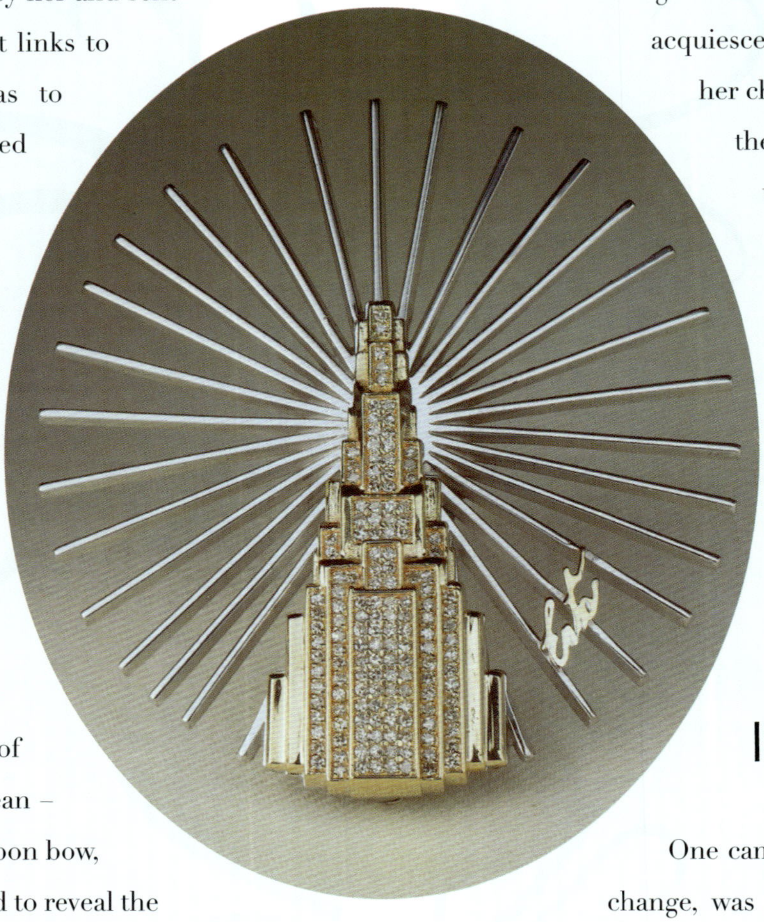

CONTRACT TERMINATED

Erté stated that *Harper's Bazaar* editor Carmel Snow 'not only wanted to supervise my work, but to impose her own ideas' on it. For a man who never let anyone watch him work, apart from his cat (or cats), this must have been a blow. She had decided to 'abridge his freedom of action', he said. He tried to acquiesce, and carried on for a short time, giving her choices of cover drawings. But it signalled the end of Erté's liaison with the magazine, which ended in 1937. One of his last covers was *Seagulls* (1935, *see* page 157). It was an unhappy split, Erté disconsolate for his abrupt dismissal from a magazine for which, he said, 'I truly had spilled my guts' (*Erté: Fashions by Erté* (Academy Editions, 1972), Introduction).

PHOTOGRAPHY VS ILLUSTRATION

One can understand that Carmel Snow, wanting change, was drawn to the newness of Cassandre's striking posters, but it was photography that excited fashion editors for fashion shoots and front covers. British fashion writer Colin McDowell stated in *The Sunday Times* in 2005 that at this time fashion magazines changed from being aspirational, promoting glamour and sophistication, to 'a catalogue of available merchandise', a quote attributed to the fashion columnist Diana

Manhattan *brooch, 1979–90, gold, silver, diamonds, depth: 6 cm (2¼ in)*

Manhattan Mary V, *1989, embossed serigraph, 69.9 x 50.8 cm (27½ x 20 in)*

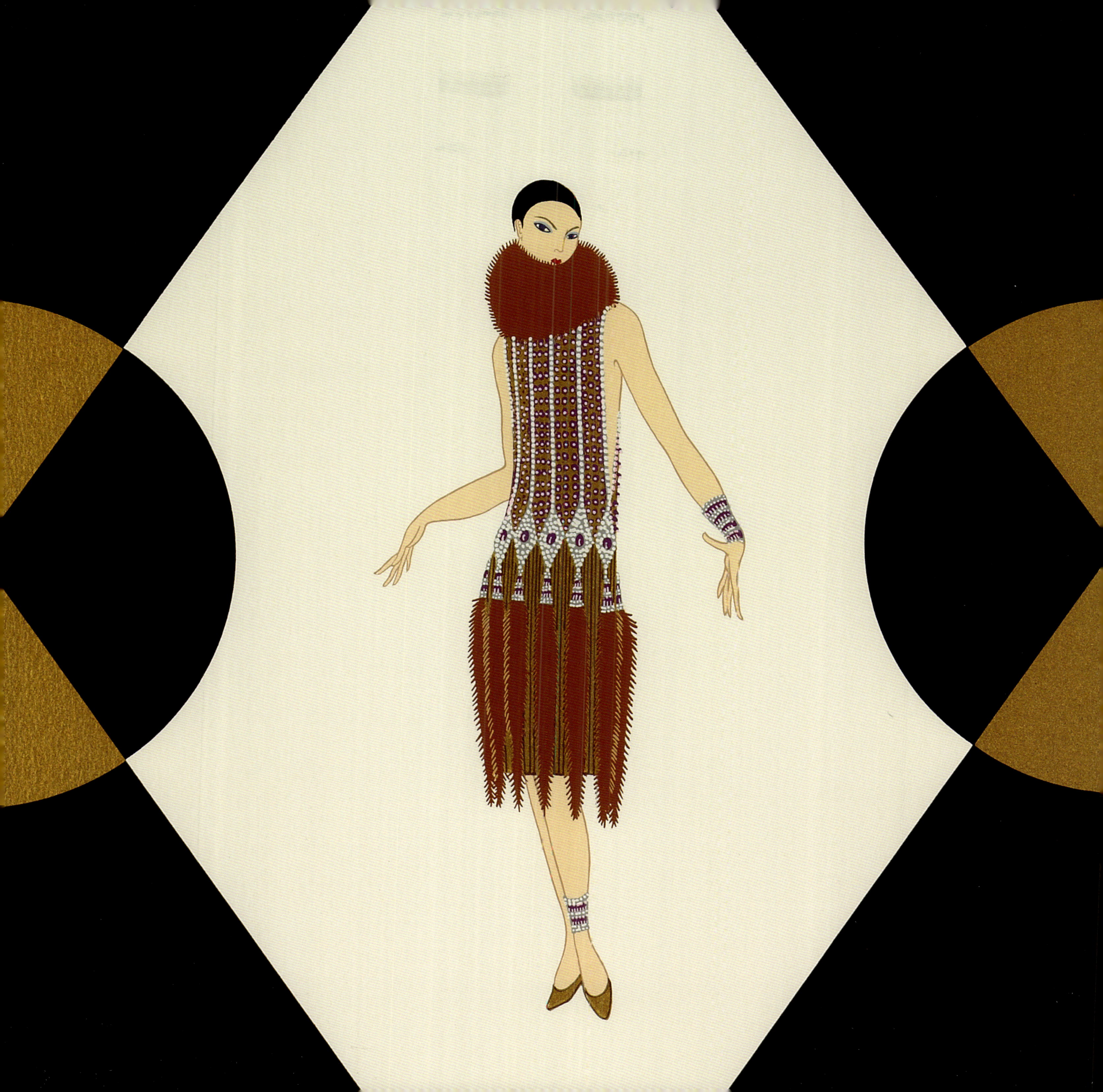

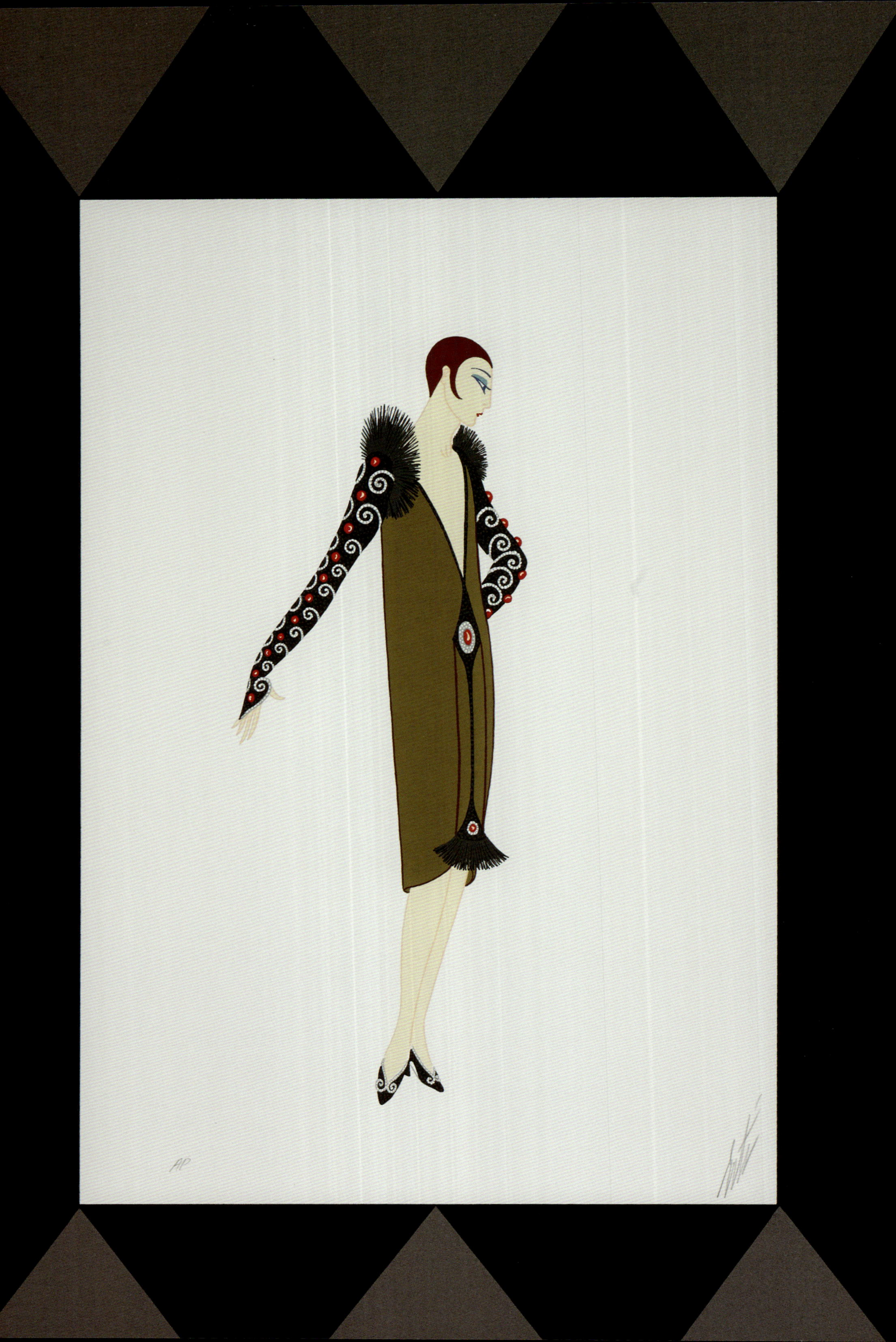

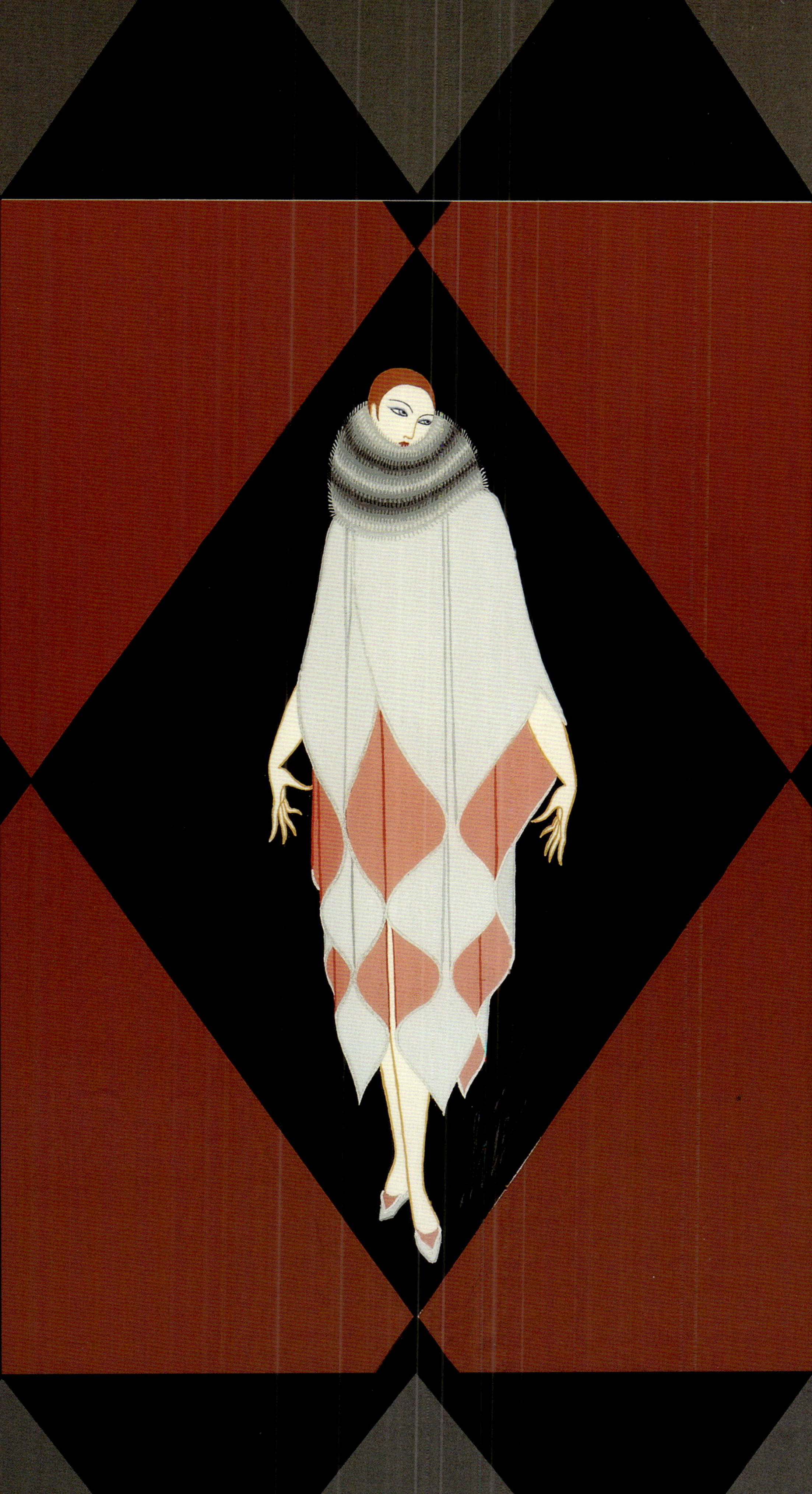

Vreeland (1903–89), working at *Harper's Bazaar* under Carmel Snow from 1936, and later moving to edit American *Vogue*. This explains why Erté's aspirational fashion costumes, loosely based on current trends, were considered to be from a bygone era.

1931: COLONIAL EXHIBITION, PARIS

At a time when America was recovering from the economic downtown created by the Wall Street Crash, Europe was only a few years away from the Second World War. The Colonial Exhibition of May–October 1931 in Paris highlighted French colonial power as trustworthy and dependable. Thousands visited. There were large-scale mock-ups of African, Arab, Asian and Polynesian buildings. Within the buildings indigenous people from each nation demonstrated their local crafts and traditions. Erté loved it and visited it often for days at a time. One exhibit struck him more than others, a mock-up of a temple at Angkor Wat, Cambodia (the largest religious temple in the world). In 1922 this temple had been his inspiration for the sets and costumes for the ballet *The Treasures of Indo-China*. Its opening performance was held at the Alcazar Theatre, Marseilles, a suitably colonial-style French port town in the south of France. From there it toured throughout Europe and the USA.

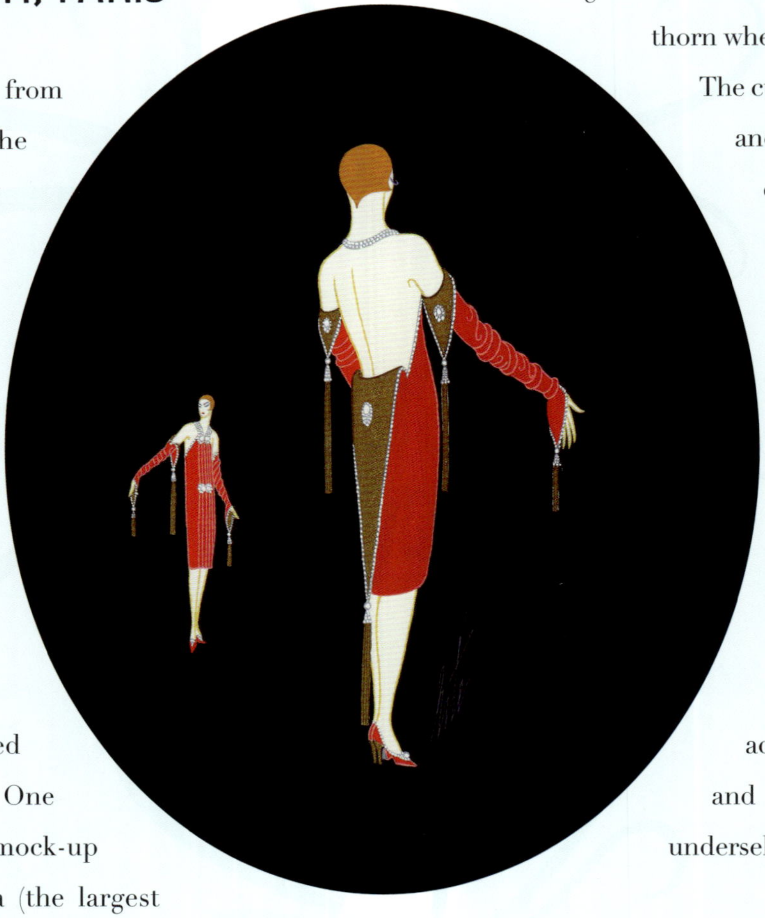

DEATH OF PRINCE NICOLAS

An unfortunate accident in spring 1933 resulted in the loss of Erté's closest friend, companion and business partner, Prince Nicolas Ouroussoff, his distant cousin whom he had met in 1914. At their house on the outskirts of Paris a young and inexperienced gardener had been engaged. Nicolas was pricked by a thorn when showing him how to prune their roses. The cut became infected, septicaemia took hold and Nicolas was taken to a Paris clinic. His condition worsened. Erté stayed with him during this critical period, putting an extra bed in the private room so that he could stay with him all the time. After 15 days the infection had spread throughout his body. Nicolas died on 4 April 1933, with Erté at his bedside. His death had a traumatic effect on Erté. His partner had been both his companion in life and in business for 25 years. Without business acumen, Erté found himself in debt, and worse, making poor business deals underselling his value.

PARIS UNDER OCCUPATION

When Paris was declared an 'open city' on 14 June 1940, following the outbreak of the Second World War, Erté had intended to leave it for a safer location. However, his mother,

(Previous, left) **Manhattan Mary II**, *1979, lithograph/serigraph, 59.4 x 43 cm (23⅜ x 16⅞ in)*
(Previous, right) **Manhattan Mary IV**, *1989, embossed serigraph, 69.9 x 50.8 cm (27½ x 20)*

(Above and right) **Costume designs for Manhattan Mary**, *1927, gouache, approx. 65 x 45 cm (25½ x 17¾ in)*

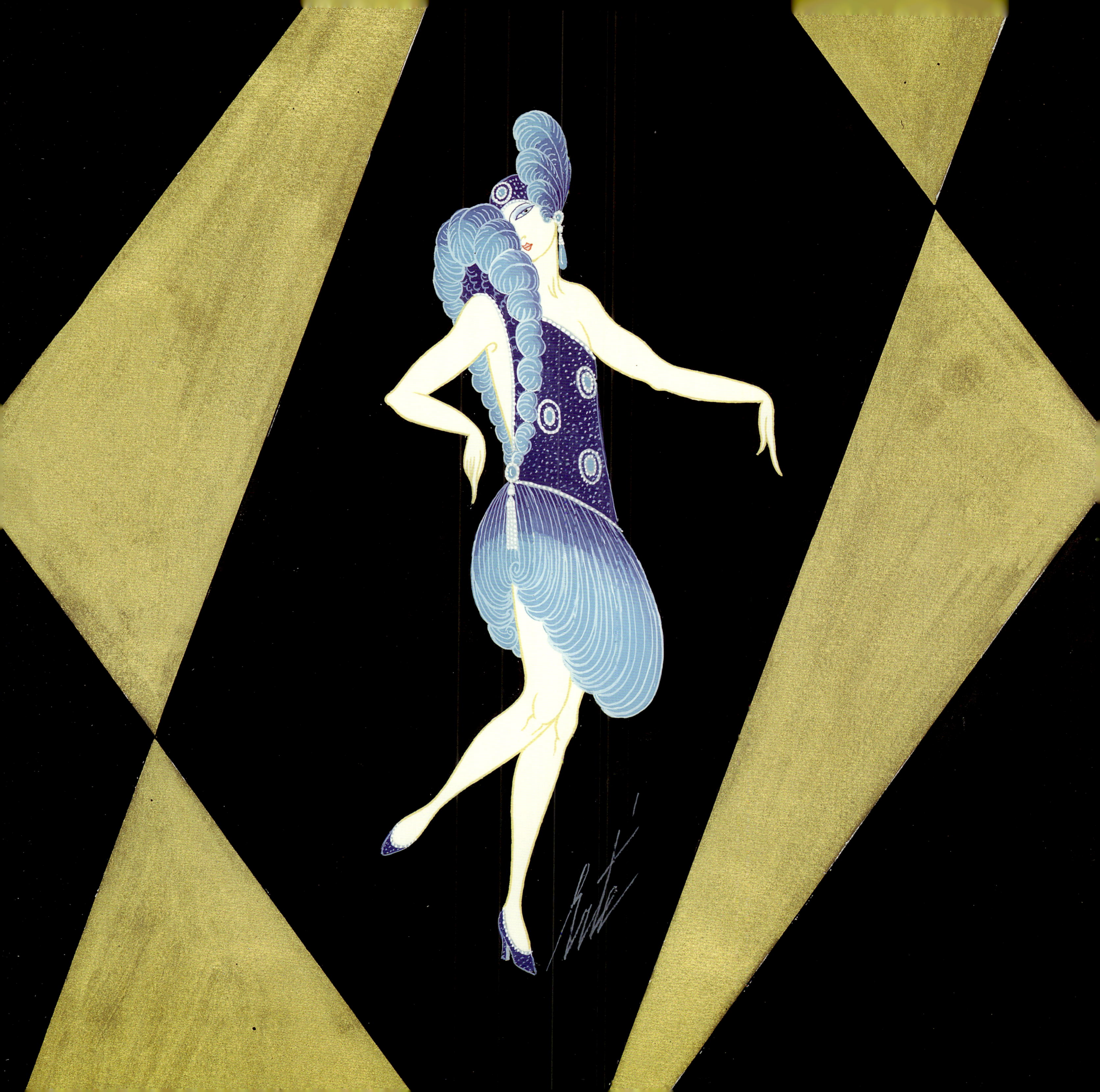

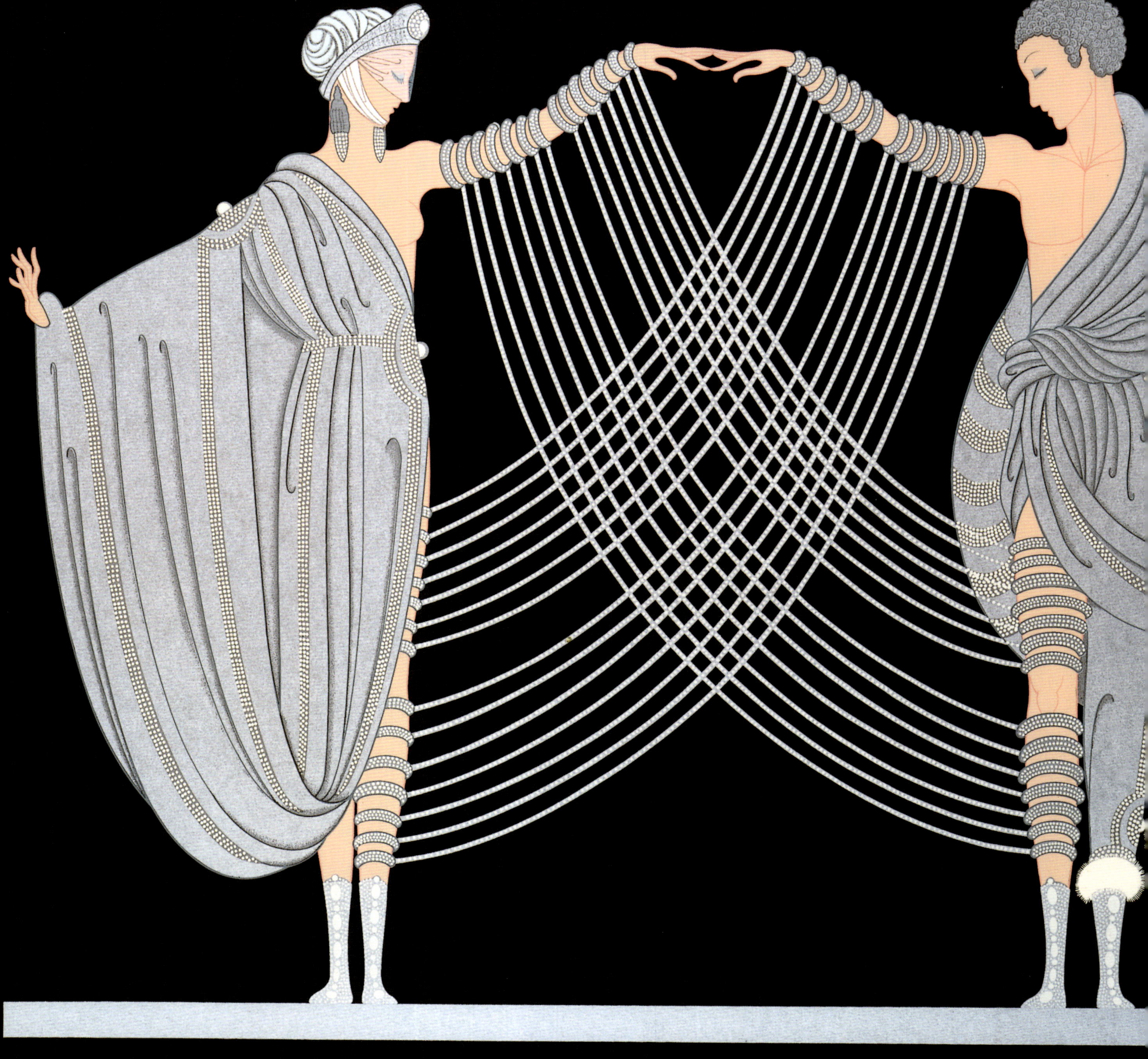

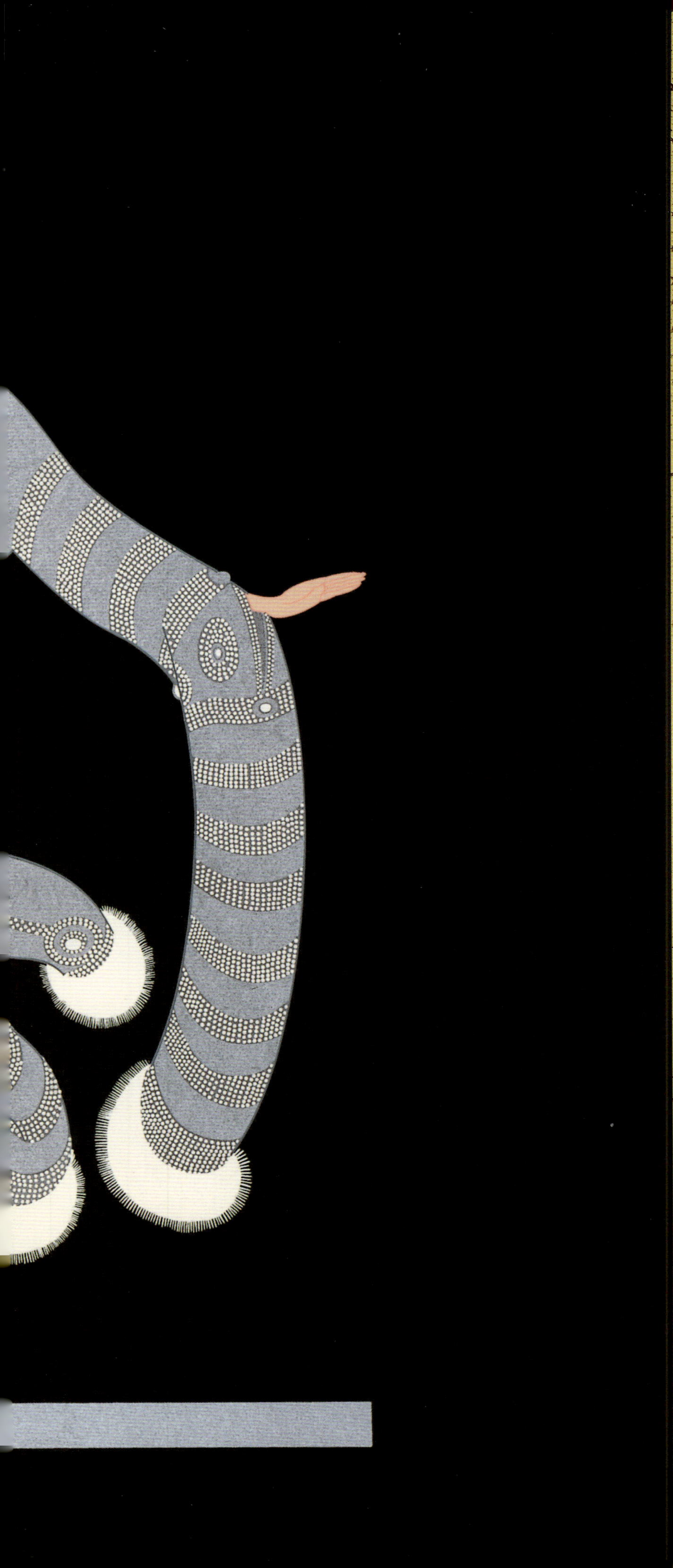

unable to move from her Paris nursing home in Boulogne-sur-Seine, meant his plans had to change, and he stayed. Erté described only German cars on the city streets while Parisians used their bicycles, bicycle-taxis (cycles with sidecars) or the Metro. He remembered the long queues for food, and everything in short supply. He recalled women wearing 'platform sandals', wooden shoes with wooden platform soles, and large 'cloth-draped' hats and short skirts. Surprisingly, perhaps, all the couturiers with the exception of Chanel, who closed her fashion house for the duration of the war, remained open for business. Entertainment venues at first closed, then gradually re-opened, as the German occupiers wanted a 'Gay-Paree'. Erté was permanently in work. He designed sets and costumes for *Phi-phi* at the re-opened Théâtre de Bouffes Parisiens (*see* page 89). The costume for Madame Phidias would be the model for ballets at the Lido, and for *Dans Notre Miroir* at the re-opened Bal Tabarin, and later for an Erté bronze sculpture *Tanagra* (1988, *see* page 90), a limited edition of 500. He worked on operettas at the Theatre Marigny, and at the Apollo, the Théâtre des Capucines and the Théâtre des Nouveautés. However, Erté had to make do without his excellent business partner, the costumier Max Weldy, who had left Paris in late 1940, taking up residence in America in January 1941.

COFFEE FOR CONTRACTS

With little to eat – Erté's regular diet included swedes and turnips, like the rest of occupied Paris – and his small weekly meat ration given to his adored cat Micmac, he, like others, survived on a meagre diet. Occasional dinner parties held by his

Marriage Dance, *1984, embossed serigraph with foil stamping, 73.7 x 86.4 cm (29 x 34 in)*

friend, the couturier Germaine Bruel, were exceptions, where wonderful food was served. He never asked from where it was obtained. But Erté's one passion that he found hard to work without was the taste of real coffee. And so he made a deal with every show producer or theatre director who had access to it, that his show contracts included a good supply of fresh coffee. As Erté put it, things gradually got better in Paris, particularly through a black market network. And the city's cultural life flourished with ballets, exhibitions, opera, theatre and concerts. One of Erté's last commissions before the cessation of war was to design the window displays for the Grand Magasins Printemps department stores on a monthly basis. When the armistice was announced, Erté and two of his closest friends in Paris took a three-week celebratory cycling holiday.

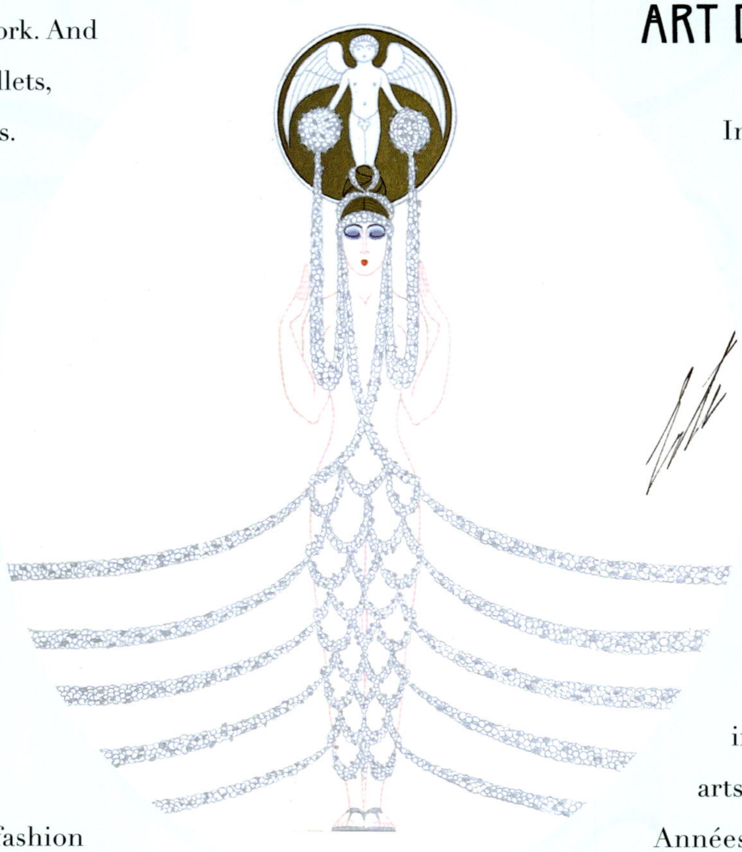

1940S–50S

One reads little about Erté and fashion illustration during the 1940s and 50s. His style of illustration had gone out of fashion, one could say from the moment his contract with *Harper's Bazaar* ceased, but his flair for theatrical costume and set design was in great demand across Europe, even through the years of the Second World War. Theatrical productions included operettas, opera, revues and musical comedies, ballets and television productions such as Rossini's *Il Barbiere de Siviglia* for French television in 1945. In England he designed several productions for the Opera House, Blackpool, for pantomimes such as *Puss in Boots* at the London Palladium in 1949, and for productions at London's Victoria Palace and the Hippodrome.

ART DÉCORATIF REVIVAL

In the 1950s a revival of interest in the architecture and decorative arts of Art Décoratif of the 1920s–30s first appeared in novels. The first time the term 'Art Deco' appeared in print in English was in *The Times* on 2 November 1966, in a news feature written by Hilary Gelson. She wrote about the 'nostalgic return to the design trends of the Twenties'. Her article was titled *Art Deco* and related to a revival of interest in 1920s fashion and decorative arts, instigated by an exhibition 'Les Années 25' in the Pavillon de Marsan at the Musée des Arts Décoratif in Paris, which looked back to the Art Décoratif era of the 1920s. Erté's work played a commensurable part in that exhibition. He took part after the encouragement of a friend Jacques Damase (b. 1930). The catalogue of the exhibition had the subtitle 'Art Deco'. Further references to *Les Arts Deco* appeared in French publications. Consolidating this trend, the English

Triple costume design (centre) for 'Marriage' in Les Mariages, *George White's 'Scandals', New York, 1924, gouache, 39.1 x 29 cm (153⁄8 x 113⁄8 in)*

Triple costume design (centre) for 'Golden Wedding' in Les Mariages, *George White's 'Scandals', New York, 1924, gouache, 38.7 x 28.5 cm (15¼ x 111/8 in)*

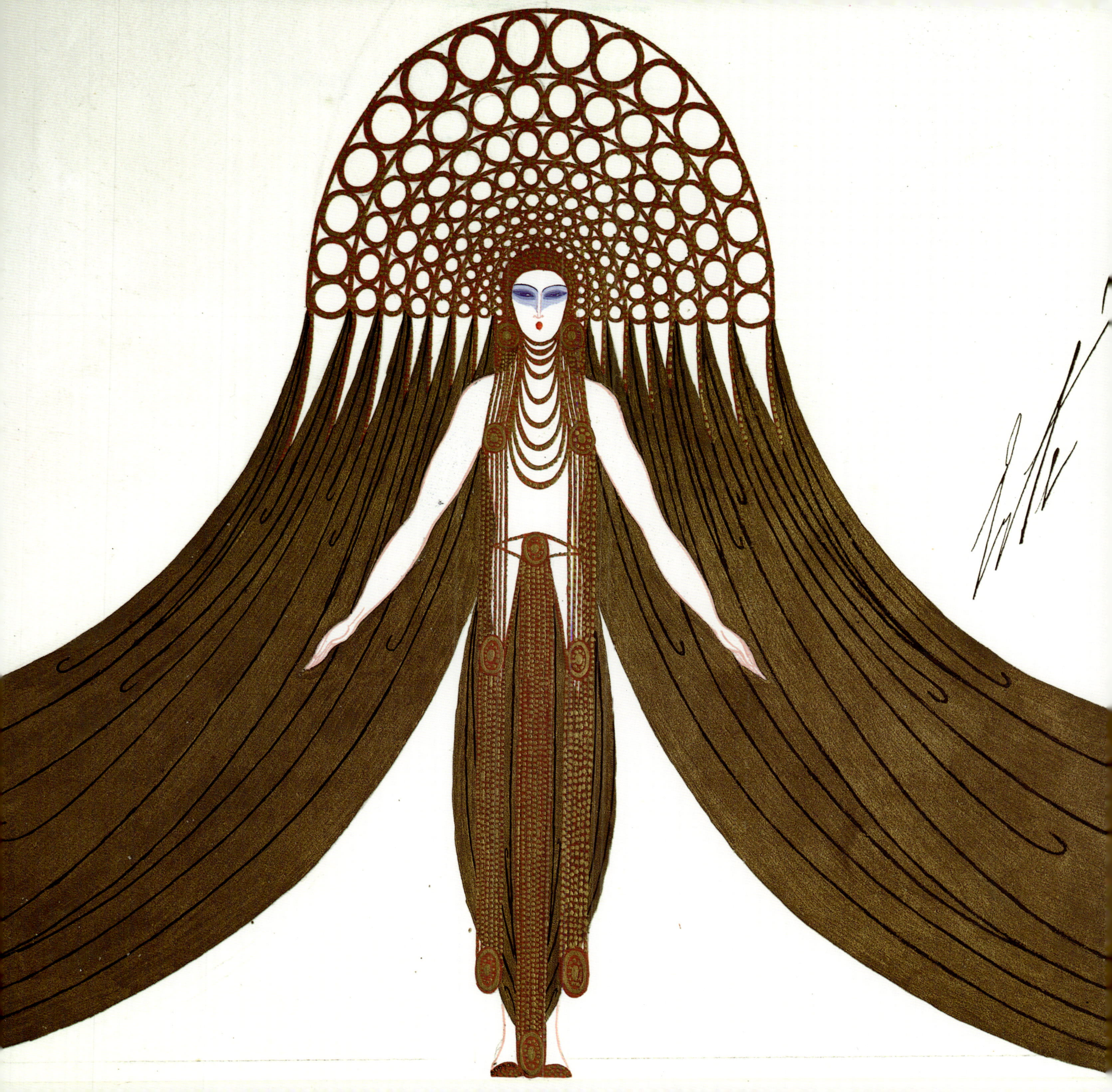

writer Bevis Hillier (b. 1940) published *Art Deco of the 20s and 30s*, in 1968. He analysed what the style was, its history and the new revival.

ERTÉ ON ART DÉCORATIF FASHION

Erté visited the 'Exhibition of 1925' at the Pavillon de Marsan, Paris, in 1966. He was struck by the contrast of fashion dress on display that purported to represent the Twenties era. As he put it, he was surprised by the 'misleading anachronism in the design of the wooden mannequins', more nineteenth to early twentieth century in shape. They were dressed in clothes created by the top couturiers of the Art Décoratif period but the silhouette looked wrong: 'The shape of all these figures was that … the bust slanted forward, the bottom backward.' It changed the shape of the original designs, making the clothes look quite different to the way the dresses were actually worn in the Twenties.

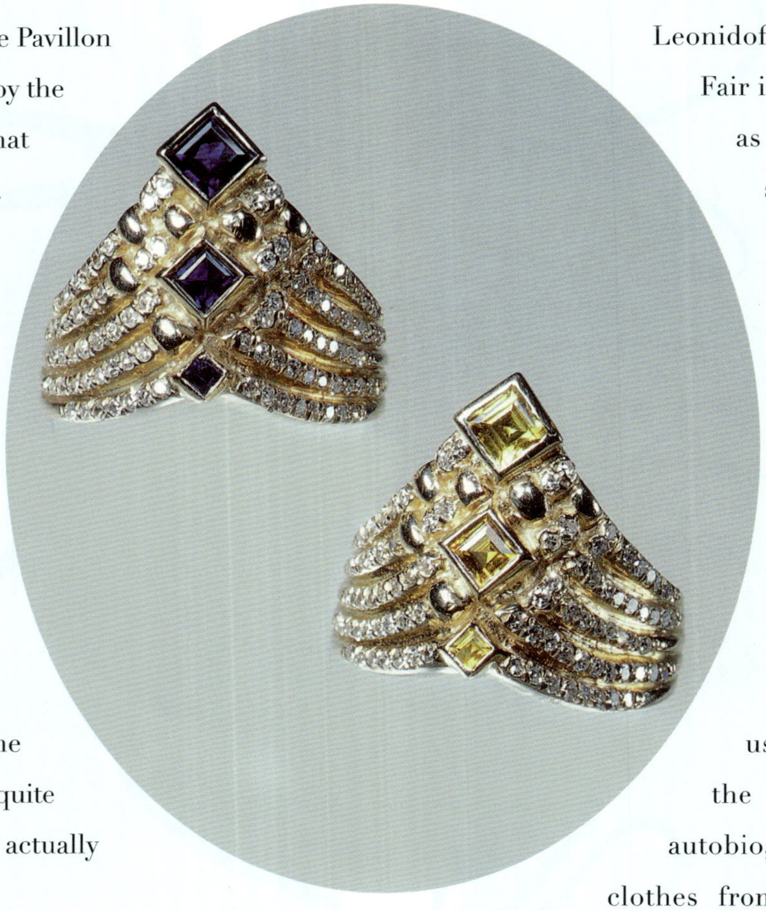

EXPO '67, MONTREAL

From 11–30 July 1967 the major entertainment at Expo '67 in Montreal, Canada was a musical revue 'Flying Colors', devised and produced by Romanian-born American Leon Leonidoff (1894–1989), founder of the Isbe Russe Ballet Company, and producer of hundreds of spectaculars at Radio City Hall, New York. Erté was commissioned to design the sets and costumes. 'Flying Colors' starred the veteran French actor, entertainer and singer Maurice Chevalier. Erté had first met Chevalier in 1918, and previously worked with Leonidoff on *Wonderworld*, at the 1964 World's Fair in New York. 'Flying Colors' was billed as the 'largest of all Stadium spectaculars', seating 25,000 people. Erté was the right man for spectacular sets and costumes but the budget did not match his ideas for the show. The original proposal to have the modern dresses made in Paris by his friend, the French couturier Pierre Balmain (1914–82), fizzled out. The small budget meant the stars' costumes were made in New York with Erté using ready-made rented costumes for the rest of the cast. In his 1975 autobiography he mentions hunting through clothes from Hollywood rental studios. When the director of one supplier asked, 'Is he the real Erté', it was the 'last straw' for him. Curiously, this Expo show would put the spotlight back on Erté. His name had largely been forgotten but today design historians categorize the Montreal Expo '67 show as the beginning of the revival of interest in Erté.

Douceur *rings, c. 1979–90, left: gold, diamonds, blue sapphires; right: gold, diamonds, yellow sapphires*
Erté wrote that he was aware of Byzantine art as a child in St Petersburg and stated that Persian/Byzantine art was a major influence on his work – such as the turban motif in these rings.

Byzantine, *1985, embossed serigraph with foil stamping, 88.9 x 64.8 cm (35 x 25½ in)*
This serigraph was inspired by the 1929 gouache costume design for Mélissinde in *La Princesse Lointaine*.

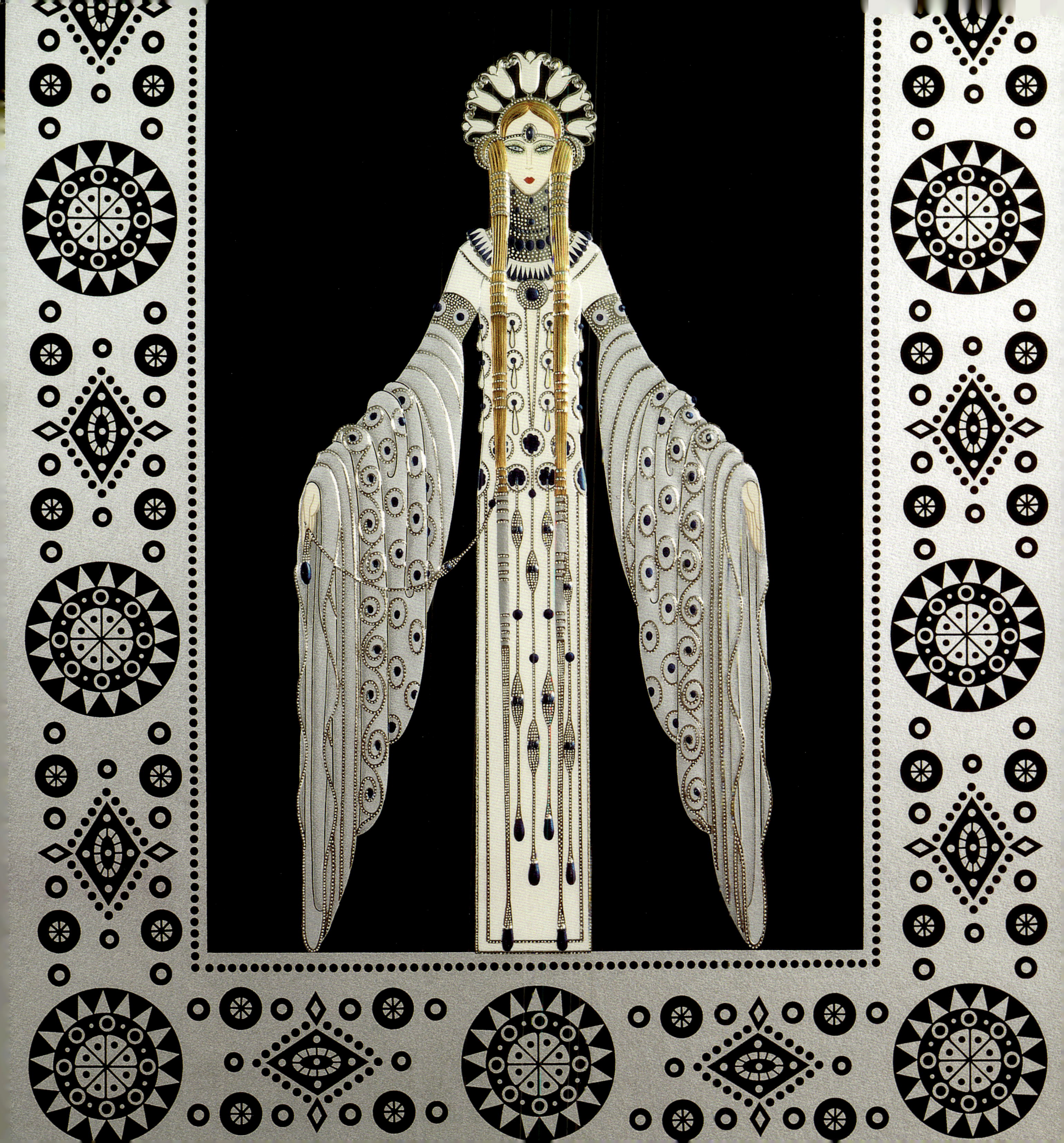

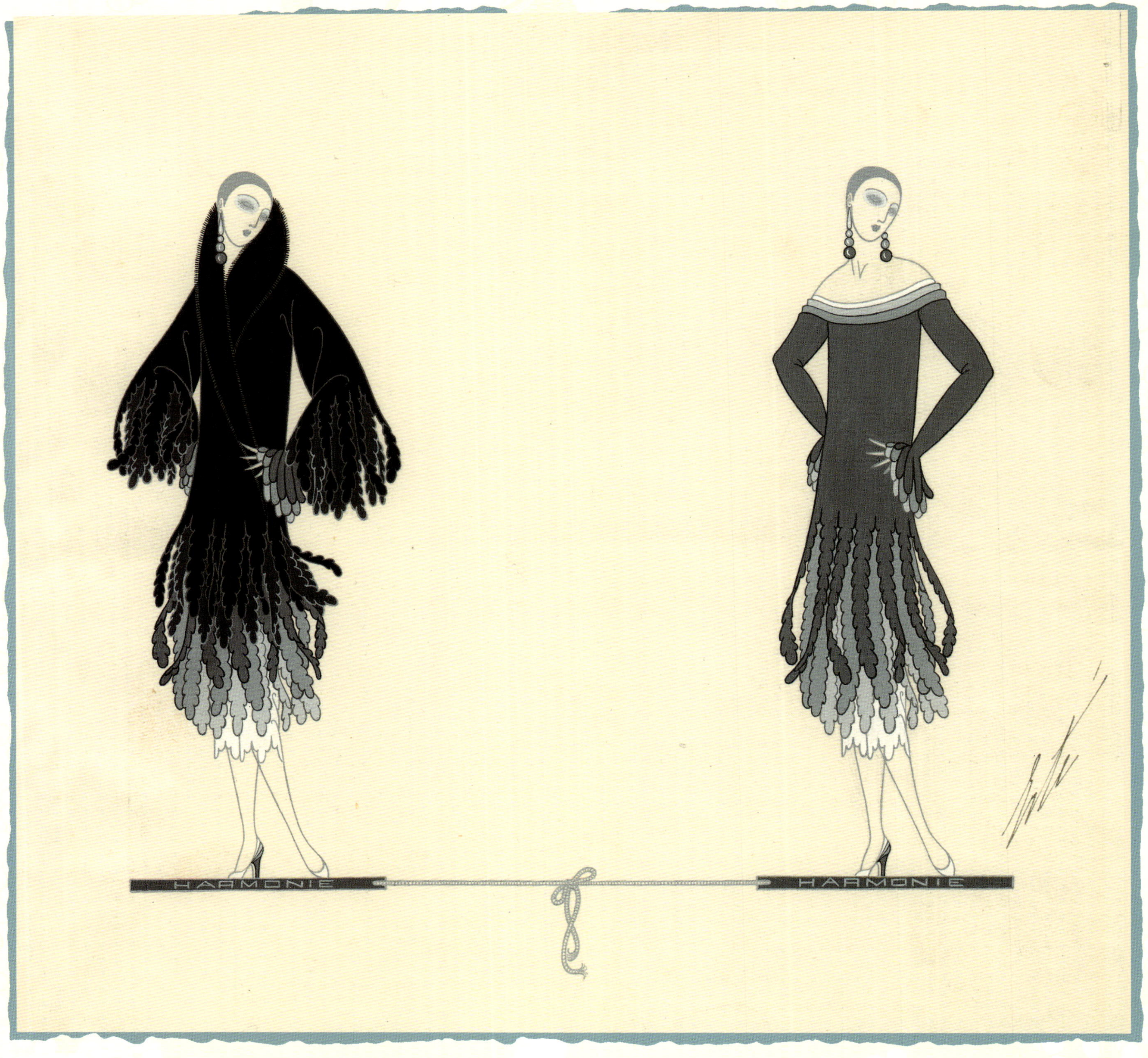

2 Harmonie, 5 et 6, *1926, pen and ink, 34.5 x 24.8cm (13½ x 9¾ in)*

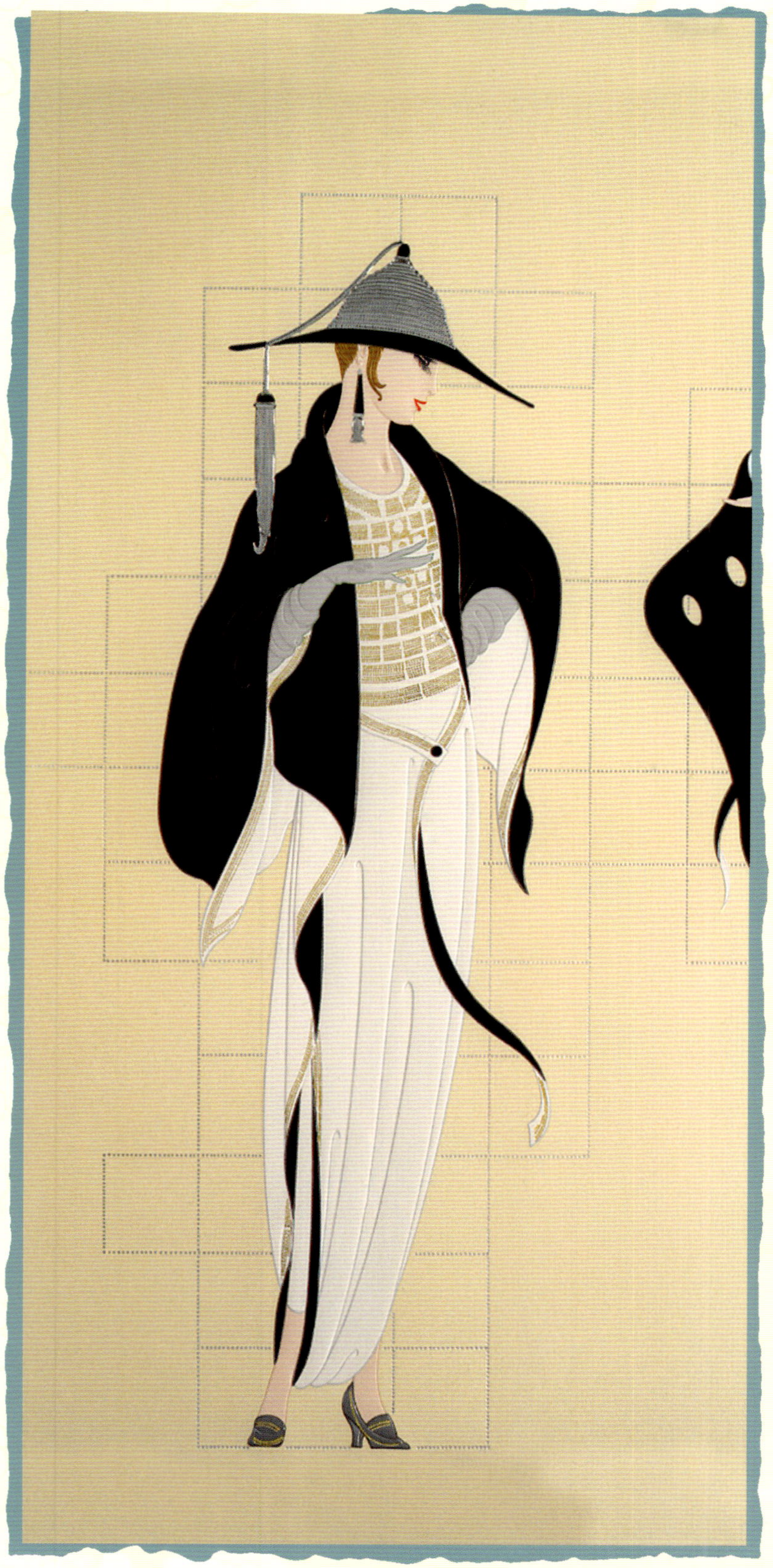

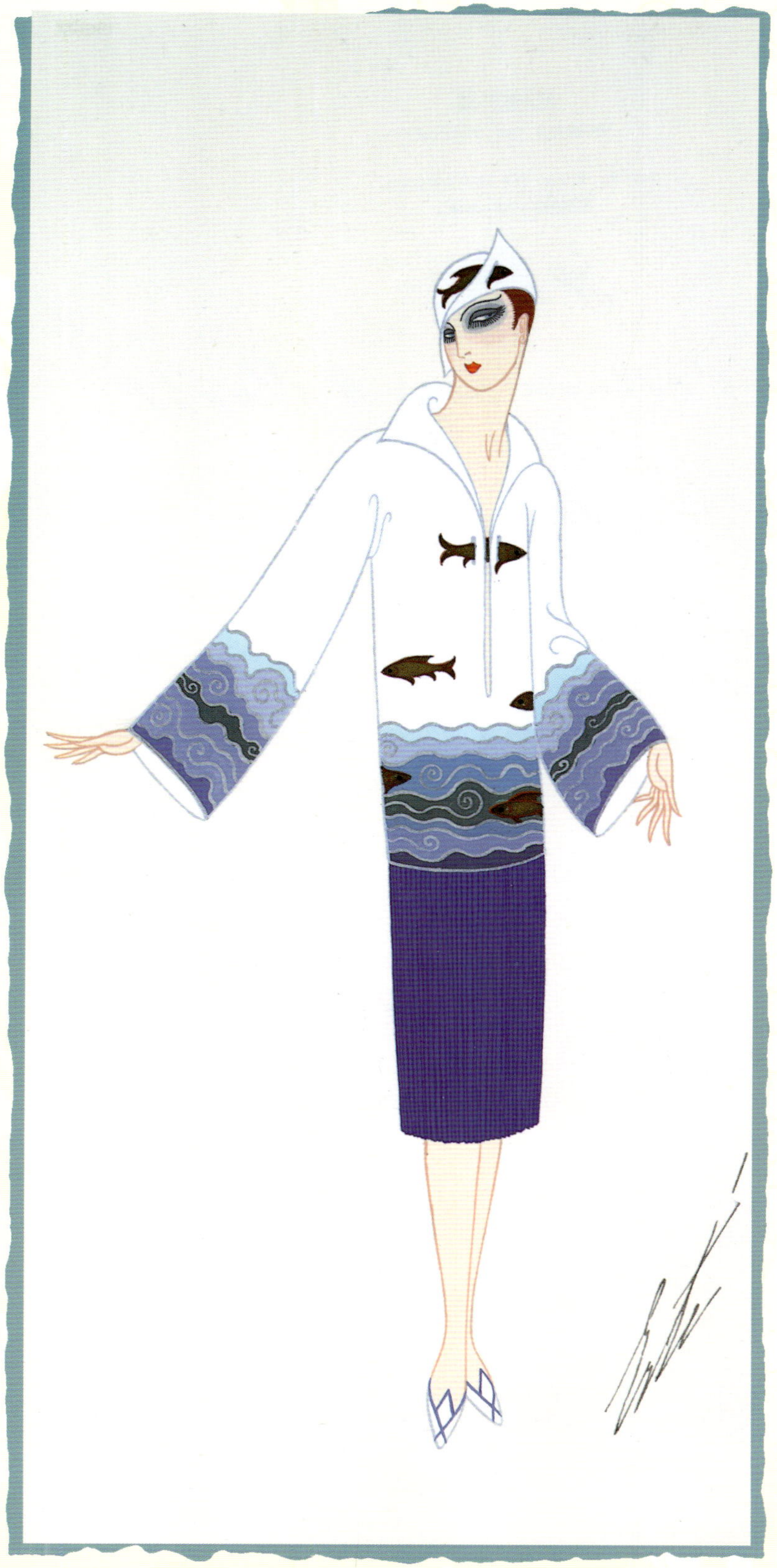

Haute Couture, *1987, serigraph, 96 x 70 cm (37¾ x 27½ in)*

Design for Davidow, *New York, 1928, gouache, 38.7 x 28.6 cm (15¼ x 11¼ in)*
Erté's sense of fun is evident in this fashionable dress in white, blue and green. The wide border at the hip and on the sleeves echoes seawater waves, and colourful fish swim through the design. Erté later used fish in his jewellery designs.

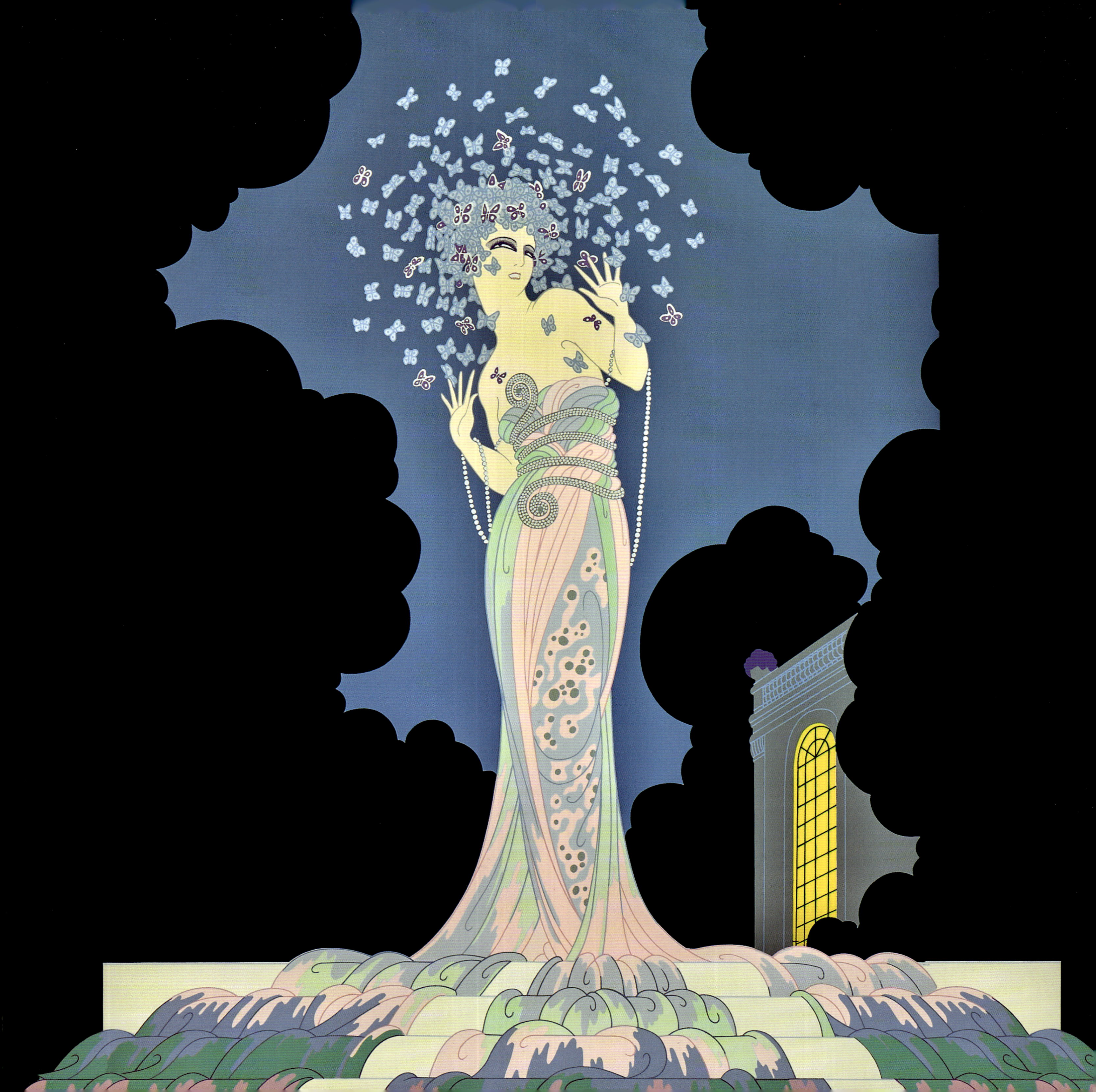

TECHNIQUES

Erté's earliest technique was his use of pen and Indian ink, or predominantly gouache (often including metallic pigments), to create illustrations and fashion designs, for Paul Poiret's studio in Paris, or editors of New York's *Harper's Bazaar*. In addition, he created costume and set designs for revues, plays, operas and films in the same media. Years later, from the 1970s, a revival of interest in his works of the late 1960s led to him appraising them anew, going back to an earlier image and exploring its characteristics in a different medium; he learned new skills to create a series of limited edition lithographs, serigraphs (more usually known as 'screen printing' or 'silkscreen printing'), bronze sculptures and jewellery based on his original works. In the later intervening years Erté also experimented with more abstract forms of sculpture, with his 'Formes Picturales'.

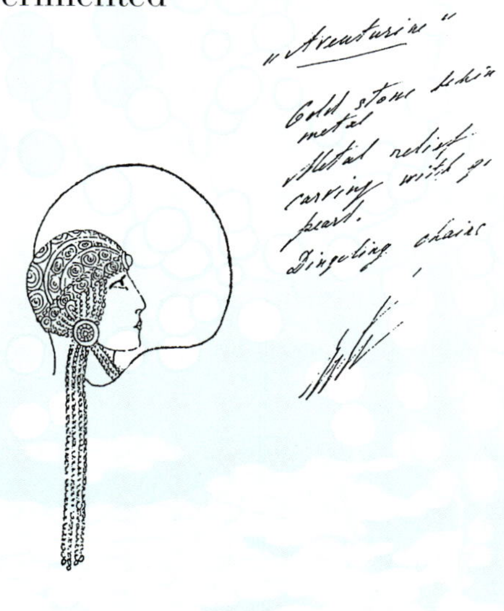

SOLITUDE

For Erté, life was always full, particularly when working. He had his method of controlling each place he worked, from the design of the room to the situation of his desk and chair. He always insisted on solitude – no one could watch him at work, except his cat (or cats). In the background, classical music would be playing, perhaps Bach or Mozart, Ravel or Schumann. He particularly loved working late into the night, 'I have always loved working at night. No one interrupts me. No telephone calls disturb my train of thought. I feel I have unlimited time. One bright lamp (its bluish light helps me to see the true colours), illuminates the drawing on which I am working.'

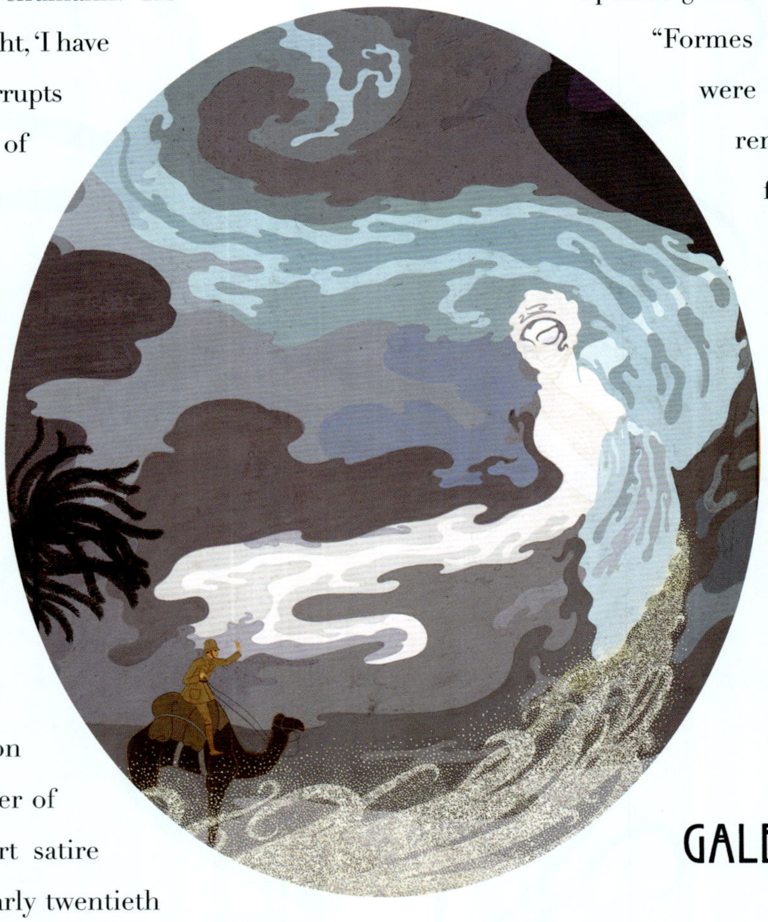

ERMYNTRUDE AND ESMERELDA

In 1968 Erté was approached to create illustrations for a novella *Ermyntrude and Esmerelda*, written in 1913 by Lytton Strachey (1880–1932), a founder member of the Bloomsbury Group. It was a short satire highlighting the sexual taboos of the early twentieth century. It took the form of a conversation by letter between two 17-year-old girls using synonyms to describe making love and having babies. Strachey had written it for the entertainment of his close circle of friends. Erté created 17 two-tone illustrations for the book's first edition, published in 1969 by Stein and Day, and more for a 250 limited edition publication.

FORMES PICTURALES

From an idea Erté formed whilst half-asleep, sunbathing on a beach in Majorca in 1960, his unique three-dimensional sculptures *Formes Picturales* ('pictorial forms') were created. He said he had 'a sudden vision of a strange shape composed of sparkling shimmering colours. This was the birth of my "Formes Picturales".' The sculpture-paintings were created by Erté in cardboard then remodelled in metal by a blacksmith and finally coated by Erté in thick oils. He used a variety of materials including wood, wood roots, iron, copper and duraluminium, and pieces of coloured glass and enamel on copper. These are extraordinary pieces. He explained the concept as 'not completely abstract; they express a thought, an emotion, a mood or a natural element' (*Erté: Things I Remember*, 1975).

GALERIE ROR VOLMAR, PARIS

When 20 *Formes Picturales* were completed (1960–64), Erté's thoughts turned to exhibiting the sculptures under a different name, to free up any expectation associated with his illustrative work. As he put it, artists tended to be pigeon-holed into a particular type of work. At 70 years of age he wanted to be like a young artist starting a new venture. His friends disagreed and

(Previous page) **Fantasia**, *1982, serigraph, 83,8 x 63.5 cm (33 x 25 in)*
(Above) **Armide ou Le Mirage**, *1917, gouache, 29.5 x 40.6 cm (11½ x 16 in)*

Sandstorm, *1985, serigraph, 19.7 x 52.7 cm (7¾ x 20¾ in)*

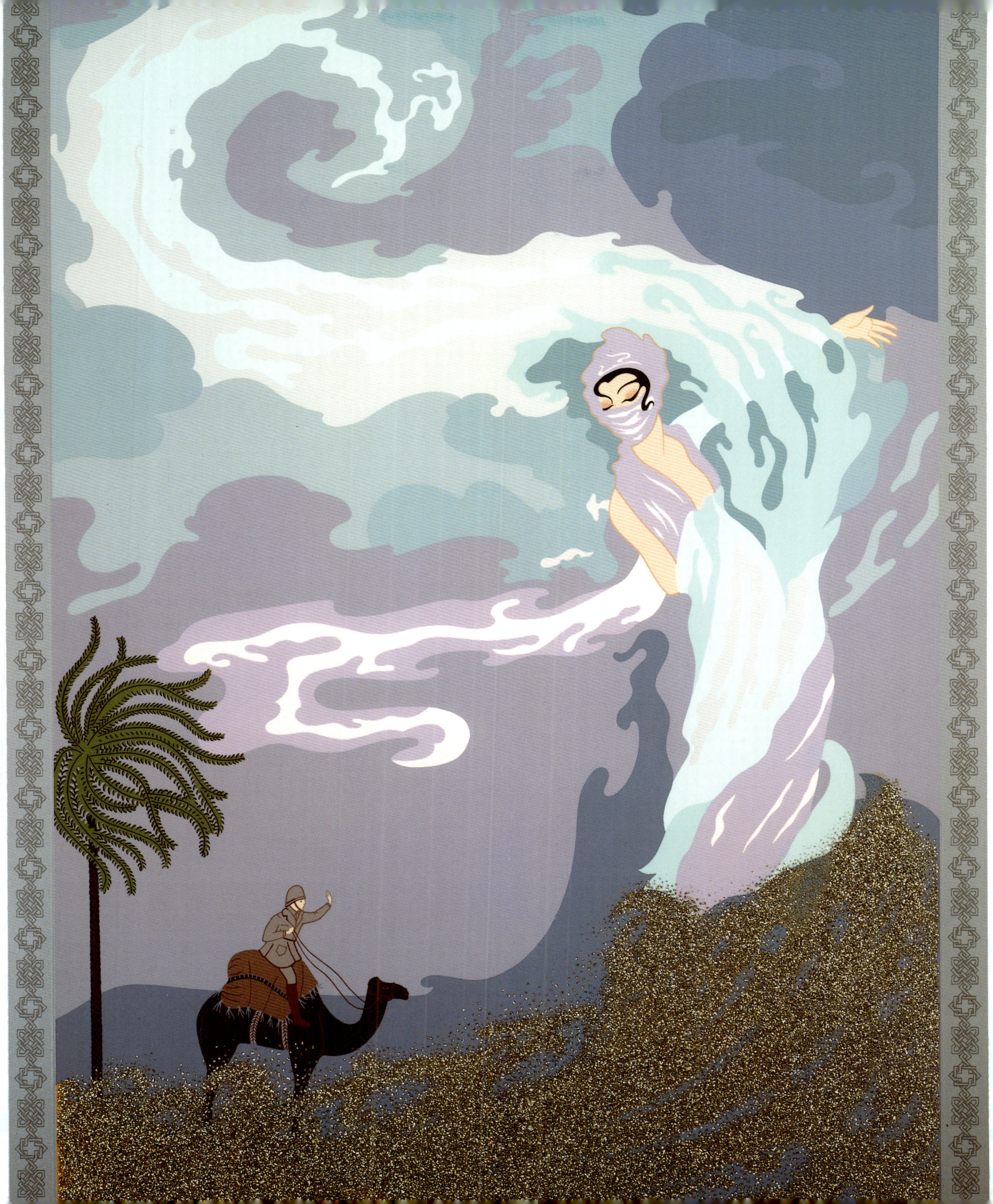

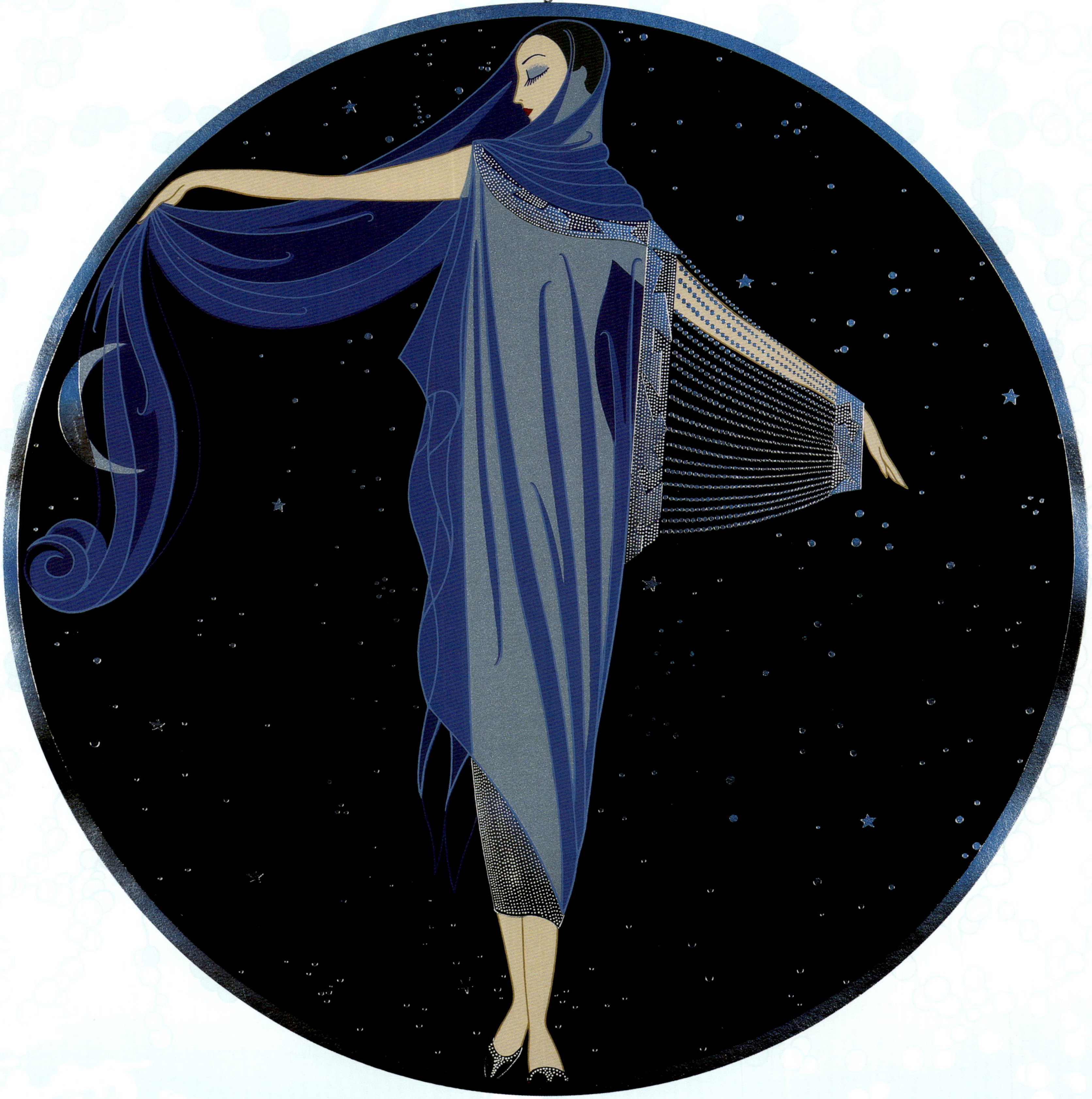

persuaded him to exhibit under his own name. He later stated that he regretted taking their advice. His *Formes Picturales* were exhibited at Galerie Ror Volmar, Paris in February 1964 under Erté's name, with favourable reviews. Later, from 1979, he returned to his sculptural shapes and utilized them for a series of jewellery pieces, such as the exquisite *Ombre et Lumière* brooches, in silver, with blue sapphires, amethysts, rhodolite garnets and mother of pearl; miniature echoes of the *Ombre et Lumière* (1964/65), *Formes Picturales* in copper, glass, stained glass and lacquer.

ERIC ESTORICK

The American-born New Yorker Eric Estorick (1913–93), a wealthy art collector and owner of the Grosvenor Gallery – the largest art gallery in London – renewed Erté's career in the late 1960s, introducing him to new audiences around the world. Eric and his wife Salome ('Sal') became Erté's exclusive world agents through their company Sevenarts Limited, securing, it is said, $100 million per annum. Erté's work was exhibited globally through the Grosvenor Gallery. Eric, Salome, and their son and daughter became family to him. In his career Estorick had aimed to create an 'internationally minded art emporium'. He had travelled to Russia many times in the early 1960s to bring new art to Europe, most notably exhibiting 'Aspects of Russian Art' at his gallery. In 1967 Eric and his wife met Erté. The meeting dramatically changed Erté's fortunes as Estorick, in the capacity as Erté's agent, negotiated lucrative contracts for a series of lithographs, followed by serigraphs, limited edition jewellery and bronze sculpture editions. Erté, in good health and with an inimitable desire to learn new techniques, agreed to the work.

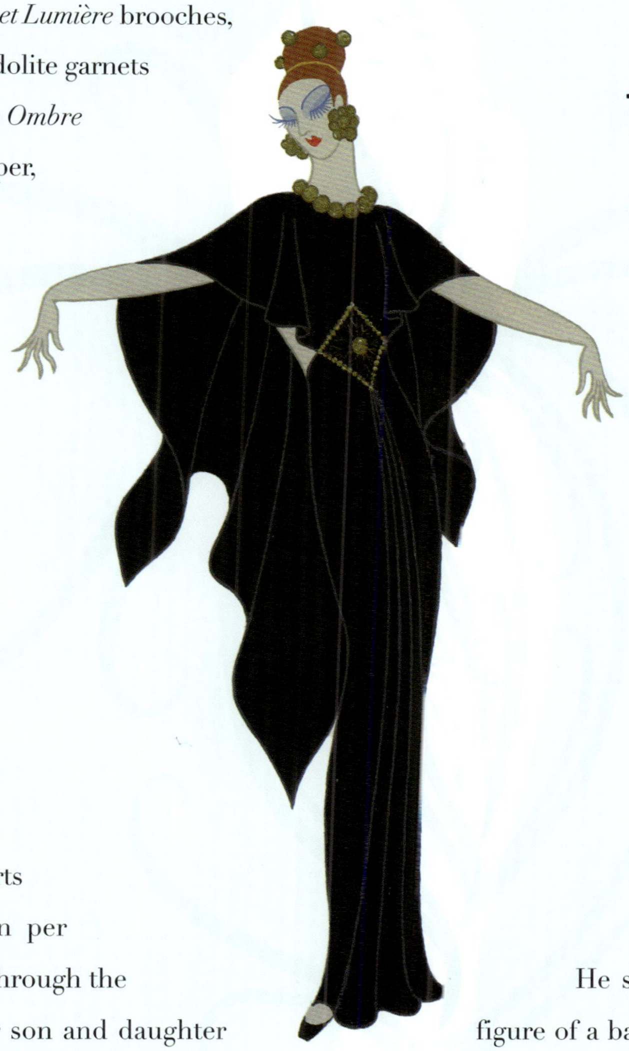

THE ALPHABET SERIES

The Alphabet series of 'human figure' letters was begun by Erté in 1927, in gouache, with each letter of the alphabet created from one or two figures of feminine feline forms. Erté stated that his first-ever series of alphabet drawings and paintings had actually been produced when he was a young child learning the alphabet but these are no longer extant. Eric and Salome Estorick wanted to show a complete *Alphabet* series at the Grosvenor Gallery in London. When Erté unwrapped his artworks, two letters were missing; he had neglected to make an 'L' or a 'Q'. He started work immediately. The 'L' was an exotic figure of a bare-breasted woman – nipples highlighted in red – wearing a revealing leopard-print costume. Her jewelled collar matched the collar of the sleek leopard lying at her feet (*see* page 186). 'L' became the most popular letter when the series took the form of limited edition lithographs (*see* pages 7, 185–87). The 'Q' was formed from the shape of the heads, bodies and tail feathers

Moonlight, *1984, serigraph with foil stamping, 49.8 x 50.8 cm (19½ x 20 in)*

Robe de Soir, *an evening dress for Norio Souzoke, 'Collection of Robes, Tokyo', 1975, gouache and metal paint, 37.5 x 27.3 cm (14¾ x 10¾ in)*
This timeless evening dress echoes Erté's luxurious evening-wear fashion designs from the 1920s.

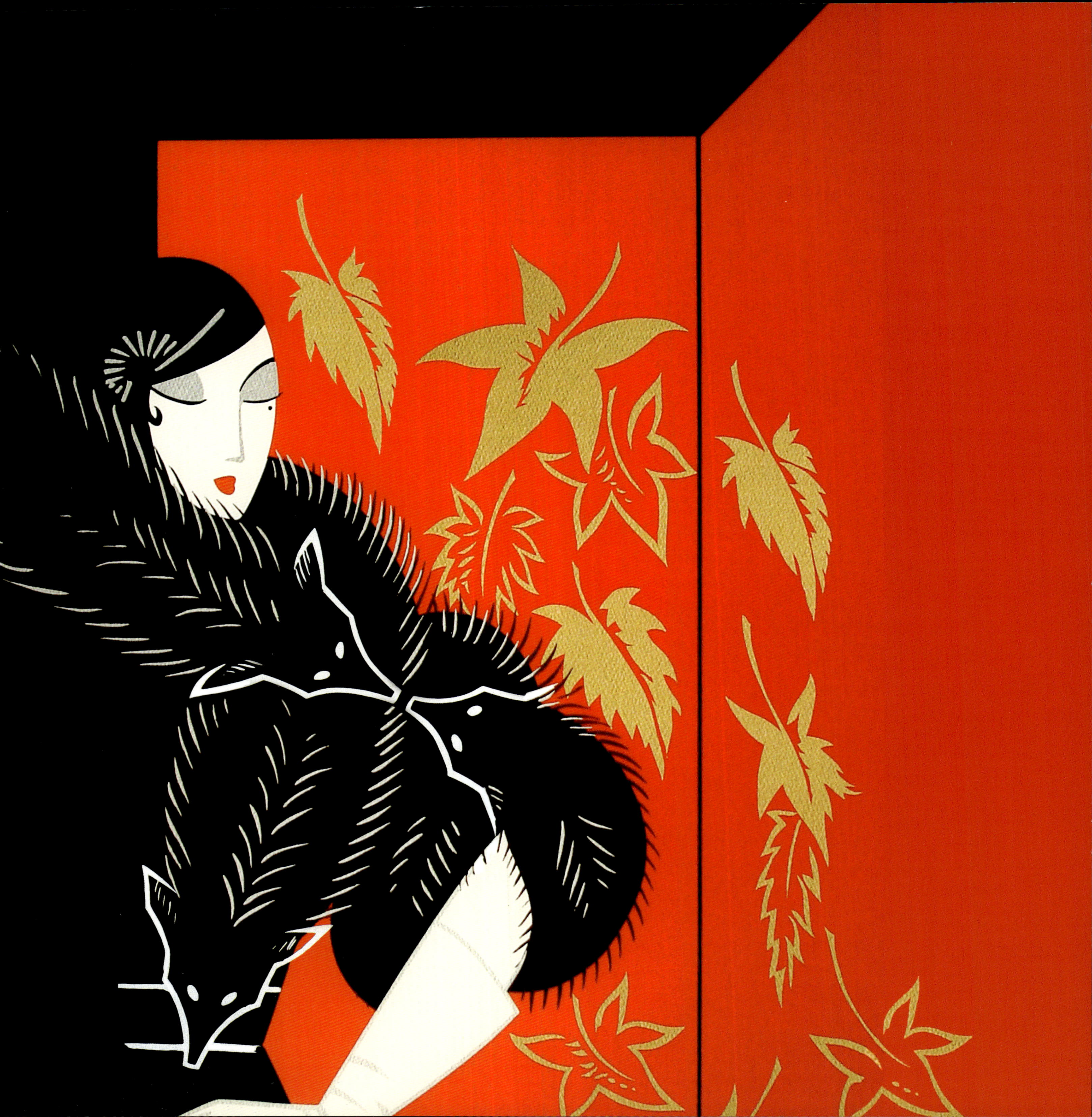

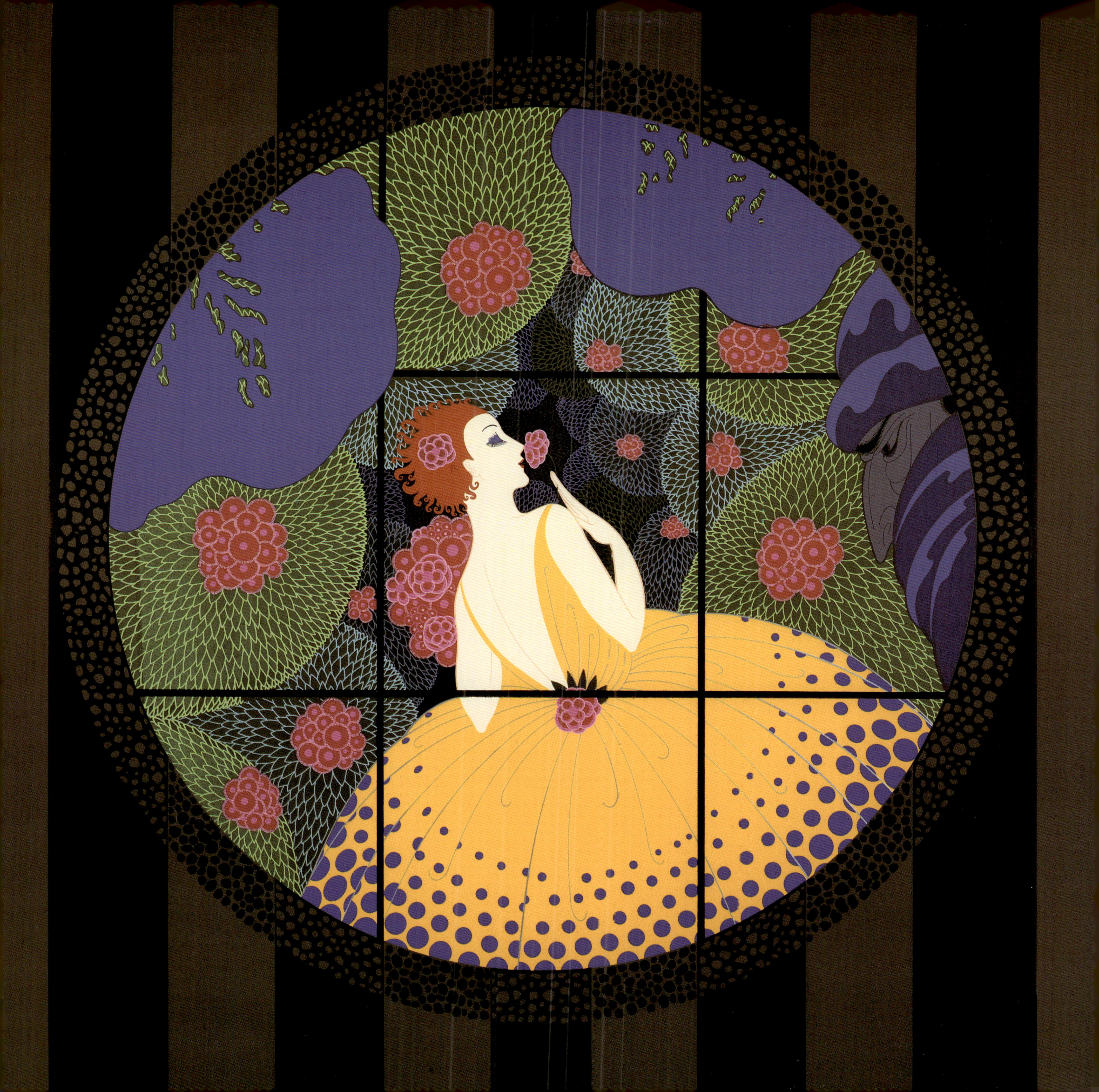

of two exotic birds (*see* page 186). At the centre was the outline of a figure that loosely resembled Leonardo da Vinci's *Vitruvian Man* (*c.* 1490). Of the letters, 'K' was slightly more risqué (*see* page 186), and raised attention when later produced as a bronze sculpture. One can see in the *Alphabet* letters, such as 'B', formed from a naked woman enwrapped by a sinuous snake, traces of Art Nouveau, particularly in the femme fatale's hair, and in 'J', 'K' and particularly 'P', more Art Nouveau than the short cropped modern bob associated with Art Deco. The letter 'Z' is informed by both decorative styles (*see* page 187). Erté commented that *The Alphabet* series was the most successful of all his works.

AN OUTSTANDING YEAR: 1968

The year began with a successful exhibition of Erté's work at the Neues Kunst-Zentrum Gallery in Hamburg, Germany in January 1968, arranged by Sal and Eric Estorick. Erté had last visited Hamburg with his mother in 1910. The newspaper *Die Welt* reported that 'Erté is the world's genius of presentation…. A master of pleasures for extravagant enjoyment.' This was followed by a retrospective in Chicago at the Sears-Vincent Gallery, also organized by the Grosvenor Gallery, and sponsored by the Chicago Opera House. For Erté the highlight of 1968 was in New York, at a substantial exhibition of his work at the Metropolitan Museum of Art. Two of its curators, John McKendry (d. 1975), and Polaire Weissmann, head of costume department, had purchased a complete collection of Erté's original illustrations – 179 works – the previous year, from the Grosvenor Gallery exhibition in New York, the first time, according to Erté, that any museum had bought a complete collection of an artist's work.

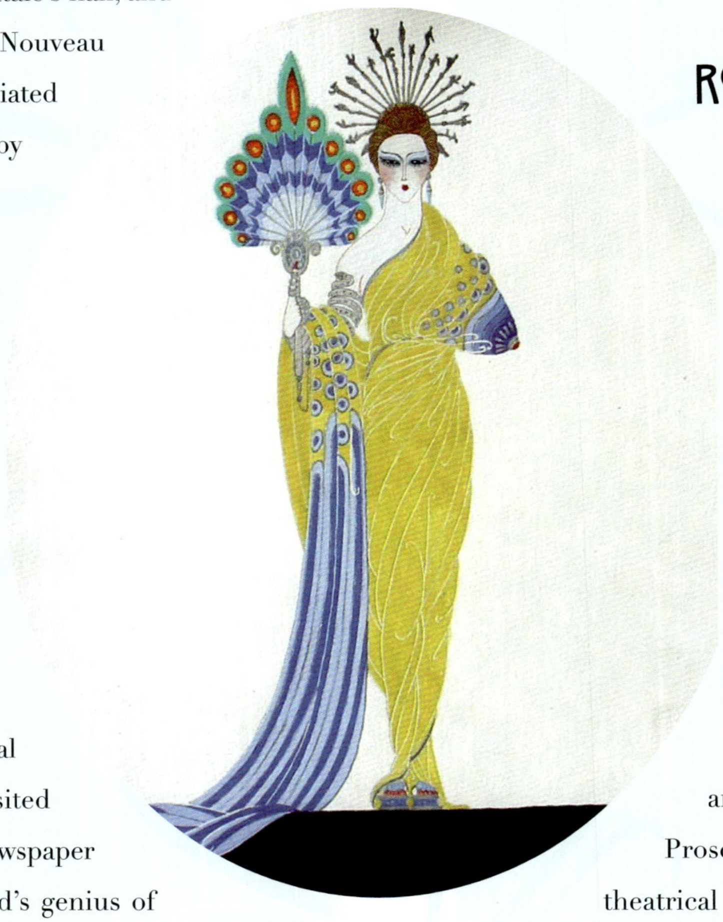

ROLAND BARTHES

The reaction to the Metropolitan Museum exhibition was far-reaching. An Italian publisher, Franco Maria Ricci, having seen the exhibition, wanted to publish a book on Erté. The book, one of a series *I segni dell uomo*, would be written by the French art critic and philosopher Roland Barthes (1915–80). It was published in Italian in 1971, followed by an English edition in 1972, and a French edition in 1973. To coincide with an exhibition of Erté's work at the Gallerie Proscénium, Paris – an art gallery focused on theatrical productions – and a French television programme about his life, an advance copy of Barthes' book was on display with text available to read. Erté was ecstatic about Barthes' summation. One extract read:

Before becoming well known artists must pass through a small mythological purgatory: it must be automatically possible to associate

(Previous, left) **Furs,** *1974, serigraph, 43.2 x 54.6 cm (17 x 21½ in)*
(Previous, right) **Winter Flowers**, *1983, serigraph, 83.8 x 73 cm (33 x 28¾ in)*
This is based on Erté's January 1921 *Harper's Bazaar* cover.

(Above) **Aphrodite**, *1920, gouache and metallic paint, 33 x 26.9 cm (13 x 10½ in)*
(Right) **Athena**, *1986, embossed serigraph with foil stamping, 88.9 x 66.8 cm (35 x 26¼ in)*
As you can see, strangely 'Aphrodite' becamce 'Athena' when she was translated into serigraph format; Erté's *Aphrodite* serigraph is altogether different (*see* page 96).

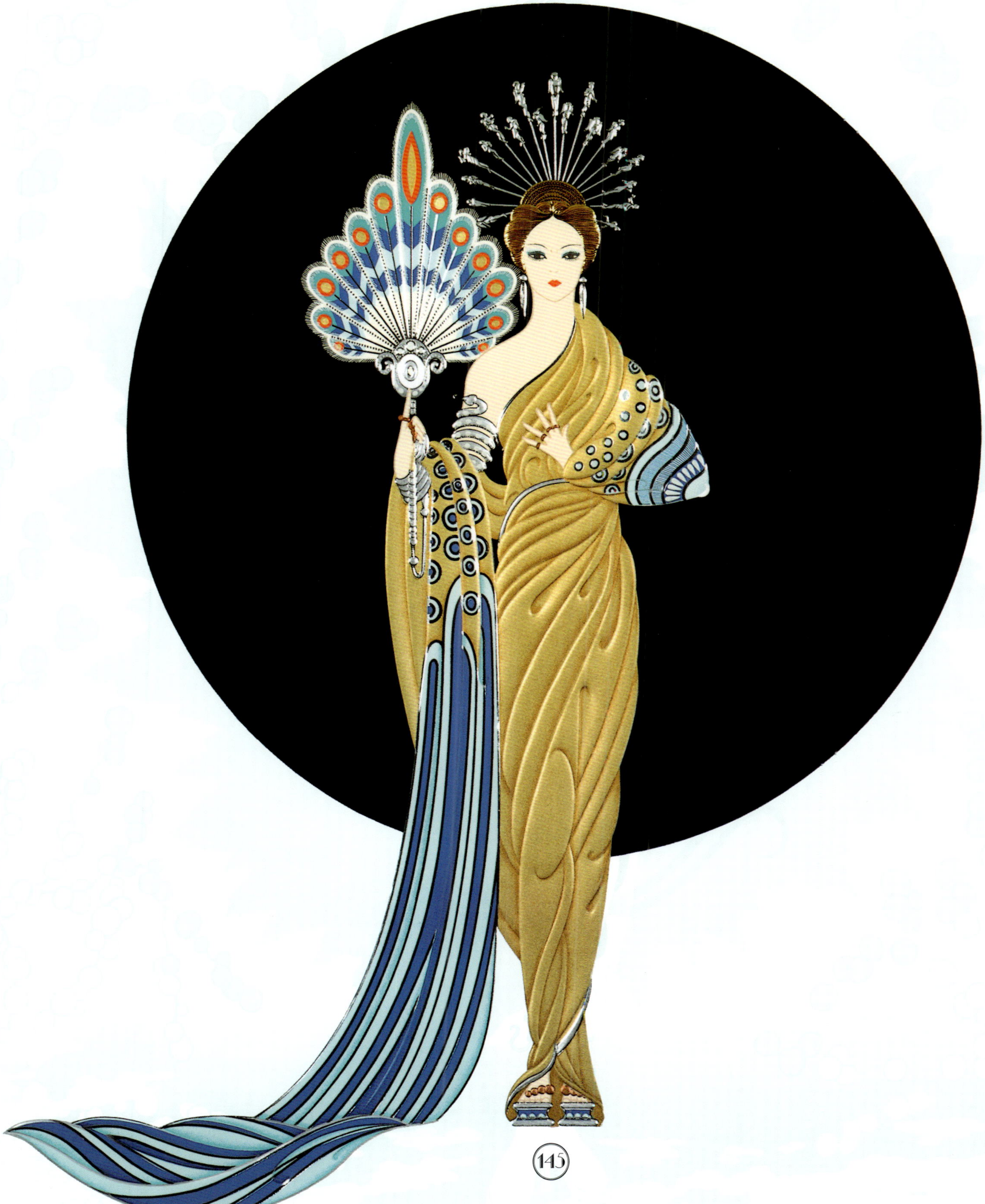

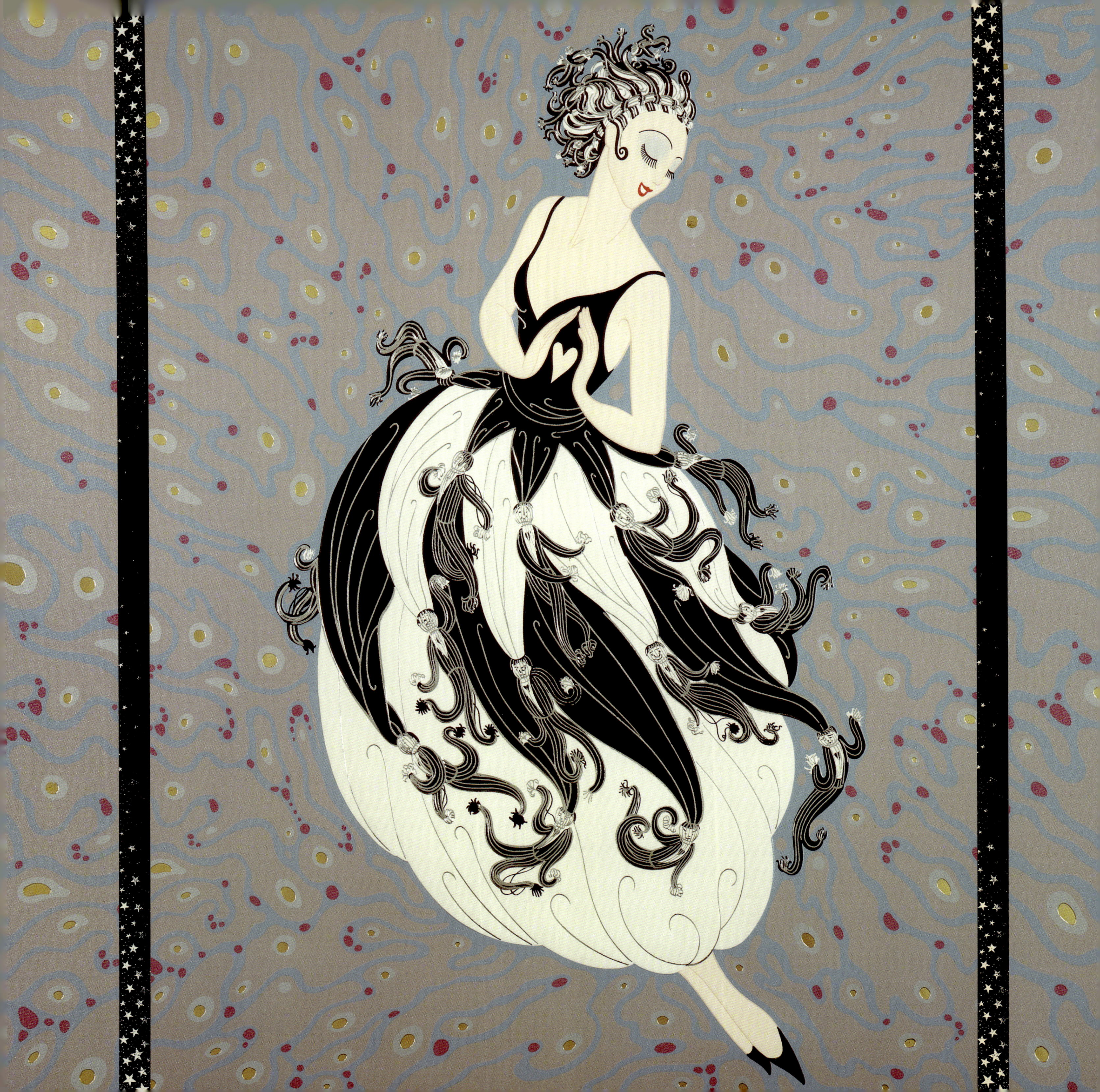

them with an object, a school, a fashion or an era of which they are, or so it is said, the precursors, the founders, the witnesses of the symbols; in a word it must be possible to categorize them without further effort.... Erté's purgatory is Woman.

A critic followed up on Barthes' text, observing that 'Erté exalts and magnifies Woman ... the heroine according to Erté, is a desirable object, fascinating, exacting and terribly frivolous.' Erté was delighted. In 1971 the book brought him a new audience of art lovers in Italy with many exhibitions from Milan at the beginning of the year to Parma and Palermo, Sicily, culminating in October in an exhibition in Rome at the Galleria Marino in the Piazza Navona.

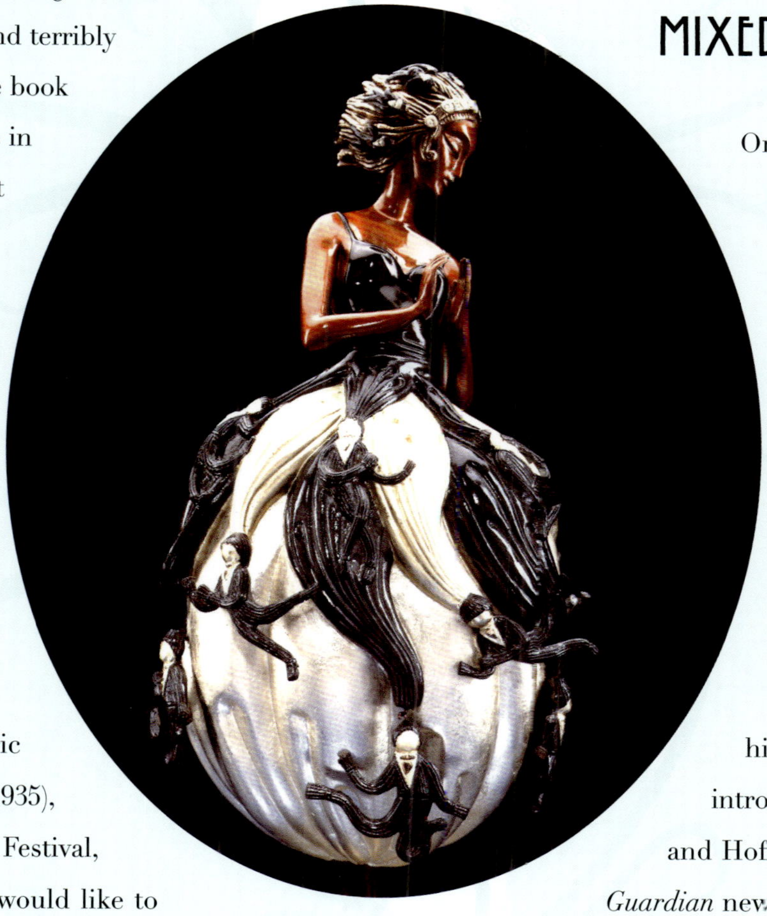

DER ROSENKAVALIER AT GLYNDEBOURNE, ENGLAND: 1980

In July 1978 Erté's agent and friend Eric Estorick was approached by John Cox (b. 1935), artistic director of Glyndebourne Opera Festival, in East Sussex, England, to ask if Erté would like to design the sets and costumes for the comic-opera *Der Rosenkavalier*, ('The Knight of the Rose'), by the German composer Richard Strauss (1864–1949), and librettist Hugo von Hofmannsthal (1874–1929), first performed in 1911. When offered the contract, at a fee much below his normal acceptance, Erté agreed because he stated he had been waiting all his life for someone to ask him to design this particular opera. Erté was by now 86 years of age. Strauss had set the opera in mid-eighteenth century Vienna, the period of Empress Marie Theresa (1717–80). Erté preferred to set in the 1850s, the period of Emperor Franz Josef I (1830–1916), to stay away from knee breeches and hose.

MIXED REVIEWS

On 4 January 1980, Erté delivered his finished designs for four sets, 76 costumes and a carpet design for *Der Rosenkavalier* at Glyndebourne Opera Festival. One bedroom set was decorated with pink satin quilted walls. The production opened in July and the setting and costumes received mixed reviews. The arts critic of the London newspaper *The Observer*, Peter Heyworth, suggested that Erté had not much concerned himself with authenticity and in fact had introduced vulgarity to the 'world of Strauss and Hofmannsthal'. Edward Greenfield of *The Guardian* newspaper felt Erté's sets worked very well but criticized some of the costumes, including one referred to as 'a vulgar pink costume complete with pearl-encrusted snood'. Fortunately critics' criticisms did not deter the audiences from embracing the production and the enjoyment of Erté's set and costumes. His visual interpretation was repeated again in the summer production of 1982.

Tuxedo *(with added borders), 1986, embossed serigraph with foil stamping, 78.1 x 55.9 cm (30¾ x 22 in)*

Tuxedo *sculpture, 1986, bronze, 53.3 x 21.6 x 17.8 cm (21 x 81/2 x 7 in)*

BACK TO WORK

Far from retiring from work, Erté was reaching a new peak in his long career. Apart from demand afresh for theatrical work, his time was taken up with learning new techniques, new methods of graphic printing (lithography and serigraphy) and the intricacies of creating jewellery design, as well as learning how to create a sculpture maquette in order to create bronze sculptures using the timeless *cire perdue* ('lost-wax') process. He achieved each challenge with a quiet charm, an inquiring mind and the ability to adapt, change and create a new highly successful business. To read about the techniques he used during his career shows the versatility of the man.

A CHANGE OF DIRECTION

With new interest in Erté's work emerging from the late 1960s, he looked back to re-appraise his earlier works, and adapted some of them to new media. A gouache painting would be redesigned for a lithograph, a serigraph or a bronze, thus making lucrative limited editions for a new audience of collectors. A figure illustration in an original pen and Indian ink sketch or a gouache from earlier decades could be remade into a bronze figurine or a piece of jewellery, retaining the original characteristics but in a new mode. For this Erté needed to learn new skills. It excited him and, with the help of professional colleagues in print and sculpture production, he succeeded in building another very profitable career.

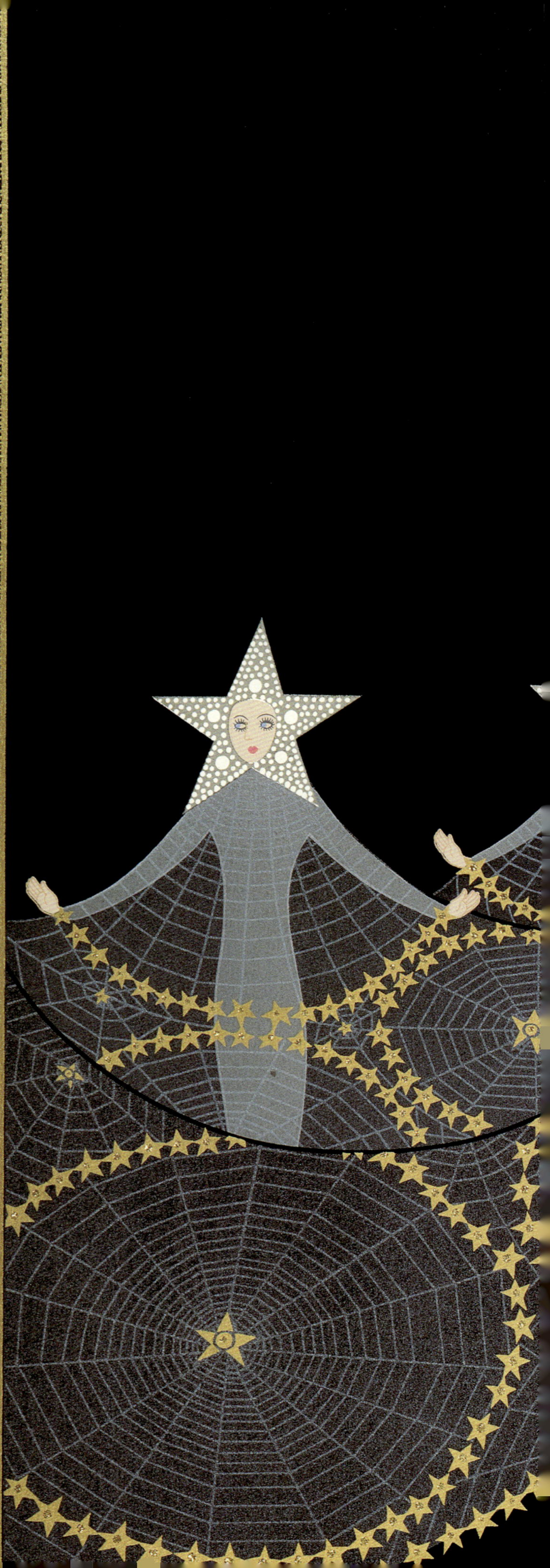

Queen of the Night, *1985, embossed serigraph with foil stamping, 72.6 x 83.8 cm (28½ x 33 in)*

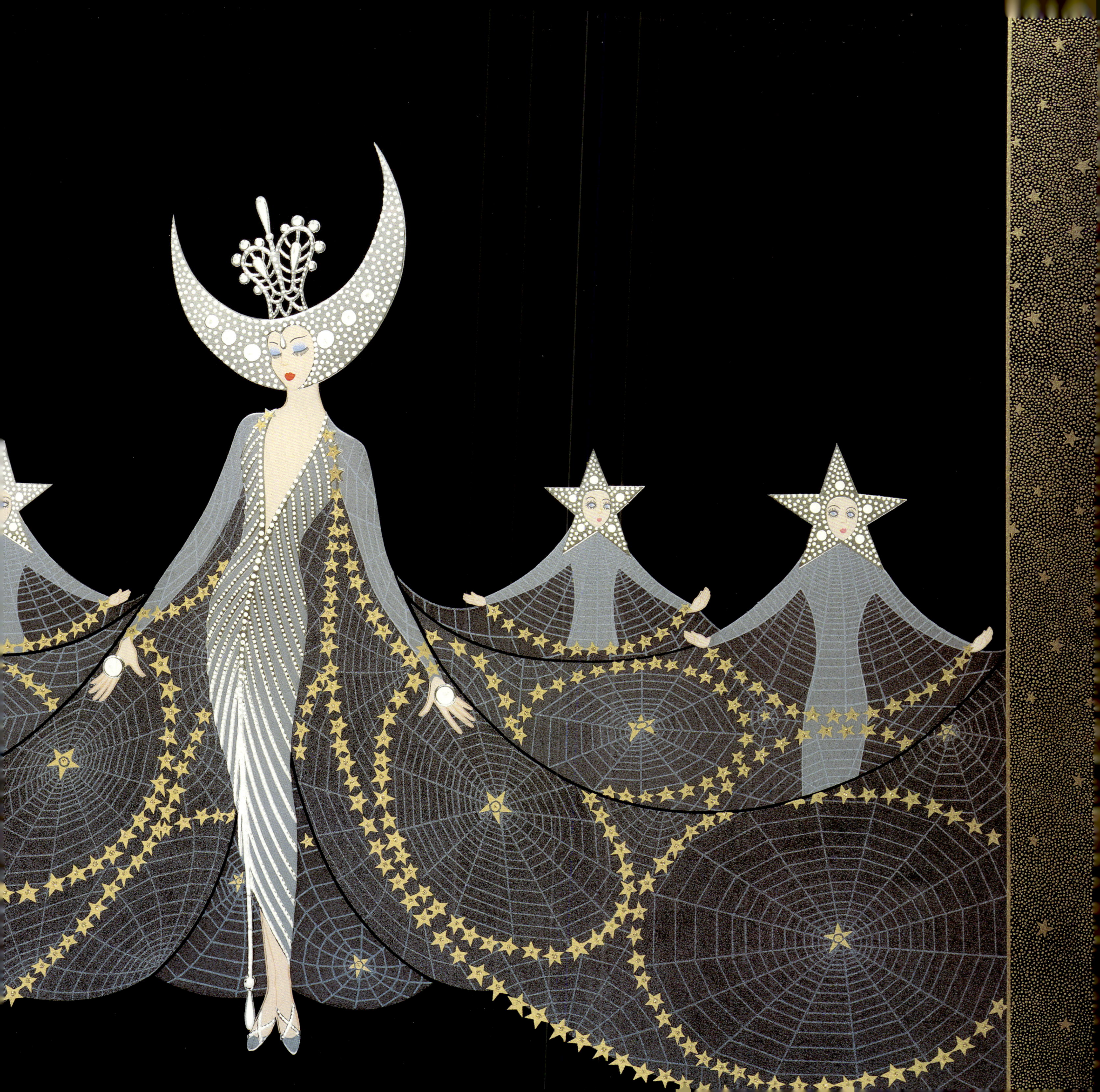

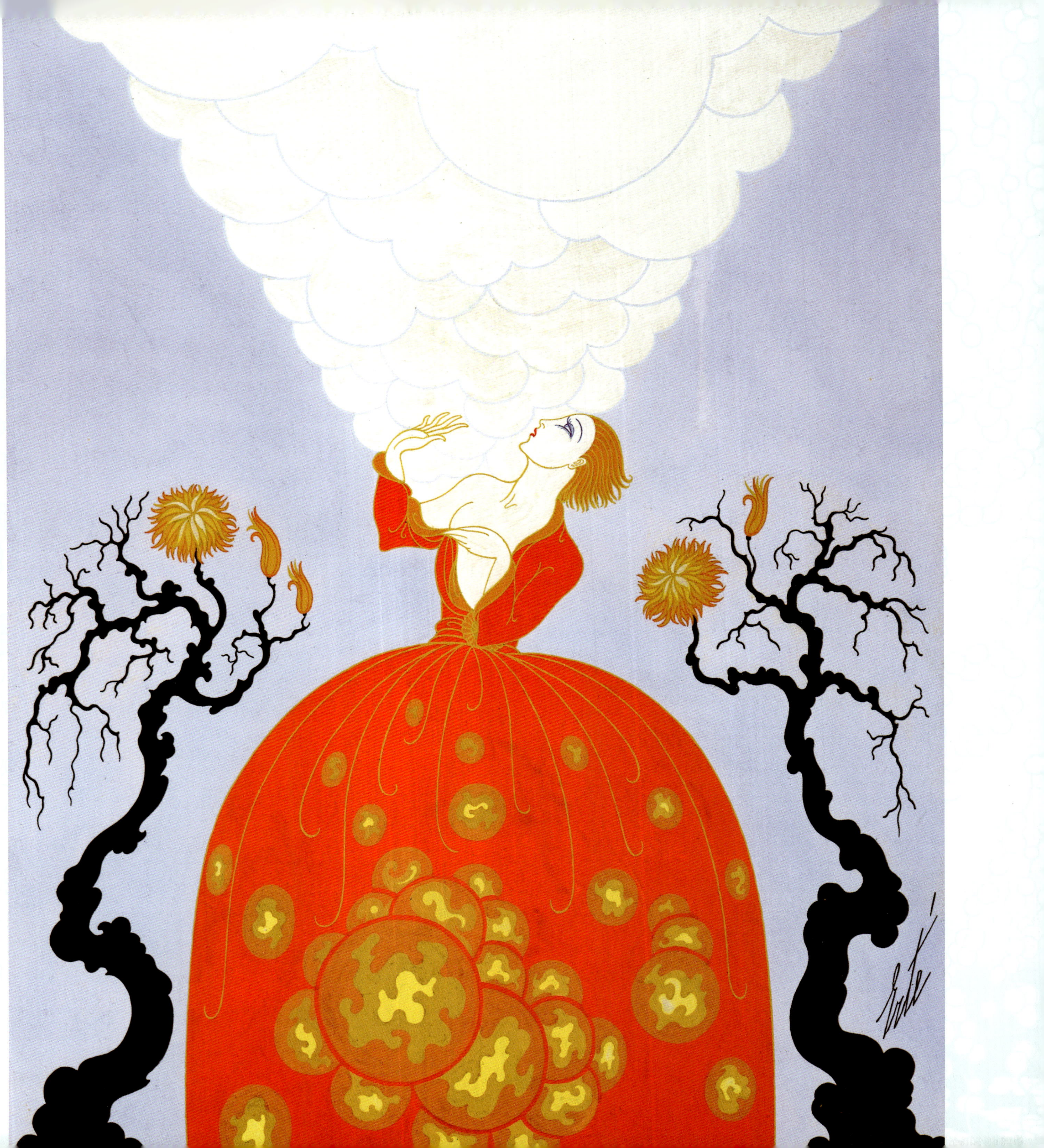
Erté

FROM GOUACHE TO BRONZE

It is said that Erté only once created a fine art painting in oils as he did not like the medium, preferring the density and consistency of gouache or tempera paint. Gouache is a solid-colour opaque watercolour medium. Its pigments are bound together with glue, and its texture and solidity is perfect for illustrations created for graphic reproduction and thus favoured by illustrators, designers and commercial artists. The colours range from the softest pastels to vibrant rich tones, and include metallic gold and silver and deepest black. Erté used these extensively. Erté's magazine covers for *Harper's Bazaar*, from 1915–38, were created in gouache. Each original was sent to the editor who later returned it to Erté. For other commissions, such as musical revue costume designs, Erté kept the original work but sent an exact copy, made by his copyists. Many of Erté's original gouache designs were later created in sculptural form.

METAL EXPERIMENTS

In 1936 Erté experimented with metal for costumes, 30 years before the French couturier Paco Rabanne (b. 1934) created a sensation with a metal and plastic mini-dress in 1967. Erté instigated it. For a ballet titled *Metal*, produced at the Bal Tabarin, Paris, Erté designed all the costumes out of aluminium.

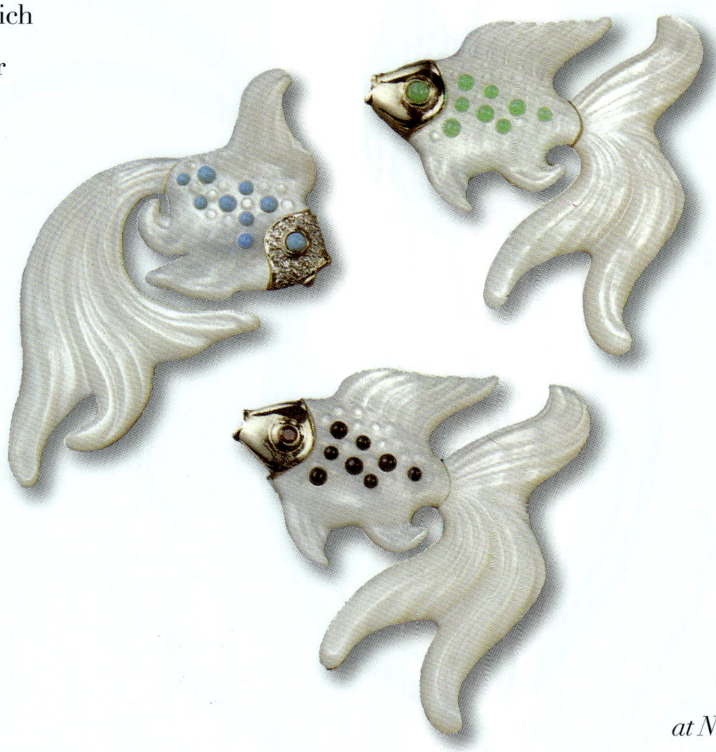

DEFINING THE FEMALE BODY

Erté's designs are intrinsically associated with his diverse manipulation of the female human form. He transformed woman-as-bird in the exotic costume for *L'Oiseaux Merveillieux* (1927, *see* page 172 left), at the Folies Bergère, Paris; provided a subtext of woman-equals-caged-bird in *Bird in a Gilded Cage* (1989, *see* page 172 right); or contorted the female figure to create letters or numbers. The designer commented that when he started painting seriously, in the early years of study in St Petersburg and at the Académie Julian in Paris, he was 'dazzled' by the human figure and saw hundreds of objects as anthropomorphic shapes taking on 'human contours'. He carried this through to his *Numerals* (*see* pages 182–83), and *Alphabet* series (*see* pages 7, 185–87). He defended his portrayals: 'If I have treated the human body in a static manner and represented it in symmetrical figures, it is merely as a reaction against my habit of expressing movement' (*Erté at Ninety: The Complete Graphics*, 1980).

NEW CREATIONS

Erté gained much pleasure from rethinking and reworking his early originals, but his characters never lost their 'woman as object' attributes, trapped in a vision of women that was

The Heat and the Clouds, *cover design for* Harper's Bazaar, *July 1926, gouache, 40.6 x 29.2 cm (16 x 11½ in)*

Chimera *brooches, c. 1979–90, clockwise from top left: mother-of-pearl, gold, silver, diamonds, turquoise; mother-of-pearl, gold, silver, chrysophase; mother-of-pearl, gold, silver, ruby, black onyx*

discarded by the Feminist movement in the 1970s. Erté carried on regardless. His *Blossom Umbrella* (1924), reworked as a serigraph in 1979, is echoed by *Pink Lady* (1980, *see* page 8). There is an edge to the latter but the character's femininity prevails.

FIRST LITHOGRAPHS

It was Eric and Salome Estorick who suggested to Erté in 1967 that he might like to make a series of lithographs. It would make his art available to a wider group of collectors through a series of signed limited editions. As Erté recalled, 'This graphic work has attracted a vastly larger audience than could have been achieved by exhibitions of my original works for publications or theatrical and film productions' (*Erté at Ninety: The Complete Graphics*, 1982). The first series, published in 1968, was *The Numerals*, similar in format to his series *The Alphabet*. The set of prints were on the theme of numbers, 0 to 9, with the figures created from the human form or from mythical creatures. From each original, 75 numbered prints were made. The successful sales of the prints expanded Erté's audience, leading to larger print runs and different types of commercial product promotion. Both *The Numerals* and *The Alphabet* were later released as serigraphs (*see* pages 182–83, 7, 185–87) and adapted for a collection of jewellery pendants and brooches (*see* page 184). There were also a *Jewels* series of precious stones: amethyst, diamond, emerald, ruby, sapphire and topaz, and *The Four Seasons*: Autumn, Winter, Spring, Summer. From each original, 75 numbered prints were made.

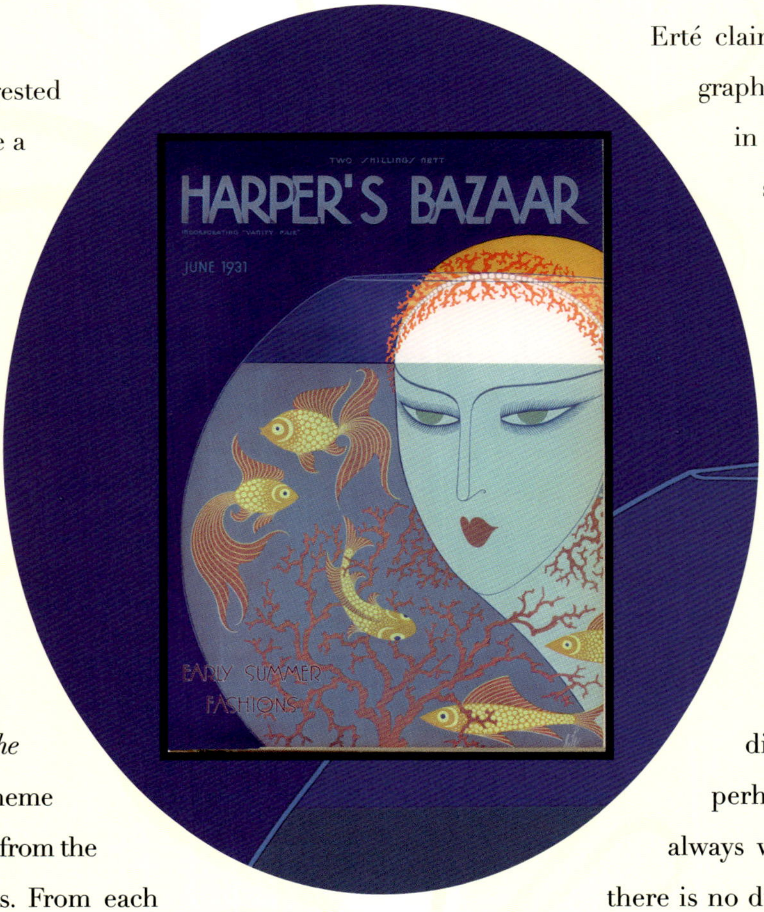

GRAPHICS

Erté claimed that his choice of subject for his graphic designs depended on the mood he was in on the day. His preference was to make a series of prints as a 'suite', a body of work where each print related to others in the suite or album. His plan was to tell a story through the compilation of prints. It would, of course, be of more interest to serious collectors and museum curators, too, to invest in a coordinated group rather than a sole print. Although many of the early works are reworked in graphic prints, sculptures and jewellery, Erté did not directly work across the media. This is perhaps surprising: 'Although I am almost always working on projects in different fields, there is no direct relationship between the different kinds of work I do,' he stated. What he liked most was to have variety, to work on a theatrical production, then on graphics, then jewellery design, and then sculpture. He outlined his strategy: 'I work on each project as an individual problem,' without considering them as a homogenous body of work (*Erté at Ninety: The Complete Graphics*, 1982).

Harper's Bazaar *cover, June 1931 (from* **Aquarium**, *1923, gouache, 35.6 x 30.5 cm/14 x 12 in)*

Fish Bowl, *1977, serigraph, 50 x 37 cm (19¾ x 14⅝ in)*
The mannequin face reflects the composition of earlier works such as the *Bain du Soleil* cover design for *Harper's Bazaar* (June 1930) and the refinement of the marble *Sleeping Muse I* (1909–10) by Constantin Brancusi (1876–1957).

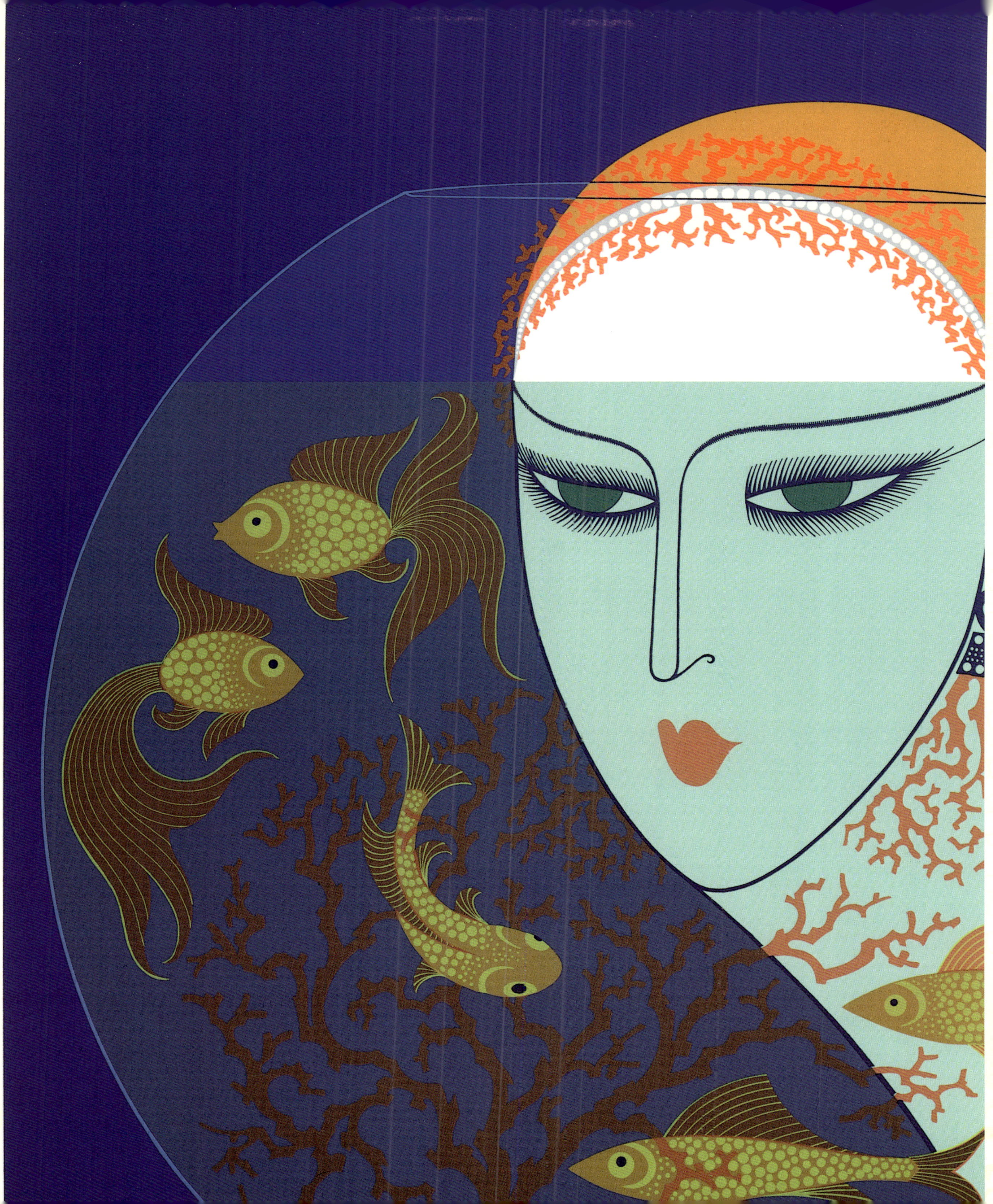

MANHATTAN MARY REAPPEARS

The 1927 success of New York impresario George White's *Manhattan Mary* (26 September 1927 – 12 May 1928), a Broadway show about White's 'Scandals' revues, resurfaced in Erté's lithographs, *Manhattan Mary* in 1979 (*see* page 102), each in a series of 300 limited editions plus artist's proofs. The show was now a historic note in Broadway history but the costumes were fashionable again following the 1970s Art Deco revival era. Erté's theatrical costumes were usually just that, theatrical, embellished, often barely-there dresses or sumptuous fantasy costumes. But for the original *Manhattan Mary*, the clothes were fashionable for the period and highly wearable. Exhibiting works from this show in 1972 he stated: 'The costumes for this production were modern dresses of that period and even today … I noticed that one of them was exactly like a dress I had seen a few days previously in the show of one of the leading Parisian couturiers' (*Erté: Fashions by Erté* (1972), Introduction).

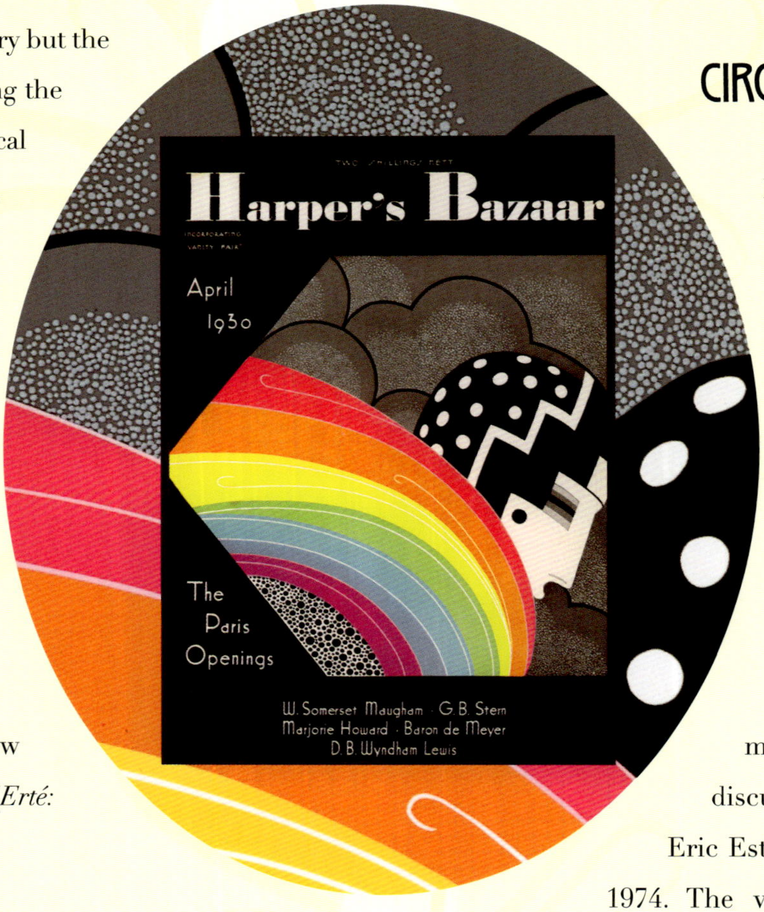

COMMERCIAL VENTURES

The success of *The Numerals* led to Erté designing a playing card pack for the black Russian cigarette brand 'Sobranie', made by the Gallagher cigarette company in London. Each twin-pack included a copy of a short biography of Erté. Special editions were presented in 'The Erté Playing Cards Presentation Box'. The advertising copy promoted it as 'A True Collector's Item from Sobrane [sic] of London'. The advertisements were placed in a variety of magazines including *Illustrated London News* (Saturday 31 December 1983, Issue 7025).

CIRCLE FINE ART CORPORATION

In 1974 Jack Solomon Jr. (1928–2011/12), owner of Circle Fine Art Corporation and the lithography studio American Atelier, approached Erté to offer a contract to publish the artist's graphic designs as serigraphs, colour prints using a silkscreen process. Erté was not familiar with this technique but was enthused and excited by the project. He had lost none of his desire to explore new methods to print his graphic designs. After discussion with Erté's agents, Salome and Eric Estorick, the contract was signed in April 1974. The venture was a success, creating new collectors of Erté's work, as well as widening the scope for established collectors of graphic design. In *Erté at Ninety: The Complete Graphics* (1982) – a *catalogue raisonné* of 207 works from 1968–82 – Solomon lists four factors that he believed made Erté's work so successful. First, the vibrancy of rich colour, deep inks and bold, elegant line, and the exotic and erotic mixed with

Harper's Bazaar *cover, April 1930 (from* **L'Arc en Ciel** *gouache, 1929, 38.1 x 27.9 cm/15 x 11 in)*

Tempest, *1978, serigraph, 61 x 43 cm (24 x 17 in)*
This colourful serigraph recalling the 1920s Jazz Era and fashion for the 'garçonne' look, was based on one of Erté's *Harper's Bazaar* covers.

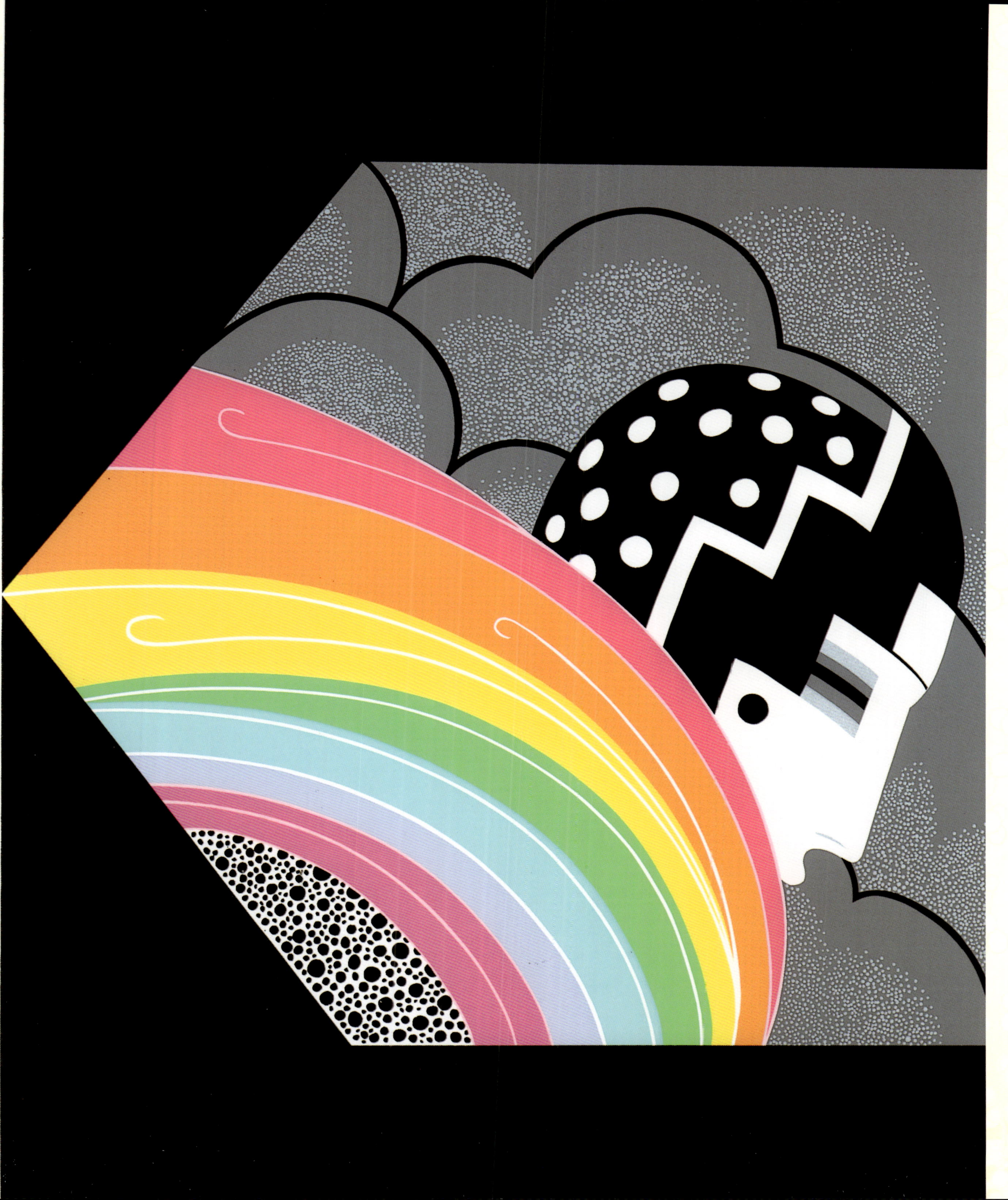

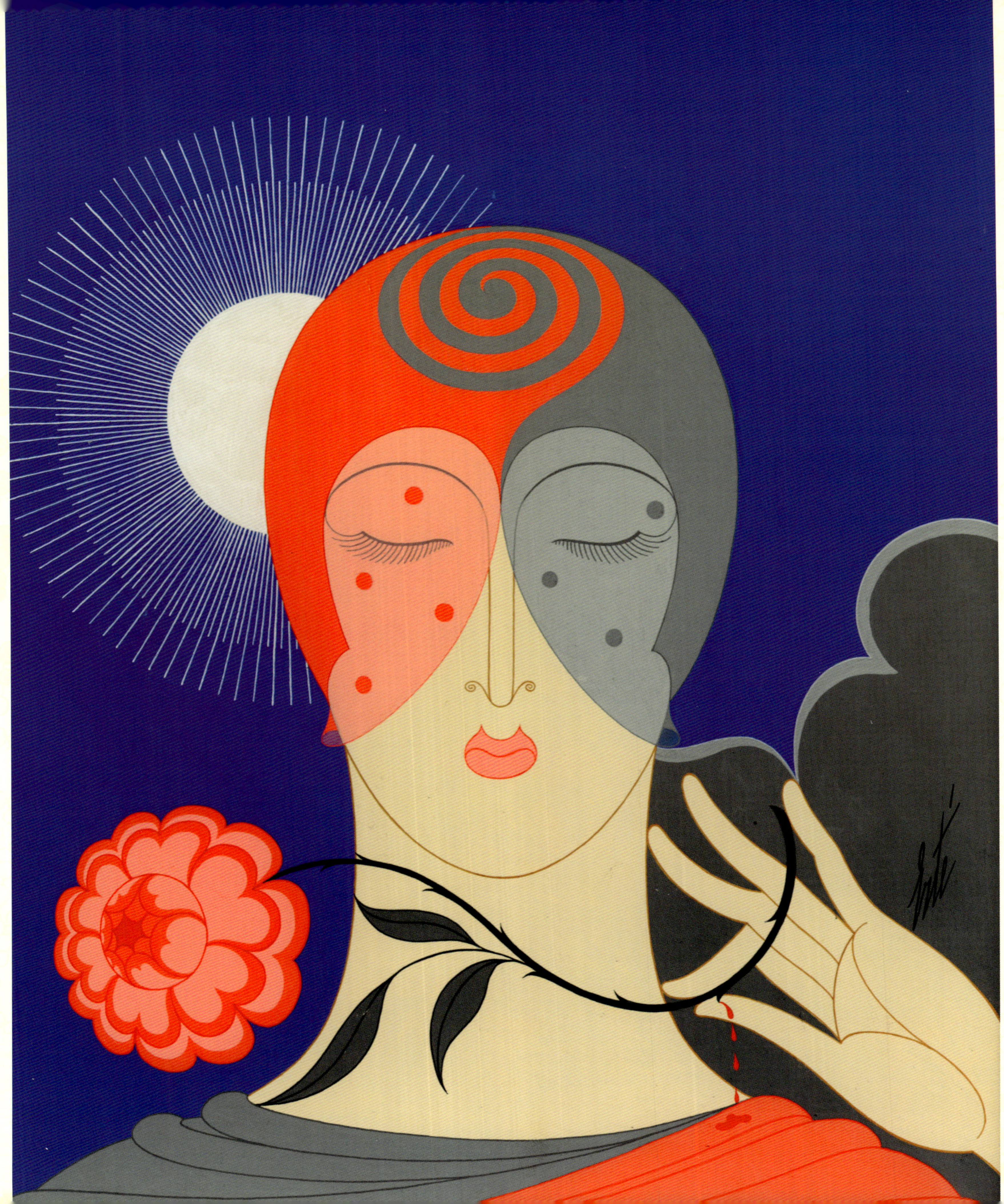

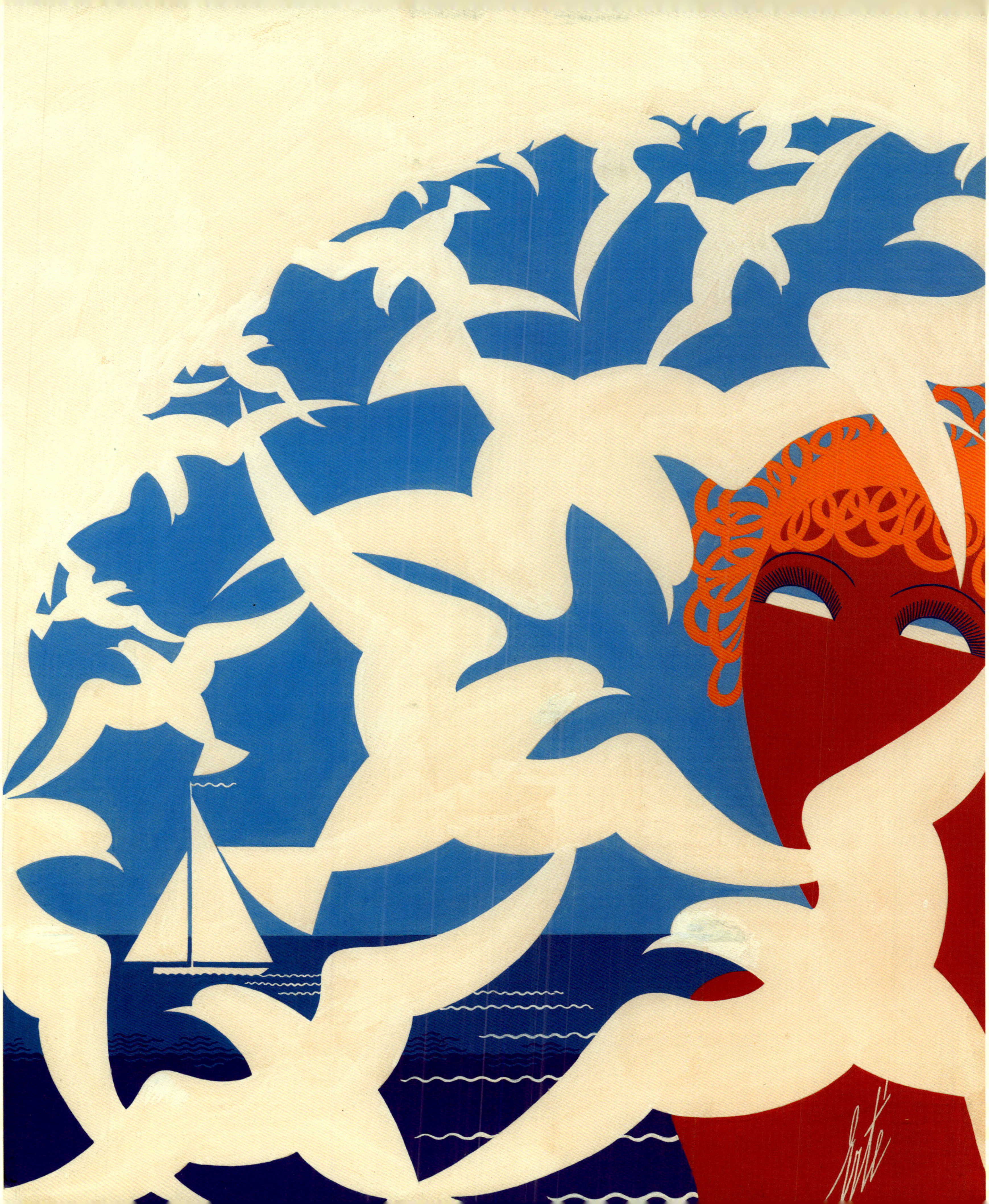
Erté

romanticism and wit; secondly, Erté's method of using a hard line to define details, followed by clear, flat colour infill; thirdly, innovation, unafraid to experiment with new methods; and lastly, that people *love* Erté prints, not like, or admire, but *love* his work, which keeps his name at the forefront of graphic design.

SERIGRAPHY

When Erté was introduced to the method of serigraphy he found it an exciting experience, drawing on new ideas and creativity to bring a fresh perspective to his earlier works and to create new works. Serigraphy, also known as silk-screen printing, entails the reproduction of an original painting, although not necessarily an exact copy of the original, which remains the artist's decision. Serigraphy, a higher quality of reproduction than lithography, is used for limited edition printing. The serigraph screens are destroyed when the edition is completed to ensure no further copies are made. A cut stencil is attached on to a silk screen that has been stretched on a wooden or metal frame (today it is more common to use a polyester sheet rather than silk). *Black Rose* (1975, *see* page 80), gives an idea of the stencil layering. Erté created a maquette, which could be a pen and ink drawing with written notes on colour, or a complete artwork. He made his serigraphs larger than the original drawings or gouache, and 15 to 20 colours were used. His collaborators, Jackson and Eunice Lowell of Chromacomp Inc., New York, the best fine art printing studio in the 1970s and 80s, created special machinery that could hot-stamp larger images. Erté described this as 'roughly equivalent to designing a gown of stainless steel and taffeta that is both practical and beautiful'.

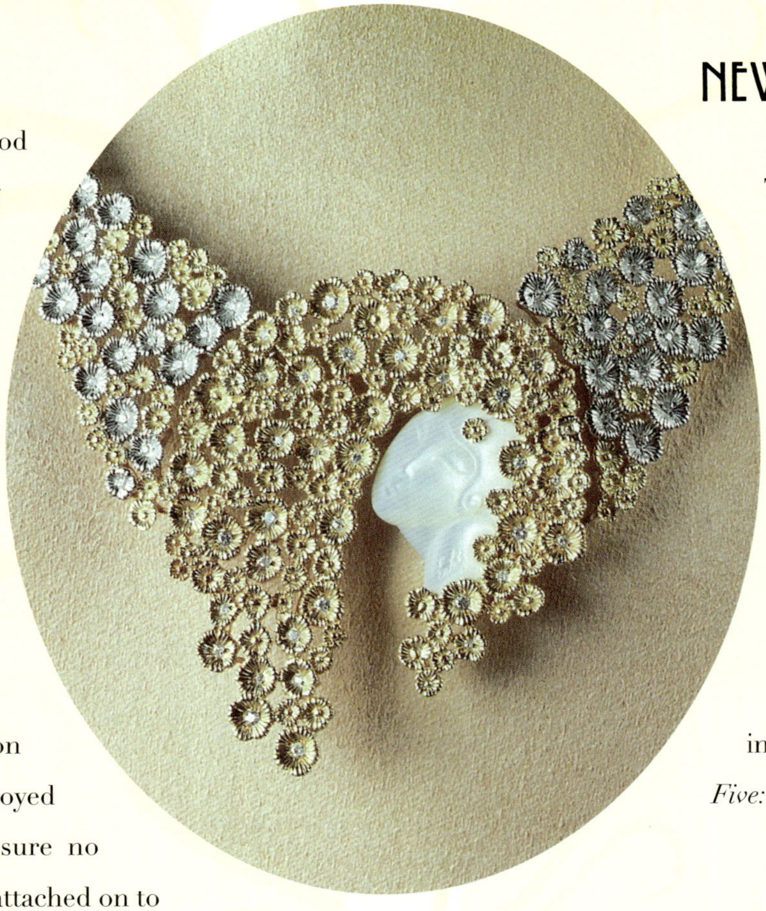

NEW GRAPHICS 1982–87

The development of printmaking techniques introduced a finer quality to Erté's graphics, which he appreciated. He followed the printing process of his works at every step. Coming late to the graphics medium, he appreciated what it was achieving for him, 'graphics ... is a form of expression very close to my heart because it was the medium with which I made my reappearance in the broad international world of Art' (*Erté at Ninety-Five: The Complete Graphics* (1987).

COLOUR AND TEXTURE AT PLAY

The addition of an embossed surface or foil embellishment to give the serigraph the effect of a bas-relief needed new processes to ensure perfect reproductions. Erté's use of high quality rag paper added complexity to the print process but it

(Previous, left) **Optimism and Pessimism**, *cover design for* Harper's Bazaar, *1929, gouache, 38.1 x 27.9 cm (15 x 11 in)*
(Previous, right) **Seagulls**, *cover design for* Harper's Bazaar, *July 1935, gouache, 36.8 x 27.9 cm (14½ x 11 in)*

(Above) **Rainbow in Blossom** *necklace, 1988, gold, silver, diamonds, mother-of-pearl*
(Right) **Rainbow in Blossom**, *1977, serigraph, 46 x 34 cm (18 x 13½ in)*
The flower decoration of this serigraph is an echo of Erté's gouache *Movementes divers* (1930), a flowery textile design. The mannequin head is a trademark Erté face illustration.

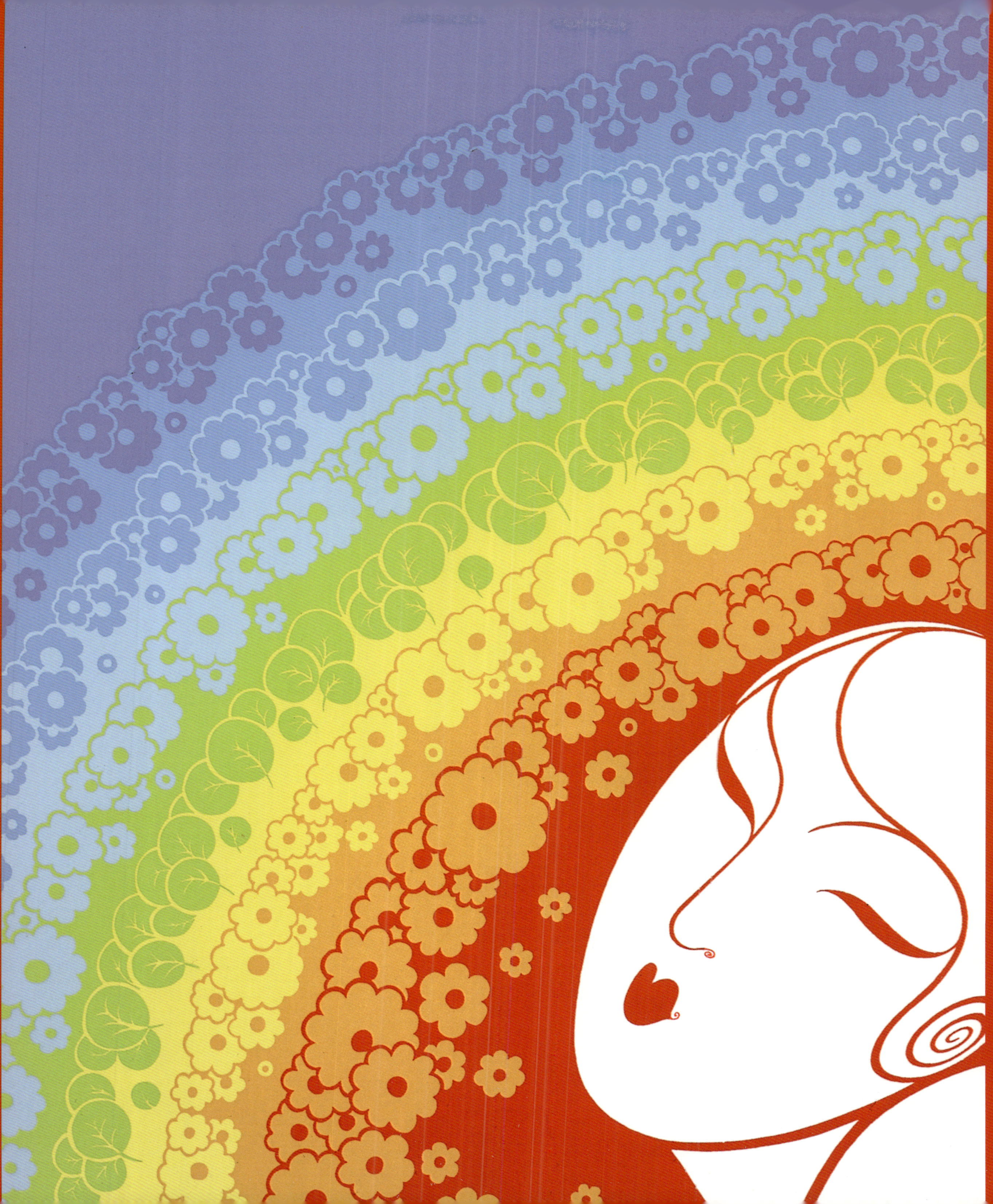

produced remarkable results, such as the snowy background of *The End of Romance* (1981) and the floating background of *Tuxedo* (1986, *see* page 146). The pointillist backdrop – separate dots of colour – of *Rose Dancer* (1984, *see* page 29) was created by spattering the background area with four different paint colours, followed by stamping on silver and gold at random. A sculpture, *Rose Dancer* (*see* page 28), loosely modelled on this serigraph, was produced in 1988. The resulting sophistication of this technique, that produced the spectacular starry night backdrop in one of Erté's last works *Star Spangled Night* (1990, *see* page 110–11), shows how accomplished he had become.

MARRIAGE À LA MODE

In his serigraphs, Erté also built up layers of colour pigment to create three-dimensional enamels and lacquers. This technique was used for the border patterns of *Fringe Gown* (1985, *see* page 162) and *Veil Gown* (1985, *see* page 163), both from 'The June Brides Suite' series. Several layers of translucent ink, especially developed to produce a see-through alabaster effect, created the bride's veil. It is fascinating to compare Erté's various marriage-themed designs; others include those from 1924 for George White's 'Scandals' revue *Les Marriages:* the lavish triple costume design for 'Golden Wedding' (*see* page 131), the barely-there triple costume design for 'Marriage' (*see* page 130), and his spectacular *Opening Curtain*, which integrated female dancers within the hanging curtain panels, a creation perhaps unique to Erté at this time. Other later serigraphs dealt with this theme too, such as *Marriage Dance* (1984, *see* pages 128–29), from the 'Love and Passion Suite' limited edition series.

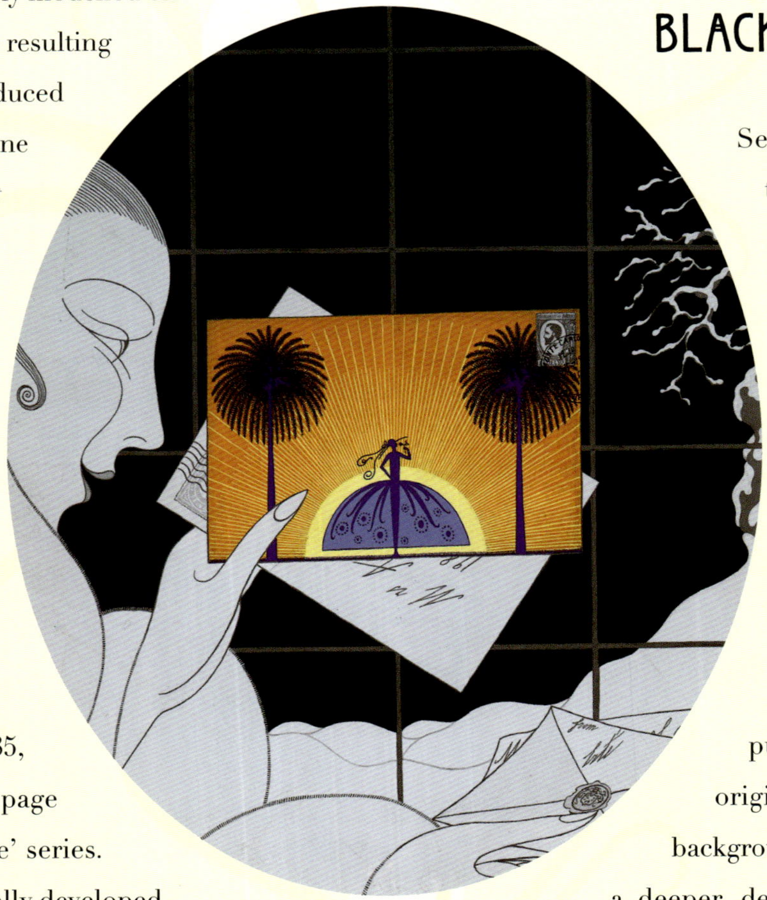

BLACK PAPER PICTURES

Serigraphy introduced a further element to Erté's designs, the use of black paper and a new printmaking technique. Erté's graphics were usually printed on high quality paper, his 'rag paper', as he called it. His colleagues suggested printing on black paper, a new innovation. Print publishers would steer away from black due to flaws or damage in handling. However, Erté was keen to explore the medium, as were his publishers, because so many of Erté's original designs were set on black backgrounds. The serigraphy process allowed for a deeper, denser black background, which thrust focus on to the figures. *Aladdin and his Bride* (1984, *see* pages 70–71), is an example that shows how the black background throws a spotlight on the spectacular robes and headdresses of the pair. Look again at *Marriage Dance* (1984, *see* pages 128–29), and the composition of *Starfish* (1986, *see* page 85). Reading Erté's comments on his working methods, one gets the instant

Riviera, *cover design for* Harper's Bazaar, *Christmas 1927, gouache, 40 x 29.8 cm (15¾ x 11¾ in)*
On this cover Erté featured a 'postcard' of the sunshine of the French Riviera where he was living, illuminating the cold winter of New York.

Surprises of the Sea, *1982, serigraph, 83.8 x 63.5 cm (33 x 25 in)*
Erté created many fantasy marine scenes, particularly for the 1923 stage show *Les Mers*. In *Surprises of the Sea* he visualizes a vessel, its prow pushing through the waves. On board a young woman is framed by sun-yellow rays.

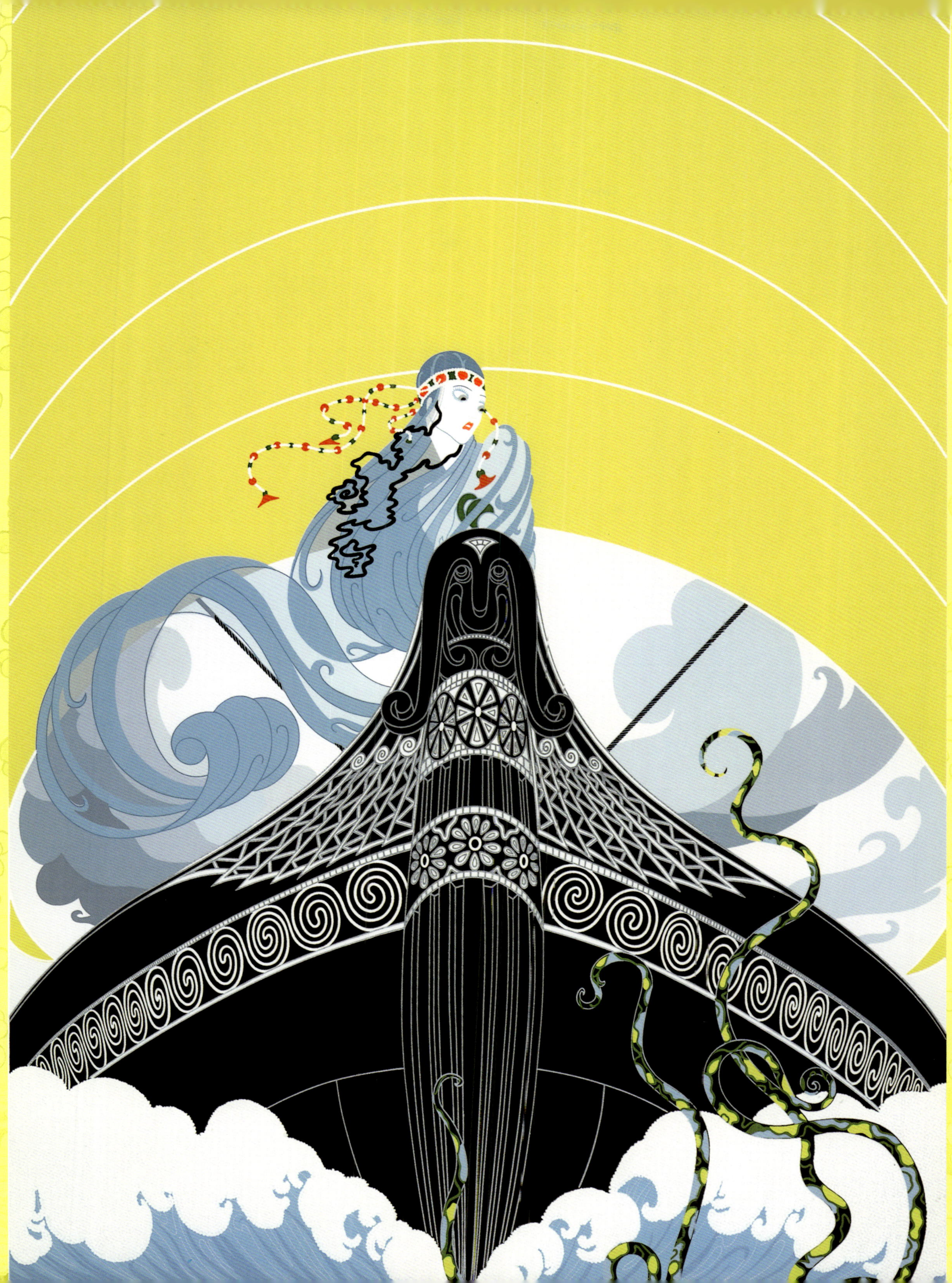

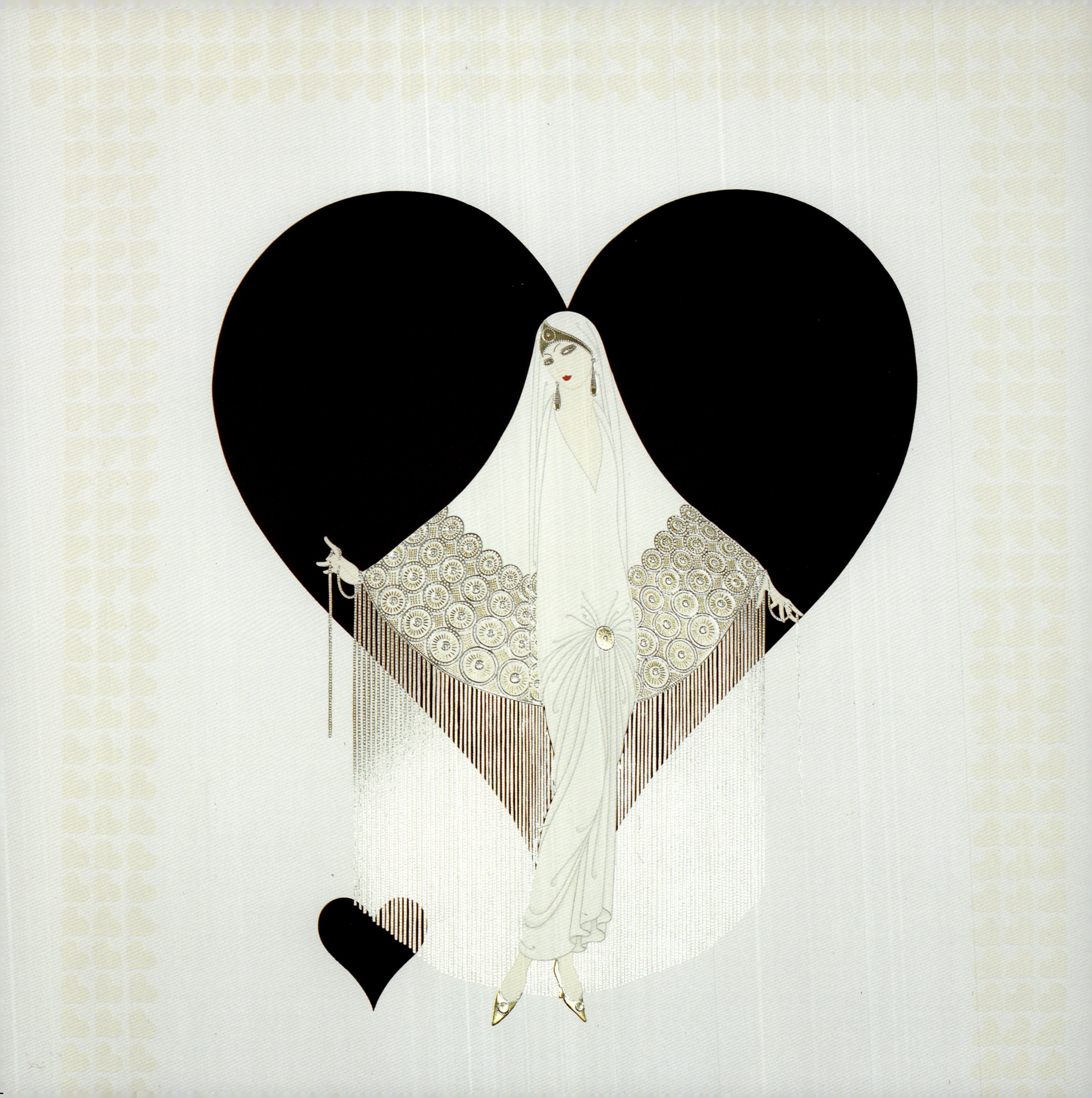

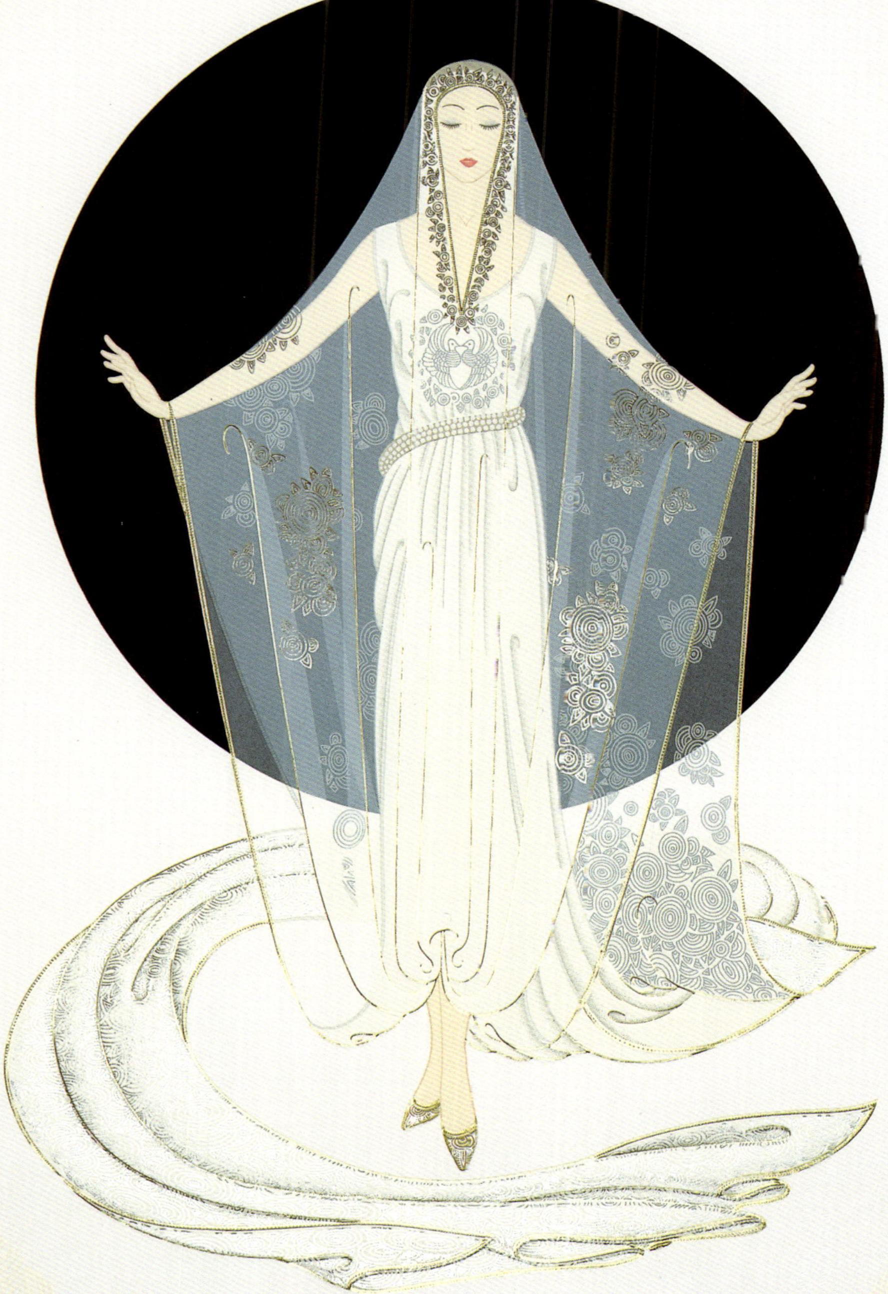

impression that he loved the intricacies of each process. He had great patience, working through a problem to get the result he wanted by whatever means available.

ORIENTALISM REVISITED

Orientalism, the term given to describe Western interest in aspects of Middle Eastern, Asian and Indo-Chinese culture, particularly visual culture and decorative arts, had emerged in the middle of the nineteenth century. As a child Erté had been interested in the original forms of Oriental, Byzantine and Asian visual culture, and the classical civilizations of Greece and Rome. He had translated this into fabulous fantasy costumes for the theatre. From the 1970s he reappraised these original gouaches and drawings to create a series of graphic prints. They are some of his most stunning illustrations, painstakingly transferred to the laborious time-consuming method of serigraphy, which took months to create one design.

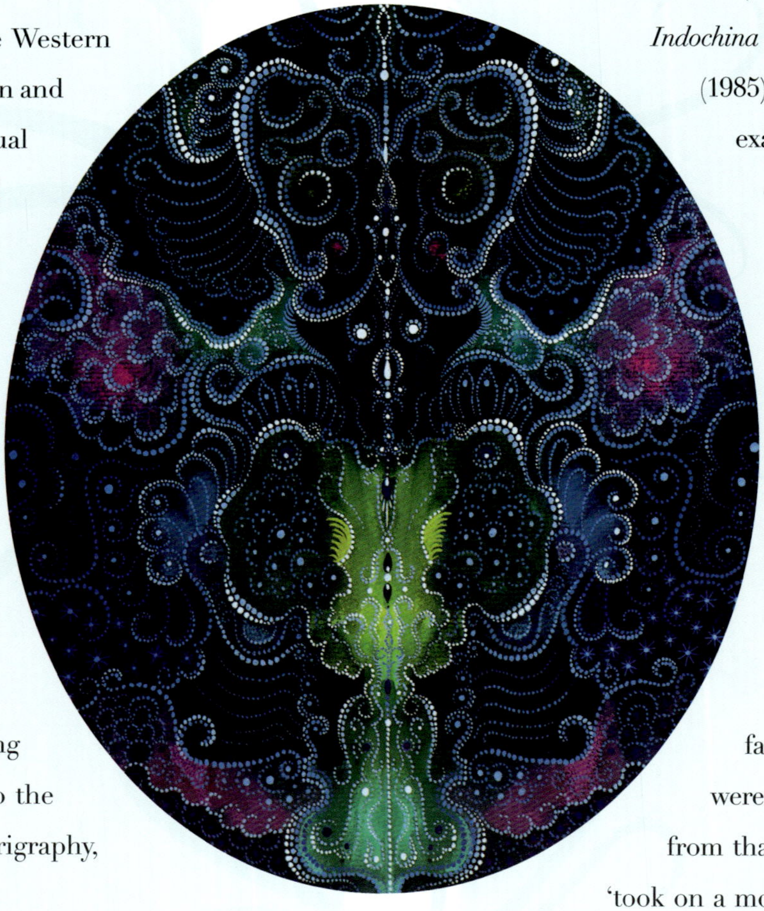

HISTORICAL FANTASIES

Examples of Erté's Orientalism explored a liberal approach to historical accuracy. But these were some of his finest fantasies, like the extraordinary coloured feathers that stretch across the paper in the serigraph *The Nile* (1982, *see* pages 14–15). In *Athena* (1986, *see* page 145) and *Aphrodite* (1985, *see* page 96), one can see Erté playing freely with the antique, and in *Gown Orientale* (1989, *see* page 87), creating his own translation of bygone fashion. This serigraph, one of a pair with *Cape à la Russe* (1989, *see* page 86), in the 'Ensemble du Soir Suite', has an echo of his Russian past. The exotic *Indochina* (1984), and *Red Sea* (1984), with *Byzantine* (1985) and *The Egyptian* (1986) are further examples of Erté's remoulding of national costume characteristics. The European-style *Le Harem Moderne I* (1990, *see* page 88) was one of his final interpretations.

ON MALE FASHION

An arbiter of fashion, Erté stated often that he did not see fashion as a uniform to be adhered to but a style adapted to the individual. He thought that fashionable clothes for men and women were balanced until the nineteenth century. But from that time he considered that men's clothes 'took on a monotonous and sadly frightening rigidity' (*Erté: Fashions by Erté*, 1972). He abhorred social events where the women were adorned in jewels and fabulous dresses whilst the men were all in black 'looking like an army of head waiters'. His fabulous serigraph *Top Hats* (1975, *see* page 65) rather makes the point. It is one of his most famous and most popular graphic designs, a summation of the glamour of the earlier Art Deco era.

(Previous, left) **Fringe Gown**, *'June Brides Suite', 1985, embossed serigraph with foil stamping, 97.8 x 77 cm (38½ x 30¼ in)*
(Previous, right) **Veil Gown**, *'June Brides Suite', 1985, embossed serigraph with foil stamping, 97.8 x 77 cm (38½ x 30¼ in)*

(Above) **Curtain design for Phantasm**, *1928, gouache, 49.8 x 31.7 cm (19⅝ x 12½ in)*
(Right) **Costume design for Ganna Walska in Manon,** *Chicago Opera Company, 1922, gouache, 40 x 30 cm (15¾ x 11⅜ in)*

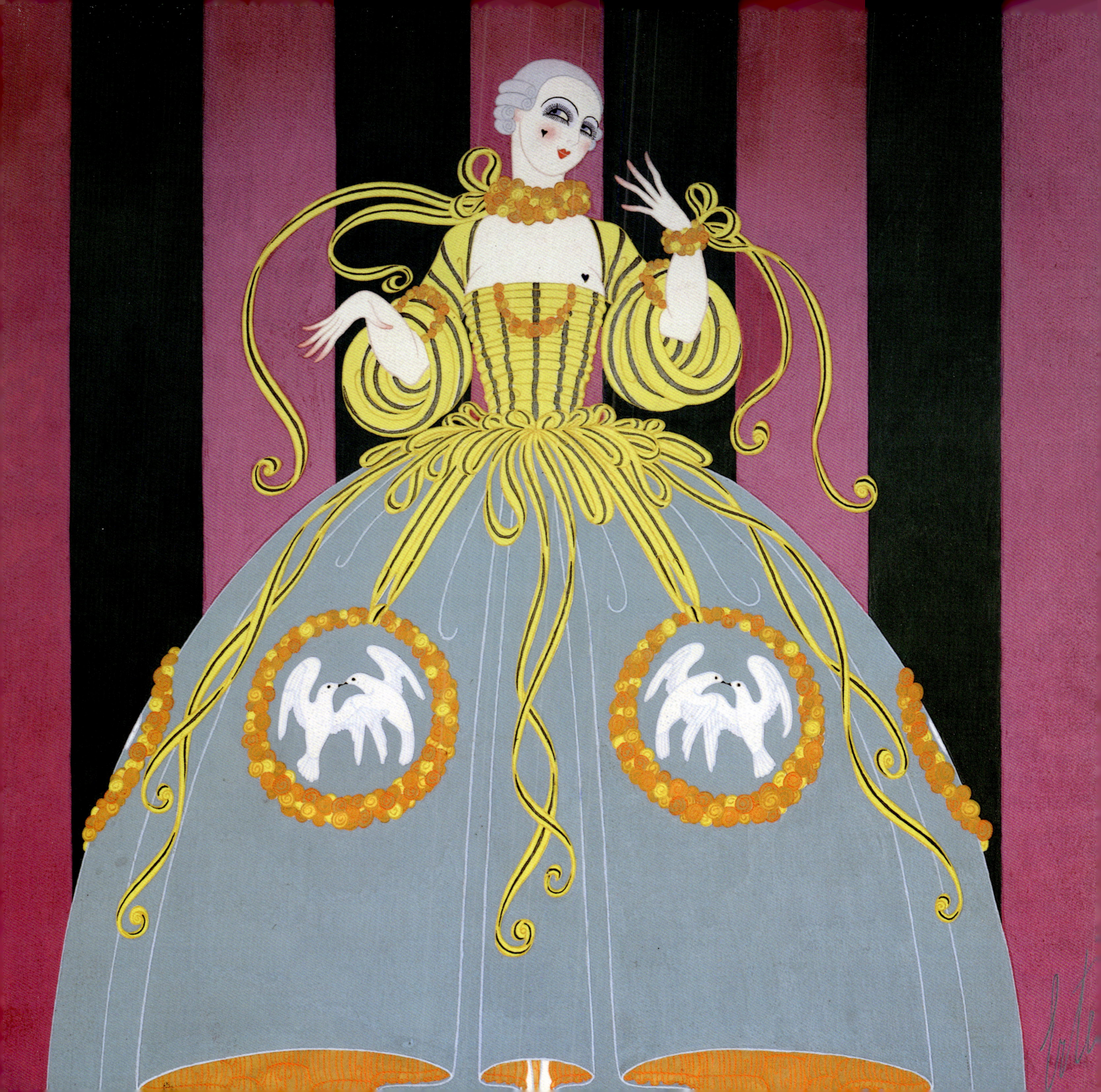

LUCRATIVE THEMES

To capitalize on the Erté name and interest in the diverse aspects of his work, lithographs and serigraphs were put together in 'suites' of works, from two to as many as 26 per suite. This created a new dimension for collectors, to appropriate a whole set, such as 'June Brides Suite' (series of two), 'The Twenties Remembered Again' (eight works) or 'The Alphabet Suite' (series of 26).

ART DECO SUNBURST

Sunrise (1984, *see* page 192), from Erté's 'The Sunrise/Moonlight Suite' series, is a semi-circular embossed serigraph, printed in a limited edition of 300. Its content echoes the cloud formation, and sunburst – an emblem of Art Deco – of Erté's earlier *New Bridges for the Seven Seas*, the remarkable *Harper's Bazaar* cover design of March 1919. The other, complementary, work in the suite is the circular *Moonlight* (1984, *see* page 140).

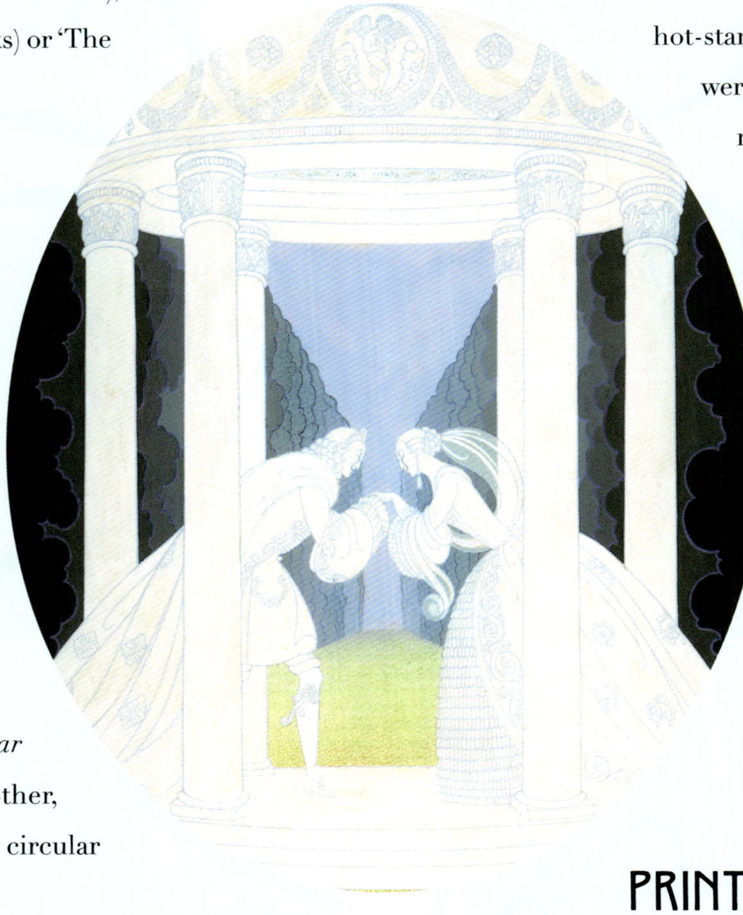

NOT PRINTING TO THE EDGE

In the introduction to *Erté at Ninety-Five: The Complete New Graphics* (1987), the artist explains the decisions he needed to make when reworking earlier illustrations, from gouache to serigraph. He used the examples of *Circe* (1985) from 'The Myth Suite' and the serigraph *Enchantress* (1986) because they both feature columns either side of the central image. The problem was that the two images, originally created in gouache, spread out to the edges of the sheet. This is not practical in serigraphy, due to the vulnerability of the surface edges, especially hot-stamped or embossed surfaces, which these were going to be. Following Erté's premise to re-work, possibly alter, earlier images when using a different medium, he chose to add columns either side of the image, as in *Circe* and *Enchantress*, which were integral to the female costume and headdress design. This follows on from Erté's earlier works, where the backdrop or surrounding ephemera relates to the costume of the character represented. In addition, this method left blank paper borders for handling the work. It solved the problem of fragile edges.

PRINTING TO THE EDGE

Erté, having stated his preference to not print to the edge of serigraphs, due to fragility, made exceptions for some works where artistic expression did not yield in deference to saleability. One of them is perhaps his most remarkable Art Deco image, the serigraph *The Angel* (1983), taken directly from the *Angel Harpist*, the costume

Les Trois Chemins, *1921, gouache, 35.6 x 26.7 cm (14 x 10½ in)*

Souvenirs, *cover design for* Harper's Bazaar, *1922, gouache, 36.2 x 26.9 cm (14¼ x 10⅝ in)*

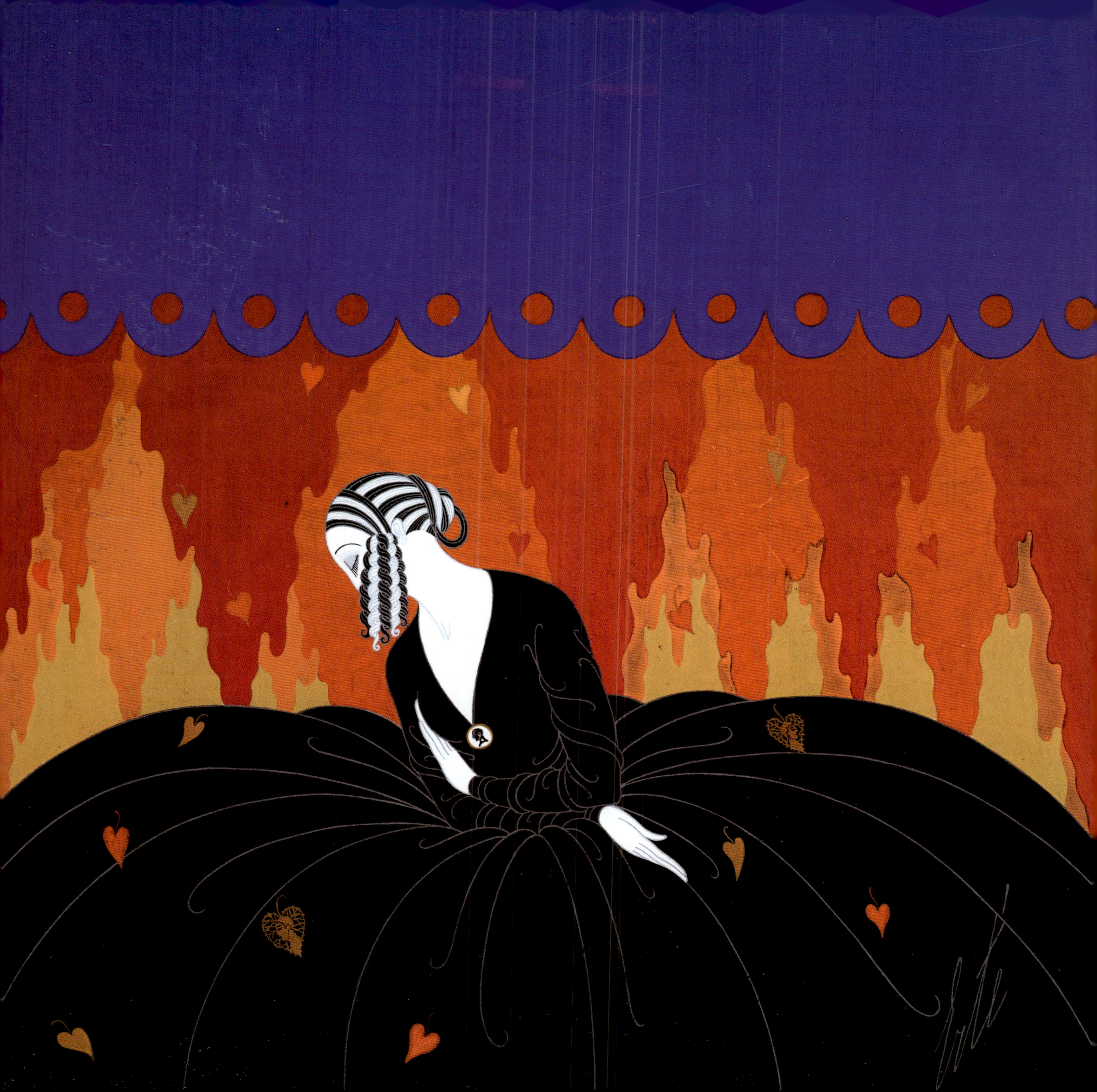

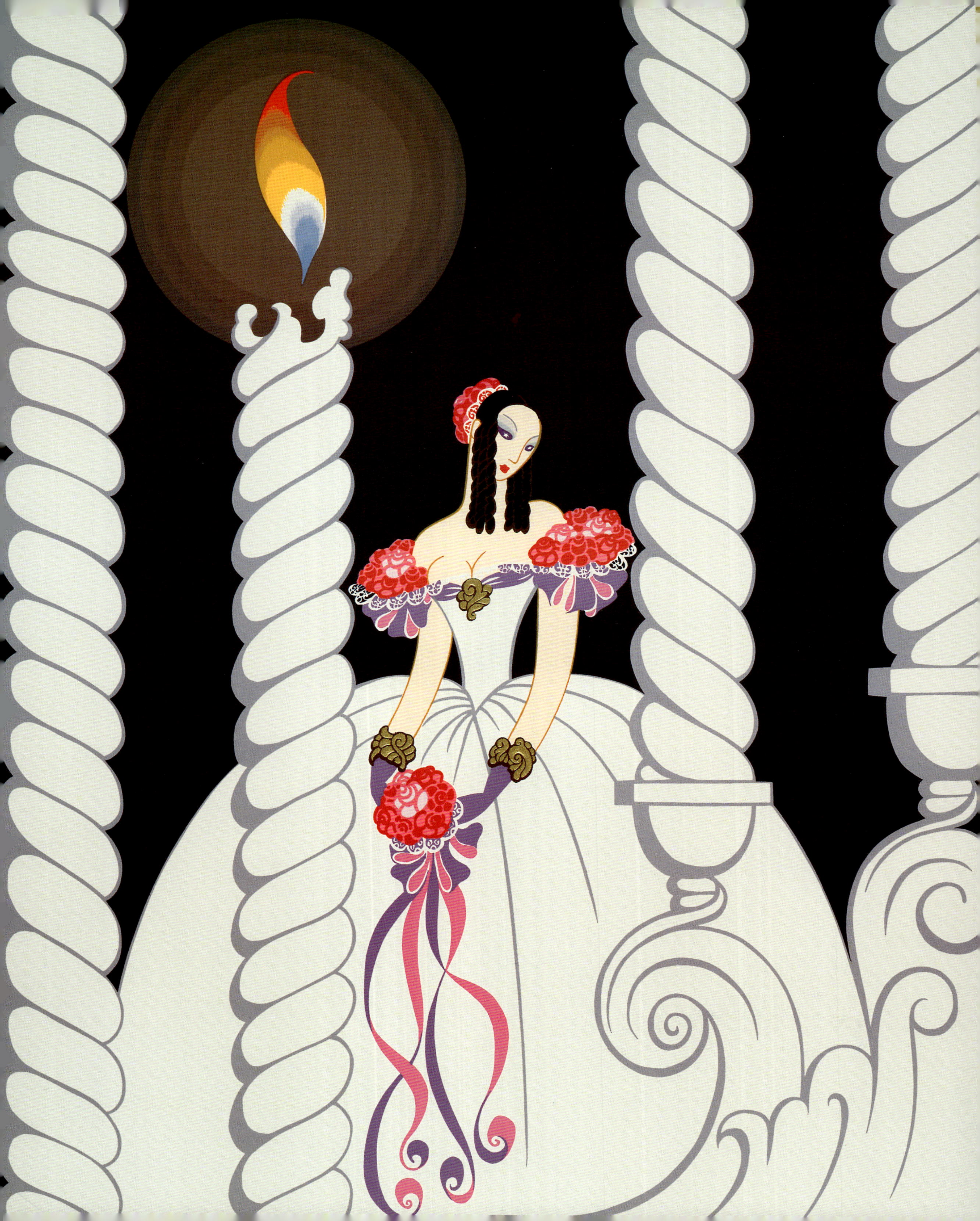

design for *The Blues* (1926, *see* page 102–3), created for George White's memorable Broadway 'Scandals' revue (the kneeling position of the 'Angel', bears resemblance to the Angel Gabriel in Leonardo da Vinci's *The Annunciation*, *c.* 1472). The other two serigraphs that Erté printed to the outer edge of the paper were *The Mystery of the Mask Suite*, and *Queen of the Night* (1985, *see* page 149), a stunning embossed serigraph with foil stamping.

REVERSED PAIRS

Erté dismissed the idea of making the serigraphs *Statue of Liberty Day* (1986, *see* page 108), and *Statue of Liberty Night* (1986, *see* page 109), as a pair of reverse images, due to the complication of in which hand Liberty would hold the flamed torch. But for other serigraph images he was flexible, 'to allow varied and endlessly imaginative settings for each image'. He created two versions of the feminine *Rose Gown* (1989, *see* page 20) and *Roses de Nuit* (1989, *see* page 21) in different colour-ways. The striking 'Diva Suite' of 1984 illustrated *Diva I*, a light-skinned woman on a black background, and *Diva II*, a dark-skinned woman on a pale ground, both embossed serigraphs with foil stamping. Similarly, *Emerald Vase* I (1986) on a pale background is reversed in black in *Emerald Vase* II (1986). Striking examples of reverse image within the same frame are *Adam and Eve* (1982), and *Aladdin and his Bride* (1984, *see* pages 70–71). Sometimes he would choose to alter the original image even further by printing on a different coloured paper.

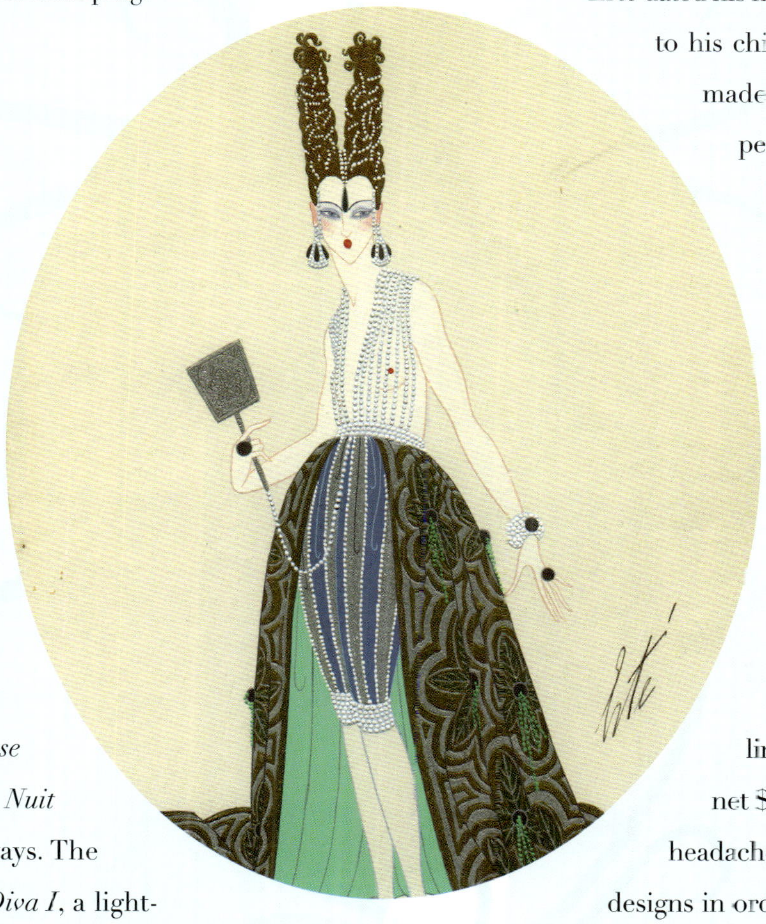

THE BRONZE SCULPTURES

Erté dated his first three-dimensional creations right back to his childhood, when at the age of five he had made a theatre of characters from empty perfume bottles with fabric offcuts glued on. His work in furniture design, jewellery and theatrical costumes also realized his illustrations in three dimensions, as did his *Formes Picturales* exploration of metal sculptures. But in 1980 Ronald K. Parker, President of the American company Circle Fine Art Corporation, contacted Erté to suggest creating a signed limited edition collection of bronze sculptures. This was a lucrative commission. One limited edition of 300–500 sculptures would net $150 million to $200 million. Erté's biggest headache was choosing from tens of thousands of designs in order to pick 24 for the first collection. The decision was taken to make it a 'fashion and fantasy' series. *An Evening in 1921*, a dress design for *Harper's Bazaar*, symbolizing the glamorous fashions of the 1920s was one, and *Firebird* was another from the original group. The sales success of the first collection led to the second collection of 18 works entitled *Images in Bronze*, focusing on theatre, fashion and fantasy.

La Traviata, *1982, serigraph, 57.8 x 45.1 cm (22¾ x 17¾)*
Erté was involved with *La Traviata* in many ways, including a 1952 production with controversial surrealistic costumes. In 1985 he created a playing cards pack. When laid out numerically, by suit, highlights from the opera unfolded.

Costume design for la Belladonne, in Les Fleurs du Mal, *1917, gouache, 25.4 x 16.5 cm (10 x 6½ in)*

GETTING HIS HANDS DIRTY

For some designers and illustrators, the making of bronze works from original drawings might signify leaving the work to professional sculptors. Not Erté. He envisaged the finished result in three dimensions right from the beginning. It was his working method to comprehend the complete design of any work in his mind before putting pen or paintbrush to paper. This dated from his earliest study of fashion design. Of course, some of his original works lent themselves to three-dimensional transference more than others. Although he was aware of the process of making bronze sculptures, he did not realize just how complex, complicated and difficult it was. One must admire Erté, at 87, learning a new skill and perfecting it. From the preliminary drawing to making an armature (the 'skeleton' for the clay) to making the clay model, Erté controlled the creative process. A plaster cast was made from his clay model, and a rubber mould made from the plaster cast. The bronze sculpture was made using the *cire perdue* method, centuries old, in use in ancient times. In 1980 Erté spent many hours at the foundry when first production began.

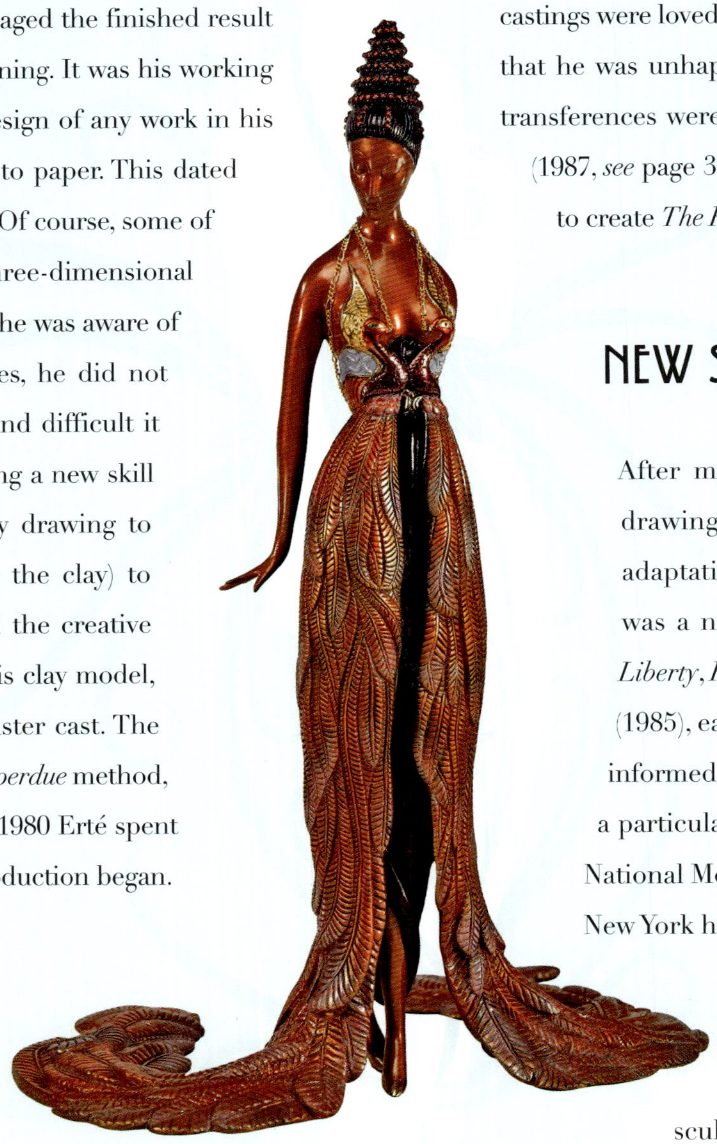

A SUCCESSFUL SERIES OF SCULPTURES

Erté chose a top-quality, expensive form of bronze work, using chemical patination, or sometimes the 'cold painting' method, whereby a colour is painted on to achieve a particular patina. He enjoyed this process from a painter's perspective, choosing the right colour, texture and finish for each piece. From 1980 to 1990 he used four different foundries: Joel Meisner & Company Foundry, New York; Fine Art Acquisitions Foundry, Los Angeles; the Renaissance Foundry, Connecticut; and the Tallix Foundry, New York. Not all castings were loved by Erté. For *Ibis*, after 35 castings Erté decided that he was unhappy with the head. It was changed. But most transferences were successful. *The Firebird* embossed serigraph (1987, *see* page 31 left), in a limited edition of 300, was adapted to create *The Fire Dancer* sculpture (*see* page 31 right).

NEW SUITES SERIES

After making bronzes inspired by his earliest ink drawings and gouaches, Erté broke away from his adaptation of earlier works to create a new series. It was a new direction. The *American* series, featured *Liberty, Fearless and Free* (1984); *Peace* (1984); and *Justice* (1985), each in a limited edition of 500. The trilogy was informed by Erté's respect for American values. He had a particular empathy with the copper Statue of Liberty National Monument on Liberty Island, at the entrance to New York harbour. It was a gift from the people of France to commemorate the centenary of the American Declaration of Independence in 1886. The statue was designed by French sculptor Frédéric Auguste Bartholdi (1834–1904). Erté admired Bartholdi's work but for his own version added 'movement' through the angle of Liberty's body, the flowing drapes of her dress and the angle of the torch. The *Liberty, Fearless and Free* led to a request for 50 ten-foot versions of it,

Feather Gown *sculpture, 1990, bronze, 43 x 30 x 20 cm (17 x 12 x 8 in)*

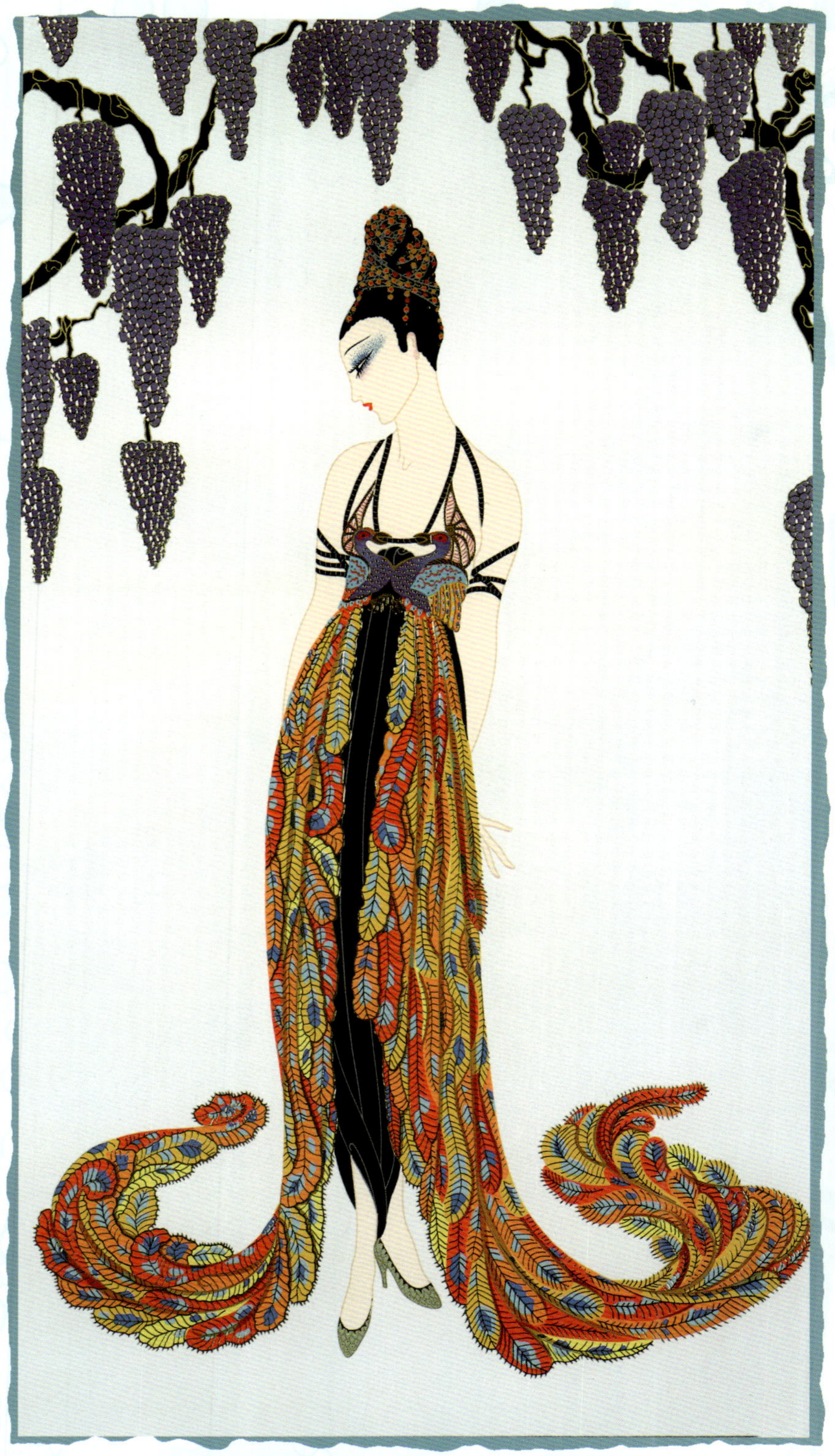

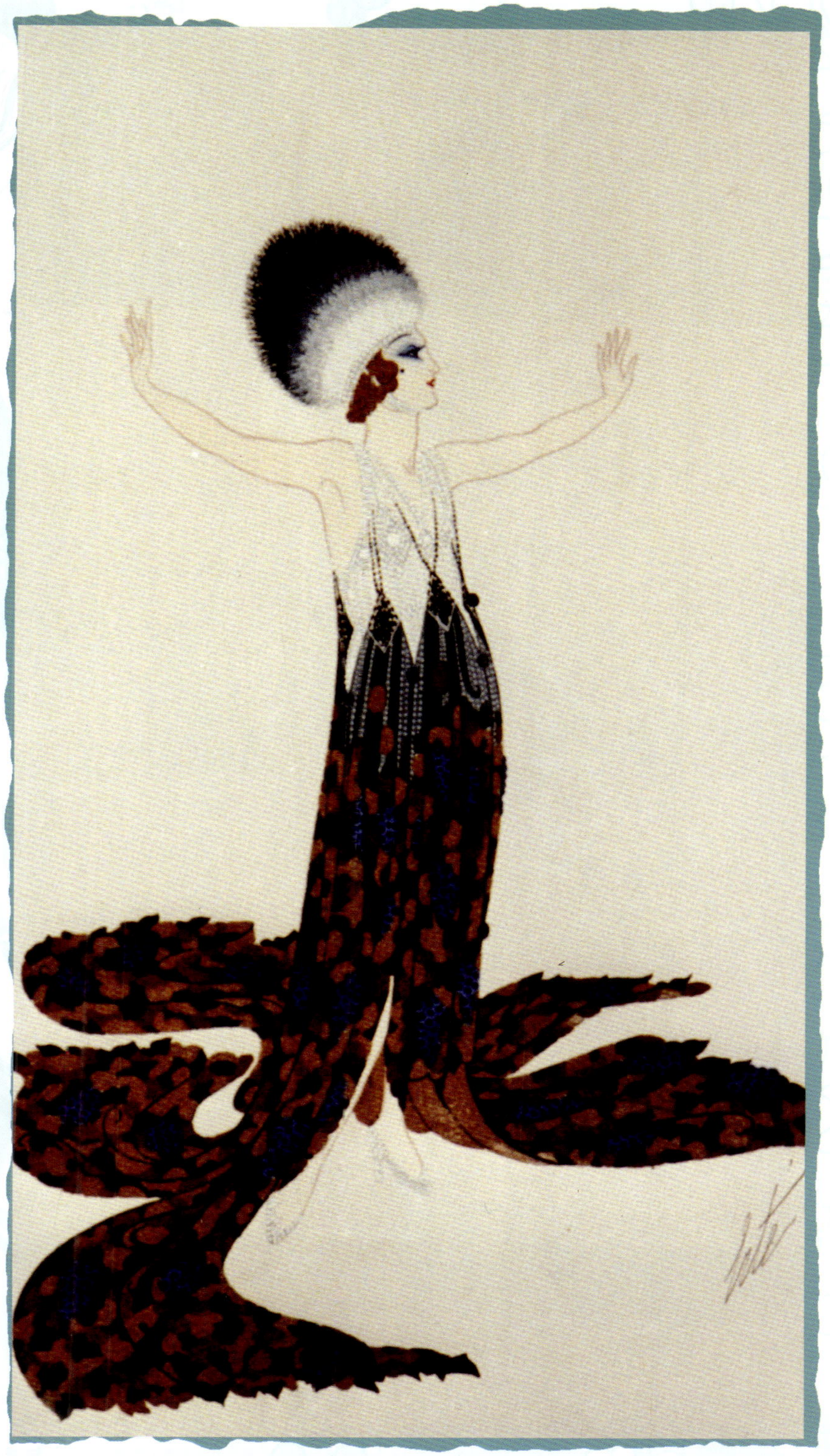

Feather Gown, *1985, embossed serigraph with foil stamping, 75.2 x 52.1 cm (29½ x 20½ in)*

Robe de la Fête, *costume design for Gaby Deslys, 1919, gouache, 31 x 23.5 cm (12¼ x 9¼ in)*
Though this dress seems to feature leaves rather than feathers, one can see strong similarities between this costume and the later serigraph and sculpture *Feather Gown* (1985/1990).

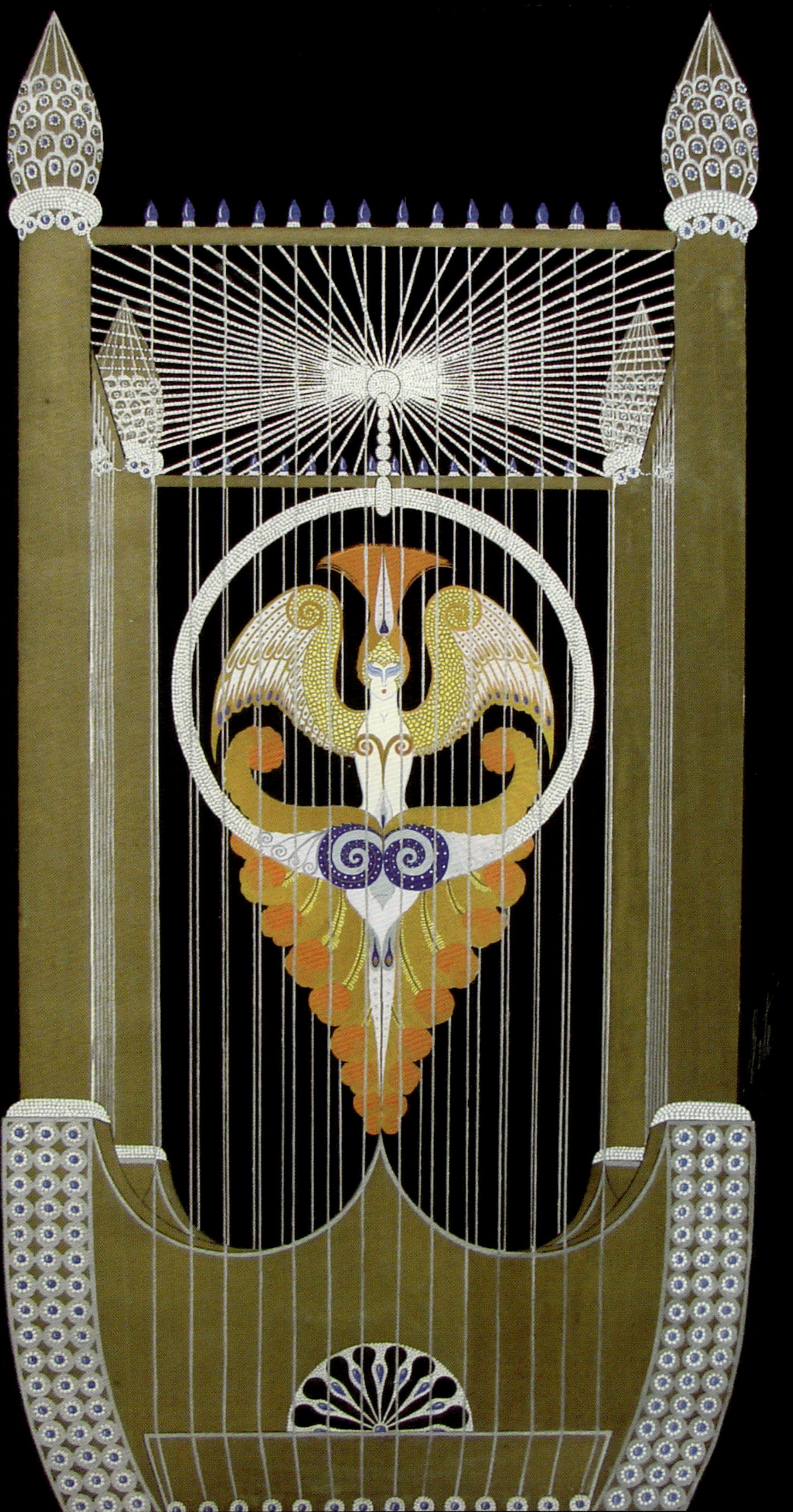

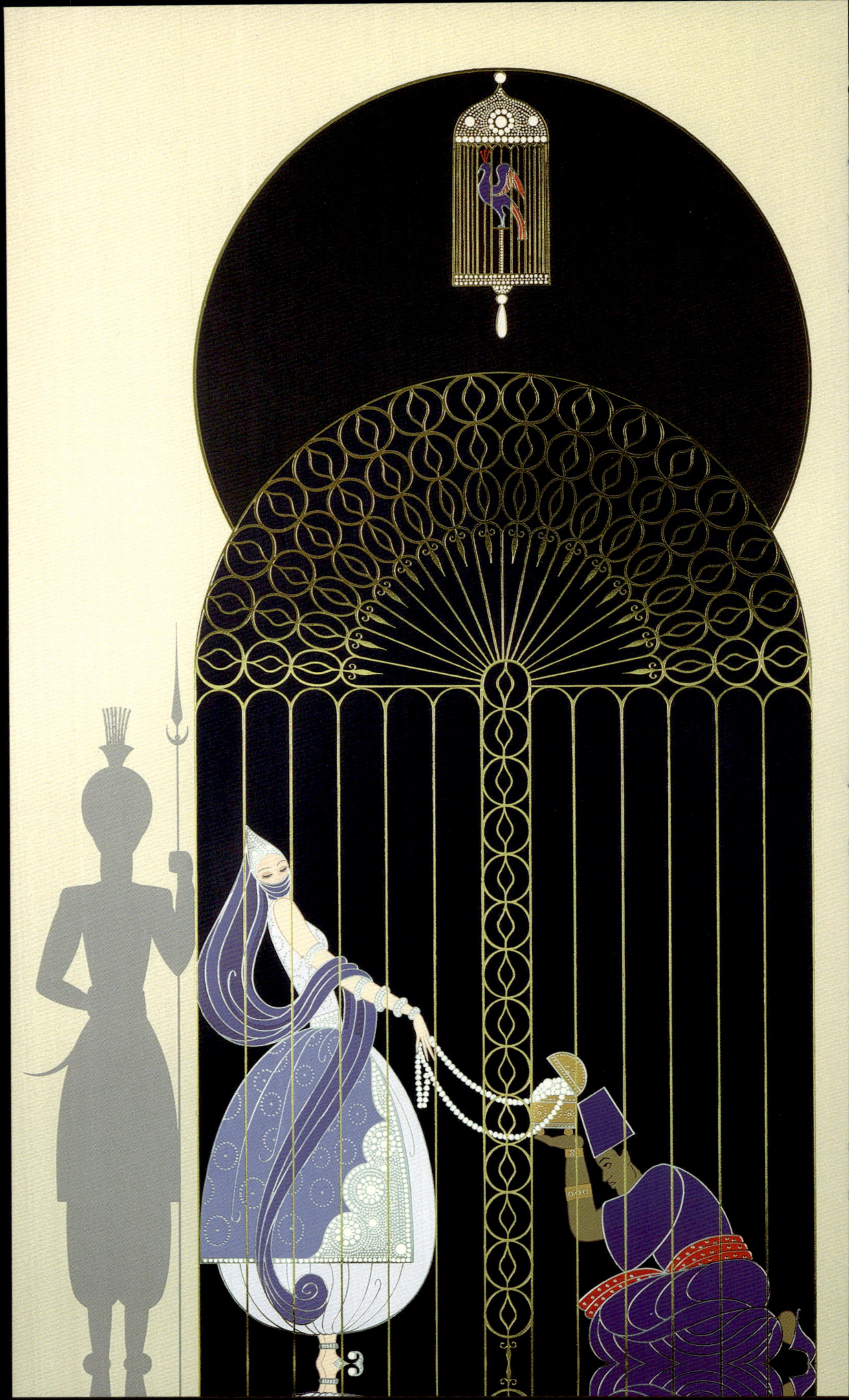

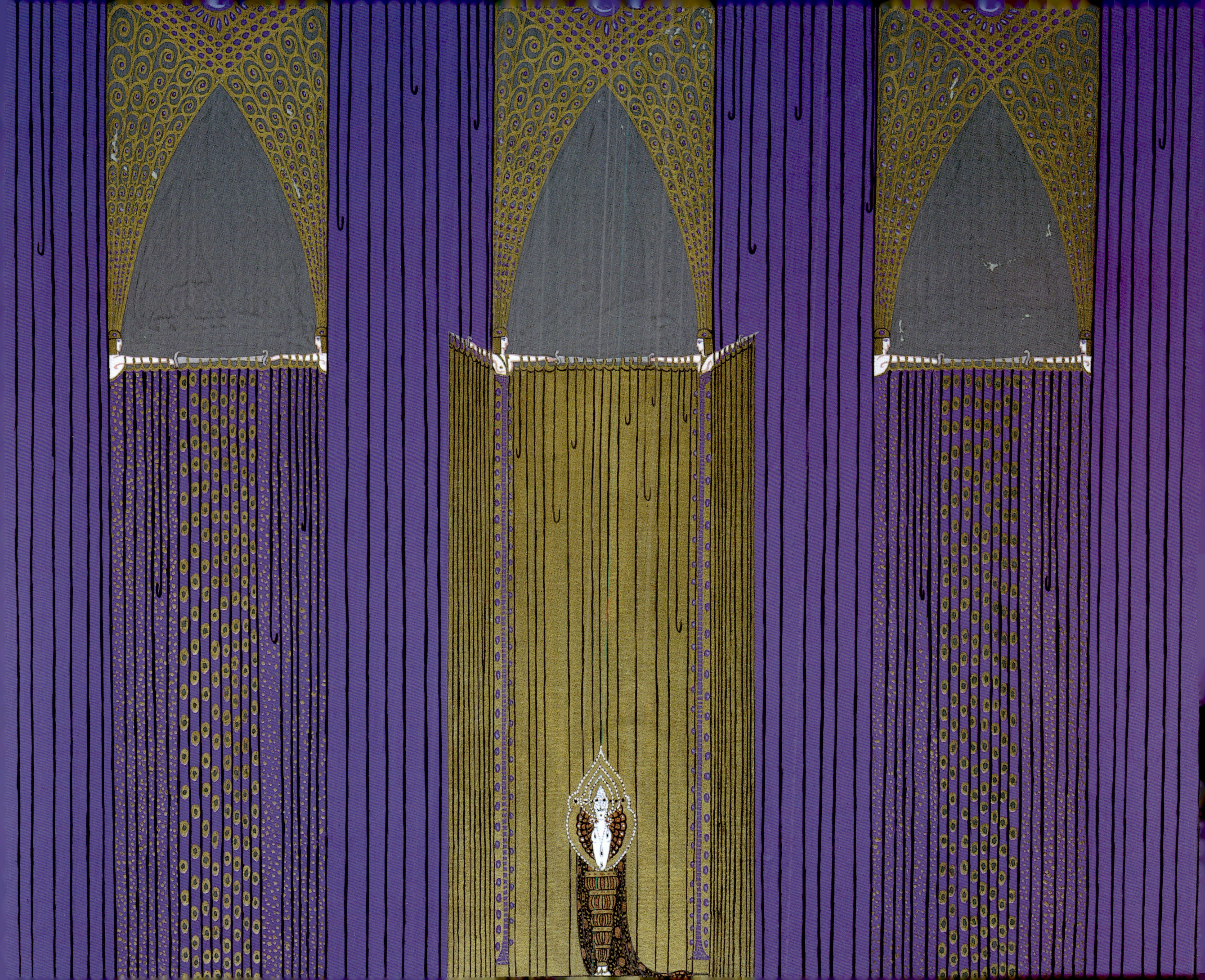

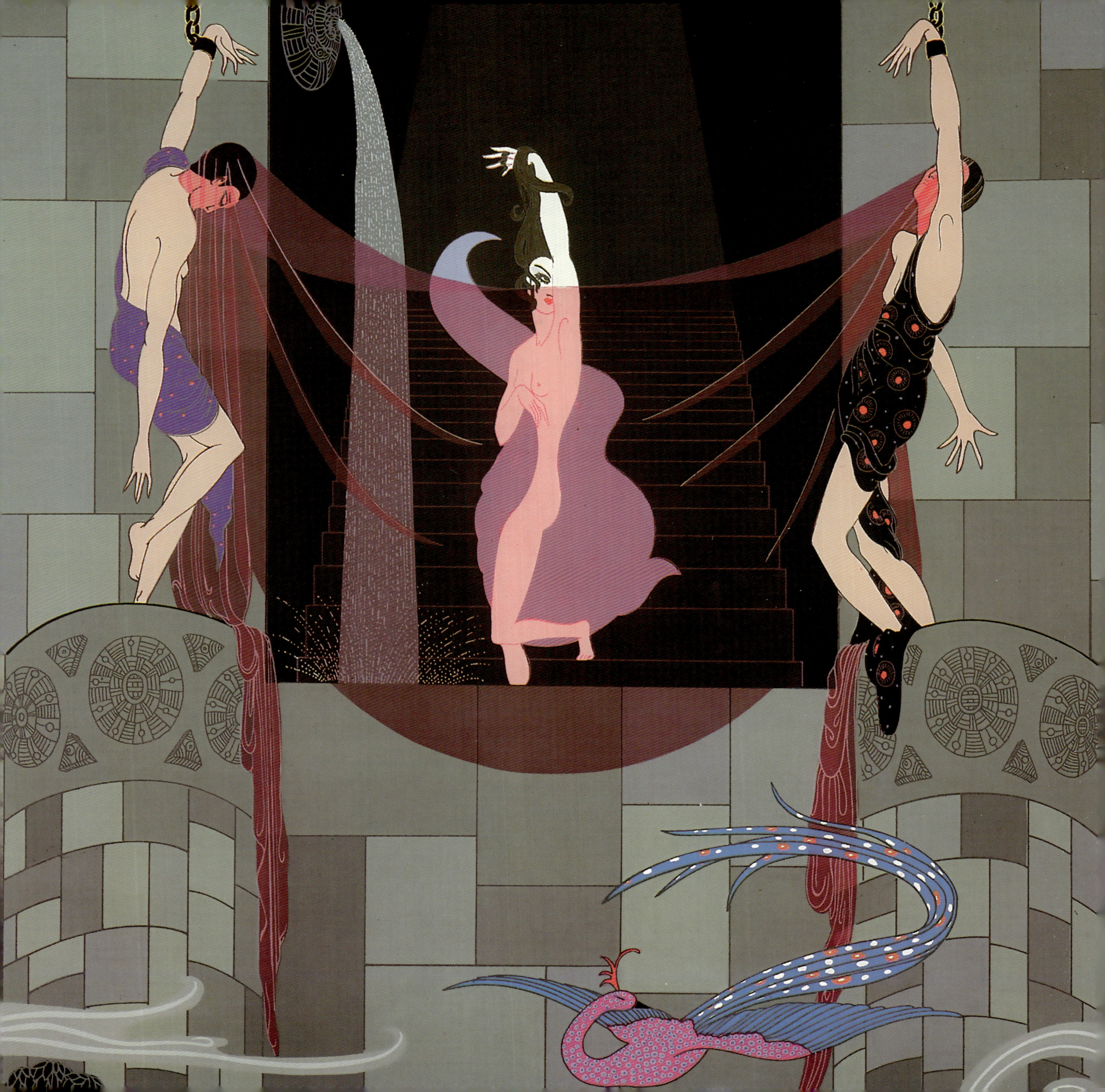

one for each American State. The Hoheb Studio in New York up-scaled the original clay maquette and the Meisner Foundry cast them in bronze. The work inspired the serigraph 'Statue of Liberty Suite': *Statue of Liberty Day* (1986, *see* page 108), and *Statue of Liberty Night* (1986, *see* page 109), published to coincide with the 200th anniversary of the American Declaration of Independence.

STATUE OF LIBERTY PRINTS

Each design created for a serigraph was a new challenge for Erté, his printers and publishers. He wanted to push the limitations of serigraph printing and its visual content. For the 'Statue of Liberty Suite' he wanted a day scene, *Statue of Liberty Day* (1986, *see* page 108) and a night scene, *Statue of Liberty Night* (1986, *see* page 109), possibly adapted from the earlier *Fire* (1984), in the 'Four Elements Suite'. He referred to the assignment as 'an epic story in itself' (*Erté at Ninety-Five: The Complete Graphics*, 1987). It took him and his team two years to complete the pair. Erté agreed to the suggestion that the images should face each other but later changed his mind. He did not want 'Liberty' holding the torch in her left hand because 'left in Latin is sinister'. Elements such as fireworks in the *Night* scene were difficult to achieve, as were the gradations of gold colouring from bronze gold for the statue to a yellow gold for the sunburst in the *Day* scene. Other problems included the background of the Manhattan skyline silhouettes and the waves. Erté wanted the waves rising up to the statue to be a symbol 'that Liberty is always threatened from without as she moves upward towards her goals'. Reading about the various problems to be worked through gives an understanding of how each layer of the serigraph had to be considered in relation to the whole work and the months of work that went into achieving the result Erté had envisioned at the start.

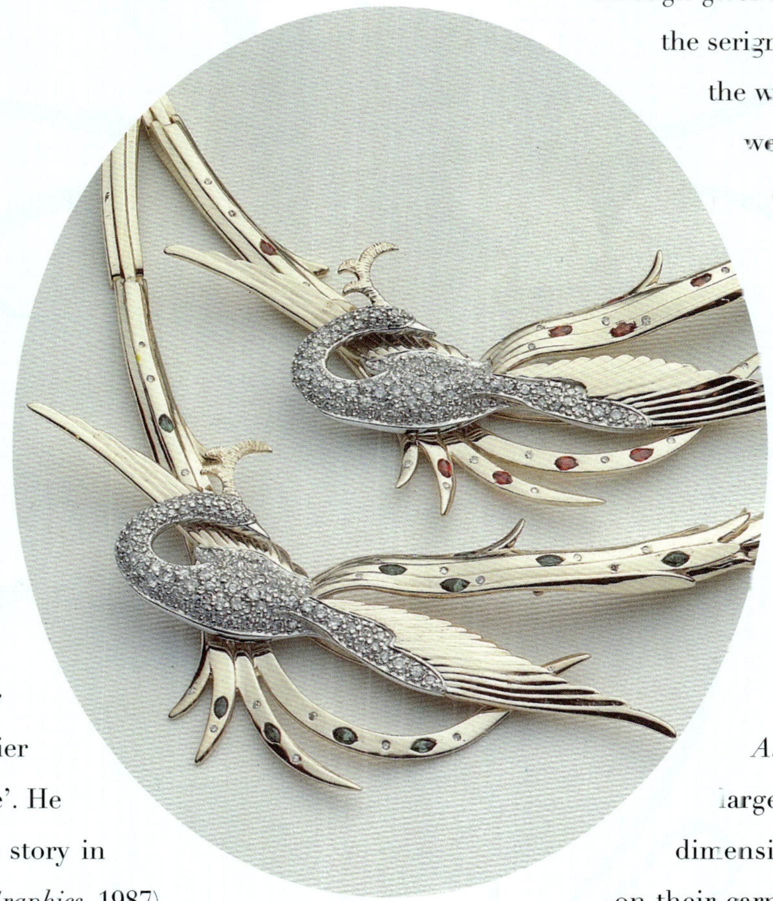

A LUCRATIVE ALPHABET

In the 1980s a bronze sculpture collection, based on the *Alphabet* series, was introduced, with adaptations to some of the costumes and additions to the series, such as *Alphabet Lady* (1989, *see* page 180). The larger forms of the original two-dimensional figures focused public attention on their carnal content. For example the letter 'K' reproduced as a bronze sculpture was deemed erotic. Erté justified his concept of a near-naked girl (her arms and legs forming part of the 'K'), wearing only a necklace, stockings and long gloves, chained to a column with a statue of Cupid on top, defending it as a symbol of a woman's captivity in love, bound to another person. Roland Barthes commented that for

(Previous, left, left side) **L'Oiseaux Merveillieux**, *1927, gouache and metallic paint, 55.9 x 37.1 cm (22 x 14½ in)*
(Previous, left, right side) **Bird in a Gilded Cage**, *1989, serigraph, 99 x 69 cm (39 x 27 in)*
(Previous, right) **Set design for The Golden Fables**, *George White's 'Scandals', New York, 1926, gouache, 38.1 x 29.2 cm (15 x 11½ in)*

(Left) **The Chaste Susanna**, *1980, serigraph, 43.2 x 33 cm (17 x 13 in)*
(Above) **Juno** *necklaces, c. 1979–90, gold, diamonds, rubies/emeralds*

Erté 'femininity is sinuous', a cultural or cult form of beauty. Conversely, when Erté created his bronze sculpture *The Three Graces* (1987), he clothed them, unlike the ancient Greek originals. Erté recalled that during his childhood visits to the Hermitage Museum he was impressed by ancient Greek sculptures and the beauty of the 'marvellously draped human forms'. The flow and movement of the drapery inspired him. One can see this love of drapery in this sculpture group and the embossed serigraph *Three Graces* (1985).

UNISEX LOOKS RETURN

Early on in his career Erté's first stab at criticizing the uniformity of men's fashion led to a backlash in the press. He advocated a unisex fashion in the late 1920s, the first designer to make the suggestion. The pen and ink drawing *Modern sports dress for men and women* (1929), is a visual interpretation. One can see in his drawings, such as the *Charleston Couple* (1980) (from 'The Twenties Remembered Suite'), his preference for attention-grabbing male dress. In the 1970s, probably bolstered by the return to men's 'peacock' fashions, in suits, shirts, ties and accessories, and the 'flower-power' ideology embraced by the younger generation of the era, Erté returned to fashion design, long absent from his repertoire, with a series of 'unisex' tunics.

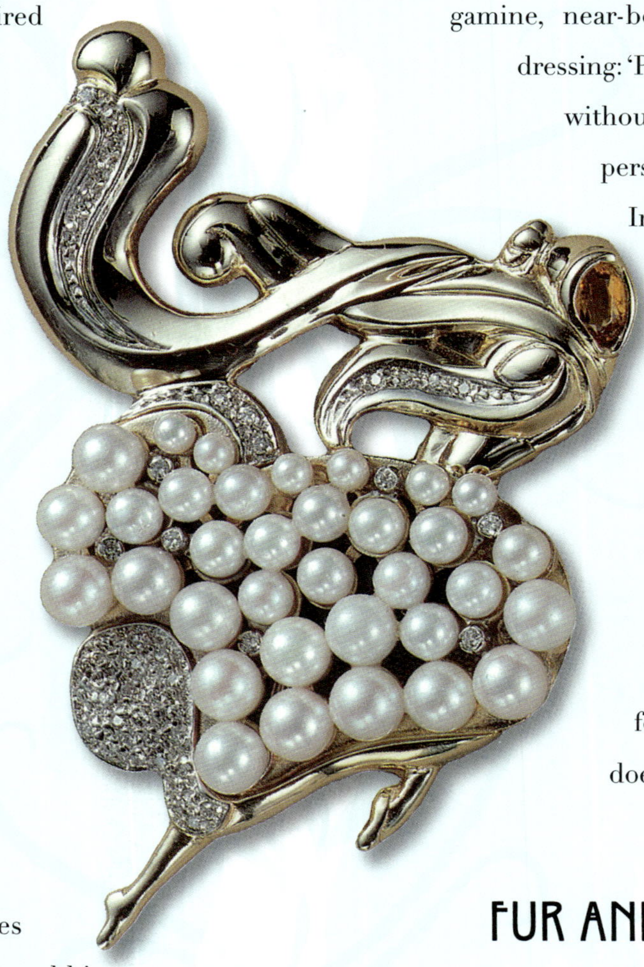

THE IDEAL WOMAN

Erté's drawings and gouache artworks established his personal look for women. His design technique revolved around a slim, elegant silhouette. He did not design clothes for larger women. His ideal model was slim, not too curvaceous, preferably with gamine, near-boyish looks. He had a mantra for dressing: 'People should not blindly follow fashion without taking into account their personalities' (*Erté: Fashions by Erté* (1972), Introduction). He believed that everyone should dress according to their own character and shape to achieve with clothes, as an aid, their real personality. 'I designed models out of my own imagination without any precise objective. The result was that they became sources of inspiration for the fashion trade.' However, 'The ideal dress, the epitome of elegance, is for me one which five or ten years later does not seem to be ridiculous.'

FUR AND FEATHERS

'I have a great affinity with fur and feathers,' stated Erté in a 1982 interview with Suzy Menkes on fashion for *The Times* newspaper. He put his extensive use of fur down to the many theatrical costumes he had designed. Worn by a society woman, fur was a symbol of wealth. In the theatre or on film it was a

Iris *brooch, c. 1979–90, gold, diamonds, citrine, pearls, D: 6 cm (2¼ in)*

The Pursuit of Flore, *1985, embossed serigraph with foil stamping, 83.8 x 67.3 cm (33 x 26½ in)*

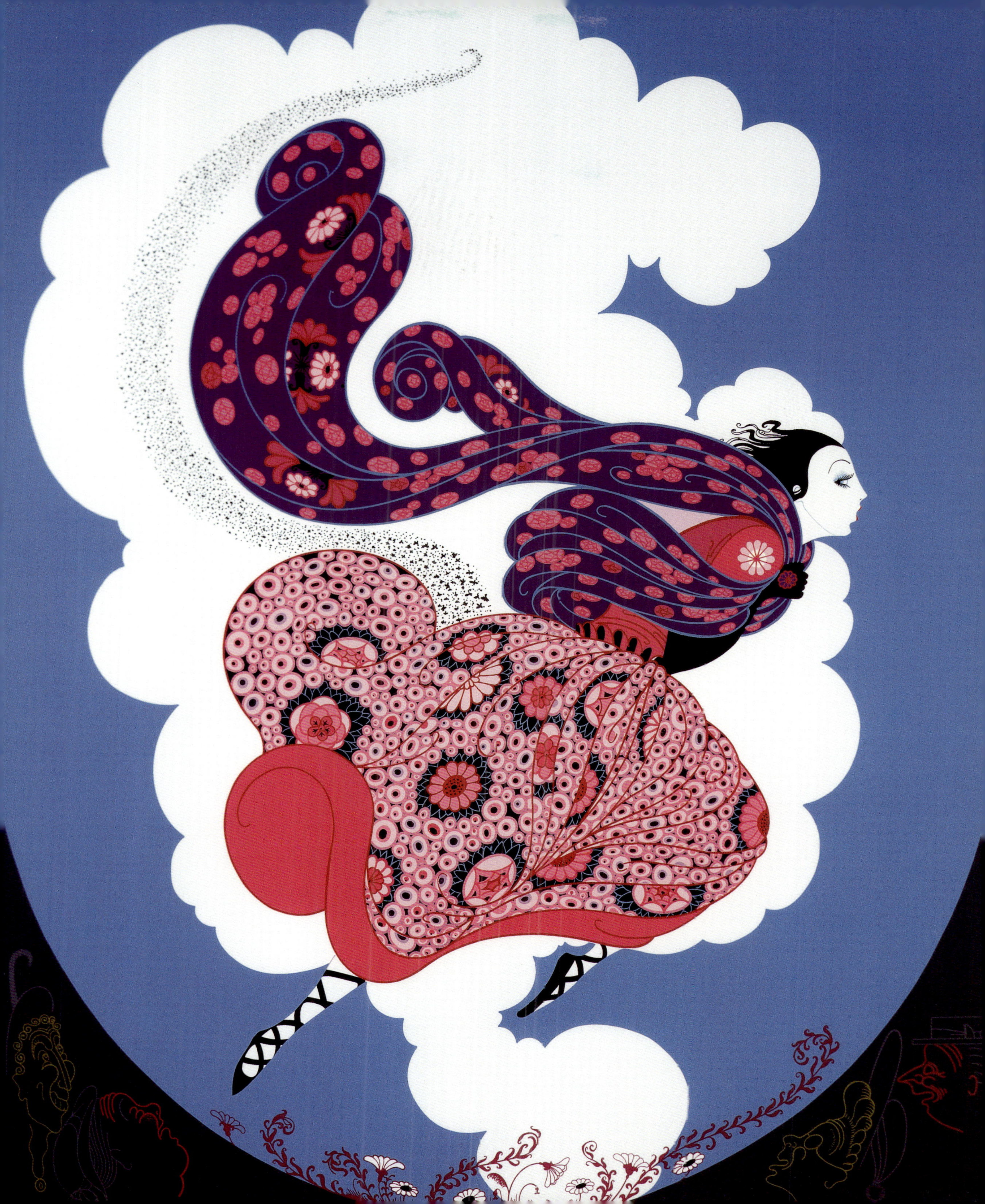

good prop to define the status of a character, as were feathers, from peacock feathers loved by *fin-de-siècle* aesthetes to the plumed hats and feather boas of the Twenties generation. Fur and feathers were aids, visual techniques to symbolize a specific a period in time through fashion.

CREATING SENSUALITY

Erté took the use of fur and feathers further, allocating their use to symbolize characteristics of exotic otherness. The bronze sculpture *La Femme à La Panthère* (1981), a female figure half-woman, half-feline holding onto a snarling panther by a golden chain was, in his words, a technique to convey the 'sensuous and dangerous' (*Erté: Sculpture*, 1986). The work was informed by Erté's successful 'L' letter from 'The Alphabet Suite' (*see* page 186). What else stands out? One of his earliest fur designs for Paul Poiret was featured, without Erté's signature, in *Harper's Bazaar* in January 1915, captioned, 'In times of peace the Parisienne would revel in this sumptuous ermine wrap....'

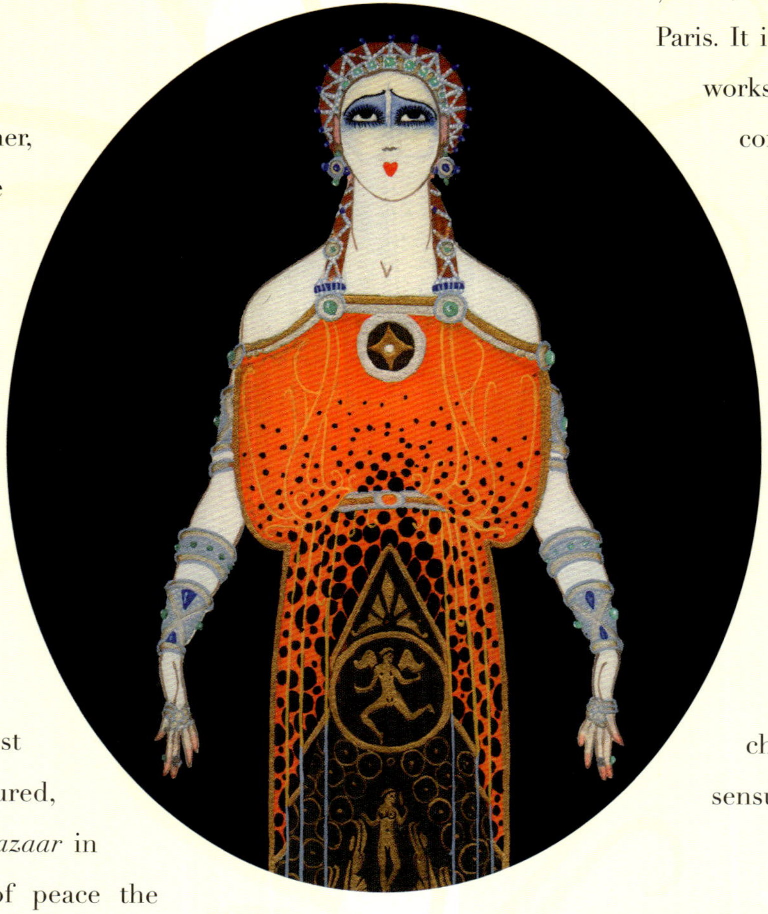

One could argue that the majority of female costumes Erté created for the stage and for film were sensuous. He had a gift for creating visually appealing theatrical clothing that bordered on fantasy. He adapted many to serigraph in later years. A 1919 costume design for actress Gaby Deslys *Robe de la Fete*, (*see* page 171 right), informed Erté's fantasy bird-feather dress in the serigraph *Feather Gown* (1985, *see* page 171 left). It was made into a bronze too, *Feather Gown* (1990, *see* page 170), one of his last works. Another bronze, *Ibis* (1983) was revised from a lavish pink-feathered costume, Erté's original design for a scene from *Les Oiseaux* ('The Birds') 1941, at Léon Volterra's music hall, the Lido, in Paris. It is interesting to consider in Erté's later works that although attitudes to women considerably changed between 1920 and 1990, Erté continued to rework original designs of women as sensual fantasy: the seductress, temptress and slave, young maiden and desirable beauty.

Erté carried this sensual creativity through to his stage and screen sets. For example, looking at photographs of sets for the Metro-Goldwyn-Mayer film *Paris* (1926), the dining room set is swathed in leopard skins, draped over chairs and side tables, creating a vision of sensual luxury, near-decadence, for the scene.

A SYMPHONY IN BLACK

Erté concocted fabulous fantasies of women – he preferred fantasy to reality in all his works – although some were based on people he had seen or knew. His technique was to make the woman and the clothes desirable. The sophisticated,

Costume design for Thaïs, *3rd Tableau, 1920, gouache and metallic paint, 30.5 x 24.4 cm (12 x 9½ in)*

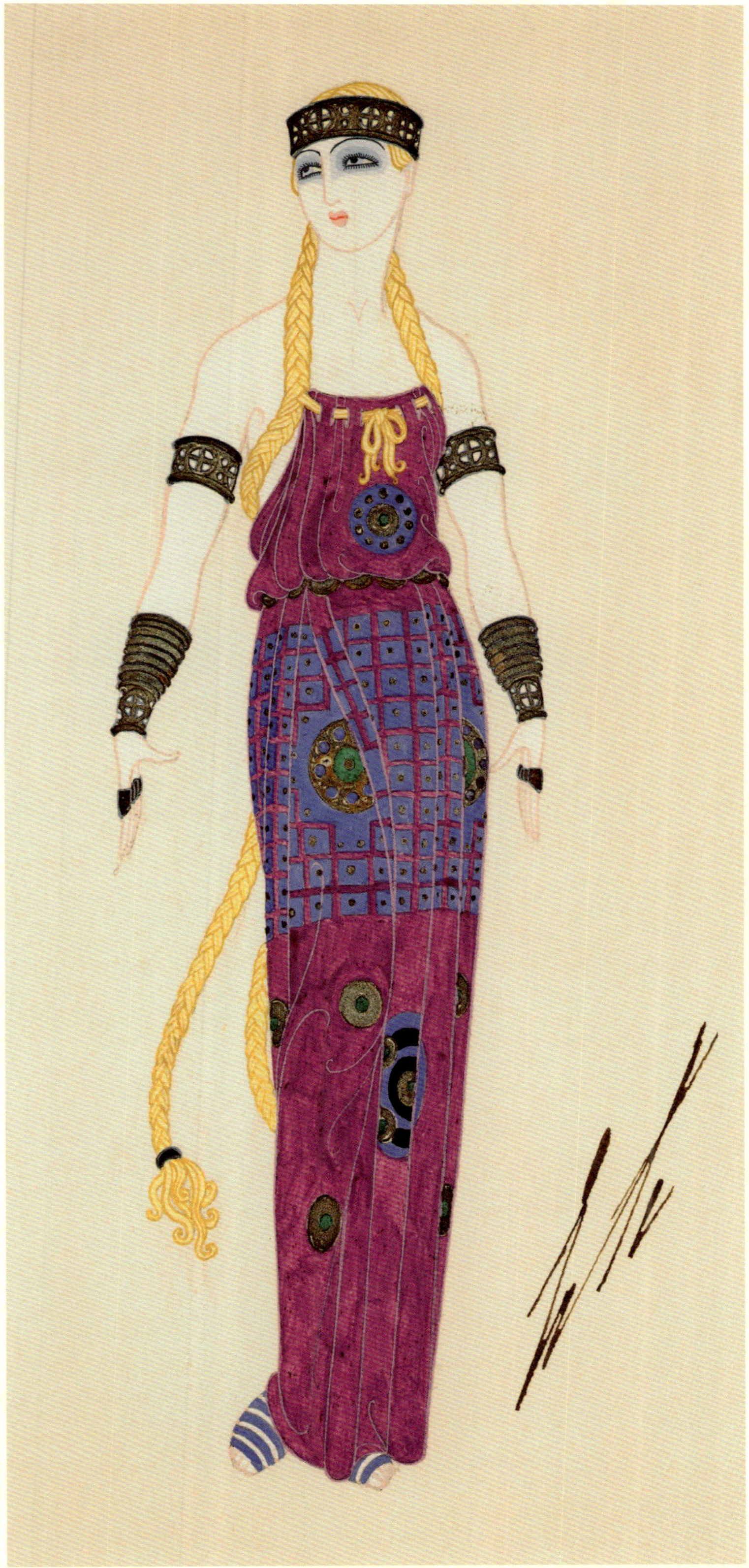

Femme Scandinave, *costume design for the film* Restless Sex, *Cosmopolitan Films, 1919, gouache, 36.2 x 26 cm (14¼ x 10¼ in)*

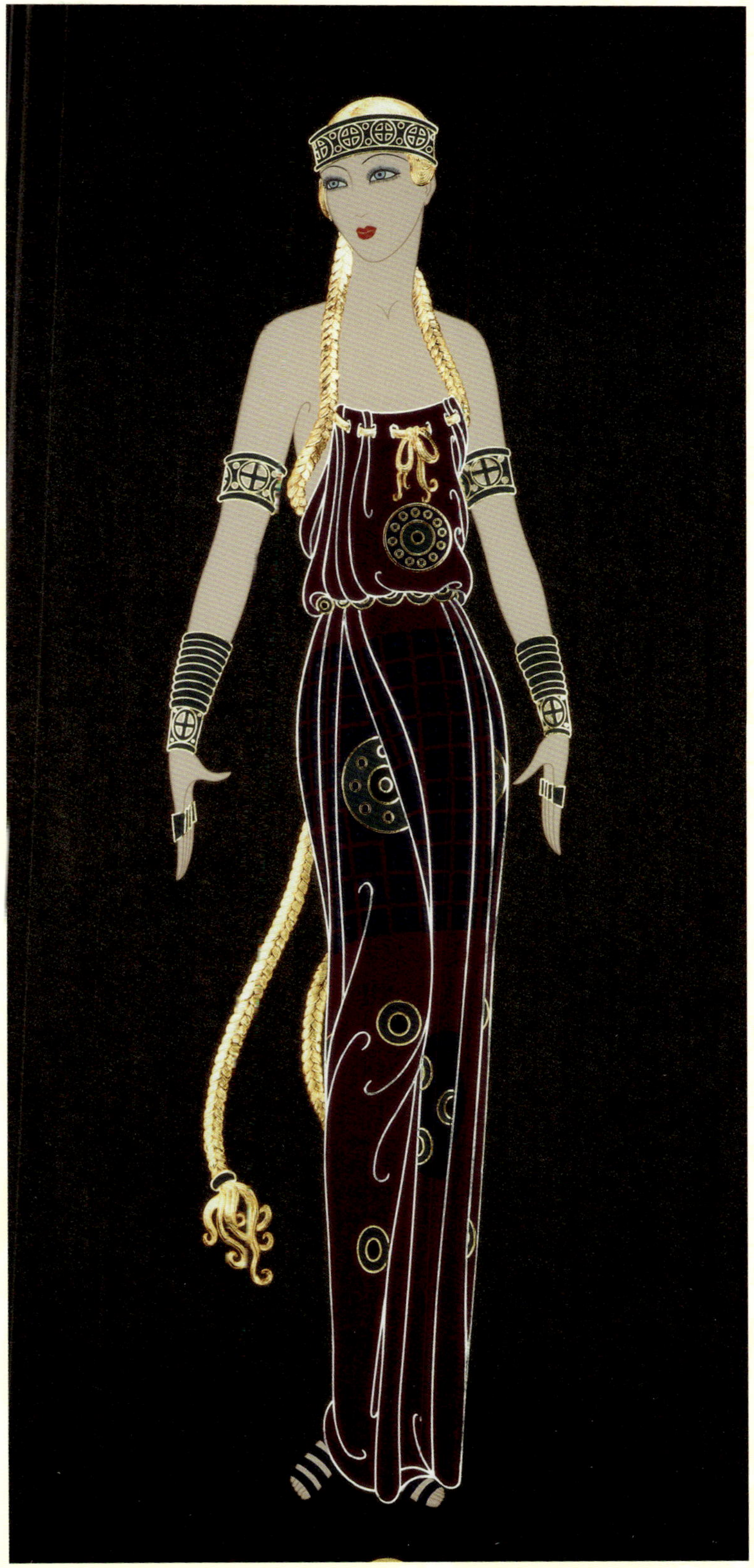

Scandinavian Princess, *1990, serigraph, 104.8 x 64.1 cm (41¼ x 25¼ in)*

elegant woman in the sculpture *Elegance* (1980, *see* page 68), also utilized in the serigraph *Symphony in Black* (1983, *see* page 67), was a re-make of Erté's costume design *Symphony in Black* (1938) for the 'London Symphony' show at the London Palladium in the same year. (*Symphony in Brown*, 1938, is from the series). The woman is adorned in a figure-tight evening dress, triple fur arm wraps, ornate headdress and jewels. She stands with her sleek greyhound who wears a bejewelled collar and lead. The woman and dog (not the costume) may have been instigated by Erté's memory of a chic slim woman with her Borzoi dog 'as thin as its mistress', its collar and lead matching the colour of its owners clothing, whom he saw in Biarritz in 1913, 70 years earlier. The serigraph was created in reverse image too, in *Ebony and White* (1982, *see* page 66). On elegance, Erté remarked, 'When I started out on my fashion career, I believed that a woman's Three Graces were beauty, charm and elegance. Of the three, I think, elegance is paramount. Elegance is an innate quality, it cannot be acquired.'

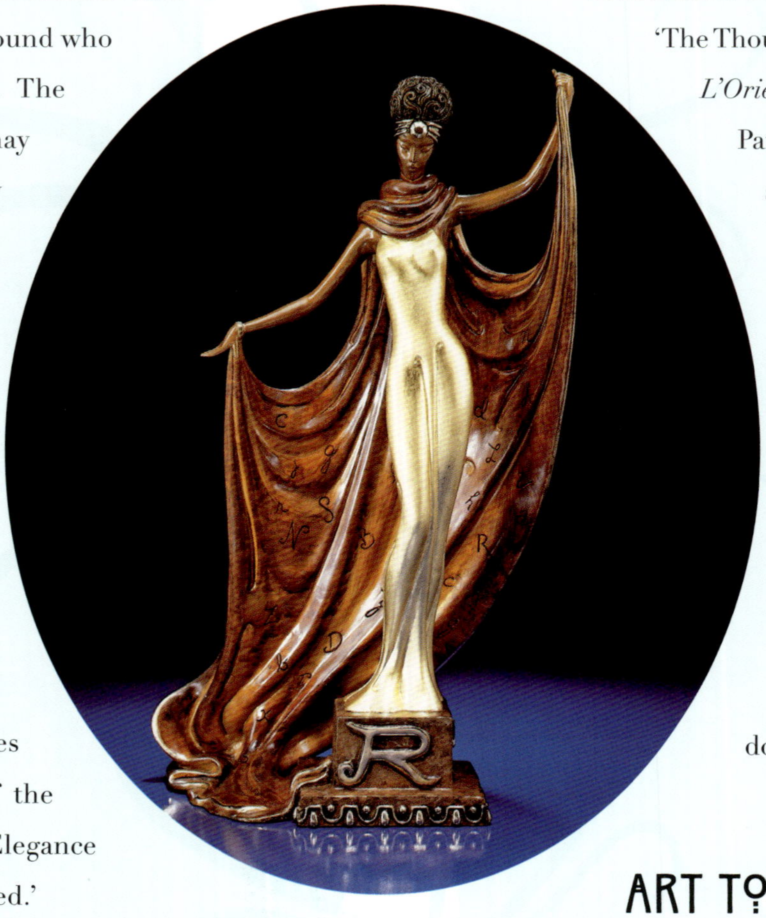

NAKED AMBITION

And what of Erté's techniques in theatrical costume design? He created many costumes that suggested that the spectator was seeing naked female bodies but his use of illusion, realized in the choice of materials, suggested more nudity than there actually was. Erté's costume designs on paper were often little more than a light decoration of the naked body, particularly for revue shows like the Folies Bergère in Paris. But those who wore them stated that they were well made, stayed in place and were comfortable. The *Diamond Statue* (1917), a costume in 'The Thousand and Second Night at Baghdad', for *L'Orient Merveilleux* (at the Femina Theatre, Paris, 1917), was made entirely of dazzling strung beads, formed to make spiders webs and scrolls. Some costumes, such as the triple costume design for 'Marriage' (1924, *see* page 130), for George White's *Les Mariages* revue looked little more than strings of spangles, beads and fake pearls. So, too, with the costume *Les bijoux de perle* (1983). Erté stated that his technique was to concentrate on one aspect of the body and work upwards or downwards from it.

ART TO WEAR

In 1979, Jack Solomon, with Erté's lithograph production underway, saw an opening for jewellery inspired by Erté's illustrations, another commercialization of Erté's style. In the 1970s, particularly in Britain and the USA, there was a strong demand for Art Deco jewellery, particularly amongst the

Alphabet Lady *sculpture, 1989, bronze, 48.3 x 25.4 x 19.1 cm (19 x 10 x 7½ in)*

Alphabet Cloak, *1968, gouache, 38.1 x 24.8 cm (15 x 9¾)*

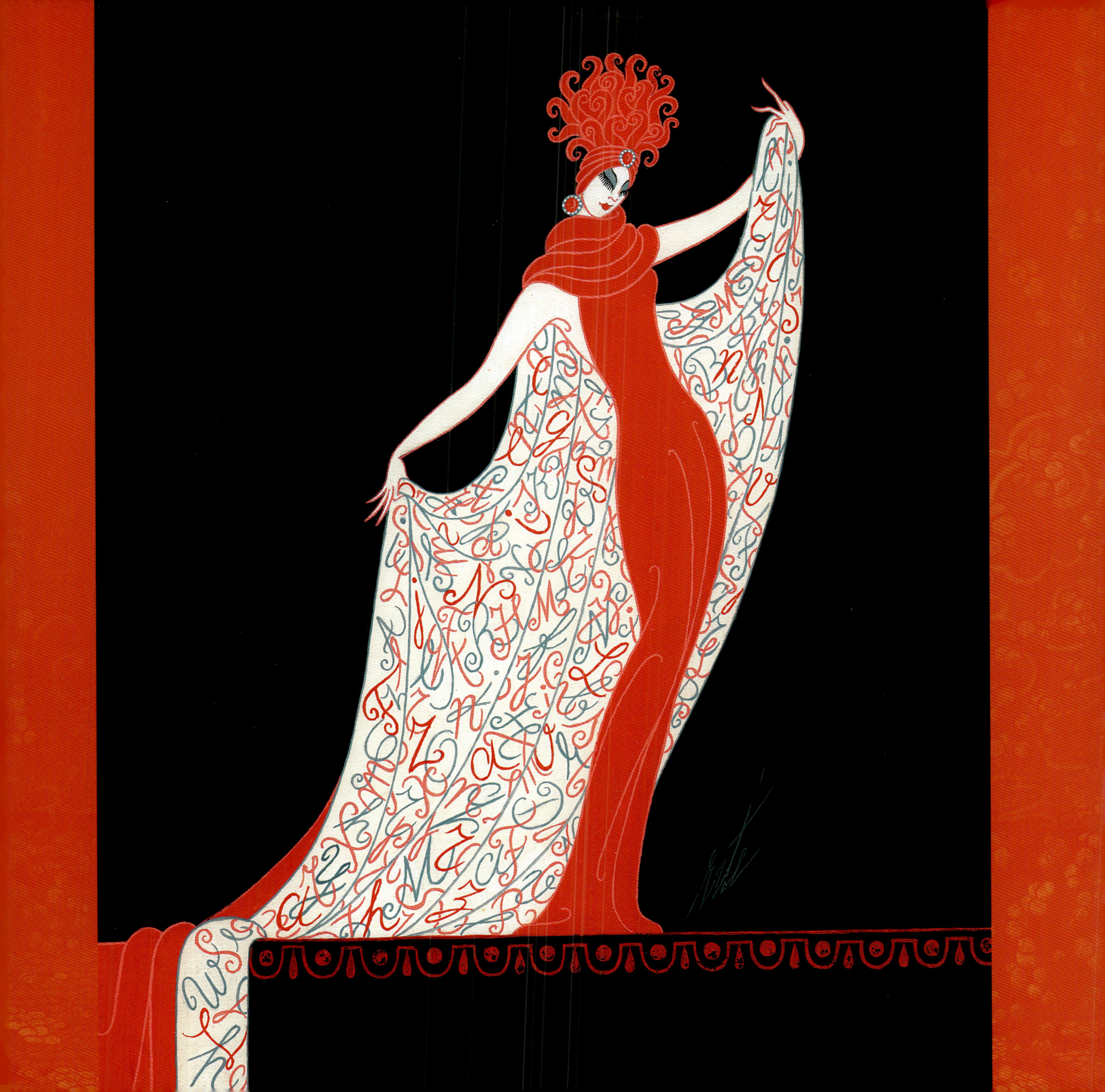

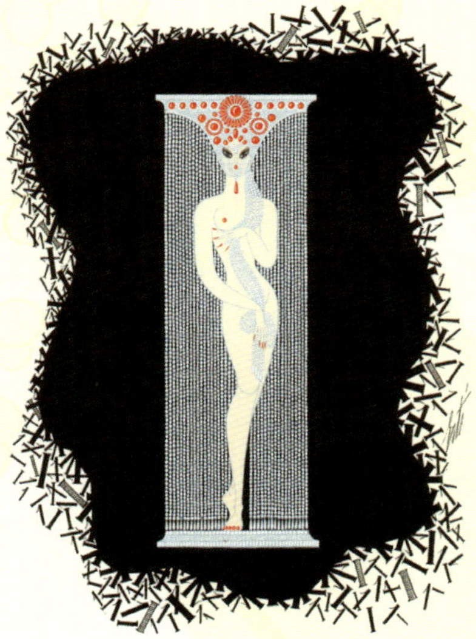
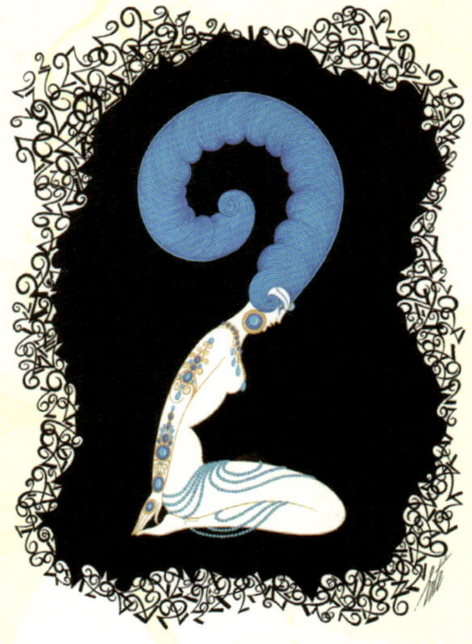
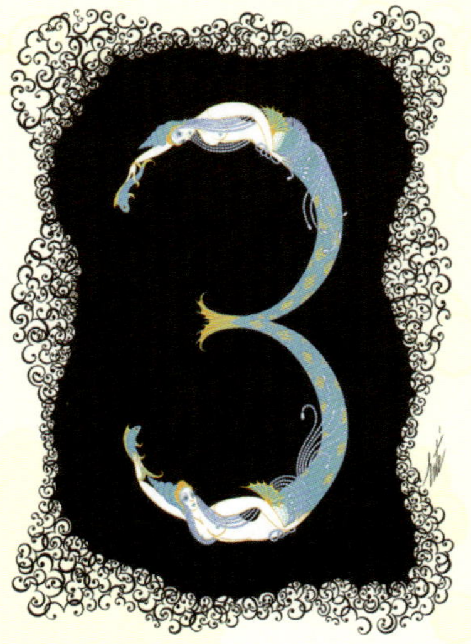
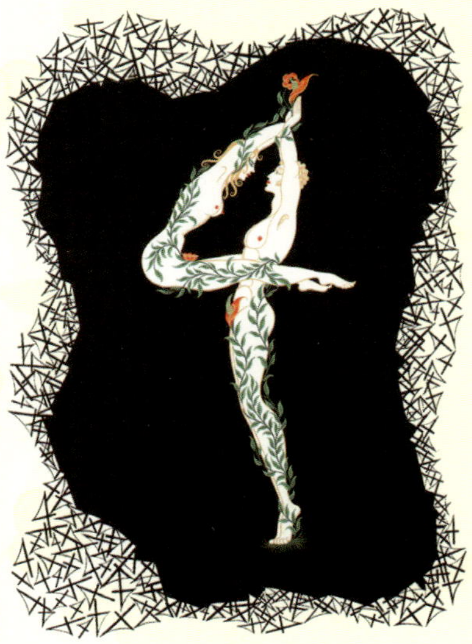
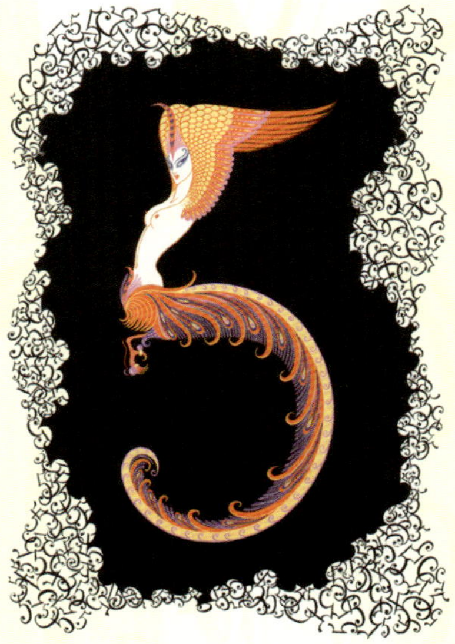
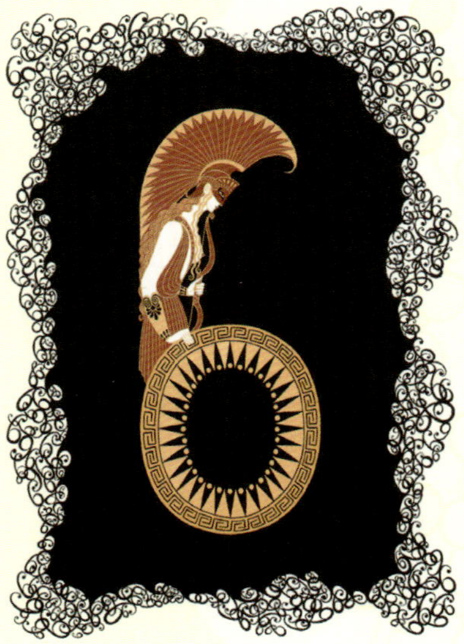
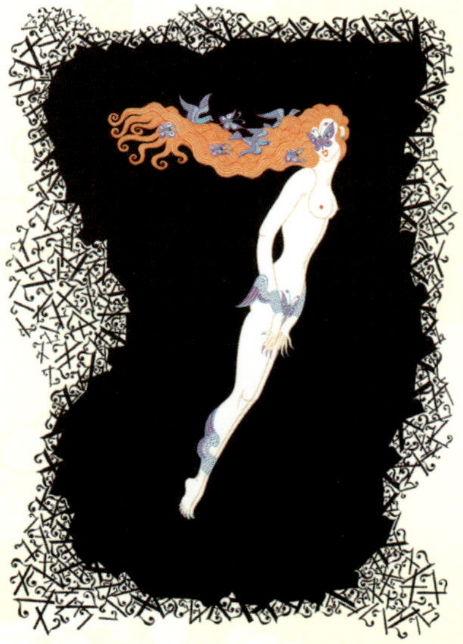
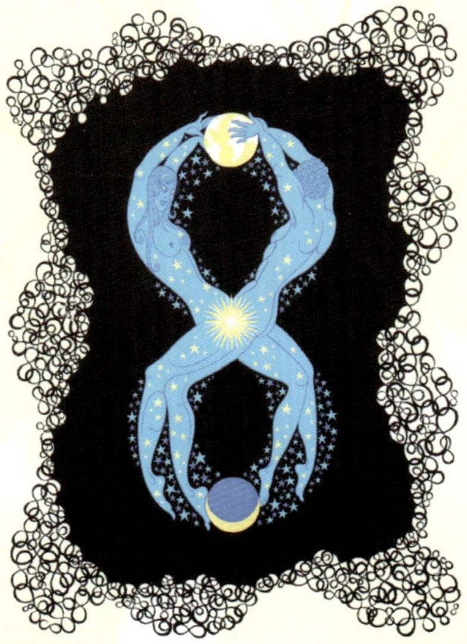
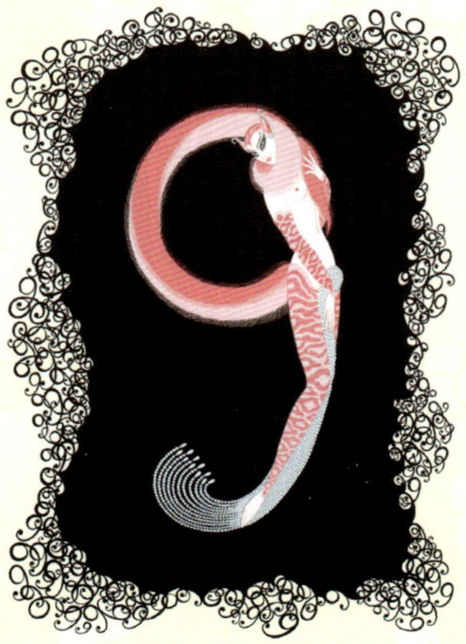

younger generation tapping into the glamour of the Twenties and Thirties. It excited Erté. He had realized a small show of limited edition jewellery at an exhibition of his art works in London at the Electric Gallery, South Molton Street, London in 1975 but Solomon's proposal was on a larger scale. For it, Erté needed to learn the complexities of jewellery design and the pleasure of re-working two-dimensional art into three-dimensional forms. A drawing, *Design for Coral Earrings* (1932) in gouache and metal, illustrates Erté's natural talent for jewellery design. He created a serigraph of the character of 'Giulietta' (1983), from the opera *Tales of Hoffman*. The character, a femme fatale, wears a seductive leopard print Directoire-style dress. She drips with jewels. For the brooch/pendant jewellery created from this image, only the head and shoulders were used. Re-named *Salome*, the design focused on opulent gemstones, using rubies, diamonds, silver, black onyx and mother-of-pearl.

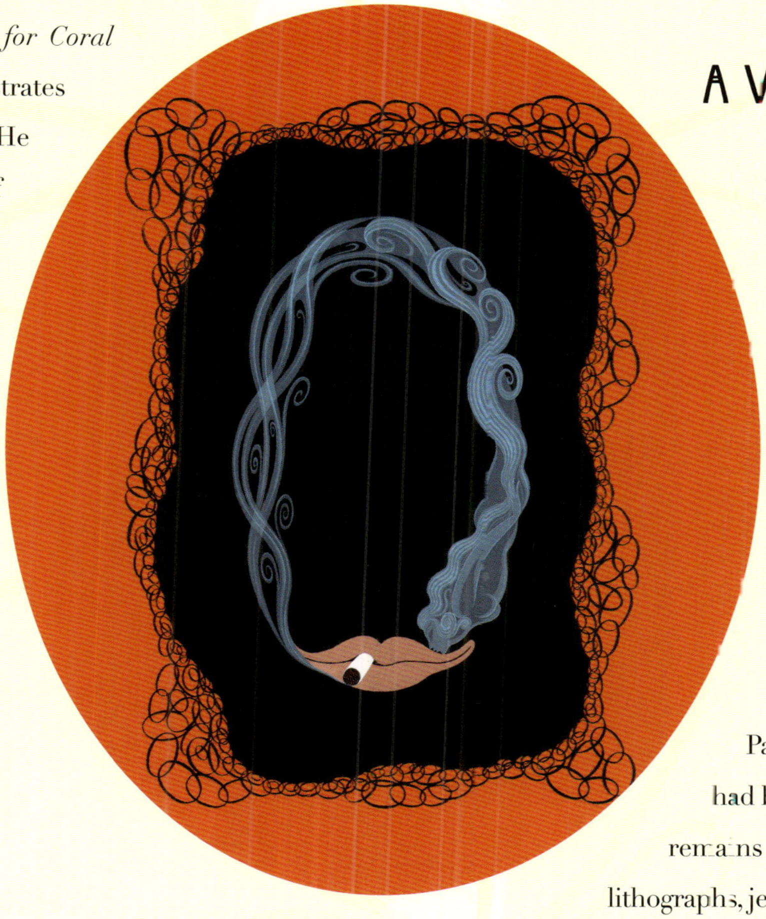

ERTÉ'S 'CHILDREN'

In 1982, in *The Times* interview, white-haired and in his ninetieth year, Erté was asked about his vast collection of over 20,000 works on paper. He said, 'I love them all equally. They are all my children and I am a good father'. Following his death, newspaper obituaries sought to sum up an extraordinary man who defined an era of glamour, perfect manners and high society. Erté had great stamina, which he put down to a good diet and regular exercise in the form of walking. His eyesight remained pin-sharp and his mental agility to take on the challenge of new enterprises, such as lithography and bronze-making, delighted him.

A VIABLE BUSINESS

Limited edition commercial productions had re-launched Erté; he became a collectors' focus. Apart from the first lithographs made in limited editions of 75, the following lithographs, serigraphs, jewellery and bronzes were created in greater limited editions. It widened the collectors' circle and made Erté a name to collect. His early theatre and film costumes, languishing in a prop room in Paris or Hollywood, were searched out. Erté had become a hot-property saleable brand. He remains so to the present day with serigraphs, lithographs, jewellery and sculptures sold at high prices.

COLLECTABLES

From the moment Erté stepped into the world of lithography and serigraphy he became collectable. Prior to 1979 he had

(Left and above) **The Numerals: 0–9**, *1980, embossed serigraphs, approx. each 42.5 x 31.7 cm (16¾ x 12½ in)*

retained the majority of his original works, stored away. Bringing back to life the originals in limited edition prints of 300 to 500 allowed private collectors to buy series and suites of his works. He is noted amongst the great artists of graphic design. During Erté's era a group of artists defined avant-garde illustration: the pioneering Czech graphic designer Alphonse Mucha, the masterful Frenchman Henri-Toulouse Lautrec, the Swiss Théophile Steinlen (1859–1923), and the Italian Manuel Orazi (1860–1934) plus Cassandre from the Ukraine, alongside the Russian Erté. All were exceptionally talented.

DEATH OF AN ICON

In March 1990, whilst on holiday on the island of Mauritius in the Indian Ocean, Erté suffered kidney problems and flew home to Paris. Weeks later, on 21 April, he died in the city's Cochin Hospital. It was a short illness that did not blight his 97 years of life. He was buried at the Cimitière de Boulogne-Billancourt, Hauts de Seine, Paris. At his death, obituary writers remembered him for his diverse ability to design couturier-quality clothes and 'Liberace' showbiz glamour costumes for musical revues. Some picked up on the male–female ambiguities found in his illustrations and costumes and his personal cross-dressing enjoyment – no one would forget his silver lamé 'Clair de Lune' costume covered in pearls, worn to a fancy-dress ball at the Sporting Club, Monte Carlo in 1922 – during his early professional years in Paris, dressed in sumptuous clothes designed for women but worn to greater effect by him.

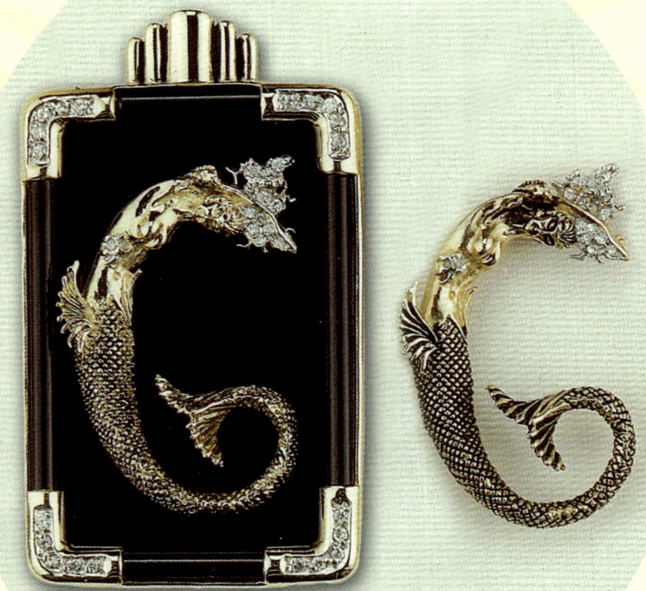

ERTÉ ON ERTÉ

Asked many times if he saw himself as the 'Father of Art Deco', Erté rejected any association with a particular period, except for his childhood interest in Persian miniatures. Writing in the early 1980s he stated:

Although I strongly reject the idea that my work in necessarily tied to the Art Deco period of the Twenties, because it is entirely personal and has, as I have said, its roots in Eastern miniature painting of my heritage, neither is there any direct connection between my graphics and the world of today. My work is not realism at all.
(*Erté at Ninety: The Complete Graphics,* 1982)

For the graphic artists, theatrical costumiers and stage producers who are inspired by Erté, and the many collectors and fans of his work, it is this lack of realism and focus on fantasy and glamour that makes Erté so popular today.

The Alphabet: 'G' *brooch/pendant, c. 1979–90, brooches: with frame: gold, diamonds, black onyx; without frame: gold, diamonds*

(Right and following pages) **The Alphabet: 'A–Z'**, *1976, lithograph/serigraph, 40 x 26.7 cm (15¾ x 10½ in)*
The Alphabet series was initiated in 1927. Erté created all but two letters – L and Q – in gouache. Years later he added the missing letters to create a new series of successful works in lithograph/serigraph (*see also* page 7).

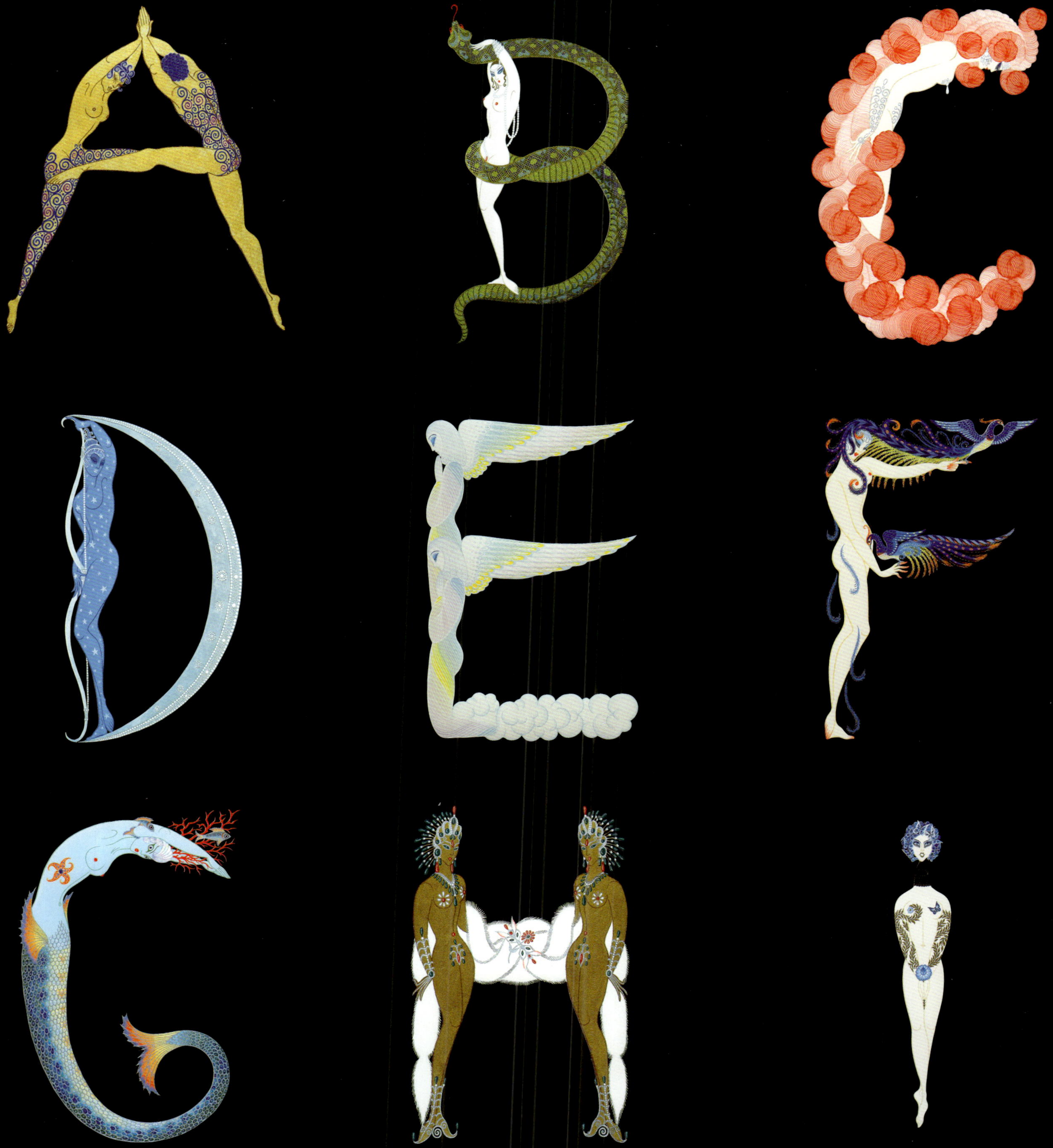

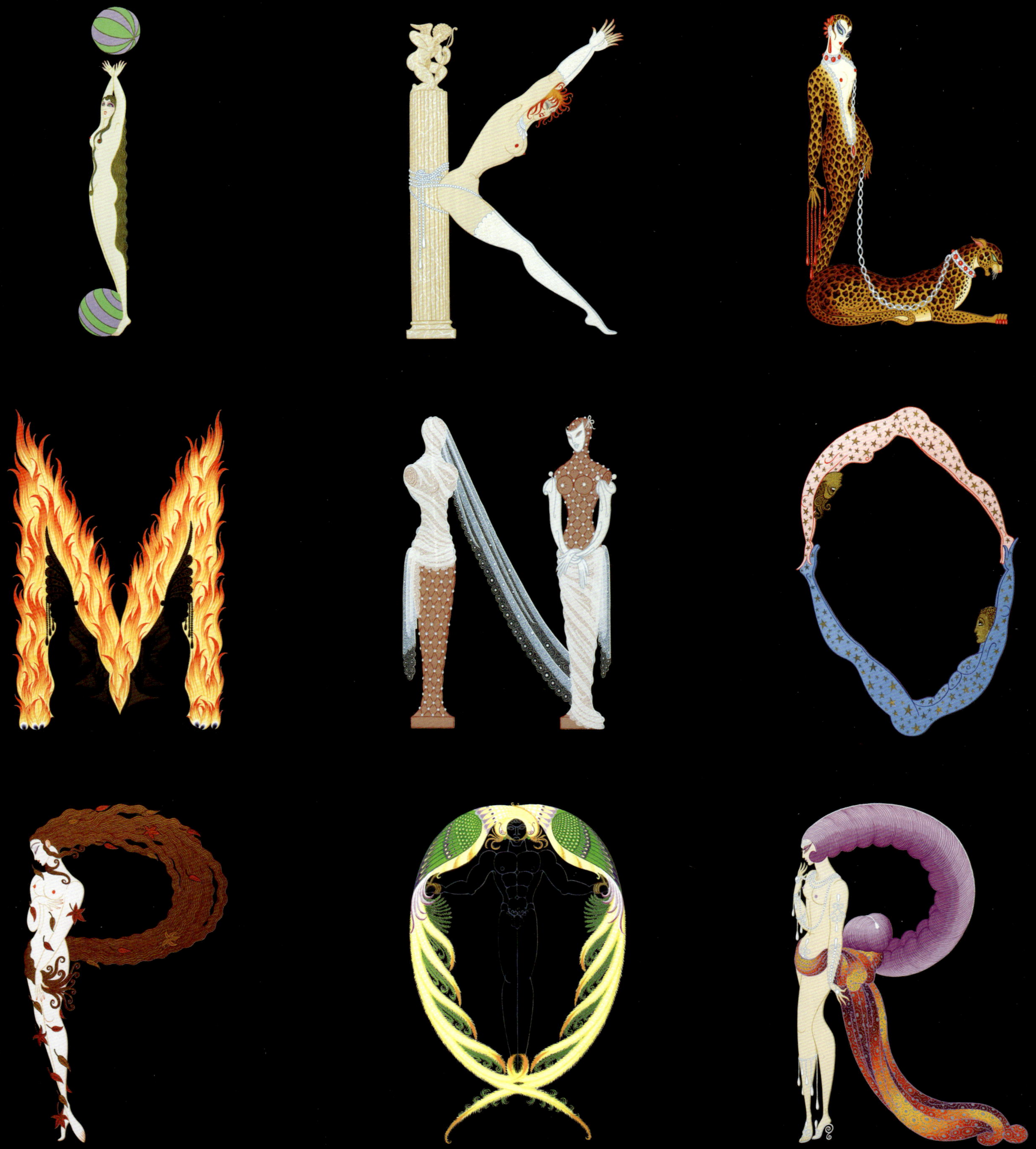
I K L
M N O
P Q R

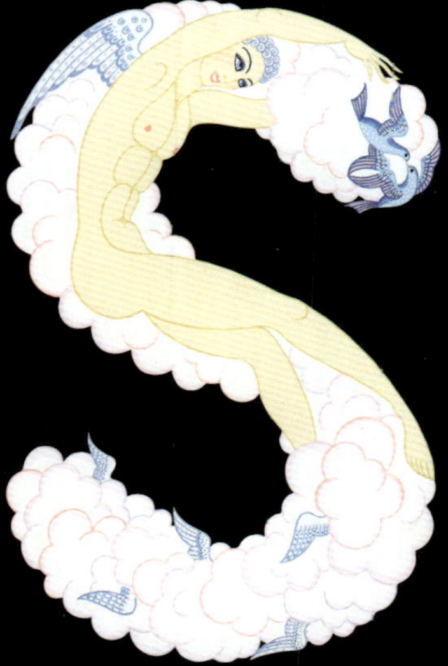
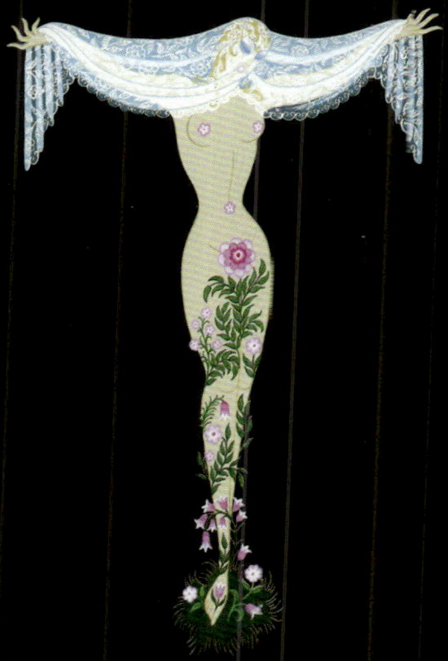
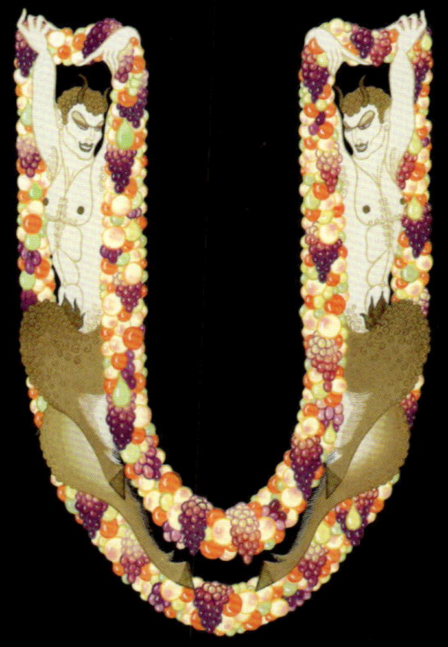
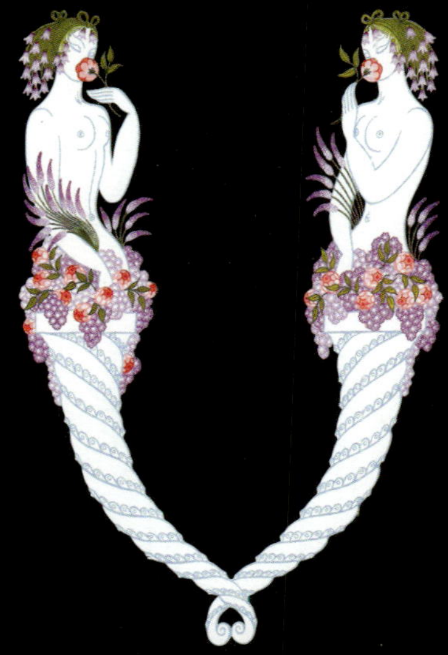
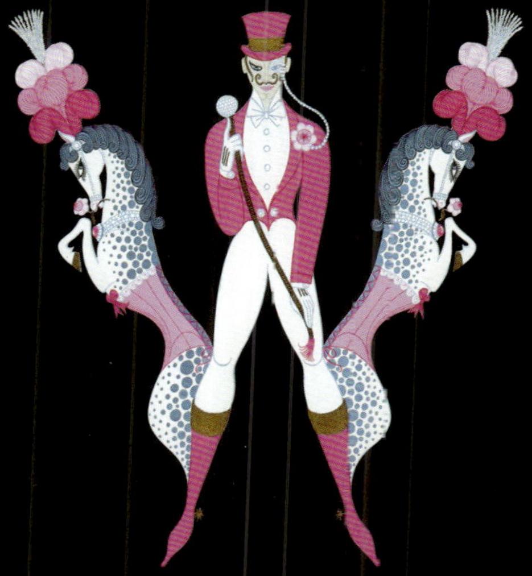
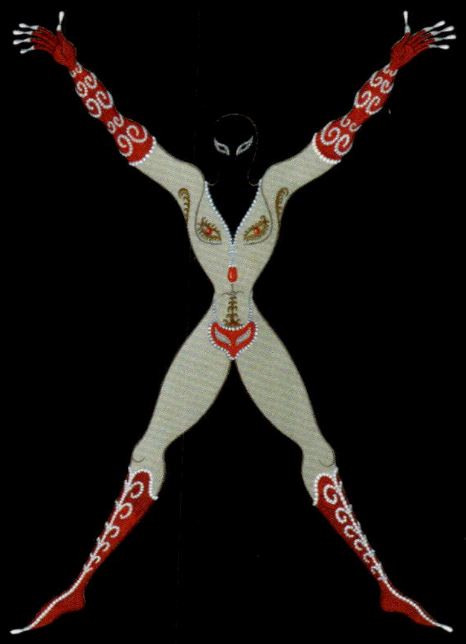
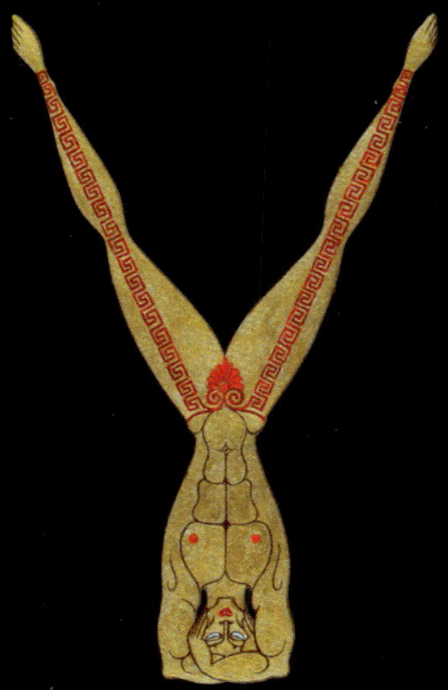
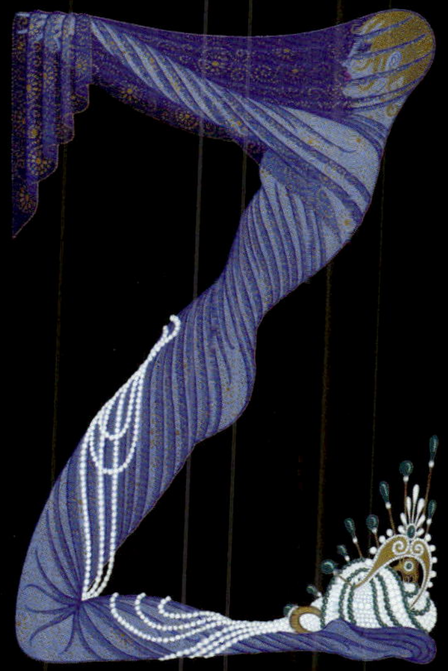
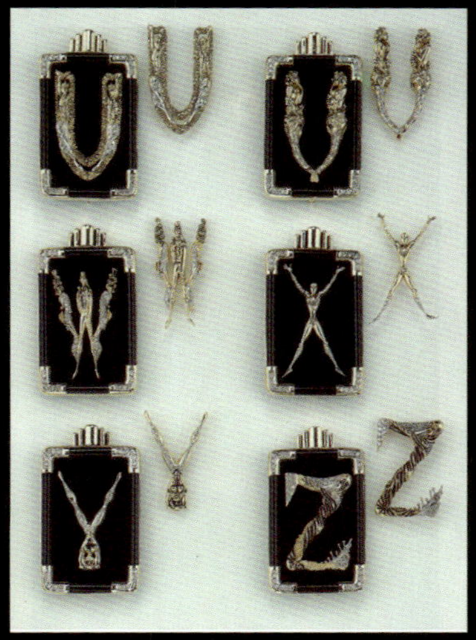

FURTHER READING

Barthes, R. *Erté*, Franco M. Ricci, Milan, 1972

Battersby, M. *Art Deco Fashion: French Designers 1908-1925*, Academy Editions, London; St Martin's Press, New York, 1974

Benton, C. & Benton, T. & Wood, G. (Eds.) *Art Deco 1910–1939*, V&A Publications, London, 2003

Bingen, S. & Sylvester, S.X. & Troyan, M. *MGM: Hollywood's Greatest Backlot*, Santa Monica Press, California, 2011

Blum, S. *Designs by Erté*, Dover Publications Inc., New York, 1976

Bowman, S. *A Fashion for Extravagance: Art Deco Fabrics and Fashions*, Bell & Hyman, London, 1985

Duncan, A. *Art Deco Complete*, Thames & Hudson, London, 2009

Ercoli, G. *Pochoir Art Deco*, Rizzoli, New York, 1989

Erté. *Erté Fashions by Erté*, Academy Editions, London, 1972

Erté. *Erté: Things I Remember, An Autobiography*, Peter Owen Publishers, London, 1975

Erté. *Erté*, Academy Editions, London, 1978

Erté. *Erté's Theatrical Costumes in Full Color*, Dover Publications Inc., New York, 1979

Erté. *Erté's Costumes and Sets for Der Rosenkavalier in Full Color*, Dover Publications Inc., New York, 1980

Erté, (Romain de Tirtoff). *Erté's Fashion Designs: 218 illustrations from 'Harper's Bazaar' 1918–1932*, Dover Publications, Inc., New York, 1981

Erté. *My Life/My Art, An Autobiography*, E.P. Dutton, London, 1989

Erté. *Erté: Art to Wear: The Complete Jewelry*, Penguin Books Ltd, London, 1991

Estorick, E. *Erté: The Last Works: Graphics, Sculpture*, Penguin Books, London, 1992

Greenhaigh, P. *Ephemeral Vistas: The Expositions Universalles, Great Exhibitions and World's Fairs*, 1851–1939, Manchester University Press, Manchester, 1988

Hillier B. *Art Deco of the 20s and 30s*, Studio Vista/Dutton, London, 1968

Hillier, B. *Art Deco Style*, Phaidon Press Ltd, London, 1997

Kobel, P. *The Birth of Film to the Triumph of Movie Culture*, Little Brown Book Group, London, 2007

Lee, M. (Ed.). *Erté: Sculpture*, Weidenfield and Nicolson, London, 1986

Lee, M. (Ed.). *Erté at Ninety-Five: The Complete New Graphics*, Weidenfield and Nicolson, London, 1987

MacKenzie, J.M. *Orientalism: history, theory and the arts*, Manchester University Press, Manchester, 2011

Ormiston, R. & Robinson, M. *Art Nouveau: Posters, Illustration & Fine Art from the Glamorous Fin de Siècle*, Flame Tree Publishing, London, 2009

Raulet, S. *Art Deco Jewelry*, Thames & Hudson, London, 2002

Riding, A. *And the Show went On: Cultural Life in Nazi-occupied Paris*, Gerald Duckworth Co. Ltd, 2012

Robinson, M. & Ormiston, R. *Art Deco: The Golden Age of Graphic Art & Illustration*, Flame Tree Publishing, London, 2008

Said, E.W. *Orientalism*, (first published 1978), Penguin Books Ltd, 2003

Skinner, T. *Art Deco Era Textiles Designs*, Schiffer Publishing, Atglen, Pennsylvania, 1998

Soloman, J (Ed.) *Erté at Ninety: The Complete Graphics*, Weidenfield and Nicolson, London, 1982

Spencer, C. *Erté*, Clarkson N. Potter, Inc., New York, 1970

Strachey, L. *Ermyntrude and Esmeralda*, (Illustrations by Erté), Blond, London, 1969

Tibbetts, J. *Erté*, Bison Books Limited, London, 1995

Weill, A. *La mode Parisienne: La Gazette du bon ton (1912–25)*, Bibliothèque de l'image, Paris, 2010

Costume design for Ganna Walska in Tosca, Act III,
Chicago Opera Company, 1920, gouache, 29.2 x 20.3 cm (111/2 x 8 in)

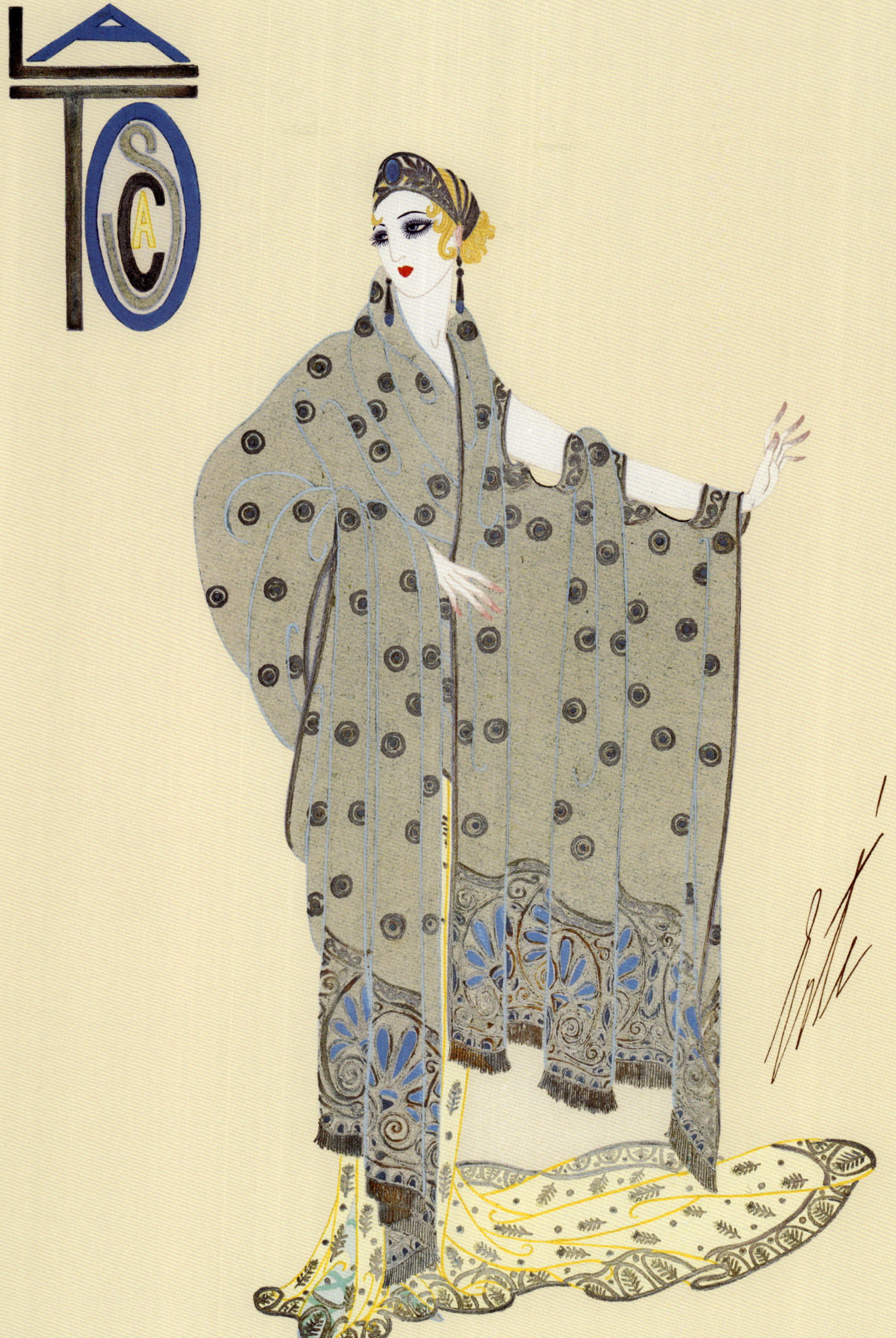
LA TOSCA

INDEX

Page numbers in *italics* indicate illustrations.

(Following page) **Sunrise**, *1984, serigraph with foil stamping, 34.9 x 55.2 cm (13¾ x 21¾ in)*

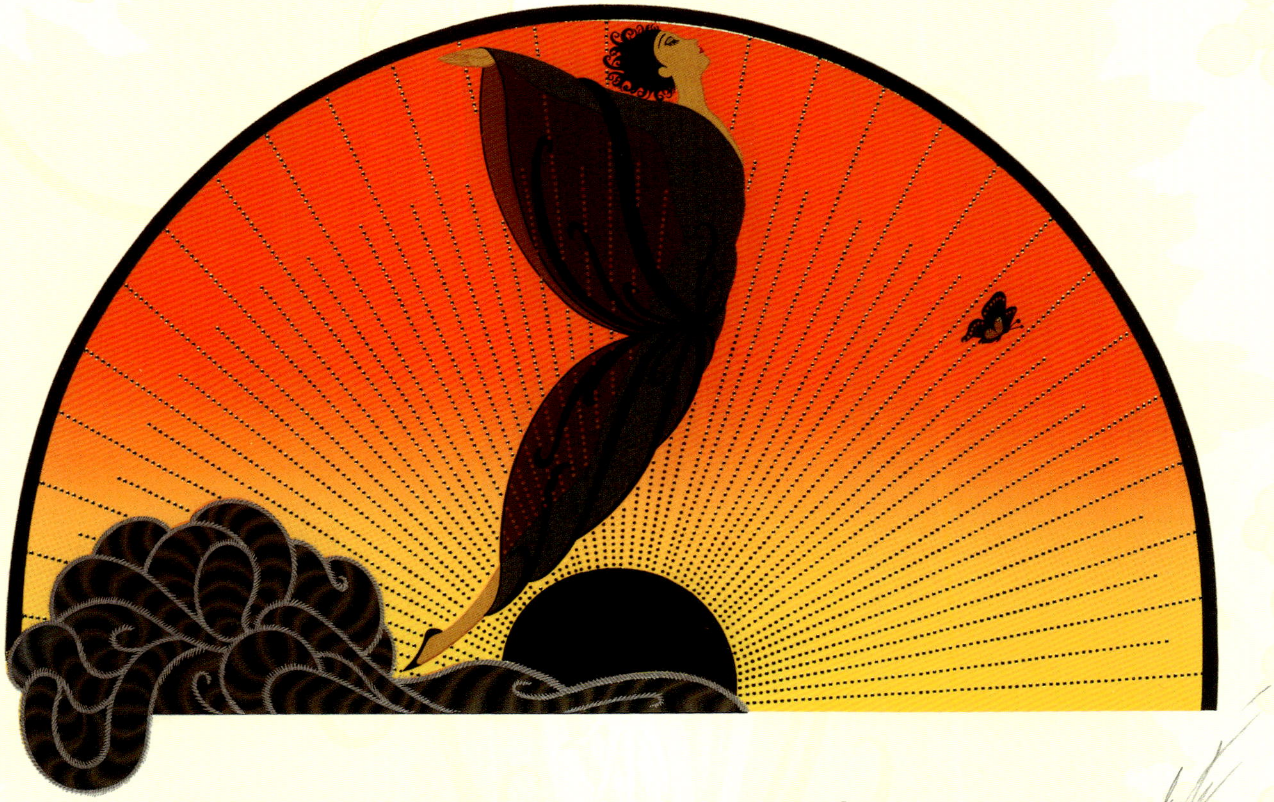

For further information about **Erté, art deco**
and associated arts please visit our blog:

blog.flametreepublishing.com